ALSO BY JAMES LOEFFLER

Rooted Cosmopolitans: Jews and Human Rights in the Twentieth Century

The Most Musical Nation: Jews and Culture in the Late Russian Empire

The Law of Strangers: Jewish Lawyers and International Law in the Twentieth Century

A Jew in the Street: New Views on European Jewish History

EXCEPTIONAL HATRED

EXCEPTIONAL HATRED

ANTISEMITISM AND THE FIGHT OVER FREE SPEECH IN MODERN AMERICA

JAMES LOEFFLER

METROPOLITAN BOOKS
HENRY HOLT AND COMPANY
NEW YORK

Metropolitan Books
Henry Holt and Company
Publishers since 1866
120 Broadway
New York, New York 10271
www.henryholt.com

Metropolitan Books® and m® are registered trademarks of
Macmillan Publishing Group, LLC.
EU Representative: Macmillan Publishers Ireland Ltd., 1st Floor, The Liffey Trust Centre,
117–126 Sheriff Street Upper, Dublin 1, D01 YC43

Distributed in Canada by Raincoast Book Distribution Limited

Library of Congress Cataloging-in-Publication Data

Names: Loeffler, James Benjamin, author.
Title: Exceptional hatred : antisemitism and the fight over free speech
in modern America / James Loeffler.
Description: First edition. | New York : Metropolitan Books, 2026. |
Includes bibliographical references and index.
Identifiers: LCCN 2025051409 | ISBN 9781250806079 (hardcover) |
ISBN 9781250806086 (ebook)
Subjects: LCSH: Antisemitism—United States—History—20th century |
Antisemitism—United States—History—21st century | Freedom of speech—
United States | Hate speech—Law and legislation—United States
Classification: LCC DS146.U6
LC record available at https://lccn.loc.gov/2025051409

First Edition 2026

Printed in the United States of America

10 9 8 7 6 5 4 3 2 1

For my family

Democracy is always a beckoning goal, not a safe harbor. For freedom is an unremitting endeavor, never a final achievement.

—Felix Frankfurter

The entire world rests on the tip of the tongue.

—Yiddish proverb

CONTENTS

EXCEPTIONAL HATRED

Introduction

Flames pierced the August darkness. Hundreds of men marched through the university quad, two abreast, their torches forming a burning line against the night. Their chants rose in a deep growl: "Blood and soil!" and "You will not replace us!" Then came the slogan that would define Charlottesville: "Jews will not replace us!"

As the parade reached the University of Virginia's iconic Rotunda, the men mounted the front steps, then streamed down to the plaza behind. There they found a small band of students forming a human chain around a statue of Thomas Jefferson. The mob swarmed them, lunging with their torches, cursing and screaming. The students shouted back their own slogan—"Black lives matter!"—before ducking their heads to avoid bursts of pepper spray. Within minutes, violent chaos consumed the plaza—the beginning of a weekend of blood and mayhem.

Seven years later, I walked into a Charlottesville courtroom located steps away from the site of a Confederate monument, now removed, that had drawn the torch-bearing mob to town. The jury faced me from the far end of the room, the judge perched above them on his dais. Over his head hung a portrait of Thomas Jefferson, for whom the building had once doubled as his local church. After taking my oath, I settled into the witness box for *Virginia v. Dix*.

The Commonwealth of Virginia had finally begun prosecuting hundreds of those white supremacist protesters on felony hate crimes charges. Six men had already pleaded guilty to violating a state law banning the use of burning objects to cause reasonable fear of injury or death. The seventh, Jacob Dix, chose to go to trial. As a University of Virginia professor of history and Jewish studies, I had been called as an expert witness to decode the hate symbols and slogans brandished on that August night back in 2017.

My testimony began smoothly. After entering my academic résumé into the record, the assistant prosecutor guided me through the evidence: the Nazi and Klan symbolism of nighttime torch marches, the neo-Nazi hate chants, and the "88" on Dix's T-shirt—code for "Heil Hitler." These facts demonstrated intent.

Then came the cross-examination. The defense attorney began by mocking my credentials. Did I really know the Russian language, as noted in my résumé? Was I an expert in Jewish *and* American history? And law? He challenged my interpretation of the symbols as antisemitic. After all, 88 appears on sports jerseys; Vikings used torches for burial rites. Wasn't this all subjective?

Then he veered into new territory. "Is hate speech illegal under Virginia law?"

"No," I answered. Hate speech enjoys constitutional protection unless it threatens or incites violence.

He pounced. "What if a group of protesters were to, say, gather on the University of Virginia grounds and chant 'From the river to the sea,' how would you interpret that?"

The question was a trap. That very day, another courtroom was hearing cases from the recent UVA Gaza encampment. Now I was being asked to choose between equating student protesters with violent white supremacists or conceding that hatred lay in the eye of the beholder. I wanted to reject the question as improperly argumentative. I wanted to describe the students I know who are terrified by that slogan, and the other students I know who see it is a plea for justice. But I was there as an expert witness, not a lawyer or a teacher.

I took a breath and gave my reply. "How I would interpret it would depend on the context. 'From the river to the sea' appears in the Hamas 2017 Charter, an Islamic terrorist group that calls for the eradication of Israel," I said, but if students chanted it on a public university campus, then "that would still be protected speech."[1]

I braced myself for the next attack. To my surprise, he retreated. The prosecution clarified on redirect that threatening speech is not protected by the First Amendment. Then they rested their case.

In that exchange, I came face-to-face with the subject of this book. American democracy stands at a precipice, besieged by authoritarian politics, resurgent nativism, and populist demagoguery. These forces, once relegated to history, now threaten our pluralistic society and its defining commitments to freedom and equality.

Against this backdrop of democratic erosion, America finds itself consumed by a national crisis over antisemitism and free speech—one that both reflects and accelerates this broader collapse. From college campuses to congressional hearings, from immigration courtrooms to social media platforms, polarizing arguments rage over what counts as hate speech and what the law should do about it. The consequences of this debate are devastating. Lives are upended. Dissent is criminalized. Fear stalks Jewish and Palestinian students alike. Meanwhile, the horrors of war and terror grind on in Israel and Palestine, each fresh tragedy deepening the fractures in American civil society.

Yet the further we descend into political crisis, the more clarity eludes us. Grievance, hypocrisy, and weaponization replace honest discussion. We argue endlessly over whether antisemitism is worse on the right or the left. We proclaim our commitment to fighting hatred while applying it selectively. We champion free speech until confronted with speech we despise—and minimize the claims of those wounded by words. Why has antisemitism become the focal point for all these debates in this moment of profound division and polarization? Why has it become our exceptional hatred?

"It is the exception that proves the rule," Cicero remarked in an ancient Roman trial of his own. The exception defines the normal. When we make an exception, whether in law or culture, we do more than carve out a special category. We also expose the limits of the system. The exception invites comparison. It questions difference.

This is a book about exceptions. It is a book about antisemitism, a puzzlingly old species of hatred that does not conform to the standard rules of racism and religious bigotry. It is a book about free speech, the principle we herald as democracy's bedrock, and hate speech, the specter that haunts it. And it is about American exceptionalism, the myth that our nation's singular political experiment can embrace absolutist free speech while escaping its consequences.

Since World War II, antisemitism has erupted into the center of public life at three moments when American democracy confronted its deepest contradictions about race, religion, and national identity. First, in late-1940s Chicago, where anti-Jewish riots sparked *Terminiello v. Chicago* (1949) and *Beauharnais v. Illinois* (1952), cases that redefined free speech at the dawn of civil rights. Second, in 1970s Skokie, where a planned neo-Nazi march forced America to reckon with Holocaust memory after the civil rights era. Third, in Charlottesville in 2017, where torch-bearing white supremacists met Black Lives Matter protesters—and where our current era of antisemitism began.

Much of this history has long been forgotten, and even stories we think we know read differently after Charlottesville and October 7 and Gaza. Centering antisemitism in America's free speech story provides an alternative history that moves beyond the facile narrative of individual freedom triumphing over government censorship. We can see not only what was gained through the vast modern expansion of civil liberties, but what was lost in terms of minority protection and equality.

This approach also provides a new vantage point on antisemitism itself. Inhabiting the strange borderland between American hatreds, antisemitism weaves racial and religious elements into seductive myths of power and difference. This very complexity has led many to discount anti-Jewish prejudice as tangential to color-based racism, while others isolate it to the point of disavowing any possibility of comparison. Both responses are mistakes. Understanding antisemitism requires grappling with both its distinctiveness and its profound entanglement with American ideas of race and religion.

In the aftermath of Charlottesville's terror and violence came the statements. "As a public institution, we value diversity, inclusion, and mutual respect," declared University of Virginia President Teresa Sullivan, the very antithesis of the hate on display during the march. She went on to denounce the "racist, anti-immigrant, homophobic, and misogynistic chants." Remarkably, her first response to this explicitly antisemitic riot made no mention of Jews or antisemitism. She was not alone. None of the twenty-five statements issued by the presidents of other Virginia colleges and universities in the immediate aftermath said anything about Jews or antisemitism. Even more striking were the words of Charlottesville public school superintendent Dr. Rosa Atkins, who vowed to stand with "our Latino, Muslim, bisexual, transgender, Christian, and Black students." Jews went unmentioned.[2]

What had happened? It might be tempting to attribute these elisions to progressive ideology, except that none of these speakers would qualify as political progressives, much less radicals. Rather, they were centrist liberals who evidently did not know where to place Jews or antisemitism within their framework of American diversity. Accustomed to thinking of Jews as simply a predominately white religious community, they struggled to grasp the realities of Jewish vulnerability in America.

Progressives also struggled with antisemitism after Charlottesville. At UVA, the Minority Rights Coalition announced its goal of fighting white supremacy in all forms—then refused to admit the main Jewish campus group unless those students cut ties with a pro-Israel organization. To join the fight against antisemitism and racism, the Jewish students were required to pass a political litmus test on Israel and Palestine, regardless of their individual views on the conflict. Months of negotiation produced a bizarre compromise offer. The Jewish student group could join as an adjunct, nonmember affiliate. This second-class status perfectly captured Jews' ambiguous place in America's color-coded racial categories—demonized as non-white by racists yet unrecognized by anti-racists as a minority deserving full solidarity.

While Charlottesville disclosed the contradictions of the Left, it launched a new era in the conservative politics of racism and antisemitism. President Trump's infamous comment about "very fine people, on both sides" became the defining moment—a refusal to condemn the antisemitism on the right that revealed both his disregard for truth and his willingness to appease white nationalists.[3]

Yet lost in the fury over his whataboutism was how it marked the beginning of the Right's new strategy: ignore right-wing antisemitism while weaponizing accusations of left-wing Jew hatred. Beginning with his 2019 executive order, Trump targeted universities as havens for antisemitism disguised as anti-Zionism. In the Trumpian inversion that deemed antiracism racist, civil rights law unlawful, and diversity a radical plot, fighting antisemitism became a potent tool for dismantling liberalism while shielding his own supporters from scrutiny.

Liberals today still struggle to fit antisemitism within their framework of racism, while progressives and conservatives instrumentalize it to serve different political ends. For some conservatives, mere public association with pro-Palestinian activism is grounds to suspend habeas corpus. For some progressives, the crimes of Zionism are enough to excuse antisemitism. Between these camps stand many Americans uncertain over how to identify antisemitism or respond to it beyond platitudes about tolerance.

The differences between these positions matter. The cynical weaponization of antisemitism by an ultra-conservative American government employing the levers of state power to punish dissent is not the same as the ideological dogmatism of the far left. Those liberals who slip into reactionary centrism, cheering punitive assaults on higher education in the name of combating antisemitism, are not the equivalent of the illiberal right they unwittingly enable. Yet what they all share is easily overlooked. In a faltering democracy torn apart by questions of national identity, Jews have become the screen onto which Americans project their fears and fantasies about the very meaning of pluralism in our society.

These patterns long preceded October 7, 2023, but burst into view after Hamas's attack and Israel's subsequent war in Gaza. Antisemitism became an ideological obsession, challenging First Amendment principles and inflaming national debates over the boundaries of free expression. Neither the scale of suffering and atrocity abroad nor the repressive policies emerging at home should obscure the fundamental question before us: how to balance free speech with equal protection when democracy itself stands imperiled.

Ladies and gentlemen of the jury, look above your heads, said the defense attorney in *Virginia v. Dix* as he began his closing argument. You will see the portrait of Jefferson, and over there are Madison and Monroe. "All three of those men stood right in this room, right where you're sitting." We owe them our freedom, he continued, and above all: the freedom of speech. "The First Amendment was not put in place to protect popular views; the exact opposite. The First Amendment is in place to protect the unpopular view, protect the view that nobody wants to hear, to protect the view that everyone thinks is ugly. That's why we have the First Amendment."

Let's talk about those three men, countered the lead prosecutor. They wrote our Constitution, but they also knew that "the Constitution is not a suicide pact." In our law, we limit free speech to prevent peril and fear. "You're not allowed to yell 'Fire' in a crowded theater," she reminded the jury. "And our General Assembly has decided that you cannot burn an object for the purpose of intimidating people in a manner that will have placed them in reasonable fear."

The reason, she explained, is that "this beautiful nation of ours, this country that we love" also has "an ugly, ugly history." Drawing the connection between freedom's limits and equality's promise, she continued: and that is why we have laws to protect the equal rights of African Americans from Klansmen and Jews from neo-Nazi attacks that "put our Jewish community in fear."

Each of these closing arguments invoked history as its authority. Each contained a measure of truth. We defend dissent to protect democracy. We balance rights to preserve equality. Yet the law pursues not the triumph of one principle over another but the delicate calibration of their equilibrium.

To ground our judgment, we turn to the past. Every legal dispute springs not only from abstract commitments but from concrete historical experience. History can trap us in amber—freezing our imagination of what law is and what justice might be. Yet it can also liberate us, revealing how different things once looked, and thus how we remain free to choose our path.

What we need now is a history that makes sense of our bewildering moment—one that neither romanticizes the First Amendment as tyranny's eternal antidote nor accepts hate speech as freedom's inevitable price. We must understand how free speech has been weaponized by racist ideologues seeking to undermine equality, how close American law has come to banning hate speech, and why those efforts ultimately failed. Most important, we need not only history's lessons but its questions: Where does free speech end and hateful discrimination begin? How do we calculate the harm in hatred? Does history offer an urgent warning about where unbridled antisemitism can lead—or merely a trapdoor into moral panic?

This new history begins in America in the mid-1940s, a time when intensifying antisemitism collided with a nascent civil rights movement confronting a resurgent far right. In *Terminiello v. Chicago* (1949) the U.S. Supreme Court took up the case of a renegade priest convicted of sparking a riot with an antisemitic speech. The 5–4 decision to overturn his conviction relied on a technicality but revealed a court bitterly divided over the First Amendment at a time when American democracy was considered under threat from the communist left and fascist right.

Resolution came three years later in *Beauharnais v. Illinois* (1952), when the Court heard the case of Chicago's leading white supremacist propagandist—the very man who had instigated one of the worst anti-Jewish riots in American history. This time the justices voted 5–4 to uphold his conviction under Illinois's "group libel" law. The decision opened the door to constitutionally valid restrictions on racist speech. Yet the anticipated legal revolution never materialized. These forgotten cases linger on the margins of American constitutional law. Recovering them reveals that the civil rights framework we inherited was not the only way liberalism might have evolved.

The unresolved questions of the late 1940s resurfaced in 1970s Skokie, Illinois, during another American reckoning over free speech and civil rights. For two years, Holocaust survivors and town leaders fought unsuccessfully to block a neo-Nazi march through their town. The ACLU, which took the neo-Nazi side, lost half its membership.

The saga, which generated three different Supreme Court cases, forced America to grapple with still more fundamental questions: What lessons should American liberalism draw from the Holocaust? Do minorities deserve protection from hateful speech that doesn't incite violence? How should individual rights be reconciled with minority group protection? The Skokie affair yielded an unexpected answer. Rather than banning hate speech, American law birthed a new category: hate crimes.

Finally, this history turns to Charlottesville in 2017 to examine why law failed to prevent tragedy and how the collision of racism and anti-racism propelled America toward its current crisis. The story unfolds in three acts: the unsuccessful attempts to stop the deadly rally; the campus debates over free speech and Israel-Palestine that fractured any unified response to white supremacy; and the 2021 civil trial *Sines v. Kessler*, where nine victims sought justice from the organizers of the violent rally.

Charlottesville shocked the American conscience with its vicious display of raw antisemitism and racism. Yet it also exposed a profound tension *between* these two hatreds—how they intersect, diverge, and compete for moral attention. Since October 7, 2023, that relationship has become a battleground. Americans now clash over the very meaning of civil rights, the definitions of racism and antisemitism, and whose suffering matters most. The story of Charlottesville serves not merely as prologue to this moment but as a key to decoding our present pathologies of race, religion, and democracy.

Dix v. Virginia ended in a hung jury. It was a legal disappointment, but a perfect symbol of our law's unfinished business of grappling with antisemitism and hatred. That task begins with revisiting the history recounted in these pages.

PART I

THE 1940s

1

Someone Else's Skin

On Tuesday afternoon, September 4, 1945, a crowd of more than 150,000 people lined the Atlantic City Boardwalk to catch a glimpse of the pride of American beauty. Forty young women planted like aquafauna on motor floats glided down a four-mile parade course, accompanied by a twelve-thousand-person escort including marching bands and honor guards, with a navy jet flyover. The event marked the beginning of the annual Miss America pageant, a weeklong national spectacle that melded the patriotic and the prurient. Contestants posed in bathing suits provided by the Catalina Swimwear company as the media breathlessly relayed their measurements. Yet these sex symbols were also subject to a strict code of modesty. The chaperoned young women were required to be unmarried, to abstain from alcohol and tobacco, and to avoid male contact—including their fathers—for the duration of the contest. The competition rules also specified one other form of purity. Only women "of the white race" could enter the pageant; a full genealogy was required as part of the application. African American women were welcome to compete in their own separate event for the title of Miss Sepia America.[1]

Miss New York City, Bess Myerson, a twenty-one-year-old, five-foot-eleven, fair-skinned brunette, passed the whiteness test. Yet her Jewishness marked her at every turn as a very different sort of American from the usual blond, white Protestant contestants. Basya, as she was known in her Yiddish-speaking home, was the second of three daughters of working-class immigrants who had come from tsarist Russia shortly before World War I. She grew up in a tight-knit community of families living in the Sholem Aleichem Houses, a Bronx cooperative housing complex founded by members of the Workmen's Circle, a Jewish socialist fraternal order. After studies at the New York City High School of Performing Arts, she majored in music at Hunter College. A first attempt at modeling ended badly when a top agency executive dismissed her with a comment that she lacked "all-American" looks. She graduated in June 1945 and went to work as a summer camp counselor in Vermont. In mid-August came an urgent telephone call from home. She had been invited to compete in the Miss New York City contest; her sister had surreptitiously entered her photos. Reluctantly, she returned home for the competition. Two weeks later, she was on a train bound for Atlantic City.[2]

Even before the Miss America contest began, Myerson's Jewishness emerged as a problem for the organizers. Pageant director Lenora Slaughter quietly urged her to change her name. Why not "Betty Merrick" or "Betty Meredith"? Hollywood would be more likely to come calling. Many Jews before her had done the same. Myerson hesitated, tempted by fame, torn by guilt. Pride finally held her back. "I knew I had to keep my name," she recalled later. "To have given up my name would have been like masquerading in someone else's skin." The unexpected look of panic in the older woman's eyes confirmed her decision. "I knew suddenly that I was not dealing with just a name change, that I was dealing with Lenora's fear."[3]

In Atlantic City, Myerson was also enveloped by fear. Whispered comments and sharp glances were followed by rumors that pageant leaders and corporate sponsors aimed to sabotage her chances. "Watch yourself," warned a friendly journalist. Hostility bred strategic creativity. Embracing her unusual profile, Myerson presented herself as the "beauty with brains." In 1945, for the first time, the pageant awarded the winner a $5,000 scholarship, a nod to changing notions of American womanhood. For her pageant booklet page, Myerson eschewed a bathing suit shot and instead submitted a photo of herself in her graduation cap and gown. Stage and screen were not for her. "I just want to teach music," she told the press.[4]

Tensions intensified after she won the bathing suit competition and dazzled in the talent section by playing the Grieg piano concerto followed by Gershwin's "Summertime" on the flute. Word spread of behind-the-scenes debate about the prospect of a Jewish winner. On Saturday, September 8, the day of the finals, several judges received threatening phone calls. "We do not want a Jewish Miss America," an unidentified male voice declared. "And if you do vote for her, you will never be invited back again."[5]

The pressure campaign failed. That evening a national radio audience tuned in to watch her cruise to victory. At the announcement "Bess Myerson is Miss America," the crowd erupted in shouts of joy. Cries of "Mazel tov" were even heard inside the Atlantic City theater. "Beauty is a power," marveled one newspaper columnist. The Nazis had plunged the world into war by claiming that "blonde Aryans were the preordained rulers of the universe." Now America gilded its battlefield victory with the selection of a Jewish brunette, a latter-day Queen Esther, to personify American democracy.[6]

America's "tall, dark, and delightfully different" beauty queen spent her first month performing vaudeville shows up and down the East Coast. She interspersed these stage performances with well-publicized visits to wounded veterans and breezy interviews with syndicated newspaper columnists. *Life* magazine blasted her image across America in a photo spread. Fan mail piled up at her parents' home in the Bronx. In October she was announced as the new face of the U.S. war bonds campaign, now rebranded as Victory Loans, to help defray the costs of World War II and support returning veterans. In early November she led a military parade through downtown Washington, DC, and visited the White House to sell a bond to First Lady Bess Truman. When she dropped by the gallery of the U.S. Senate, the floor proceedings were paused as the senators delivered a standing ovation.[7]

Behind the scenes of this triumphant tour, however, the resistance persisted. Several corporate sponsors refused to hire a Jewish spokesmodel.

The Ford Motor Company reneged on its pledge of a gift of a new automobile. The Catalina Swimwear company withdrew its promised contract and scholarship offer. While touring the South, Myerson was greeted by hotel signs that read "No coloreds, no Jews, no dogs." At one Veterans Administration hospital, the mother of a badly wounded serviceman blocked her from entering his room. "My boy doesn't want to see you," she berated her. "I don't want you near him. Because of the Jews, we got into this war. Because of the damn Jews, my boy was maimed. We would have been better off if Hitler had killed every last one of you people."[8]

The final straw came at a Southern country club where Myerson was scheduled to appear on behalf of the Miss America scholarship fund. As she descended the stairs from her changing room, wearing an elegant New York fashion gown, she froze midstep. Down below, a voice could be heard saying that a terrible mistake had been made, "This is a restricted country club. We do not have Blacks and we do not have Jews." Turning around, she marched back up to her room, shed her dress, and left that night. Myerson took the train back to New York City, crying and defeated. The victory tour was over.[9]

Myerson's fast rise to fame and private confrontations with hatred neatly captured the ambiguous Jewish position in America at the dawn of the postwar era. Growing public acceptance concealed rampant private discrimination. Few laws directly targeted Jews, most of whom were treated as white by law, and yet an unwritten code of rules barred them from whole swaths of society. The invisibility of that animus made it no less powerful. White appearance spared most Jews the extraordinary evils of segregation yet did not exempt them from a different colorless racism. Myerson was eligible to compete in a segregated beauty contest, even suitable in the eyes of some to embody American nationhood, yet she could not escape the taint of Jewishness. Having volunteered to become an all-American icon, she found herself caught between image and reality. "There seemed to be no way to fight back," she recalled, "I was trapped in the disguise I myself had agreed to wear."[10]

Every argument against hatred involves the defense of difference.

The underlying humanity we all share must be acknowledged even though we belong to different groups. Yet what if the nature of that difference is itself contested and ambiguous? That philosophical question formed the central political problem of modern Jewish history. Where did Jews belong in a world carved into rigid categories of nation, race, and religion? Their collective identity defied such boundaries, weaving together sacred tradition, ancestral lineage, ethnic culture, and the shared experience of global diaspora.

Bess Myerson's encounters with antisemitism in the fall of 1945 generated an identity crisis. To defend herself from discrimination, she needed to explain to herself where she belonged in the racial and religious categories of American society. In her own eyes, she was not white. That term she reserved for Protestant Anglo-Saxons and European Catholics. Yet she had just won a segregated beauty contest as a white woman.

In her befuddlement and disillusion, Myerson had glimpsed the root contradiction at the heart of American democracy. The nation premised on a grand experiment in human freedom was built upon deep-seated hierarchies of race and religion. The fact that most Jews had landed legally on the white side of the American racial ledger only compounded the ironies of antisemitism. Rather than being a land free of the kind of hatreds that stalked Jews in Europe, America possessed its own distinctive tradition of antisemitism. That is what Myerson grasped in her moment of degradation.[11]

AMERICA'S JEWISH HISTORY begins with a story of Christian fear. In September 1654 a ship bearing twenty-three Jews fleeing the Portuguese Inquisition in colonial Brazil made port in New Amsterdam. Their arrival so alarmed the Dutch governor, Peter Stuyvesant, that he promptly wrote his superiors at the Dutch West India Company back in the Netherlands seeking approval to expel the newcomers. Doing so would ensure that these members of "the deceitful race—such hateful enemies and blasphemers of the name of Christ—be not allowed to further infect and trouble this new colony" with their "abominable religion" and "customary usury and deceitful trading with the Christians." Some eighteen languages were spoken in the streets of the city over which he presided, including those of enslaved Africans and local Iroquois, yet Jews, in his view, represented a unique affront and grave danger to the future of the European colony.[12]

"Is there anything in the world that more unites and connects the hearts of men," wrote another Dutch colonial official in 1614, "and on the contrary more separates the hearts of men and creates larger hostility than religious difference?" Of all the lines that divided early modern Europeans—save gender—none cut as deeply as religion, creating chasms wider than those between enslaved and free, colonist and native, poor and rich. Christianity not only defined the West's self-image as a superior civilization, it also provided the ethical and legal justification for the pursuit of global empire. The Dutch staked their claim to territory in the name of Christian authority; the same held true elsewhere in colonial North America. "Propagating Christian religion to such people, as yet live in darkness and miserable ignorance of the true knowledge and worship of God," read the 1606 Virginia Company royal charter, "may in time bring the infidels and savages, living in those parts, to human civility." The fact that these lands and their inhabitants were "not now actually possessed by any Christian prince or people" permitted their subjugation.[13]

Even the seventeenth-century Puritans, themselves refugees from religious persecution by the Church of England, feared the Jews, banning them from the New England colony until "the happy day of their conversion." These words came from the preeminent seventeenth-century Puritan intellectual Reverend Cotton Mather, a man who liked to sit in his study wearing a skullcap and asked his flock to address him as "Rabbi." They reflected how the Christian doctrine of supersession—that Christians had replaced Jews as God's elect—animated the early American imagination.[14]

The same theological obsession with Jewish difference bequeathed the emerging modern Atlantic world its most pernicious idea: race. For the first fifteen hundred years of their history, Christians regarded Jewishness as a mental error that vanished in the baptismal font. Even supposed Jewish physical traits, such as the fabled medieval "foetor judaicus," or "Jewish odor," that Jewish bodies were said to emit, magically disappeared upon conversion. Then, in the fifteenth century, European Christians began to reimagine Jewishness as a permanent fact of biology. Confronting a large population of *conversos*, descendants of earlier waves of forced Jewish conversions to Christianity, Spaniards promulgated new laws premised on *limpieza de sangre*, "blood purity," to separate the impostor "New Christians" from authentic "Old Christians." Family genealogy became the means to certify untainted Christian descent and check the spread of "Judaizing" heresy. This novel form of anti-Judaism triggered the Spanish Inquisition in 1478, followed by the 1492 expulsion of Spain's entire Jewish population, and then the banning of Judaism in Portugal and its colonies, a policy that led to that desperate voyage to New Amsterdam.[15]

The new genealogical thinking haunted generations of Jews and their descendants throughout the European colonial world. It also provided the theological matrix within which modern racism was born. As they conquered the Americas, European slavers and colonists transposed creed into color, recasting Amerindians, African slaves, and others of mixed lineage as physical and spiritual inferiors. In the process, "Christian," the original term for European settlers, slowly morphed over the course of the seventeenth century into "white."[16]

The gradual invention of whiteness left Jews in early colonial America ambiguously positioned between race and religion. Their ancient Middle Eastern origins, distinctive ethnoreligious identity, separate laws, and non-Christian status led other Europeans and Americans—and many Jews themselves—to regard Jews as a separate racial group (the term "ethnicity" would not appear until the mid-twentieth century). Yet most European Jews also coded as physically white by virtue of their light skin color, sparing them the legal classification and discrimination faced by indigenous peoples and African slaves.[17]

Color and creed mattered enormously in colonial America, but so, too, did money. Economic motives drove colonial settlement and racial slavery alike. They also conditioned the new European spirit of religious tolerance. "We would gladly have" ordered the Jews to be expelled so that the colony "would not be infected any more by any Jewish nation," Stuyvesant's superiors replied to him, "as we foresee from this the same difficulties which you anticipate." Alas, they explained, financial calculus trumped religious conviction. Some Amsterdam Jewish merchants owed a "large amount of capital . . . to the Company," they explained, and the same men willingly vouched for their distressed brethren. Hence the Jews in New Amsterdam must be allowed to remain and trade in order to repay the Jewish debts provided that "the poor among them shall not become a burden to the company or to the community but be supported by their own nation."[18]

Economic tolerance proved a double-edged sword. In the money-hungry world of early modern capitalism, profit motives encouraged pragmatic inclusion of Jews and other religious minorities deemed economically useful, like the French Huguenots. Still, paid protection required wealthier Jewish patrons to underwrite the cost of toleration for poor Jews. Philanthropic capitalism hardly cured prejudice. In fact, transactions of this sort contributed to the perpetuation of medieval stereotypes about Jews and money that would recur throughout modern history. Upon learning of the deal to permit the Jews to remain, Reverend Johannes Megapolensis, the head of the Dutch Reformed Church in New Amsterdam, bitterly complained, "These people have no other God than the unrighteous Mammon, and no other aim than to get possession of Christian property."[19]

Even those eighteenth-century English colonial leaders who did espouse tolerance did so for mercenary reasons. Roger Williams, the founder of Rhode Island, a figure renowned today as a paragon of religious freedom, insisted on "liberty of conscience" and separation of religion and state as the bedrock principles of modern government. Yet he, too, presumed Christianity's superiority and openly professed "a spiritual war" against "the Jewish, the Turkish and other Pagan and Antichristian religions." Toleration for Williams was less an ethical precept than a missionary strategy. The best way to convert Jews, he believed, was to tolerate them. This conversionary scheme led him to allow the first organized Jewish community to be established in New England in 1677, though without equal rights.[20]

The same spirit prevailed over the next century, as small numbers of Jews arrived from the Spanish and Portuguese Sephardic diasporas, joined by a trickle of central European Ashkenazi migrants. These traders and artisans clustered themselves in the port cities of the mid-Atlantic and upper South. Synagogues appeared in New York (1730), Savannah (1733), Charleston (1749), Newport (1759), Philadelphia (1782), and Richmond (1789). Jews in this period never amounted to more than a few thousand people, equivalent to less than one twentieth of one percent of the entire population of British North America. That tiny number meant that early American Jews were absorbed into, and to varying degrees accepted by, the European Protestant population. Though suffering under a range of legal disabilities alongside other dissenting religious sects like Quakers and Baptists, they also found themselves spared the persecution and violence characteristic of Jewish life in eastern Europe at that time.[21]

The American Revolution heralded a revolutionary change in Jewish status. For the first time in human history, Jews found themselves citizens of a country in which religious equality was a precondition for democratic politics. In the 1786 Virginia Act for Religious Freedom, Thomas Jefferson famously asserted that "the natural rights of mankind" guaranteed that "no man shall be compelled to frequent or support any religious worship . . . nor shall otherwise suffer on account of his religious opinions or belief." The same language passed into the 1787 U.S. Constitution, with its ban on religious tests for federal government office holding, and the First Amendment's Free Exercise and Establishment clauses.[22]

These radical new ideas of individual rights arrived accompanied by a strain of Protestant Hebraism. Many founders looked to the Jews as Christians' spiritual stepbrothers, descendants of the "Stock of Abraham," as George Washington described them, who deserved respect on account of their shared biblical patrimony. In his 1790 letter to the Newport Jewish community, Washington lauded the fact that mere "toleration" had been replaced by true "liberty of conscience" and "inherent natural rights" and promised that "everyone shall sit in safety under his own vine and fig tree, there shall be none to make him afraid."[23]

There was truth to this lofty statement, which went on to become a prized token of American Jewish belonging. Unlike Europe, where the fight for Jewish rights would define the character of liberalism and citizenship well into the twentieth century, American democracy implicitly postulated Jewish equality from the start. Still, Washington's rhetorical flourish counted for far less than it might seem today for three reasons. First, when the Founding Fathers spoke of religious freedom, they had chiefly in mind Protestant freedom from the Church of England. Some went further in imagining a pan-Christian country without an official national church. While many American Christians aspired to grant non-Christians equal status, just as many, if not more, assumed that civil rights for Jews would lead to their eventual conversion.[24]

Second, the Constitution's religion clauses applied only to the federal government, leaving each state free to establish its own laws on religion. A patchwork of Jewish rights consequently emerged. Georgia removed its Christian-only provision for public office holding in 1789, yet Connecticut did not do so until 1818. North Carolina took another fifty years after that, and New Hampshire followed last in 1877. Even the arc of these dates proves deceptive. The act of political disestablishment—the formal removal of the church from an official, sanctioned role in state government—did not prevent the maintenance of a host of other state laws that enshrined Christianity in public life through education, government holidays, public prayer, and the notorious Sunday Sabbath laws, which forbade all business on the Christian day of rest. Together these laws placed a heavy burden—both socially and economically—on Jewish shoulders, undermining the vaunted claims to full equality.[25]

Last, across the nineteenth century, various political leaders campaigned to Christianize the U.S. Constitution. Among them was former U.S. president and Massachusetts congressman John Quincy Adams, who in 1844 proposed a constitutional amendment to make "clear and explicit acknowledgement [of] the Lord Jesus Christ as the ruler of this nation." Christian nationalists were driven by both evangelical zeal and a gnawing identity crisis. The United States had begun as an immigrant country peopled in the minds of its leaders by white Protestant settlers from western Europe. The 1790 Nationality Act restricted citizenship by naturalization to "free White person[s]." Yet colonial expansion brought more Native Americans and Mexicans within its boundaries, joined by Chinese and Japanese laborers and millions of Irish Catholics and other Europeans, including a hundred thousand German Jews from the 1820s onward. This new diversity radically challenged the American demographic compact and its racialized system of citizenship. What finally brought the country to the breaking point, however, was the root conflict over the presence of slavery in a liberal democracy.[26]

The Civil War continued the curious pattern of animus and acceptance that had characterized the American Jewish experience since colonial times. With Northerners and Southerners alike viewing the conflict as a divinely ordained battle for the country's soul, Christian anti-Jewish prejudices surfaced across the divided country. In the North, General Ulysses S. Grant infamously barred Jews "as a class" from the Tennessee military zone based on nefarious stereotypes about Jews as war profiteers, and the Union Army refused to accept non-Christian chaplains. Yet after Jewish protest, both bans were quickly rescinded, and President Abraham Lincoln also rebuffed calls to Christianize the Constitution. Some seven thousand Jewish soldiers fought in the Union ranks, part of a pattern of Jewish military service dating back to the American Revolution.[27]

Similar dynamics prevailed in the South. The Confederate Secretary of State Judah Benjamin, of Sephardic ancestry and himself a slave owner and prominent proslavery advocate, faced continual anti-Jewish harassment even as he rose to the highest ranks of the Southern leadership. Some two thousand Jewish men followed his call to take up arms in defense of the Confederacy. In the war's wake, Jewish Southerners displayed varying reactions to Jim Crow segregation and white supremacy. Some quietly resisted anti-Black racism, allying with their Black neighbors. Others acquiesced to the prevailing Jim Crow hierarchy to secure their own racial status and deflect anti-Jewish prejudices.[28]

Then there was the Virginia-born sculptor Moses Ezekiel, who produced some of the most iconic Confederate war memorials. Son of an Ashkenazi father and a Sephardic mother, the Richmond-born Ezekiel fought as a teenager in the Civil War. He launched his postwar artistic career in 1873 with a bas-relief, *Israel*, that depicted the Jews in exile after the Roman destruction of Jerusalem as an allegory for the evils of hatred more generally. "Art is the solvent of prejudice," Ezekiel wrote of the sculpture's meaning. But much of his own art belied those words. Ezekiel's proudest achievement was the Confederate War Memorial at Arlington National Cemetery in Virginia that depicts a weeping, loyal female slave holding a Confederate soldier's child. The monument's Latin inscription praises the "Lost Cause," the noble defense of Southern freedom from Northern tyranny, a staple of the white supremacist narrative that emerged in the Civil War's aftermath.[29]

At the same time, Ezekiel created the country's first great monument to religious freedom. At twenty-four feet tall and thirteen tons, the statue *Religious Liberty* now stands on Independence Mall in Philadelphia. The marble sculpture depicts a toga-clad woman wearing the ancient Phrygian cap of freed slaves and holding a copy of the U.S. Constitution. It was commissioned in 1876 by the B'nai B'rith Jewish fraternal order to commemorate the one hundredth anniversary of American independence. Writing to invite President Grant to the dedication ceremony, the B'nai B'rith president, Simon Wolf, praised America for granting its Jews a unique redemption. "No class of citizenship has been made happier by religious liberty than the Jew, for that denial of that liberty in other lands has been the cause of endless persecution and misery." The framing of anti-Jewish hatred as a strictly religious affair ignored the fact that in the tumultuous era of postwar Reconstruction, many Americans had come to revile the Jews not for their religion but for their race.[30]

In these postwar years, a new biological antisemitism arrived from the old country. The United States has brilliantly solved the problem of "Judaism, a phenomenon that negates everything that is purely human and noble," observed the "patriarch of antisemitism," Wilhelm Marr, from Germany in the 1860s. "The North American state does not recognize the Jews as such," he explained to his German readers, and consequently the Jews as a group quite naturally disappeared via "race-mixing" into "the state majority" of white Christians. America's success presented a useful model for a German society embroiled in debates about whether to grant its Jews civil rights. German Jews must abandon their objectionable beliefs and practices and dissolve themselves into the Christian majority, Marr argued, for true democracy to emerge.[31]

By 1873, however, he had changed his mind about both Jews and democracy. "Alien domination has been forced upon us," he wrote that year in his bestselling pamphlet *The Victory of Jewry over Germandom, Considered from a Non-Religious Point of View*. It was not the belief system of Judaism but the Jews themselves that represented the greatest challenge to the freedom of Germany and humanity as a whole: "For 1800 years, the Jewish nation fought against the Western world," and now the "sociopolitical phalanx" of "Jewish power" had conquered every arena in modern life—government, culture, advertising, newspapers, business, even the church—turning non-Jews into "slaves." Old-fashioned religious disputes counted for much less than innate biological differences. Jews constituted a "Semitic" race, a pseudohistorical term Marr adopted from linguistic anthropology to lend his theory a scientific aura. At times he even borrowed from American racism to christen the Jew as a racial anomaly: "the White Negro."[32]

It was not long before Marr's new word migrated across the ocean to a post–Civil War American society in the grip of a profound societal crisis. The efforts to reconstruct American democracy along the lines of racial egalitarianism triggered lethal violence and biological racism, best reflected in the appearance of the Ku Klux Klan and Jim Crow segregation laws. It was then that the doctrine of white supremacy, itself born out of Christian anti-Judaism, first began to display elements of overt anti-Jewish racism. Much of white supremacy's racial myth centered on an imagined Anglo-Saxon purity said to be possessed by western and central Europeans. Jews and Catholics were both deemed racially inferior, along with African, Asian, and indigenous people.

Yet racial antisemitism differed from conventional racism in two key respects. While colonized, colorized people were deemed racial inferiors, antisemitism endowed Jews with a strange superiority and vast, sinister power. And the very fact that the most modern Western Jews (Ashkenazi and Sephardi alike) had abandoned traditional markers of difference—dress, language, male beards, and physical mannerisms—and did not differ in color from their European and American neighbors only lent them a shadowy image as racial chameleons, or, in Marr's coinage, "White Negroes."

This dynamic was already on display in 1877, the year a national controversy erupted at an exclusive hotel resort in upstate New York. The family of Joseph Seligman, a teenage immigrant from Germany who had worked his way up from traveling peddler to prominent financier, was abruptly denied entrance on grounds that Jews were no longer welcome as guests. In what would become a hallmark of American antisemitism, the proprietor denied that he hated all Jews, only those "Liberals" like Seligman who "absolutely threw overboard the Hebrew Bible and Moses" and shed their beards and kosher diets in a vain attempt at camouflage.[33]

Two years later, the New York banker Austin Corbin declared his intention to ban all Jews from his Coney Island hotel. "Personally, I am opposed to Jews," Corbin told a reporter in 1879. "They are contemptible as a class, and I never knew but one 'White' Jew in my life." He followed this pronouncement with a short-lived plan for a Society for the Suppression of the Jews. "If this is a free country," Corbin declared, "why can't we be free of the Jews?"[34]

The answer was that such discrimination was at that time illegal. In the wake of the Civil War, the Fourteenth Amendment enshrined the principle of "equal protection" in American constitutional law. In a series of related federal civil rights laws passed between 1866 and 1875, Congress extended the umbrella of protection across the entire citizenry, covering voting rights, property rights, and "the right to equal enjoyment of public accommodations and amusements" for all "citizens of every race and color." These bold laws were designed to secure the rights of African Americans facing ongoing violence and dispossession, especially in the American South.

Whether these laws might have helped combat antisemitism remained an untested proposition, for the Reconstruction-era civil rights system did not last long. As part of a series of landmark cases in 1883, the U.S. Supreme Court ruled that Congress lacked the authority to ban racial discrimination by private individuals. Federal law "cannot possibly cover the whole domain of rights appertaining to life, liberty and property," wrote

Justice Joseph Bradley. Such matters were left to the states to decide for themselves. That decision opened the door to decades of legally enforced racial segregation across the American economy and culture in the name of states' rights. It also meant that after 1883, a Jew-free hotel or country club was wholly constitutional.[35]

The new anti-Jewish racism coincided with a major change in the very size and shape of Jewish America. In 1880, Jews numbered only one half of one percent of the American population. Over the next few decades, more than three million Jews from eastern Europe arrived as part of a larger wave of European immigrants drawn by the expanding American industrial economy. These Yiddish-speaking, religiously traditionalist Jews stood out far more than earlier Sephardic or German immigrants. Now, as they poured into cities at ever-increasing rates, some American Protestant elites glossed their migration in dystopian terms. "We are in the hands of the Jews," warned the writer and historian Henry Adams, grandson of John Quincy Adams, in 1899. Lock up your wealth in gold, he counseled, lest you risk "the burglar, the Jew, the Czar, the socialist, and above all, the total, irremediable, radical rottenness of our whole social, industrial, financial and political system." Adams's roster of enemies suggested the conglomeration of extremes associated with Jewishness: rapacious capitalism and revolutionary radicalism; unsurpassable power and gross degeneracy. The solution to this mushrooming threat could only be violence. "Bombard New York," Adams fantasized in a letter to a friend, "I know no place that would be more improved by it. The chief population is Jew"—of Russian origin—"and the rest is German Jew."[36]

Adams's Northeastern patrician racial snobbery echoed across other sectors of American life, particularly in the ranks of the Populist Party in the South and West. These agrarian radicals opposed banks and federal monetary policies, which they viewed as intrinsically detrimental to farmers and laborers. At the peak of their brief period of influence in the 1896 presidential election, the Populists trafficked in an unadulterated antisemitism rife with conspiracy theories. An *Associated Press* correspondent covering their St. Louis convention that year observed "the extraordinary hatred of the Jewish race. It is not possible to go into any hotel in the city without hearing the most bitter denunciation of the Jews as a class and of the particular Jews who happen to have prospered in the world."[37]

Even those philosemites who denounced this rising current of antisemitism often acquiesced to its core postulates. Writing in *Harper's* magazine in 1899, Mark Twain disavowed all prejudice against Jews but concluded that antisemitism stemmed from natural reactions on the part of American Christians to Jewish financial prowess and cunning. The fault ultimately lay with the Jews themselves. "You will always be by ways and habit and predilections substantially strangers—foreigners—wherever you are," he told his Jewish readers, and "that will probably keep the race prejudice against you alive."[38]

Still, few American antisemites could countenance the idea of a violent suppression of Jewish life. There would be no European-style pogroms or mass terror of the kind directed at African Americans. Instead, they chose the softer technique of restriction. That meant, in the first instance, attempting to close the country's doors to Jews, along with other undesirable racial inferiors such as Italians, Slavs, and Asians. From 1898, the federal government classified Jewish immigrants as members of the Hebrew race and soon imposed onerous health and literacy tests to restrict their numbers. Tellingly, the architects of the modern immigration system initially instructed border officials to classify Jews separately from Christian immigrants hailing from the same country. In the case of "the Hebrews," inquiring about religion should be used "as a means of distinguishing race." Even when that practice was abandoned, officials expressed befuddlement over how to classify "the Hebrews . . . a clannish people, with certain tendencies for money getting that are thought to be racial characteristics" and "often afflicted with disease" despite generations of intermarriage that had diluted their "native blood." Regardless of Jewish protests, these ambiguities persisted, culminating in policies that would drastically curtail all immigration in the aftermath of World War I.[39]

Meanwhile, the idea of restriction gained traction in other sectors of American society. From the early twentieth century, real estate deeds and neighborhood covenants often explicitly barred property sales to

Jews along with African Americans and other non-white minorities. Hotels and clubs explicitly advertised that Jews were not admitted. Law firms, banks, hospitals, and other elite professions systematically rejected Jewish job seekers, sometimes openly. Elite public and private universities instituted restrictive admissions policies targeting Jewish enrollment. As in Europe, fears and fantasies about the unnatural Jewish presence in key areas of society—business, media, law, medicine, education, culture—bred antisemitic myths. Time and again, Jewish overrepresentation was mistaken for diabolical predominance.

In response to this discrimination, a new Jewish self-defense organization emerged in 1913 under the auspices of B'nai B'rith: the Anti-Defamation League, dedicated to securing "justice and fair treatment to all citizens" and halting the "pernicious and un-American . . . defamation of the Jewish people." The immediate pretext for its creation was the arrest and subsequent conviction of the Atlanta Jewish businessman and communal leader Leo Frank, a B'nai B'rith member, who was falsely accused and wrongly convicted of the murder of Mary Phagan, a thirteen-year-old white girl who worked in his family's factory. After the Georgia governor commuted his sentence, a frenzied mob broke into the prison and proceeded to lynch Frank. His murder marked the beginning of a revived Ku Klux Klan movement, which now expanded its remit from anti-Black terror to a battle against Jews, Catholics, and other non-Anglo-Saxon immigrants.[40]

The "only safeguard" against the spread of antisemitism, argued Sigmund Livingston, the ADL's founder and a German-born Chicago lawyer, was to endeavor to keep the Jewish name in "good esteem." Since in his view antisemitism stemmed from the harmful stereotypes circulating with ever greater frequency thanks to the new popular culture and mass media, the ADL initially focused its efforts on the problem of "the caricaturing and defaming of Jews on the stage, in moving pictures." In 1914, the group wrote every state educational superintendent across America to request that they remove *The Merchant of Venice* from schools because of its negative Jewish images. They joined with the Central Conference of American Rabbis, the National Council of Jewish Women, and the National Association for the Advancement of Colored People to combat the proliferation of films that featured patently offensive depictions of Jews and Blacks, including D. W. Griffith's 1915 *The Birth of a Nation.* "No other instrument in modern civilization is so widespread in its influence and makes so profound an impression upon the child-mind" and the "unmatured, ignorant" masses now flocking daily to the movie theaters, the 1915 ADL annual report stated. The next year they began a national campaign to create state laws barring "the publication and distribution of discriminating advertising matter." This campaign marked the first effort to ban hate speech in American law.[41]

The idea of halting discrimination in the form of speech also surfaced in the early strategy of the American Jewish Committee, founded in 1906 by wealthy Jewish New Yorkers to protect the "civil and religious rights of Jews" at home and abroad. Its leader, the prominent constitutional lawyer Louis Marshall, worked hard to secure the passage of the New York 1913 Civil Rights Act, designed to fill the gap left open by the U.S. Supreme Court's invalidation of earlier Reconstruction-era civil rights laws. Among its provisions was a law rendering it a crime to discriminate based on "race, faith, creed or color" in advertisements for hotels and resorts. Yet in a pattern that would recur throughout later periods of Jewish civil rights history, Marshall declined to use the law once it was passed. Pressing public legal demands in the name of the Jewish people risked affirming myths of Jewish power and clannish self-interest. In a liberal society, he insisted, there could be no such thing as "distinctly Jewish interests with respect to matters of government." The best defense to antisemitism was to render Jews invisible in the public eye. As for responding to outright manifestations of antisemitism, it was far better to rally "wholesome public opinion" through "quiet, unobtrusive" means, including statements emanating "from non-Jewish sources."[42]

That technique was on display in the crisis that enveloped American Jews at the tail end of World War I. As the 1920s dawned, nativism and anti-communism led to a precipitous rise in antisemitism. American society was flooded with "concerted anti-Jewish propaganda," as modern mass media—books, pamphlets, and newspapers, along with films and radio—began to circulate antisemitic invective on a national scale. The worst offender was automobile titan Henry Ford, who in 1920 began using his *Dearborn Independent* newspaper to publish a steady stream of articles depicting Jews as arch-Bolsheviks bringing revolution to American shores, promoters of interracial sexuality, polluters of American culture, and capitalists preying on the American worker. Many of these pieces, which included excerpts from *The Protocols of the Elders of Zion*, the nefarious Russian antisemitic forgery, were then published in book form in a four-volume series, *The International Jew* (1920–22).[43]

Three different libel lawsuits were filed against Ford by individual Jews slandered in his pages. Yet the leaders of both AJC and the ADL blanched at the idea of waging direct legal battle against the industrial giant. The ADL opted instead to coordinate a public statement in 1921 condemning antisemitism "as un-American and un-Christian," signed by 116 "citizens of Gentile birth and Christian faith," including President Wilson, W. E. B. Du Bois, and Jane Addams, without mentioning Ford by name. The AJC's Marshall, meanwhile, quietly negotiated a public apology to put the matter to rest. In a statement drafted by Marshall, Ford implausibly disclaimed any prior knowledge of the hateful remarks and settled the individual lawsuits. After shuttering his newspaper, Ford proceeded to privately support numerous domestic extremist groups in the lead-up to World War II while developing warm relations with the Nazi regime.[44]

Another reason for Jewish civil rights groups' hesitation to pursue litigation against overt antisemites was the rising free speech movement. Even though the First Amendment expressly prohibited Congress from "abridging the freedom of speech," American courts displayed little respect and even less recognition for free speech before 1920. The law chiefly focused on protecting the right to private property as the most sacred individual right. It was only after World War I that the Supreme Court first identified freedom of expression as a fundamental constitutional right. That process began with early court battles over anti-draft protests and the 1919–20 "Red Scare," with its massive arrests and deportations targeting socialists, communists, and anarchists.

What most drove the free speech movement, however, was less war-related censorship than labor disputes. The American Civil Liberties Union, founded in 1920, focused on the promotion of free speech principally in order to defend radicalism and labor rights, including the right to strike and form labor unions and advocate political revolution. Where constitutional law had once upheld slavery, segregation, and laissez-faire capitalism on grounds of protecting the supremacy of private property, now free speech advocates insisted that preserving democracy from violent revolution or political violence necessitated speech and assembly freedoms.[45]

The centrality of economics to this idea of free speech was encapsulated in one line written by Supreme Court Justice Oliver Wendell Holmes Jr. in 1918: "The best test of truth is the power of the thought to get itself accepted in the competition of the market." In these words, a new theory of free speech was born. The "marketplace of ideas" model imagined society as a commercial exchange where open competition winnowed falsehood from truth. Absent a "clear and present danger," like "falsely shouting 'fire' in a theatre and causing a panic"—a line also coined by Holmes just six months earlier—the First Amendment not only permitted but required troubling and offensive ideas to be disseminated to the public. Taken together, Holmes's two dicta expressed the modern American philosophy of free speech. The search for truth must be balanced against the preservation of public safety. Barring mortal danger, the government should refrain from using its coercive power to silence speech.[46]

In 1923, when Boston's mayor tried to ban Klan meetings, the ACLU explicitly cited this rationale in the organization's defense. "We are just as much opposed to the Ku Klux Klan as you are," the New England branch wrote in response. But the civil rights "of the enemies of civil liberty as of its friends must be protected" from the government's attempt "to suppress by force the ideas and influences most disliked." The law drew a line "between word and deed" that must be safeguarded from government encroachment absent mortal danger.[47]

But when does offensive word cross that line into dangerous deed? That question surfaced in the legendary opinion of Holmes's Jewish colleague Justice Louis Brandeis in the 1927 case *Whitney v. California*. Addressing whether the State of California could pass a law to ban communist speech that threatened public welfare, Brandeis captured the dilemma neatly. "It is the function of speech to free men from the bondage of irrational fears," he wrote in his concurrence to the decision upholding the conviction of a political activist, and public "order cannot be secured merely through fear of punishment." The problem, as he identified it, is that there is no fixed legal "standard by which to determine when a danger shall be deemed clear; how remote the danger may be and yet be deemed present, and what degree of evil shall be deemed sufficiently substantial to justify resort to abridgement of free speech and assembly as the means of protection." Hence the predicament facing all those who would stop antisemitism by means of law. If prejudice is irrational, Brandeis suggested, then free thought is the best antidote to hate speech. Yet what if fear-fueled expressions of hate inflict great terror and grievous harm on Jews themselves? How is law to measure fear and correlate it to danger and injury?[48]

These questions became even more urgent in the 1930s with the ascent of organized political antisemitism. As economic depression ravaged society, a burgeoning network of individual demagogues and political groups began to weave various elements—Christian anti-Judaism, white supremacist racism, populist radicalism, anti-communism, and nativist isolationism—into a new radical right. By the mid-1930s, the ADL noted the existence of well over a hundred avowedly antisemitic fascist groups operating across America. At their head stood Father Charles Coughlin, an outspoken Catholic priest, and Gerald L. K. Smith, a charismatic Protestant preacher. From his perch in suburban Detroit, Coughlin developed a massive following through his nationwide radio broadcasts, which featured impassioned defenses of isolationism laced with virulent Jew hatred. During the Great Depression, Smith entered politics as a follower of Louisiana Governor Huey Long's "Share Our Wealth" populist campaign. After Long's assassination in 1935, Smith shifted into isolationism, then antisemitic extremism. In 1942 he founded the Christian Nationalist Crusade, with early support from Henry Ford, and then launched the America First Party in 1943. Others followed suit, including America's great hero the transatlantic aviator Charles Lindbergh. After visiting Nazi Germany in October 1938, where he accepted an award from Adolf Hitler just days before Kristallnacht, Lindbergh returned to the United States blaming Jewish control of American media and government for the prospect of global war.[49]

Such sentiments found ready ears in the late 1930s. The new field of public opinion polling immediately yielded disturbing data. A 1938 survey indicated that 36 percent of Americans believed Jews held too much power in the country, while 83 percent opposed changing restrictive immigration quotas to permit Jewish refugees to settle in the United States. Even once isolationist attitudes plummeted in late 1941 after Pearl Harbor, Americans grew still more fearful of Jews. In 1942, nearly a quarter of respondents in one survey named Japanese Americans as a "menace to Americans," while 18 percent identified German Americans, and 15 percent said Jews. Two years later, the numbers had flipped: 24 percent named Jews as America's most dangerous internal enemy, while Japanese and Germans registered only 9 percent and 6 percent, respectively. A 1944 study also revealed that over 50 percent of Americans claimed Jews held too much influence in business and government, and 25 percent believed Jews were less patriotic than other Americans. One third told pollsters that they would join or sympathize with an antisemitic political campaign.[50]

These attitudes did not penetrate mainstream politics in the form of the antisemitic parties common to interwar Europe. Smith's unsuccessful runs for the U.S. Senate in 1943 and the White House in 1944 on the America First Party ticket achieved only negligible results. Yet contemporary reports suggested that even the government employees charged with running the war effort frequently approved of Hitler's policies vis-à-vis European Jews. Those attitudes were partly responsible for keeping America's gates closed to desperate Jewish refugees and forestalling U.S. military action to stop Hitler's death machinery. They also stymied Jewish attempts to raise public awareness of the extent of Jewish suffering in Nazi Germany.[51]

Where antisemitic beliefs became concrete social realities was on the streets of the country's largest cities. Despite a lack of attention from the mainstream press, urban anti-Jewish violence skyrocketed during

World War II. From Boston, New York, and Chicago came daily reports in 1944 of vicious beatings of Jews of every age and appearance. Schoolchildren were a particular target of youth gangs and fascist elements. Synagogue vandalism and cemetery desecration spread across America. This violence was accompanied by another surge in antisemitic publications, radio broadcasts, and other media.[52]

Most alarming, the end of the war brought evidence of an increase in antisemitism across American society. In Uhrichsville, Ohio, for instance, a V-E Day celebration on May 8, 1945, turned into a riot when some seven hundred elementary and high school students proceeded from a school assembly into the streets, where they vandalized a clothing store owned by a recently discharged Jewish navy veteran and painted his car yellow. It took a police escort to rescue him from the mob. Street attacks were accompanied by an alarming trend of new restrictions in higher education. Alongside the long-standing quotas in effect in medical schools, the American Dental Association in 1945 considered a proposal to impose quotas on Jewish admissions to dental schools to rectify the "racial and geographical imbalance" in the profession. The *Journal of Clinical Psychology* launched its first issue that year with a similar call to reduce the number of Jews.[53]

While Father Coughlin had retreated from the national stage, Gerald Smith continued to crisscross the country seeking to build a political movement. In Congress, Mississippi Senator Theodore Bilbo repeatedly attacked the Truman administration's Fair Employment Practices Ordinance, designed to prevent hiring discrimination, as a Jewish conspiracy. "I am a great admirer of the Jewish race," he said in a floor speech on July 6, 1945; "Jesus Christ was a Jew. Some of my associates are Jews. But there is a certain class of 'kike' Jews in New York, organized with the CIO—Congress of Industrial Organizations—and the Negroes in a drive to cram this piece of legislation down the throats of the American people."[54]

A few months after Bilbo's speech, a survey of active duty American servicemen revealed that more than one fifth believed Hitler was right in his views and supported his policy of murdering Jews. Overall, a poll of polls, based on fourteen independent surveys conducted that year, indicated that 25 percent of Americans held antisemitic views, 25 percent opposed such views, and 50 percent had no fixed opinion on the subject. Americans hated Hitler, but a disturbingly high number also hated Jews. In between the two groups lay the half of the country who could not decide (or did not care to share) what they thought of their Jewish neighbors.[55]

In the face of these developments, American Jewish rights defenders struggled to formulate a coherent legal response. Should they seek new laws to outlaw antisemitic groups and ban hate speech? Or would such legislation only jeopardize fundamental civil liberties? How did the struggle against antisemitism relate to the fight against racial segregation? One of the first answers came in the form of a 1946 ADL national campaign to promote tolerance under the title "You Can't Be Beautiful and Hate." The slogan was cued to the group's newest spokesperson, Miss America 1945, Bess Myerson.

IN NOVEMBER 1945, Bess Myerson marched into the Midtown offices of the Anti-Defamation League with a proposal. Instead of selling Victory Bonds, she wanted to fight for civil rights. Myerson had fond memories of accompanying her father to public protests in support of workers' rights, anti-fascism, and racial equality. She had grown up in a New Deal household that lionized President Roosevelt and Mayor Fiorello La Guardia. Now the work of justice beckoned. It was time for a Tolerance Tour.[56]

The two young men who greeted her there, Arnold Forster and Benjamin Epstein, were the architects of the ADL's transformation from a small Chicago-based group into a major professional organization operating on a national scale. A fellow native of the Bronx, Forster (born Fastenberg) had earned his law degree and twice applied to work at the FBI. Rejected both times, he signed on as an ADL undercover investigator infiltrating Nazi and fascist groups in the 1930s. The Brooklyn-born Epstein had studied abroad in Nazi Germany in college, then took an MA in European history at Penn. One of his first projects at the ADL was producing a dime store edition of Hitler's *Mein Kampf*, published in 1939 to showcase the true character of Nazism to an ignorant American public.[57]

Besides framing antisemites as the enemies of democracy, Forster and Epstein sought to counter hate speech not by legal action but by flooding America with positive messages of tolerance and social harmony. Their strategy was shared by a bevy of other groups that worked with the ADL, including the Jewish Labor Committee, the American Jewish Committee, and the American Jewish Congress. During the war, this loose coalition began spending huge sums to showcase Jewish virtue and battlefield valor along with advertisements emphasizing that racial and religious discrimination threatened national unity. We must "unleash the power of printed and spoken word—weapons of truth and decency for our protection," announced the ADL in 1945, calling for "a coordinated defense program, involving professional techniques and mass media geared to reach all the 136 million American men, women and children." The effort involved a massive advertising campaign, with 65,000 radio spots, 2,000 newspaper inserts, 9 million pamphlets, 40 million comic books, and lectures reaching 30 million people.[58]

All this cultural production reflected a singularly liberal faith in the benevolent power of messaging. Fed the right media diet, the reasoning went, Americans would shed their ignorant hatreds for a more positive view of their own minorities. "We leave no media of public expression untouched," explained an AJC official, "whether it be a program of billboards, posters, car cards or newspaper ads. The national weeklies, the pulps ranging from westerns to mysteries all have been enlisted in the fight against anti-semitism and the forces of hate." A belief in the power of education to inculcate democratic values was a bedrock assumption of American liberalism at the time. In practice, however, education meant less civics lessons than entertainment. "Democracy can be fun," read one memo describing the campaign's recruitment of popular songwriters to write radio spots; "jingle advertising can sell democracy just as well as it sells Pepsi-Cola," it went on, before quoting this cringeworthy lyric: "You can get good milk from a brown-skinned cow; the color of the skin doesn't matter anyhow."[59]

What was most striking about this joint campaign was its anonymity. Very few of these millions of statements explicitly mentioned Jews or antisemitism. Instead, they spoke euphemistically about the un-American evils of racial and religious hatred. The messages were often presented by front groups or liberal Christian allies to avoid the appearance of Jewish self-interest. This all-American rhetoric served another purpose. In a society already saturated with anti-communist rhetoric from the conservative right that often masked antisemitism, linking civil rights too openly to Jews risked accusations of communist sympathies.[60]

As a result, the largest publicity campaign against antisemitism in history kept both the problem it sought to eliminate and the people it aimed to protect hidden from the very country it hoped to influence. The same pattern characterized the Tolerance Tour dreamed up for Bess Myerson. The woman who brokered Myerson's deal with the ADL was the legendary publicist and advertising executive Claire Wolff. Together, Wolff, Forster, and Epstein devised a national speaking tour focused on community centers and high school audiences. It would be run through a front organization, the American Lecture Bureau, which they had invented precisely to keep the Jewish ties undisclosed.[61]

In February 1946, Myerson debuted her new campaign in Chicago with a rousing public speech written by Epstein that emphasized the power of beauty and the ugliness of hate:

> A person with a hateful soul never can be beautiful, because hate is a corroded disease which affects everything you do . . . The seeds of prejudice are unwittingly planted in the minds of children by their parents. The children have a genuine desire to do the right thing. The biggest job of all lies in educational systems of the country.

Myerson spoke at countless events in the city that week, including visiting the Altgeld and Cabrini public housing projects, urban communities then in the throes of social conflict over race and real estate. Her multiple appearances in the city would eventually bring her in front of nearly a hundred thousand Chicagoans.[62]

The Tolerance Tour continued that spring across the U.S., with stops in Boston, Hartford, Philadelphia, Erie, Buffalo, and Chicago once more. At each venue, Myerson spoke passionately from Epstein's script, adding her own embellishments. Yet she never mentioned her own encounters with antisemitism. In fact, it would be decades before Myerson publicly acknowledged her personal experiences with antisemitism at Atlantic City and afterward. Even as she denounced racial and religious hatred as un-American and campaigned for tolerance, her pain remained concealed behind a facade of white skin and Jewish achievement. Instead of speaking forthrightly about the depths of discrimination, she emphasized a simplistic lesson of tolerance, often drawing on her meetings with veterans. "I had taken democracy for granted until then. I'd never done any serious thinking about it and then when I saw Negros and Gentiles and Jews dying together, I wondered why they couldn't live together." At other times, she stressed that studying with Black students at New York's High School of Performing Arts and Hunter College had taught her the absurdity of racism. If Americans simply agreed to end public school segregation, she told the *Chicago Defender*, the African American newspaper, all discrimination would end in no more than a decade and a half.[63]

In performing her uplifting narrative, Myerson sounded a few blatantly false notes. In an April speech, she stressed that she had won the Miss America contest "because there was no racial or religious discrimination." Glossing over the pageant's racial segregation, she stressed its respect for diversity: "When I came to Atlantic City I found . . . that nobody cared about your religion or your ancestry, or whether your parents spoke with an accent." Not surprisingly, she made no mention of what had prompted the educational tour in the first place.[64]

In June 1946, the major Jewish national civil rights groups convened a two-day summit in Chicago to address mounting antisemitism. Myerson arrived at the tail end of her tour to speak at the launch of a new joint ADL-AJC campaign. The visit coincided with the announcement of a new *Famous Funnies* comic book about her tour. The graphic biography follows Myerson from Hunter College through the Atlantic City pageant, including a scene where she visits a dying African American veteran. At his bedside she weeps, exclaiming, "And some people still say that color makes a difference." After winning the Miss America contest and declining Hollywood offers, she selflessly tours America's schools with her message: Prejudice "against people because of their religion or color" is dangerous and self-destructive. "Hate breeds ugliness."[65]

A comic book for tolerance inspired by antisemitism that was silent on its heroine's Jewish identity. A proud Jewish woman who did not consider herself white yet rose to fame through a segregated beauty pageant. Myerson's moment encapsulated the contradictions at the root of American Jewish identity at the dawn of the postwar era. It was easy for Jews to speak out against the dangers of hate but harder to voice their own Jewishness in the process. The same democracy that bestowed unprecedented rights on its Jewish citizens also seemed increasingly susceptible to the very ideology that had just eradicated their European brethren. The soaring rhetoric of American liberalism concealed a deep ambivalence regarding its Jewish minority, as the campaign against bigotry deployed every instrument of influence except the most powerful: the law itself.

2

A Riot in Chicago

At twenty minutes past eight o'clock on the first Thursday evening in February 1946, the two most controversial men in America mounted the stage of the West End Woman's Club of Chicago. Instantly recognizable was Reverend Gerald L. K. Smith. Impressively tall, with rugged features and coiffed hair, clad in a dark suit and dark tie, he radiated masculine energy. Next to him stood a far more unassuming man in a priestly habit. Of medium height, bespectacled, slightly rotund with thinning hair, Father Arthur Terminiello was the newest rising star of the far right. The pair were closely flanked by three plainclothes policemen. A few steps away on the stage sat a who's who of other extremists, including Frederick Kister, head of the Christian Veterans of America; Elizabeth Dilling, founder of the radical Mother's Movement; and Eugene Flitcraft and James Dies of the Chicago Gentile Cooperative Association, which had led a Christian boycott of Jewish businesses. They had all come together to campaign for "Christian Nationalism" in postwar America.[1]

Below the stage, the room buzzed with an overflow crowd of eight hundred white men and women. Hundreds more massed outside the doors, unable to enter. Some 250 policemen ringed the exits. In the hall, a hired legal stenographer sat at a small table poised to begin her transcription. Newspaper reporters bustled back and forth. When a press photographer mounted the stage to snap pictures of the auditorium, many audience members hid their faces. Others smiled proudly at the camera.[2]

In the streets, the atmosphere was no less intense. An enormous crowd of protesters, estimated at between fifteen hundred and three thousand people, had converged outside the building at the corner of South Ashland and West Monroe, not far from the downtown West Loop, to picket the event. Jewish and African American teenagers, rabbis and priests, local civil rights leaders, members of the National Maritime Union and the International Brotherhood of Electrical Workers, and scores of young Jewish veterans, men and women still clad in their service uniforms, marched back and forth under the watchful eyes of a thick cordon of Chicago police officers. They carried signs declaring "Divide and conquer is a Nazi technique!" and "No room for Stormtroopers in our city!" Their chants were simpler and harsher: "Fascists!" and "Nazis!" Every few minutes the scrum of protesters erupted into pockets of scuffle with the rallygoers.[3]

The rally commenced inside the auditorium with a rousing rendition of "America the Beautiful," followed by the recitation of the Pledge of Allegiance and the Lord's Prayer. Then came the first of three speeches. Kister opened with a brief, fiery campaign pitch. The Republican congressional candidate stirred the crowd with talk of thirteen million Christian veterans arriving home to find their jobs filled by Jews and Blacks. It was time to bring back the troops and retake the country from "pro-Jewish" forces. The crowd cheered wildly.[4]

Next came Smith. The man once dubbed by H. L. Mencken as "the gutsiest and goriest, the loudest and lustiest, the deadliest and damnedest orator ever heard" did not disappoint. Smith laughed and roared his way through his remarks, mirthful one moment and deadly serious the next. He urged the audience to fight with all its might for "the preservation of America as a Christian nation." The "bureaucratic fascism" of the New Deal must be stopped. The illegal Federal Reserve must be abolished. All immigration must be halted. The same held for foreign aid to postwar Europe and any other policies that led to the rise of a "world government and a super state." The choice at root was a simple one for Americans: "Christ or chaos—Christian nationalism or world Communism." Which would it be?[5]

After finishing his speech, Smith grinned as he began to introduce the evening's star attraction. Just then, a loud noise was heard from outside. The streets had descended into turmoil. The ranks of picketers had swelled with late-arriving teenagers eager to face the American fascists head-on. Eggs and bottles flew toward the hall's side windows, breaking one. Inside a man leaped to his feet. "You are a god-damned liar," he shouted at Smith before the police ushered him out. After a few tense seconds, Smith resumed his introduction. He was proud to present the young face of Catholic America, Father Arthur Terminiello. The two men wrapped their arms around each other, beaming as the audience gave a standing ovation. Then, shortly after 9:30, Terminiello stepped to the podium. The next forty minutes were a watershed in the life of hate speech in America.[6]

Terminiello opened on a quiet, homiletical note. "Now, I am going to whisper my greetings to you, fellow Christians." Then he abruptly shifted tone:

> Now, my friends, nothing you hear tonight so far, nothing that I would say can begin to express the contempt I have for that howling mob on the outside . . . And nothing I could say tonight could begin to express the contempt I have for the slimy scum that got in by mistake.

Hoots and applause followed in reply, punctuated by cries of "Tell them, Father!" They say *we* belong to the "lunatic fringe," he continued, but "you remember my Savior was put on the lunatic fringe when he was brought before Herod and kept in the role of a fool."[7]

Christ's enemies of old had returned, armed with a dangerous new agenda. The disruption "that is going on right outside this hall tonight," he said, is part of the attempt "to destroy America by revolution." Do not be fooled by all this tiresome talk of democracy, he warned. "Our democracy is not a democracy but a mobocracy, ruled by Communistic

Jews." At this line audience members began to rise, nodding their heads in righteous anger. "Yes, the Jews are all killers, murderers. If we don't kill them first, the Jews will kill us," shouted one woman. "Kill the Jews," screamed another.[8]

AT WHAT POINT does private hatred become public danger? The great promise of American democracy has always been that liberal politics can neutralize the creedal passions and tribal conflicts that destroyed so many other societies. This promise was a decidedly pragmatic compromise with the dark side of human nature. In a post-Enlightenment world, society was divided into two spheres, the public and the private. In public, all citizens would be equal; in private humans remained free to love or hate as they so wished. Prejudice would never be completely eliminated, but once consigned to the private sphere it would do no grievous harm.

For much of American history, that promise was contradicted by the glaring facts of slavery, segregation, and sexism. Religious equality was undermined by the entrenchment of Christianity in public life. The law meanwhile functioned as an instrument of prejudice. The end of world war and the triumph of democracy over fascism renewed the possibility that law could finally fulfill its stated commitment to equality for all citizens. Yet the postwar drive for civil rights raised new questions about the boundaries between public and private. Is the incitement of physical violence the only danger posed by free speech? When do noxious opinions become a political danger? In an era of totalitarianism, is hate speech a threat to democracy itself?

Terminiello's Chicago speech initiated a chain of events that forced the law to reckon with these questions. From its origins as a local charge for breaching the peace to its conclusion as a Supreme Court ruling, *Terminiello v. Chicago* evolved from a referendum on the limits of free speech into a test of postwar liberalism's boundaries. In the space between Hitler's defeat and the rising conflict with Stalin, Americans confronted as never before the reality of their own antisemitism. That reckoning inspired both fear and hope in equal measure. It also spawned the great conundrum of their day and ours. Does our exceptional faith in free speech elevate American freedoms beyond those enshrined elsewhere in the world? Or, in the iconic expression born of this case, do we idolize the First Amendment at risk of converting the "Bill of Rights into a suicide pact"?

MORE THAN SEVENTY new American antisemitic organizations appeared between September 1945 and the fall of 1946, including invigorated Ku Klux Klan chapters in the South and Christian Front groups in Northern cities. They were joined by pro-fascist veterans' groups and brazenly antisemitic politicians like Senator Robert Reynolds of North Carolina, who launched a White Nationalist party. Still, it was unclear whether these extremists would coalesce into a national political movement with a charismatic leader. Among those vying for that title was Gerald Smith. With the fighting finally over, he set about rebuilding his prewar Protestant-Catholic coalition. That led him in late 1945 to join forces with Terminiello, the "Father Coughlin of the South."[9]

Arthur Terminiello was born in 1906 to an Italian immigrant family in Roxbury, Massachusetts. After studies at Boston College and ordination at St. Mary's Seminary in Baltimore, he moved in 1933 to rural Alabama. There he took up a traveling mission serving twenty Southern counties, a territory of some 11,000 square miles with only four Catholic churches and fewer than four hundred practicing Catholics. Undeterred, Terminiello borrowed a page from the Protestant tent revival playbook and built his own custom miniature chapel-trailer to bring "God to the cotton-fields." St. Teresa's Mobile Catholic Chapel won its creator brief national attention as a new kind of Catholic priest, unafraid to use the latest technology to tackle the ills of modernity.[10]

Across the 1920s and 1930s, Catholic agrarians responded to the Great Depression by launching a back-to-the-land movement of farming cooperatives aimed at defeating the twin evils of urban capitalism and soul-destroying communism. Terminiello joined that effort in 1937 with the inauguration of Saint Teresa's Village, a farming settlement on five hundred acres seven miles south of Greenville, Alabama. The village eschewed money crops like tobacco, corn, and cotton to avoid the "economic credit parasite," focusing instead on "semi-subsistence farming." It also produced a broadsheet, *Rural Justice*, in which Terminiello registered his increasingly dark musings on the threats to American society. From denunciations of the "Jew Deal" and its program of "economic slavery" for Southern sharecroppers, Terminiello rapidly progressed in the early war years to calls for a true "Christocracy" to save America.[11]

The year 1943 proved to be the turning point in his journey from priest-provocateur to professional militant. The Saint Teresa venture collapsed and *Rural Justice* folded. Alarmed by the media attention, Church officials reassigned the renegade priest to a small parish in Huntsville. Convinced that Jewish interests had sabotaged his ventures and engineered his demotion, he embarked on a broad counteroffensive. In radio sermons broadcast across northern Alabama, Terminiello denounced the war effort and dismissed German "so-called atrocities" as Allied propaganda. He began crisscrossing the country, delivering speeches and collecting signatures for a petition urging a congressional investigation into "the truth" about Pearl Harbor. His 1944 pamphlet "The Cross of War" described the Japanese attack as a massive conspiracy staged by the Roosevelt administration, the British and Soviet governments, world Jews, communists, and American "liberals." It proved an instant success, reportedly selling over one million copies.[12]

In 1945, Terminiello announced "a Christian crusade" to stop the hidden "totalitarian" coup underway. In his new newspaper, *The Crusader*, he railed against the "3000 super-secret masters" of the "capitalistic Zionistic group," who had united with "Red fascism" in a "Communist-Jewish conspiracy" for a "World Empire Plot." That July he traveled to Washington to present his Pearl Harbor petition with fifteen thousand signatures to the isolationist Senator William Langer, who inserted it into the Congressional Record. In November, Terminiello launched the Union of Christian Crusaders to restore "a free and Christian America." His open calls for Black and Jewish civil rights activists to be shot on sight proved the last straw for Church leaders. At month's end, the local Alabama bishop suspended him from ecclesiastical duties. The decision came as no surprise to Terminiello, who had already resolved to retire from the priesthood and devote his energies to the new cause. A week later, Terminiello was on a plane to New Orleans to meet Smith. After two days of talks, they agreed to join forces in a national campaign.[13]

The Smith-Terminiello speaking tour began the first week of February 1946, making lightning stops in Pittsburgh, Cleveland, St. Louis, and Detroit. Day by day, the rallies grew larger. So, too, did the picket lines. In Cleveland, Terminiello punched a protester who shoved him. In St. Louis, four thousand protesters showed up, requiring the National Guard to maintain order; a bomb threat forced the event's cancellation. Terminiello and Smith later claimed that these incidents proved the dangerous intentions of their opponents.

Of all the cities on their tour, Chicago would prove the most explosive. It embodied America's tensions in their most extreme form: A strong labor movement and radical tradition dating to the Haymarket anarchists of the 1880s clashed with entrenched conservatism and a far right that included pro-Nazi elements in the German American community. Black and Jewish politicians challenged white Catholic Democratic machines, while waves of newcomers—European immigrants, Mexican Americans, Puerto Ricans, Japanese Americans, Southern Black migrants—competed for scarce housing in a growing metropolis. This volatile mix had repeatedly erupted in racist violence and labor riots throughout the city's history, creating a cycle of conflict that marked Chicago for generations.

A year earlier, Smith had begun scheming to turn Chicago into the stage for his greatest drama yet. He confided to Terminiello his plan to draw his Jewish communist enemies into confrontation, thereby exposing their "program of physical terrorism." To that end he deliberately chose to locate a rally on the Near West Side, a former Irish and German immigrant neighborhood increasingly populated by Jewish, African American, and Mexican families. He blanketed the city with circulars and mailings, inviting followers to join him for a martyr's mission. I will speak in Chicago, he warned, "or be killed in the attempt."

By baiting their enemies into revealing their true face, Terminiello and Smith aimed to show guileless Americans the violent fate that lay in store for them.[14]

At the West End Woman's Club of Chicago, Terminiello continued his speech with the theme of Jewish violence. Did you know, he asked his audience, that the Jews of Europe had begun exacting their revenge by murdering German Christians? Jewish doctors serving in the American army boasted openly of amputating German men's limbs as punishment. "Imagine men of that caliber—sworn to serve our Christian country! And we are asked to tolerate *them*!" Jewish military nurses were also part of the plot, poisoning German women and children with syphilis and typhus as retribution. Meanwhile, Treasury Secretary Henry Morgenthau's "vicious plan of vengeance" aimed to starve the babies and mothers of Germany. "They ought to starve the Jews," shouted one audience member. Another yelled: "They ought to kill Morgenthau!"[15]

Even as he named these Jewish conspirators, Terminiello played the classic antisemite's game of forswearing prejudice. With a verbal wink, he told the audience, "I am going to talk about—I almost said, about the Jews. Of course, I would not want to say that. However, I'm going to talk about *some* Jews." Every group contains good and bad people, he went on. But Christian mercy had its limit. "We must love every person, Germans and Jews, Italians, and everybody. We must not love particularly the criminals among those people . . . So it is with the Jews, we must condemn the criminals, even if they are Jews." This was no easy task. "The moment we point to a man and say that man is a Communist, or that his name happens to be Ginsberg, then we are considered to be antisemitic." Yet we must not fear to name "this danger which we face." The solution was simple: "Let us call them Zionist Jews, if you will, let's call them atheistic, Communistic Jewish or Zionist Jews, then let us not fear to condemn them."[16]

Just as he spoke these words, a loud noise sounded inside the hall. Some thought it was a bottle flying through a window. Others assumed a stink bomb. Or a knot of protesters breaking through the police line at the front doors. In the mounting fear, no one knew for sure. Terminiello seized on the interruption:

> Do you wonder why they were persecuted in other countries in the world? . . . We will not be tolerant of that mob out there . . . We are not going to be tolerant any longer of their pagan eye for an eye philosophy. We are Christians, and proud of it. We are not to be tolerant of their blasphemy.

That mob outside, he went on, is like a "snake." You don't tolerate a poisonous snake; you destroy it. "We must not be like the Apostles before the coming of the Holy Ghost," he said, invoking a notoriously anti-Jewish scene from the Gospel of John, in which Christ's disciples face a menacing Jewish mob outside their doors. "We must not lock ourselves in an upper room for fear of the Jews." His words drew frenzied replies. "Send the Jews back to Russia," screamed one man. Others shouted "Kill the Jews" and "Dirty kikes."

Terminiello closed with a rousing call to arms, an exhortation to join in a Christian crusade to oppose:

> Every attempt to breach freedom of speech in America;
> Every attempt to dilute Christianity in America;
> Every attempt to undermine the morality of America;
> Every attempt to shed American blood to promote Zionism;
> Every attempt to destroy the sovereignty of America;
> Every attempt to demoralize America;
> Every attempt to persecute our cross.

This we must do together, he thundered. "We shall carry on despite the howls of Communists, fascists, or Zionistic Jews."[17]

As Terminiello came to the end of his speech, two men sitting in the back of the room rose and slipped discreetly out the door. Raven-haired with dark eyes set under prominent eyebrows, Judge Samuel Heller looked more like a silent-era Hollywood movie star than a sitting justice of the Chicago Municipal Court. His companion, fair-complexioned and sharply featured, with a high forehead and a ready smile, was Ira Latimer, executive director of the Chicago Civil Liberties Committee (CCLC). Outside, they found a riot in full swing. Eggs, bricks, and bottles sailed through the air. There were fistfights between rallygoers and protesters. The crowd tussled back and forth with the police while injured bodies lay underfoot. A flying wedge of some forty teen boys rushed forward to test the police ring guarding the building's doors. As the police manhandled the unruly crowd, they swung their batons wildly, beating protesters. More rocks flew. The police began shoving bloodied protesters into paddy wagons.[18]

Judge Heller's first concern was for the safety of his teenage daughter Sonia, who was lost somewhere in the melee. He was also outraged at the scenes of anarchy unfolding. "This is a hell of a way to protect the city. I'm one of the suckers who have to pay taxes," Heller shouted above the noise to Latimer, whose reply launched the evening's second act: "I want to get a warrant for that priest."[19]

Despite the appearance of spontaneity, the call to arrest Terminiello was no spur-of-the-moment decision. It reflected the culmination of a yearslong effort by Chicago civil rights leaders to address the epic tide of racial violence that had coursed through the city during the war. Alongside massive discrimination in housing, hiring, and schooling, Jewish, Black, and Mexican American Chicagoans faced militant white homeowners' associations that employed arson, vandalism, and physical violence to keep their neighborhoods segregated. Black and Mexican men regularly suffered police brutality, while Jewish teens endured vicious gang beatings in Hyde Park and elsewhere. In Jewish cemeteries in Oakwood, Cottage Grove, and Forest Park, gravestones were regularly overturned, defaced, and blasted by shotguns.[20]

Behind all this hate lay a half-concealed network of organizations and fascist ideologues pumping the city full of pamphlets and flyers. "Chicago, the birthplace of the German American Bund and scene of the greatest wartime seditious activities," proclaimed *The American Mercury* in 1943, is now well on its way to becoming "the hate center of the nation and the staff headquarters for incipient American fascism."[21]

The city of hate had also become a laboratory for a bevy of new civil rights efforts. In 1943, the three principal Jewish civil rights organizations—the AJC, the ADL, and the American Jewish Congress—launched a local coalition, the Chicago Council Against Racial and Religious Discrimination. They found partners in a variety of other groups, including the ACLU, the NAACP, and the Chicago Urban League. The same year Democratic Mayor Edward Kelley established the Mayor's Committee on Human Relations to enlist community leaders to stave off the urban unrest that had just led to terrible race riots in Detroit. The most aggressive effort specifically keyed to antisemitism in the city, however, stemmed from the Chicago Commission on Antisemitism, a partnership between the American Jewish Congress and the CCLC.

Led by its longtime leader Rabbi Stephen S. Wise, the American Jewish Congress represented primarily eastern European Jews who identified with civil rights, progressive politics, and liberal Zionism. The group spent the war years pressing for an anti-Nazi economic boycott and urging American military intervention to save European Jews. The CCLC, founded by local ACLU members in 1931 to combat police brutality, had expanded under Latimer, an Ohio-born Baptist missionary, labor activist, and college professor. Operating as an ACLU affiliate, it broadened its mission to include employment discrimination, gay rights, labor organizing, and separation of church and state. In the later years of the war, Latimer pushed the CCLC toward offensive legal action against far right groups, challenging the national ACLU's moderate stance.[22]

"The most important civil liberties problem" we face today, Latimer concluded in 1944, "is the rise of anti-Negro, anti-Jewish, anti-Japanese, and anti-Mexican discrimination." Of these hatreds, Latimer singled out antisemitism, not because of any uniqueness but on account of "its use as a political weapon" to destroy democracy. "Unless the American public is forewarned and forearmed concerning the Hitler game now being played by the big-time political antisemites," he warned, "there cannot be built an anti-fascist public opinion politically powerful enough to defeat these professional Jew-baiters."[23]

Thanks to a $2,000 donation that year from the Inland Steel company heir Edward Ryerson III, reportedly the largest philanthropic gift ever made specifically to fight antisemitism, Latimer convened a series of citywide conferences that produced the Commission on Antisemitism. "It is not enough to name the antisemitism," wrote Ryerson, a white Protestant Chicagoan then serving as a private first class in the U.S. Army, "the thing becomes important when put in its democratic context." Emotional appeals to human equality counted for little, he added. You must combat "the use of antisemitism as a political weapon" by those forces who "fear the results of a functioning democracy."[24]

The CCLC board expanded to include several Jewish rabbis and labor leaders, along with Jack Fishbein, the editor of *The Sentinel*, the city's main Jewish newspaper. All shared Latimer's belief that hate speech should no longer be tolerated. "There must be a reevaluation of the meaning of free speech in relation to those who incite to racial hatred, discrimination and violence," declared the businessman Fred Ptashne, Commission on Antisemitism co-chair. The group intended to begin by focusing on one particular offender: Gerald Smith.[25]

All this talk of anti-fascism and banning hate-mongers alarmed the ACLU leadership, which had for decades defended groups like the Ku Klux Klan on grounds of strict adherence to free speech principles. Smith had also assiduously courted ACLU cofounder and executive director Roger Baldwin, who readily offered support. "No democracy with any guts in it has ever been overthrown by crackpots and agitators," Baldwin once told a skeptical colleague, "but if they are suppressed, underground conspiracy and violence are encouraged." Firm conviction shaped Baldwin's thinking. Yet politics played an equally decisive role.[26]

In the late 1930s, the ACLU had softened its earlier radicalism. Defending both ends of the political spectrum allowed it to project a centrist moderation against critics on the right. During the war, Baldwin grew increasingly worried that the CCLC had been infiltrated by communists. Too strong a focus on legislation in "support of racial minorities" would taint the entire organization as pro-communist. Latimer vigorously objected. "We are the only anti-Communist and anti-Fascist civil rights organization in town," he stressed. "These extreme right wingers who use 'red-baiting' to oppose equal rights for Negroes and Jews . . . actually push many of our foreign born, racial and religious minorities, trade unionists and intellectuals into the . . . extreme left-wing camp of revolt." True liberalism meant protecting the rights of minorities in the marketplace of speech in realistic terms.[27]

The question of how to handle Smith exacerbated this division. In late 1945, as word reached Chicago that Smith and Terminiello planned a major rally, the CCLC finally severed its ties with the ACLU. At a community-wide meeting, tempers flared as remaining ACLU leaders insisted that civil rights groups should neither block the rally nor stage a counterprotest. They went so far as to oppose a request for a public permit to picket the rally on the nearby sidewalk, arguing it would impede the speakers' right to free speech. Such views resonated with the ADL and AJC representatives. The answer to hate speech, they insisted, was neither censorship nor counterspeech, but a new strategy: silence.[28]

First formulated in 1943 by Rabbi Solomon Fineberg, the AJC's resident antisemitism expert, the "quarantine" theory held that all picketing, counterdemonstrations, and other "circus-like tactics" were dangerously counterproductive. The main goal of rabble-rousers was publicity. Just as with insolent children deprived of attention, the silent treatment would undercut the egos and antics of bigots. Any law "which forbids bigotry (including antisemitism) in broad terms is doomed to utter failure," Fineberg argued. If the public "is inclined to condemn antisemitism, the laws are not needed. If the public favors antisemitism, the laws will not work. In fact, once established, such laws can be used by reactionary forces to their own advantage."[29]

The Commission on Antisemitism vigorously disagreed. We are dealing here with "America's number one pro-Nazi," argued Fishbein. If the government refuses to act against "American fascists" threatening Chicagoans and openly calling for "insurrection," then responsible citizens must protest and pursue legal action. His colleague Avrum Tapper concurred: "It is a perversion of the First Amendment to throw the cloak of protection over the American 'ratzis,' who under the guise of 'Free Speech' and 'Free Assembly' would destroy these very liberties if they ever came into power. It seems to me that our so-called 'civil liberty purists' are Voltairean 'chassidim.'" "I may disagree with you," the French philosopher had supposedly remarked, "but I defend to the death your right to say it."[30]

In late December and early January 1946, the Commission on Antisemitism developed a two-part plan. First, the Smith-Terminiello rally would be met with a large public protest, either a counterrally or, as it turned out, a mass picket line involving a broad roster of labor unions, liberal Church groups, the NAACP, and the Jewish War Veterans of America. Next, they would convince the authorities to consider prosecuting Smith and Terminiello under the city's disorderly conduct law: "All persons who shall make, aid, countenance, or assist in making any improper noise, riot, disturbance, breach of the peace, or diversion tending to a breach of the peace, within the limits of the city . . . shall be deemed guilty of disorderly conduct," a misdemeanor crime subject to a fine of between $1 and $200. It was a small penalty, to be sure, but would send a message that hatred deserved legal sanction.[31]

To file a criminal complaint, however, required both a witness to the crime and a member of the local judiciary willing to sign the complaint. Latimer volunteered to serve as witness. That left the question of a sympathetic judge. They found their man in Samuel Heller, an independent-minded Jewish jurist. A child immigrant from tsarist Russia who had worked his way up from poverty to a University of Chicago BA, a law degree from Northwestern, and a municipal court judgeship, Heller vigorously disagreed with the "quarantine" philosophy, which he associated with the German Jewish establishment's elitism and political quietism. A staunch anti-communist who read *Pravda* in the Russian original every day to know the mind of his enemy, he had no concerns about being tagged as a leftist. But he insisted that he would participate only if he could attend the rally himself to determine whether a criminal charge was justified.[32]

Heller's caveat highlighted the crucial unknown in the entire gambit: Would the rally trigger a response sufficient to be deemed a riot or breach of peace? Even if public disorder did erupt, could the speakers be held responsible based on their constitutionally protected speech?

A game of legal chicken was at hand. Even as Latimer took steps to line up a criminal complaint, Smith and Terminiello spent the weeks before the rally carefully plotting how to use the event as a showdown over the First Amendment. Well aware of their potential legal jeopardy, the duo maneuvered to characterize the rally as a private affair. Smith's team mailed out hundreds of free tickets to local followers with instructions to bring friends. In theory, those tickets were required for entrance, making the rally a closed-door meeting. Whether it really was a private event would become a key point of debate during the subsequent trial.

A similarly canny tactic defined the speeches. Both Smith and Terminiello crafted addresses that alternated fiery appeals calculated to prompt emotional outrage with studied declarations of constitutional fealty. Terminiello proved particularly adept at stirring the audience just to the brink of physical rage while also counseling them not to engage the "mob" outside. Finally, the two men counted on the police to serve as their ally. Smith was ruthless in his handling of the police situation, Terminiello later wrote. He knew "that the police had to defend" the speakers "whether they liked it or not." Smith and Terminiello had quite a few supporters in the ranks of the notoriously racist Chicago Police Department, which explained why the 250 policemen within the hall likely outnumbered the force assigned to crowd control outside.[33]

BY THE TIME Terminiello finished speaking, at around ten thirty, police chief Ray Crane had concluded that it was too dangerous for anyone to leave the building. As the crowd waited inside, the two men led them in songs and prayers. Outside, the arrests and beatings continued, at moments approaching anarchy. The violence during that final hour would form the centerpiece of the legal trial to come. Who were the victims and who the perpetrators? Did the words inside the building stir the mayhem outside? Finally, after nearly an hour, the police formed two lines and an armored police car backed up to the hall's rear door. Terminiello, Smith, Kister, and their associates were ushered into the vehicle under heavy guard and driven to the Blackstone Hotel with sirens blaring.[34]

As the police van pulled away from the hall, Heller and Latimer reached the Des Plaines Street police station. There, minutes before midnight, they found nineteen teenagers being held without charge. Two were seriously injured, one bleeding profusely from his head, the second unconscious. Rather than providing medical care, the police sergeant was busy fingerprinting all those detained. This was troubling and absurd, Heller told the duty sergeant. "It's a dastardly thing that in the name of free speech a taxpayer has to protect a lousy skunk like Smith," while the police treated "young boys as if they were desperate criminals."[35]

Infuriated, Heller summoned his clerk, a bailiff, and another municipal judge, Oscar Caplan, and announced that he would hold court right then and there in the police station. Heller ordered the station supervisor, one Captain Graney, to process and release the teens. The nineteen demonstrators were charged with disorderly conduct, with three on counts of possessing or throwing stink bombs. Nearly all charges were eventually dropped after the policeman who swore out the criminal complaint admitted he hadn't witnessed the crimes alleged. Next, Caplan issued an arrest warrant for a policeman who had severely assaulted the injured youth. Then Latimer swore out his complaint, alleging that the riot was "caused by inflammatory speeches delivered in the meeting." Heller and Caplan signed arrest warrants for Smith, Terminiello, and Kister for violating the public disturbance ordinance. Then they went home to bed.[36]

The next morning at six o'clock, the telephone rang in Terminiello's hotel room. It was Captain Graney, calling with an announcement and an apology. He was in possession of an arrest warrant, yet he pledged that as a good Catholic "he would never serve a warrant on a priest." Twice the police captain refused to serve the warrant. Finally, Terminiello phoned him back. To spare the policeman any trouble, he and his colleagues would voluntarily appear at three o'clock that afternoon.[37]

When the three men showed up at the station, they found it roped off to keep crowds and press at bay. There they encountered Heller and Caplan in a brief, dramatic moment captured by the cameras. After booking they proceeded to the cashier's booth to make bond: $600 each for Terminiello and Kister and $500 for Smith. Throughout the process, Terminiello kept silent, but Kister and Smith seized the opportunity to parade their views. "I don't like to make attacks upon racial minorities," Kister shouted to the assembled reporters, "but the Jewish people in America, as a whole, are behaving very badly." We have come here to protect "the Irish police on the force from the Jews," Smith declared, adding, "God save America! God save the police department! It's become an awful thing when a priest of the Church is arrested and brought into court by a bunch of Russians."[38]

Back at their hotel, the public performance continued. The three held court in the dining room, posing and smiling for the press as they chatted over coffee. Then they issued a joint press release reiterating their "deep conviction that America is basically Christian." We must defend our country, they declared, from "the three most menacing non-Christian and anti-Christian elements in the world: (1) Communism (2) Imperialism (3) Zionism." Undeterred by the arrest, they stated their intention to continue their tour across all fifty states. As for the trial, justice would prevail. "We'll whip these bastards," declared Smith, "if it takes all spring."[39]

Heller, Latimer, and their colleagues were no less confident in their chances. That same evening, a Friday, a reporter called on the judge at his home. Heller interrupted his family's Shabbat dinner to give a statement. I am tired of hearing "the laments from the 'shah-shah' groups who believe we Jews should stick our heads in the ground like ostriches while Smith and his ilk carry on their hate tirades, protected by the Chicago police which these same Jews support with their taxes," he proclaimed. "Today I found out who is alive in Chicago Jewry." Then he made one other bold call: "We must have a law that will make the act of inciting hatred against any racial or religious group illegal." The trial, soon to begin, would determine the fate of this quest. "It is time, once and for all," Heller concluded, "to outlaw antisemitism."[40]

3

Fighting Words

City of Chicago v. Arthur Terminiello nearly began with a fistfight. The trio of Gerald Smith, Arthur Terminiello, and Frederick Kister sauntered into the Cook County courtroom on the morning of Wednesday, March 26, with grins on their faces. Kister treated the event like a political rally, pausing every few steps to hand out campaign flyers to the supporters who packed the gallery. Then a reporter from the Yiddish daily *Forverts* approached to ask for a copy. "Which newspaper are you from?" Kister demanded. "Show me your press card." When the reporter refused, Kister smirked. "I knew that you were Jewish from the shape of your nose." It took the court bailiff's intervention to end the altercation.[1]

Marching in behind the defendants came their celebrity attorneys, Albert Dilling and Maximilian St. George. The duo had made their names in the 1944 Washington Sedition Trial, defending a bevy of prominent American isolationists and fascists accused of advocating the violent overthrow of the government. After a mistrial was declared following the death of the presiding judge, St. George published a book claiming victory for the First Amendment over the "powerful economic and political minorities" who had aligned with "sinister antilibertarian, totalitarian and internationalist forces" to threaten America. He had now come to Chicago, St. George declared, to prevent another "legalized lynching." When a female reporter outside the judge's chambers mocked him for peddling "fairy tales" about the Chicago rally, he lunged at her in fury, fists swinging. Several pressmen jumped in front of her to shield her from assault.[2]

Faced with these provocations, city prosecutors took steps to keep the trial tightly focused on the crime itself. Assistant City Attorney A. A. Pantelis, the "dean of Greek American lawyers," was assigned as lead prosecutor specifically because he was not Jewish. At the prosecution's request, Judge John McCormack, the no-nonsense former dean of Loyola Law School, agreed to try each of the defendants separately. Terminiello would go first. Still, the chaos continued into jury selection that morning. St. George queried each prospective juror on whether they were Jewish or belonged to a Jewish organization or a labor union. By lunchtime, he had succeeded in weeding out all those he deemed "subversives." The result was a suitably "American" jury of twelve white men and women, seven Catholic and five Protestant.[3]

Opening statements began that afternoon. In a crisp, confident tone, Pantelis asked the jury to ignore all the distractions swirling around the case. This case boiled down to a single line in the municipal code, he told them. Chicago law forbids the making of "any improper noise, riot, disturbance, breach of the peace, or diversion tending to a breach of the peace." The State will show, he explained, that the defendant "provoked a riot" through his words, which "should not be protected under the mask of free speech."[4]

Father Terminiello is an innocent man of faith, countered St. George. My client has been scapegoated for exercising "that cornerstone of our liberties, freedom of speech." His words harmed no one. Nor were they even hateful. In truth, all the violence had happened *outside* the hall, St. George continued, where the vicious "Jewish terrorists" and "Communists" had gathered to target a Christian priest and his peaceful audience. As St. George spoke these lines, Judge McCormack grew visibly upset. Finally, he banged his gavel, leaped from his seat, and rebuked the attorney. You are in serious risk of contempt of court with this kind of language, he warned. Terminiello's supporters booed loudly. Turning to the gallery, the judge threatened to clear the courtroom. Glancing over at the jury box, Terminiello smiled and winked. The game was on.[5]

The antisemites "know that their remarks are frivolous," wrote the French philosopher Jean-Paul Sartre in 1944. "But they are amusing themselves, for it is their adversary who is obliged to use words responsibly, since he believes in words." Terminiello's mirthful signal let the jury in on what was really happening. Behind the court's sober facade of rules and impartiality, there raged a power struggle between an innocent American people and their evil enemy. American jurisprudence had been replaced by "the new Jewish prudence." Terminiello's pun, made in a private communication to Smith, was derived from a long-standing antisemitic trope that Judaism corrupted law. It grew out of the ancient Christian myth that Old Testament vengeful legalism had been replaced by New Testament merciful love. Play along with me, Terminiello was telling the jury, and together we will rescue justice from the law.[6]

Stereotype is the currency of hatred. Yet the value of that currency fluctuates based on the state of the moral economy in which it circulates. To prove powerful, a stereotype must resonate with the moment at hand. Now, in the mid-1940s, the trope of Jewish legalism spoke to Americans' fears about law and liberalism. At the newly founded United Nations, diplomats spoke loftily of international human rights law, which would ban discrimination and intolerance. Many Americans, including most lawyers, feared such laws would compromise American sovereignty and hand the Soviets a powerful propaganda weapon. Meanwhile, new federal civil rights policies and Supreme Court cases challenged the primacy of segregation, requiring not just the removal of racist laws but new ones banning racism itself.

Antisemitism offered a seductive conspiracy theory. Racial minorities and political radicals had hijacked the law, Terminiello and his comrades asserted, and behind these groups lay Jewish hands. Like the petty violence that accompanied it, this antisemitic myth threatened at times to overwhelm the weeklong trial. It also turned *City of Chicago v. Arthur Terminiello* into a legal referendum on postwar liberalism's ability to defeat hatred.

* * *

"THE STRUGGLE FOR Jewish equality—equality in law and equality in fact—is entering its critical stages in the United States," read "Full Equality in a Free Society," a 1946 manifesto issued by the new Commission on Law and Social Action of the American Jewish Congress. "Antisemitism in America differs fundamentally from the classical, European, prewar varieties," the text continued. "The main threat to Jewish equality comes not from the police or the bureaucracy, as it used to come in Russia, or Poland, or Germany—it comes from the forces of society itself." The business that would not hire Jews. The medical school that enforced a quota on Jewish admissions. The neighborhood barring home sales to Jews along with other minorities. The political organization that fomented anti-Jewish violence. "Anti-Semitism here is private or communal," continued the text, "not public or governmental in nature." That fact raised a core question for American liberalism: "How far should the federal government be allowed to go in defining the right to social and economic equality?"[7]

The author of these lines, Alexander Pekelis, was one of the most creative minds in the 1940s world of American law. He was also one of the newest. Pekelis arrived in New York City in 1941 as a refugee from wartime Europe. Born in Odessa in 1902, he established himself in Rome as a law professor and early critic of Italian fascism before fleeing with his family via France and Portugal to the United States. He repeated law school at Columbia University, becoming the *Columbia Law Review*'s first foreign-born editor in chief. In 1945, while working full-time as a professor at the New School, Pekelis joined the American Jewish Congress as the founding director of its new legal commission. Blessed with "the fire of prophecy," the passionate Russian-accented orator with a ready smile dazzled colleagues and audiences alike with his speeches about the future of liberalism.[8]

"Full Equality in a Free Society" laid out a comprehensive vision for postwar civil rights that would guide the next three decades of Jewish activism. It was accompanied by a burst of innovative litigation by the legal commission in support of civil rights across the country. In

California, Pekelis intervened in a federal civil rights lawsuit in 1945 with an amicus brief using sociological research to challenge the de facto segregation of Mexican American students in public schools, arguing that the "crippling psychological effects of such segregation are in essence a denial of equality of treatment." The strategy anticipated the same argument later used in *Brown v. Board of Education*. In New York City, he drafted the country's first employment anti-discrimination law. In Washington he lodged a pioneering 1946 lawsuit with the Federal Communications Commission to block an application by the *New York Daily News* for a radio license, citing a pattern of egregious anti-Jewish and anti-Black bias. In Illinois, he sued the Champaign-Urbana public school system to challenge the practice of segregating students by faith for religious instruction. Pekelis even sued his alma mater, Columbia University, for discrimination against Jewish students in its college admissions.[9]

Each of these legal moves reflected the core postulates of postwar Jewish liberalism: separation of church and state, active alliance with other minorities to end racial segregation and expand civil rights, and abiding faith in the American democratic process. To these Pekelis added a fourth idea: The law must curb private discrimination. Precisely because American Jews were not targeted by racist government laws, their experience highlighted the way in which informal bias was encoded in the structures of society. Even as Pekelis overstated his claim that Jews had never faced legal discrimination in American society, he used the Jewish case to illustrate his larger point. Corporations, hate groups, homeowners' associations, private schools and clubs, and mass media held so much real power in society that they effectively functioned as "private governments [that] hollow out the content of freedom and equality, leaving a well-polished shell." Nor was the state a neutral party, as some legal theorists held. Private discrimination depended on government acquiescence, if not indirect support. Now the time had come to untie that knot. "The United States has reached a stage of evolution," Pekelis wrote, "in which group existence and group responsibility, social discrimination, and private injustice have become crucial political and legal, and, in some senses, even constitutional problems."[10]

The same logic held for hate speech. A member of the ACLU, Pekelis viewed freedom of speech as the quintessence of liberalism. Yet he believed that the ACLU's libertarian approach to free speech as a David-versus-Goliath contest between individuals and their government missed the point. Free speech was not actually "freedom from government," but "freedom *through* government—through an enlightened and vigorous government" protecting constitutional rights from abuse by both its own representatives and private interests. "The freedom of the market of ideas," he argued, "can be lost through control—or through its absence."[11]

In October 1945, Pekelis published an influential article in *The New Republic*, "Group Sanctions for Racism." Just as libel and defamation laws protected individuals from slanderous speech, group libel or group defamation might do the same for vulnerable minorities. Extreme verbal assaults on groups in the form of knowingly false statements and mass propaganda endangered democracy as a whole. Liberals could not afford to let the toxin of hate course freely through the private sector under the guise of individual freedom. If modern government could halt business fraud and regulate food and drugs, the same could be said for the most damaging expressions of hate speech.[12]

The idea of group libel stretched back to the ADL's original efforts in the 1910s to ban racist and antisemitic publications and advertising. In the late 1930s, Jewish liberals had revived the idea to combat the unprecedented wave of fascist and antisemitic propaganda flowing through the country. Even the ACLU seriously considered the possibility before ultimately rejecting it. Pekelis aimed to consolidate these efforts into a systematic legal theory by reasoning from labor law. In response to economic changes in society, courts and legislatures recognized collective bargaining and striking as new, legitimate legal group-based rights. The same could hold for minorities since, in his view, "people singled out for attack as a group have the right to defend themselves as a group."[13]

As he had with other civil rights initiatives, Pekelis proposed a two-track approach to group libel. Draft legislation would provide a model for both states and the federal government to create laws against certain forms of racist speech and publications. At the same time, test cases using existing legislation would demonstrate the constitutionality of such statutes.

Illinois beckoned as the ideal place to pursue this quest for the simple reason that the state already possessed a group libel statute. In 1917, at the behest of African American state legislator R. R. Jackson, the state legislature had passed a law making it a criminal misdemeanor for:

> any person . . . to manufacture, sell, or offer for sale, advertise or publish, present or exhibit in any public place in this state any lithograph, moving picture, play, drama or sketch, which publication or exhibition portrays depravity, criminality, unchastity, or lack of virtue of a class of citizens, of any race, color, creed or religion which said publication or exhibition exposes the citizens of any race, color, creed or religion to contempt, derision, or obloquy or which is productive of breach of the peace or riots.[14]

The law was drafted in response to the racist film *The Birth of a Nation* and against the backdrop of the state's race riots and lynchings, notably the 1908 Springfield Race Riot, an anti-Black mob rampage in the state capital that also featured antisemitic attacks, and which inspired the creation of the NAACP. The statute addressed two distinct harms related to speech—incitement to violence and defaming a group—without connecting them. This broad language meant hateful speech could be regulated by law even when it did not cause violence. In 1941, an Illinois state court had convicted Jehovah's Witness members under the law for distributing anti-Catholic tracts, a ruling the Supreme Court subsequently affirmed. While this statute might have applied to Terminiello's newspaper, it could not be used here because the riot stemmed from a speech, not written material.[15]

Undeterred, Pekelis arrived in Chicago a week before the trial began to huddle with prosecutor Pantelis in a private meeting organized by the American Jewish Congress and the CCLC. He presented his own brief and theory of the case. According to Pekelis, Terminiello's speech plainly violated two established exceptions to the First Amendment. There was the now-classic Holmesian "clear and present danger" standard of threat to public security. Terminiello had effectively shouted "fire" with his incendiary speech. In addition, Pekelis cited a brand-new doctrine: "fighting words." In *Chaplinsky v. New Hampshire* (1942), the Supreme Court took up the case of a Jehovah's Witness street preacher who had verbally attacked a town marshal during a public altercation, calling him "a goddamned racketeer" and "a damned fascist." He was convicted of violating a state law prohibiting intentional public name-calling or offensive speech. In a unanimous opinion, the Court ruled that "the lewd and obscene, the profane, the libelous, and insulting or 'fighting' words" added nothing to public expression of ideas. These are words "which by their very utterance, inflict injury or tend to incite an immediate breach of the peace." Hence the government could limit certain low-value speech to uphold order and prevent harm.[16]

Pantelis agreed that the Terminiello case fitted both definitions of "clear and present danger" and "fighting words." The defendant had incited a riot with his words. Yet legal hurdles remained. The riot involved a large, chaotic melee in which multiple groups of protesters, some openly aggressive, clashed with rallygoers and police outside a building in connection with an inflammatory speech that took place inside. Many if not most present in the crowd likely did not hear what Terminiello said in the hall. To assign him legal responsibility required linking the hateful words to the violent outcome. Did the riot stem from his inflammatory speech to the hall audience? Or from the deliberate actions of the counterprotesters? Establishing the truth would require disentangling facts from politics.

AFTER OPENING ARGUMENTS the first day, Pantelis proceeded by introducing the full text of Terminiello's speech as evidence. A string of prosecution witnesses then described the atmosphere in the hall as Terminiello spoke. Lucille McVicker Lipman, a West Side housewife married to a Jewish CCLC board member, testified that she heard chilling calls by the crowd to kill Jews. On cross-examination, St. George accused her of being Jewish. "You've made a mistake. I am not Jewish. I am Irish," McVicker Lipman calmly responded, adding that she was a practicing Quaker. "My ancestors came from Ireland by way of Scotland and fought in Washington's army." As for the counterprotesters, "Most of the people I saw were white; they're not Jewish."[17]

The pattern repeated itself over the rest of the afternoon and into the next morning. Prosecution witness Michael Karel, a Jewish salesman, described his fear as he sat in the audience listening to the crowd around him chant "Kill the Jews!" "You're a Jew, aren't you?" asked St. George. "Yes, and I am proud of it," Karel answered, prompting the lawyer to shout, "You look like a Jew!" At that outburst, Judge McCormack sprang from his chair. Eyes bulging, cheeks red, he upbraided the lawyer. "This is an American court of justice," he said sharply. "I do not have enough strong words with which to rebuke you for making such an observation and I warn you that you should not insult Jewish witnesses in general and all the more so in my court."[18]

While St. George attacked the witnesses, Terminiello continued his game with the jury. From his perch at the defense table, he openly mocked Pantelis with theatrical winks, stage whispers about his "dirty Jew" tricks, and pantomimed gestures suggesting hooked noses. By day two of the trial, Judge McCormack had had enough. As Pantelis spoke about the Christian parable of the Good Shepherd, Terminiello stood up and interrupted, demanding to register an objection on grounds that "this man being a Jew did not believe one word of the New Testament." The judge immediately ruled him in contempt of court.[19]

Friday morning, day three, began with a heated hearing in the judge's chambers. St. George demanded a mistrial. Negative media coverage of his clients in the Chicago dailies and Walter Winchell's nightly radio broadcast had surely prejudiced the jury. Moreover, His Honor did not realize the political conspiracy behind the entire trial. McCormack rejected the motion and ordered the defense back to the court to proceed with the case.[20]

A miffed St. George returned to the courtroom and called his defense witnesses. A series of high-ranking police officers testified to Terminiello's version of events. The picketing remained peaceful for the first few hours, Captain Graney said, until a group of roughly fifty men showed up and began to lob bottles, bricks, tomatoes, and eggs at the building. None of that violent disorder stemmed from the speech inside the hall, he assured the jury. Other defense witnesses drawn from the ranks of rally attendees included the wives of Kister and Smith. Each swore that she had heard no derogatory or threatening remarks about Jews that night. Last to testify that week was Elizabeth Dilling, the ex-wife of attorney Albert Dilling and herself a prominent far right activist and defendant in the Washington Sedition Trial in 1944. As she took the stand, she tried unsuccessfully to hand Judge McCormack a dossier exposing the Judeo-communist plot behind both the riot and the trial. Her testimony was overshadowed, however, when her ex-husband took the occasion to apologize publicly for ruining their marriage with his infidelities.[21]

Terminiello's star turn began on Monday morning, April 1. In Alabama, he had earned a night school law degree in Montgomery only to fail the state bar exam. Now the would-be lawyer reveled in a chance to hold forth in court. With prompts from St. George, he breezily opined on the Talmud and the Kabbalah. Then he turned to his most extreme remarks that night. A close examination of the transcript, he insisted, showed he had not besmirched loyal "American Jews," only the "Zionistic Jews."[22]

Terminiello's invocation of Zionism highlighted the complex relationship between anti-Zionism and antisemitism even before the creation of the State of Israel in 1948. Zionism arose in the late nineteenth century as a modern Jewish nationalist movement seeking political self-determination in its historical homeland, the Land of Israel. From the outset, the movement combined both anti-colonial and colonial elements in its self-understanding and its objectives vis-à-vis Ottoman Palestine. On the one hand, Zionist leaders premised national renewal on liberation from centuries of European subjugation. The dreams of reviving Hebrew and restoring Jewish sovereignty both represented rejections of Christian supremacy. On the other hand, Zionist leaders willingly partnered with European imperial powers to repossess

Palestine and couched their claims in the colonial language of civilizational superiority vis-à-vis Palestinian Arab society. Above all, much like their Palestinian nationalist rivals, Zionists found themselves internally divided over various competing visions of land and power in the decades leading up to World War II.[23]

If Zionism was never a monolith, the same held true for anti-Zionism. Palestinian and other Arab nationalist leaders opposed the Zionist movement as an intrusive, destabilizing force in the emerging post-Ottoman Middle East. Socialist Jewish Bundists denounced its separatist tribalism and utopian character. Communist revolutionaries disparaged it as bourgeois nationalism. Reform rabbis feared Zionism's political impact on Jewish citizenship in the diaspora. Ultra-Orthodox rabbis rejected Jewish sovereignty before the messianic age. None of these and other anti-Zionisms were intrinsically antisemitic in the sense of demonizing Jewishness or Judaism. Yet each also carried stereotypes about Jews and Jewishness that could shift from principled opposition to ideological demonization. When that occurred, antisemitic anti-Zionists invoked a long-standing Western tradition of dividing Jews into positive and negative categories: good Jews as paragons of humanity, bad Jews as irredeemably evil; good Jews embodying historical progress, bad Jews blocking the path to universal salvation.[24]

Such was the case with Terminiello's use of the epithet "Zionist." His invocation collapsed a host of antisemitic images—Christ-killers, communist conspirators, racial tribalists, legalistic Shylocks, world-hungry imperialists—into a cocktail of evil Jewish power threatening America and world peace. He contrasted this enemy with loyal, faithful American Jews. The rhetorical move endowed Terminiello's hatred with the quality of virtue. Hating some Jews was not only permissible but morally necessary. In the context of the trial, it was also expedient. The doublespeak allowed him to continue the game of innocence with a wink.

Pantelis devoted much of his cross-examination of Terminiello to an attempt to puncture this pretense. A testy opening exchange quickly devolved into a heated verbal joust. Terminiello countered every question with one of his own. Pantelis pressed Terminiello to admit his most inflammatory remarks about Jews. Exposing his malice would prove that the antisemitic epithets were not principled distinctions but malicious slurs.

None was meant to apply to all Jews, he replied, returning to his distinction between "communistic Zionistic Jews" and "pagans" versus "good American Jews." What of his comment about "slimy scum"? That was "an intemperate remark" about the "Reds" and "Communists" mustering outside the hall, Terminiello insisted, not about Jews per se. The cross-examination ended in a stalemate. After a brief redirect, the defense rested its case.[25]

Last to testify in the trial were several rebuttal witnesses for the prosecution. Panthelis called a string of University of Chicago students who described picketing peacefully. Two local Protestant ministers, Reverend Kerwin Gaede of Waukegan and Reverend Paul Folino of South Chicago, testified that they had personally led the picket line. There was no covert plot. They had come to protest, not to entrap or fight. On cross, St. George assailed both as secret communists in bed with their Jewish masters.[26]

Wednesday, April 3, brought closing statements. Dilling spoke first. He warned that constitutional freedom was under assault. "The free speech situation in America" has reached the point that "if you say a single word against a bad Jew, you are labeled an antisemite." St. George adopted a more focused approach. The prosecution has failed to prove the link between the speech and the violence, he explained. The breach of peace plainly started outside the hall even before his client uttered a word inside. Then he abruptly veered once more into polemic. You cannot possibly mistake Father Terminiello for a bigot. He is a genuine servant of God who actually "loves the Jews." His speech was merely a passionate warning by a pious Christian about the dangers of godless communism.[27]

"The lawyer told you Terminiello loves the Jews," said Pantelis in his closing. "Which Jews does he love? The Jews he wants to deport to Russia?" The defendant thinks "he is a man above the law," with no "respect for the court, the judge, you or me." "Free speech does not mean libel," Pantelis told the jury, and it is not a license to commit incitement. Terminiello's true aim is to destroy the bonds of brotherhood that form this American "union of children of all races and peoples." Invoking his own story as a Greek immigrant from a war-torn land, Pantelis spoke with pride and reverence of glimpsing the Statue of Liberty upon his arrival four decades earlier. He closed with Christian scripture. Picture Jesus's Sermon on the Mount with its stirring appeal to Christians to love their enemies, he told the jury. Now contrast that scene in your mind with the image of Terminiello screaming his contempt for the "slimy scum" of Chicago.[28]

The last word belonged to Judge McCormack. His jury instructions took the form of a fifteen-minute soliloquy about the First Amendment. Free speech is not unlimited, he declared. Nor is it a warrant to disparage and incite people one against the other. Yet "only an emergency can justify repression of the constitutional right of free speech." You, the members of the jury, must therefore consider "whether there was a clear and present danger flowing from the defendant's speech that would tend to breach the peace." The mere existence of danger would not suffice. To be deemed a "clear and present" danger, he added, "the evil" in question must be "so imminent that it may befall before there is opportunity for discussion." As for a "breach of the peace," he offered a specific definition: any action that "stirs the public to anger, invites dispute, brings about a condition of unrest, or creates a disturbance, or if it molests the inhabitants in the enjoyment of peace and quiet by arousing alarm."[29]

For the next six hours and forty minutes, the jury deliberated. Then, just after nine thirty in the evening, they returned a guilty verdict. As the foreman read it out, four female jury members wept. St. George immediately moved for the judge to set aside the verdict or grant a new trial. Judge McCormack denied both motions. Terminiello was ordered to pay the fine of $100. "Your conduct towards this court suggests how you plan to target other American institutions," McCormack declared. "The time has come for the American people to look your philosophy straight in the face."[30]

Even the most thundering judicial rebuke loses something of its potency when the accompanying penalty consists of a modest fine. In truth, however, the sense of mismatch in the Terminiello verdict reflected American law's ambivalence when it came to speech-related crimes. If the purpose of the First Amendment was understood to be protecting individual free speech from government infringement and promoting the public pursuit of truth, then silencing a bigot achieved neither aim. Even a demagogue like Terminiello technically did not violate the First Amendment—only the government could do so; he merely improperly, unlawfully exploited it. Judge McCormack captured this irony in his admonition. An odious philosophy that mocked law and endangered democracy deserved not suppression but heightened public scrutiny and debate in the marketplace of ideas. That could come only through unfettered speech. Terminiello would have liked nothing more. Soon he would have his chance.[31]

AMERICA IN 1946 was a country happily finished with war but impatient with peace. A year into Harry Truman's presidency, much of the public still doubted that Roosevelt's mild-mannered successor was the man for the job. Paralyzing labor strikes, widespread consumer goods shortages, and galloping inflation plagued the economy. Controversial government-imposed price controls fostered anxiety and resentment. Violent Northern race riots and savage Southern lynchings augured poorly for postwar race relations. With midterm elections looming, the prospects for an end to the Democratic reign—and the New Deal coalition of labor, racial and religious minorities, and urban Democratic machines—seemed high. The question of what would replace it stirred fear. "Voices of disunity . . . foster fear and suspicion and intolerance and hate," Truman had warned in his January State of the Union message. "We must learn constantly to turn deaf ears to them," he counseled, lest they "destroy our harmony" and divide our people.[32]

Was it better to ignore hatred or silence it? The Terminiello verdict quickly exposed the divisions over that question within the civil rights community. With this win, *Sentinel* editor Jack Fishbein crowed, we have "crushed the false camouflage of the freedom of speech" propagated by "the pseudo-liberals with the ACLU." We must ensure that "America's little Hitlers" can no longer "spread venom without legal retaliation." His CCLC colleague Hy Ritman, a Chicago lawyer and progressive political activist, agreed. Speaking to an audience of five hundred–plus people at a posttrial victory banquet, Ritman insisted that true liberalism must defend itself from illiberal propaganda with the full power of law:

> When the demagogues and foes of freedom come into our city—these very same demagogues who would destroy civil rights and destroy the liberties of others—we do not indulge in niceties of definitions, and do not permit ourselves to be bogged down by the disinterred philosophy of Voltaire in order to escape the responsibility of positive action . . . My son and yours did not fight fascists with brochures only.

Such arguments resonated widely in progressive civil rights and labor circles, who saw clear links between prewar European fascism and the postwar American far right.[33]

Moderate Jewish liberals, however, greeted the *Terminiello* decision not with joyful cheers but quiet fury. Fiddling with the First Amendment played right into the hands of communists and fascists alike, argued the AJC's Solomon Fineberg. The "short-cuts" of censorship and militant protest would undermine democracy. "I know of only one way to end abuse of freedom of speech and that is to have no freedom of speech." Behind this lurked a more specifically Jewish fear: Targeting Jewish enemies with newfangled legal ideas would only lead to Jews being tagged as communists, triggering more antisemitism.[34]

As proof, Fineberg could point to the coverage of the case by the Chicago papers. Both the *Chicago Times* and the *Chicago Tribune* condemned the trial as a political witch hunt led by the same sinister forces that engineered the original "Communist inspired and directed riot," in the *Tribune*'s words. The *Chicago Daily News* blasted the error in prosecuting Terminiello, parroting his claim that no Jews suffered violence because of his words. The only solution, Fineberg concluded, was to maintain the "silent treatment." The ADL's Arnold Forster agreed. These "demagogues thrive on publicity." A single conviction for incitement was no license to experiment with subverting the First Amendment.[35]

Pekelis and his colleagues were undeterred by these concerns. They moved swiftly on the heels of the trial to capitalize on the victory. The first step was to propose an "anti-racial libel and hate ordinance" in Chicago. Together with his American Jewish Congress colleague Gilbert Gordon, a noted local civil rights lawyer, Pekelis approached several University of Chicago law professors to devise a pair of hate speech bills for the city. A legal ban on public meetings that incited racial hatred would carry a penalty of one year in jail and/or a fine of up to $500. A parallel law would criminalize the publication of defamatory literature. This formed part of their vision of Chicago as the laboratory for a nationwide effort on group libel. The initiative immediately drew vigorous opposition from the ACLU, which lobbied hard to defeat the draft legislation.[36]

In late May, Pekelis debated ACLU general counsel Osmond Fraenkel on a panel about "Racism and Free Speech" at the American Jewish Congress's annual conference in New York City. A cofounder of the progressive National Lawyers Guild, Fraenkel, who was also Jewish, had defended the Scottsboro Boys and other victims of racism. He strongly rejected the Pekelis plan. It was all well and good to punish Terminiello for the crime of incitement along the "clear and present danger" lines but a ban on "defamatory material against races" was bad policy and bad law. When Pekelis pressed him on whether it was possible to design a group libel law that would pass constitutional muster, Fraenkel reluctantly conceded that it was, though he offered no details. Still, he insisted, the risks of censorship far outweighed the benefits of social reform. Moreover, minority groups might find themselves targeted by their enemies with the very same laws devised to protect them.[37]

Pekelis disagreed. Cold War fears and unintended consequences should not distract from the imperative to calibrate law to the character of modern democracy. "Sometimes, what we need is freedom *from* government," he explained, but "sometimes, what we need is freedom *through* affirmative governmental action." The scourge of antisemitism was just such a case. Surely Americans recognized "the special danger" posed by "antisemitic propaganda" both to Jews and to democracy. "There is no genuine freedom," he added, "and there is no genuine democracy where the existence of the Jewish people is threatened."[38]

For all his legal ingenuity, Pekelis's argument hinged on a basic pair of questions about risk. Was American democracy uniquely threatened by antisemitism? And were the Jews of America truly in danger? That was the topic of conversation two weeks later, when he returned to Chicago to take part in the first postwar Jewish national conference on antisemitism. The two-day event, the same one at which Bess Myerson also appeared, was organized under the auspices of a new Jewish organization, the National Community Relations Advisory Council. The umbrella group aimed to bring all leading Jewish organizations together to speak with one voice on public affairs. The assembled experts included a range of lawyers, educators, psychoanalysts, and social scientists armed with survey data on the demographic profiles of antisemites.

Unfortunately, the experts quickly found themselves flummoxed by the topic at hand. No one could say for sure whether in this first year since the war's end antisemitism was getting better or worse. Growing mountains of data had yielded a complex, even contradictory picture. "Overt antisemitism," defined as organized mass political movements or national membership campaigns, had dramatically ebbed in the prior year. Based on polling, fewer and fewer average Americans openly espoused anti-Jewish sentiments or conspiracy theories. Several noxious episodes notwithstanding, antisemitic rhetoric was increasingly rare in mainstream politics on both sides of the aisle.

Yet countervailing trends remained. Some scholars still estimated that 50 percent of the population harbored some degree of antisemitic views and 5 to 10 percent qualified as violently antisemitic. Then there was the figure of nearly sixty new antisemitic extremist groups formed in the six months since the war's end. High levels of discrimination in jobs, housing, and higher education all remained nationwide. The Federal Employment Discrimination Commission concluded in 1946 that "the wartime gains of Negro, Mexican-American and Jewish workers are being lost through an unchecked revival of discriminatory practices." In Chicago itself, reports of hiring discrimination against Jews had increased by almost 200 percent over the previous year. The statistics for real estate discrimination were even worse. More Chicago Jewish homebuyers encountered restrictive covenants that year than the previous five years' numbers combined. This ambiguous account left many scratching their heads. Was antisemitism worsening or not?[39]

This confusion only intensified the debate over hate speech. If the most serious forms of prejudice were invisible, how should the Jewish community handle the overt rabble-rousers like Smith and Terminiello? Judged by donations and declared followers, their numbers remained negligible. They might easily be dismissed as cranks. Yet what was to stop their violent message from taking root among an already receptive public? The philosopher Max Horkheimer, an exiled member of the Frankfurt School, was one of many who warned that America should learn from Germany's recent history. Polling could miss the pliability of attitudes. "In the Germany of 1932 only the Nazis of the time would have been polled as anti-Semitic," he had previously observed, "but three to six years later the majority of the people would have so declared themselves." At the conference, he cited a recent study of returning American veterans in which "the same men who will have said 'I have nothing against Jews,' in one interview will say, 'To hell with the Jews,' in a later interview." We cannot ignore the fact "people ordinarily deemed pro-democratic may embrace fascist ideology under certain circumstances."[40]

If public opinion was so malleable, the AJC's Fineberg and his ADL counterpart responded, then that was even more reason to focus on education not law. Trials like that of Terminiello only provided free publicity for hatred. In a stirring speech, Pekelis pushed back. There is an "equal or greater danger," he exclaimed, in ignoring "the dynamics of demagoguery and antisemitic agitation" and the "nature of modern propaganda" in the age of mass media. Both the quarantine techniques and tolerance campaigns so favored by many of his colleagues at the conference were little more than cowardly evasions. Jews must seek avenues for robust "democratic participation in the struggle for full equality." The law offered as much; Jewish dignity demanded no less.[41]

The speech would be recalled long afterward not only for its eloquence but also for its finality. Months later, Pekelis's life was cut short in an airplane crash while he was flying home from a Zionist conference in Switzerland. With his untimely passing, group libel lost perhaps its greatest exponent in American law.[42]

AFTER HIS CONVICTION, Terminiello's fortunes quickly soured. By the fall of 1946, Smith had cast him aside in favor of a new alliance with the revived Ku Klux Klan—no fan of Catholics—in order to target a Southern audience. Back in Alabama, Terminiello failed the bar exam a second time. He launched three lawsuits—one against the state for anti-Catholic discrimination on the bar exam and two against newspapers for libel—none of which succeeded. The Internal Revenue Service sued him for tax evasion. A new plan to unite all the antisemitic groups in the country into a single white supremacist movement with the backing of the Texas oil magnate George Washington Armstrong collapsed. Humbled, Terminiello formally apologized to the Church and was reinstated to a small parish in Pensacola, Florida. Then, still defiant, he proceeded with his appeal. I will win this fight for "Christian America," he told St. George, or else "be stood up and shot, or sent away to a concentration camp."[43]

St. George began the appeals process by directly petitioning the Illinois Supreme Court to hear the case on First Amendment grounds. Finding no constitutional question involved, in January 1947 the justices sent it back down to the Appellate Court for the First District of Illinois for regular adjudication. There, St. George tried a different tack. He argued that Terminiello could hardly be charged with public disturbance for an event that did not take place in "public space." In June, a three-judge panel rejected that argument in a 2–1 verdict. The defendant's "wild, intemperate and inflammatory utterances" fitted the very textbook definition of "action tending to a breach of the peace," wrote Judge Michael Feinberg in the majority opinion. If Terminiello's speech was "not an appeal to fury and an incitement to disorder and violence," Feinberg added, "then these words lose their English meaning."[44]

In his dissent, Judge Grover Niemeyer agreed that the meeting was a private event. His chief concern, however, was with the "partisan" anti-Christian testimony of the plaintiff witnesses, especially Michael Karel, the salesman, "the only person of the Jewish race present." Based on his reading of the transcript, Niemeyer concluded, there was nothing offensive or intimidating about Terminiello's speech. It was a classic Christian style of preaching of precisely the kind the Supreme Court had validated in its decision in *Cantwell v. Connecticut*. In the 1940 ruling, the Court had overturned the conviction of a Jehovah's Witness street preacher for incitement on grounds that his verbal attacks on Catholics were a genuine expression of religious faith protected under the First Amendment.[45]

Armed with the vigorous dissent from Niemeyer, St. George filed an appeal with the Illinois Supreme Court. In March 1948, however, it affirmed the lower court's judgment. Terminiello's remarks were obviously "derisive, fighting words" that "tended to incite the majority of his audience to immediate violence against the angry mob outside," causing "innumerable acts of violence extending over a period of several hours." Without a recognized constitutional question or a split decision at the Illinois Supreme Court, Terminiello had exhausted all his regular avenues of appeal. His last option was to file a direct petition to the U.S. Supreme Court to hear the case "on cert," strictly on its legal merits as a matter of surpassing constitutional importance. St. George submitted the paperwork for that claim in September 1948.[46]

By then, antisemitism had become a subject of national discussion. Books and articles streamed forth, while Hollywood entered the conversation with films like *Crossfire* and *Gentleman's Agreement* dramatizing antisemitism as an irrational mania. Sociological and psychological studies of stereotyping and extremism proliferated. "Anti-Semitism is a powerful force in the United States today," wrote *New Republic* editor Bruce Bliven in a seven-part series, "one daily growing more serious." He hastened to add that "anti-Semitism is only one aspect, and in this country at this time, not even the most important of the vicious doctrine of racial-religious hostility. The burden the Negro is forced to bear is heavier, on the whole, than that of the Jew." The reason to focus on antisemitism was that "vicious propaganda" peddled by the likes of

Terminiello and other "salesmen of hate" threatened "our democratic society." Bliven's explanation reflected the exceptional place of antisemitism in the postwar liberal imagination. Less morally burdensome or politically sensitive than anti-Black racism, antisemitism was nevertheless laden with symbolism as evidence of where unchecked hatred could lead a society. Antisemitic words now carried disproportionate weight, as did the question of how the law should handle them.[47]

Nineteen forty-eight was also an election year. Just before Americans went to the polls in November, President Truman rallied a crowd of a hundred thousand in Chicago, warning them to heed the dangers of antisemitic propaganda. "The tragic story of what happened in Germany is all too fresh," he warned. "We know how Hitler used anti-Semitic propaganda as a way of stupefying the German people with false ideas while he reached out for power." Now, in America, "dangerous men" are waging "war on democracy" by seeking to "concentrate great economic power in their hands" and "attacking Catholics, Jews, Negroes, and other minority races and religions." On that platform, Truman narrowly won the election in a three-way race with moderate Republican Governor Thomas Dewey and Progressive Party candidate Henry Wallace.[48]

Once elected, however, Truman avoided mention of homegrown demagogues or civil rights, focusing instead on a message of Cold War national unity. What made America great, he said in his January 1949 inaugural address, was its commitment to God-given rights, including "freedom of thought and expression." Among those in attendance were the nine justices of the Supreme Court. Ten days later, they would take up the question of free speech, opening that spring term with *Terminiello v. Chicago*.[49]

4

Not a Suicide Pact

"If one is attacked as a Jew," Hannah Arendt famously declared after the Holocaust, "one must defend oneself as a Jew. Not as a German, not as a world-citizen, not as an upholder of the Rights of Man."[1]

That credo contained an important truth for the American postwar campaign against antisemitism. An antisemitic crime was not an attack in the abstract but an attack on a person because of their Jewishness—and thus an attack on Jewishness itself. To judge hate properly, then, the law must recognize difference. Any legal process that erased the Jewish identity of victims in the name of universal principles would fail to address the totality of the crime while robbing the victims of their collective dignity.

Precisely how to define that collectivity, however, remained a challenge in postwar America. Jewish identity was once more in rapid flux. The Holocaust had orphaned most American Jews, cutting away the European heartland whose roots stretched back a thousand years. Acculturation and socioeconomic mobility shifted postwar Jews ever more solidly into the white majority amid mounting racial strife. American leaders now spoke for the first time of a "Judeo-Christian tradition," a term largely invented during the Cold War to grant Judaism honorary membership in Western civilization's fight against communist atheism. The creation of Israel provided American Jews an ethnic homeland, but one where none of their ancestors had lived for two millennia. All this change only deepened existing confusion: Was Jewishness a religion, a race, a nation, or an ethnicity?[2]

These currents rippled beneath the surface of *Terminiello v. Chicago* from the outset, beginning with the Supreme Court's oral arguments on a chilly Tuesday afternoon in February 1949. Terminiello's lawyer, Albert Dilling, who took over from St. George, arrived armed with a simple argument: My client's constitutional rights to free speech, freedom of assembly, and due process have been grossly violated. You may not like his views, he told the Court, but they are not on trial. Nor is there evidence for incitement. The government's case against him rests entirely on his use of the word "scum" to describe a violent radical mob massing outside the hall.[3]

On the contrary, Chicago's appellate attorney Louis Karton insisted, Terminiello plainly engaged in deliberate incitement. The meaning of words like "scum" depended on the context in which they were spoken. Terminiello was no innocent. He belonged to the same breed of racial agitators who had just produced "the most hideous catastrophe known to history." This kind of speech led directly to race riots. "Slimy scum" fit the Court's own standard of "fighting words" to a T.[4]

As the justices probed these arguments, they hunted for the right analogy by which to compare the scenario to other speech cases. For Justice Hugo Black, a native Alabaman and former Democratic senator, and a former Ku Klux Klan member, Terminiello sounded more like a wily politician employing a bit of hyperbole than a racist provocateur. "Men sometimes make pretty warm political speeches," he observed, "in which they call their opponents 'scum.'" His colleague Justice Robert H. Jackson, not long removed from prosecuting Nazi war criminals during his stint as U.S. chief prosecutor at the Nuremberg trials, heard in the priest's rant a religious polemic. He likened the riot to a sectarian quarrel. "A speech attacking Roman Catholics might create violence before an audience of Catholics," he mused, "but a Protestant audience might not get very excited about it."[5]

Each of these analogies downgraded the conflict from an antisemitic riot to a political skirmish or religious dispute. They also recast the story as a clash between two equal parties, pushing anti-Jewish hatred out of the frame. A case about law's authority to stem incitement had morphed into a quest to apportion blame evenly between rival groups, equally powerful and determined to harm one another. That raised a question that would haunt the judicial deliberations all spring as well as the broader legal reckoning with antisemitism. In a pluralistic democracy, which posed the greater threat to civil rights: government censorship or violence directed at its most vulnerable minorities?

THE NINE MEN who sat on the Supreme Court in 1949 comprised a panel of liberals divided by their liberalism. It was not a question of politics but legal philosophy. All had been appointed by Democratic presidents, seven by Roosevelt and two by Truman. Yet during the Second World War the justices had found themselves at odds over how to interpret the Bill of Rights. The libertarian faction, led by Hugo Black and William O. Douglas, a Westerner known for his progressive views, held that individual civil liberties were absolute prerogatives that ought to be defended to the utmost from ever-growing government power. Constitutional democracy depended on checking the eternal threat of tyranny. The task of judges was to review laws to ensure that none harmed core freedoms. When the Constitution declared "Congress shall make no law" abridging free speech and other liberties, Black once said, no law meant *no law*.

Their pragmatic opponents, led by Jackson and Felix Frankfurter, cared equally about individual freedom, but they rejected positivist theories of law as a perfect system in which judges merely applied the law without shaping it through their interpretation. Liberalism was destined to evolve, and the law with it. The "Court realistically functions," wrote Jackson, "as a continuous constitutional convention, and the Constitution is always in the making at their hands." Ironically, that progressive view led Jackson and Frankfurter toward a policy of judicial restraint. Democracy required judges to defer to the will of the people as expressed through their legislature.[6]

Throughout the 1940s, these dueling sensibilities faced fierce tests in a series of cases where national security clashed with civil liberties. The military internment of Japanese Americans, prosecutions of Nazi sympathizers and Communist Party activists, and mandatory flag salutes were among the key legal controversies that produced shifting configurations on the Court. The war's end brought new challenges to the racial and religious dimensions of American citizenship, particularly involving church-state separation in public education, discrimination in private housing, and segregation. An American legal tradition that had long privileged property rights over equality under the law had reached a crossroads.

In each case, the justices debated not only the direction of liberalism, but also their own expanding power. In the 1920s and 1930s the Court had decided that the Bill of Rights applied not just to the federal government but the states as well. In making this move, the justices authorized themselves to review every corner of the American legal system. This extended jurisdiction dovetailed with a new conception of constitutional rights. In the 1937 *Carolene Products* case, the Court asserted that to prevent "prejudice against discrete and insular minorities," notably racial and religious minorities, the courts could apply a test of "strict scrutiny" when reviewing the constitutionality of laws. Having opened the door to questions of social equality, the Court began to engage directly with the question of when private hatred became public discrimination. That set the stage for a broader reckoning with how free speech intersected with minority civil rights in the postwar period.[7]

The contest of ideals and egos between the two legal factions intensified after Chief Justice Harlan Fiske Stone's sudden death in the spring of 1946. A steadily increasing number of narrowly split verdicts worried lawyers and politicians. Seeking to heal the divide, Truman passed over both Black and Jackson to name Fred Vinson as the new chief justice. A former Kentucky congressman, federal appeals court judge, and Treasury secretary, Vinson was selected for his skills as a peacemaker. His mission was to bring harmony to a group proverbially known as "nine scorpions in a bottle." The *Terminiello* case would test his ability to do so.[8]

The case also divided the ACLU. In 1946, when St. George had turned to the organization for assistance, the local Chicago leadership deadlocked over his request. While some saw an open-and-shut case of government overreach, insisting that freedom of speech required toleration for offensive views, others strenuously insisted that "no real defense of civil liberties is involved." In an era replete with dangers to the First Amendment from the anti-communist crusade spreading through American society and politics, any opportunity to defend protest and check government authority was generally worth taking. Still, given the unsavory defendant and his dubious legal representation, many wondered whether it made sense to expend organizational capital on the case. It was ACLU chief Roger Baldwin who broke the tie with a compromise. For the time being, Terminiello would remain on his own. But if the case reached the Supreme Court, the ACLU would defend him in the name of "protecting constitutional rights and principles." When the moment arrived, the Chicago branch balked at Baldwin's directive to help with the appeal and mount a legal defense committee. In the end, they agreed only to provide an amicus brief.[9]

Once in the fight, the ACLU offered a vigorous defense of free speech. If permitted to stand, wrote lawyers Osmond Fraenkel and William Rodriguez in their brief, the lower court's decision "will effectively take away the right of anyone freely to speak just as soon as there are others determined enough to express their collective disapproval of the speech to be delivered." The picketing outside Terminiello's event amounted to what would come to be known as a heckler's veto, a disturbance expressly intended to prevent a speech. Not only was the city ordinance unconstitutional, but the state had an affirmative duty to protect the speaker from the threat of mob violence. Terminiello was effectively the weaker party in the incident, and it was the responsibility of the government to defend his rights. The failure to do so risked greasing an already slippery slope to "dangerous censorship."[10]

At the American Jewish Congress, the Supreme Court case drew the opposite response. After the death of Pekelis, his legacy passed to two young lawyers, Will Maslow and Leo Pfeffer, who would emerge as titans of postwar civil rights law. Maslow championed the Fourteenth Amendment's "equal protection" clause to fight racial and ethnic discrimination, while Pfeffer pioneered litigation based on the First Amendment's Disestablishment clause to separate church and state. As *Terminiello v. Chicago* reached the Supreme Court, the Congress team continued Pekelis's work by advising Chicago's legal team.[11]

They also turned to the renowned University of Chicago First Amendment scholar Harry Kalven Jr. to help draft their own amicus brief. "Freedom of speech, particularly freedom to espouse unpopular causes, is fundamental to the health of any society," read the brief, "and particularly essential for the well-being of minority groups." To preserve "the vitality of freedom of speech requires that its boundaries be carefully delineated," it continued, especially when the speech involved is "an attempt to foment hatred of Jews." Terminiello's "slimy scum" comment formed the quintessence of "fighting words." No listeners coerced the speaker. No government censored his speech. He knowingly caused a "breach of the peace" through his behavior. The Court should affirm the conviction.[12]

While Maslow and his colleagues focused on what we would now call the incitement exception to the First Amendment, they slipped in another argument about the impact of group defamation on its victims. With "the Nazis' systematic extermination of 6 million Jews in Europe" fresh in their minds, "a vituperative attack explicitly aimed at Jews present in the audience" would have felt like an actual "recurrence of the Nazi threat in their midst." The Court should take note of "the heightened sensitivity of Jews everywhere to Nazi vilification tactics in appraising the likelihood that a defendant's 'fighting words' would result in violence." Invoking the experience of hatred, they effectively asked the Supreme Court to recognize the harm in hate speech—even absent an act of violence. In the process, Maslow hoped the case might advance public support for the group libel legislation they continued to pursue.[13]

In their respective briefs, the ACLU and the American Jewish Congress each sought to push the law toward a more proactive stance on speech. The Congress argued that the law must not allow itself to be weaponized against the victims of hatred. Protecting minorities from hateful speech meant protecting the law's own claim to be a neutral guarantor of dignity and equality. The ACLU insisted the opposite. In its estimation, it was not enough for the law merely to permit the speech rather than suppress it. The law must also protect individual speakers from the mob's caprice and malice. Both agreed that the law could not remain neutral. A choice had to be made.

As WAS THEIR custom, on the Saturday following oral arguments, the justices convened in chambers to discuss the past week's cases. "I am at sea," declared Stanley Reed, a Kentucky-born New Deal veteran who often became the swing vote on narrow splits. "This was disorderly conduct. If we come to Free Speech, he said nothing that led to incitement, and I would reverse." Black agreed, as did Frank Murphy, a former Detroit mayor, Michigan governor, and attorney general. Douglas, however, broke ranks with his traditional allies. "In this setting the speech was close to shouting 'fire'" in a theater, he announced, or lighting "a match in a forest." This case is textbook "clear and present danger."[14]

Jackson agreed. Free speech was not a license to preach hate and instigate violence. "A state ought to be able to ban the precipitation of riots," he argued, "and not have to wait until an actual riot starts." The justices seemed to be heading toward a divided opinion.[15]

Then Vinson threw a curveball. Having studied the original trial transcript, he informed his colleagues that he had discovered a different problem all the way back at the beginning of the case. In his jury instructions, Judge McCormack had incorrectly defined "breach of the peace." McCormack told the jurors that the term meant any behavior that "stirs the public to anger, invites dispute, brings about a condition of unrest, or creates a disturbance, or . . . molests the inhabitants in the enjoyment of peace and quiet by arousing alarm." This was unconstitutionally vague and broad, Vinson reasoned, particularly the phrase "invites dispute."[16]

An improper jury instruction meant that the jurors had used a faulty standard to determine guilt or innocence. The procedural error was grounds for vacating the whole conviction on due process grounds. There was just one problem. The defense lawyers had not raised such a claim in any of their filings or arguments. Searching for a way to avoid the legal gray zone of ruling on a claim that was not actually put forward by the defense, Vinson offered an unusual suggestion. They might take the rare step of dismissing the case even after having heard oral arguments without issuing an opinion, on grounds that a writ of certiorari was "improvidently granted." They should never have agreed to accept the case in the first place. Dismissing it would allow them to dispose of the matter without violating their own legal procedure.[17]

No one liked the idea of dismissing without issuing an opinion. That left the question of whether the jury instruction mistake should be considered in determining whether Terminiello's constitutional rights had been violated. Frankfurter would have none of it. "To note as error something," he protested, "that wasn't ever raised" across three state-level courts would be its own "extreme error." It was not their duty to conjure up an argument unmentioned throughout the entire judicial process. Nor would relying on a technicality spare the reckoning with the core constitutional question of free speech. Turning to the heart of the matter, Frankfurter told his colleagues that far from being a civil libertarian or political radical, Terminiello was a dangerous charlatan. In the past, Frankfurter had publicly stated his support for the First Amendment rights of the Ku Klux Klan and American Nazis on grounds that "civil liberty means liberty for those whom we do not like or even detest." In this case, however, he insisted on making a distinction between radical "ideas" and purely noxious "blackguardism." The former kind of speech possessed merit as legitimate dissent; the latter represented thoughtless abuse undeserving of constitutional protection.[18]

In making this argument, Frankfurter mixed principle and passion. As a Jewish immigrant from Austria, he was no stranger to prejudice. "I am the symbol of the Jew, the Red, the alien," he once quipped darkly. An early ACLU leader and proponent of progressive political causes, Frankfurter was relentlessly attacked by his enemies as an anti-Christian, pro-communist foreigner. Adding to the controversy surrounding his public reputation, he was an ardent Zionist who followed in the footsteps of his mentor Louis Brandeis in asserting that the movement represented a democratic effort to advance Jewish rights and national dignity.[19]

Frankfurter harbored an acute awareness that he belonged to "the most vilified and persecuted minority in history." During World War II he had devised plans for Jewish communal responses to antisemitism, and even begun to entertain the idea of group libel legislation. Yet he was equally determined not to let his own Jewishness form the basis for any argument over how the Court should interpret the law. After all, "as judges we are neither Jew nor Gentile, neither Catholic nor agnostic," he routinely stressed. It was imperative to remain free from any "sectarian biases—whether the sect be racial, religious or economic." When it came to Terminiello, therefore, he couched his position in terms of judicial restraint and deference to the democratic authority of state legislatures. Seizing on a technicality to dismiss the case, Frankfurter told his colleagues, would deny states the power to protect the public against dangerous incitement. This was not a violation of the First Amendment. The conviction should stand.[20]

A straw poll revealed that Frankfurter had pulled in not only Jackson and Douglas, but Vinson and Harold Burton to reach a 5–4 vote in favor of affirming the original judgment. Anticipating that this voting pattern would hold, Vinson assigned Douglas the task of drafting the majority opinion upholding the conviction. Sometime between February and early April, however, Douglas changed his mind for reasons that were never disclosed. His flip turned a 5–4 vote against Terminiello to one in his favor. As word emerged of the new voting pattern, Frankfurter scrambled to avert a full defeat. As a compromise, he proposed that they revert to Vinson's original recommendation and dismiss the case now without issuing any opinion. Douglas and his faction would have none of it. That left the dissenters to write their own opinions.[21]

On May 16, the justices reassembled to pronounce their verdict on the original conviction. The majority—Douglas, Murphy, Reed, Black, and Wiley Rutledge—voted to reverse it. Vinson, Jackson, Frankfurter, and Burton dissented. A packed courtroom listened as one by one the opinions were delivered, beginning with Justice Douglas. As he read out the majority opinion, it quickly became obvious that the judges had adopted Vinson's suggestion that the procedural error was grounds for vacating the conviction on due process grounds. Before even considering any constitutional questions about "fighting words," Douglas announced, the Court found that the jury instructions raise "a preliminary question that is dispositive of the case." The trial judge had erred by including the phrase "invites dispute" in his definition of a breach of the peace. A "function of free speech under our system of government is to invite dispute," Douglas said. "It may indeed best serve its high purpose when it induces a condition of unrest, creates dissatisfaction with conditions as they are, or even stirs people to anger."

> Speech is often provocative and challenging. It may strike at prejudices and preconceptions and have profound unsettling effects as it presses for acceptance of an idea. That is why freedom of speech, though not absolute, is nevertheless protected against censorship or punishment, unless shown likely to produce a clear and present danger of a serious substantive evil that rises far above public inconvenience, annoyance, or unrest.

The improper jury instruction—although not raised by the defense at any point—had changed the meaning of the underlying law that the jury was tasked with interpreting. The state courts had wrongly interpreted Terminiello's conduct by reading the law far too broadly. Even if Terminiello had not objected previously, and both his defense and the state had focused on the separate question of "fighting words," he had claimed all along that his right to free speech was violated. That was enough to justify the Court's review and reversal.[22]

Douglas's rousing rhetoric set a new standard for the Holmesian "marketplace of ideas" model of speech. His words would become a landmark statement in praise of the First Amendment. Still, his remarks were as striking for what he did *not* say as for what he did. Douglas did not declare the actual Chicago city law unconstitutional, only its improper interpretation in the jury instructions. Nor did he rule on whether Terminiello's language violated the "fighting words" standard. Instead, he eloquently defended free speech while sidestepping the legal question of its limits.[23]

Though he was the one who had first thought of this legal strategy, Vinson was so displeased by the maneuver that he authored his own dissent. "The Court today reverses the Supreme Court of Illinois because it discovers in the record one sentence in the trial court's instructions," he wrote in his opinion, "which had heretofore gone completely undetected." The Court could hardly reverse a state court's judgment based on a technical error unmentioned by anyone, including Terminiello's attorneys, throughout both the Illinois appellate tribunals and the filings and arguments at the Supreme Court. The case was argued and appealed by both parties strictly on the grounds of whether "fighting words" applied, not whether the statute itself or the judge's instructions were unconstitutional. Douglas had overreached. The majority's ruling was illogical and unprecedented.[24]

"Freedom of speech undoubtedly means freedom to express views that challenge deep-seated, sacred beliefs, and to utter sentiments that may provoke resentment," conceded Frankfurter, in his own dissent, in which Jackson and Burton joined. Yet such freedoms existed under laws. No one had stripped Terminiello of his life or liberty for his words. The trial was a civil misdemeanor case, not a criminal one. The punishment was a small fine. Why should this of all cases be the one for which the Court usurped the authority of state courts? Why should this be the first instance in 130 years in which the Court reversed a state court conviction "on a ground that was urged neither here or below"? We have "no authority to meddle with such a judgment" if no constitutional claim had been raised in the state court process. His was an impassioned argument, but a procedural one. He left the issue of antisemitism for Jackson, noting only that he shared Mr. Jackson's views "on the merits of the issue." As it turned out, Jackson had plenty to say.[25]

Jackson arrived in court toting a mammoth seventy-five-hundred-word dissent, one of the longest ever written. As he began to speak, a hush fell on the courtroom. "The Court reverses this conviction by reiterating generalized approbations of freedom of speech with which, in the abstract, no one will disagree," he began. They reach that conclusion by nearly completely avoiding any consideration of "the circumstances of Terminiello's speech." This leads to the false impression that the defendant "had spoken to persons as dispassionate as empty benches, or like a modern Demosthenes practicing his Philippics on a lonely seashore. But the local court was not indulging in theory. It was dealing with a riot and with a speech that provoked a hostile mob and incited a friendly one and threatened violence between the two." Having yanked the debate back to the harsh reality of the clash in Chicago, Jackson insisted that context was essential. An unstable situation turned violent thanks to the speaker's disregard for danger.[26]

He turned next to the trial itself. Any attempt to circumvent the hard questions of the case by resort to proceduralism was an unacceptable dodge; instead, Jackson insisted on addressing the heart of the matter. "This Court seems to regard" liberty and order "as enemies of each other and to be of the view that we must forego order to achieve liberty," he announced, taking direct aim at Black and his other libertarian colleagues. "So, it fixes its eyes on a conception of freedom of speech so rigid as to tolerate no concession to society's need for public order." This myopia must not remain unchallenged: "An old proverb warns us to take heed lest we 'walk into a well from looking at the stars.' To show why I think the Court is in some danger of doing just that, I must bring these deliberations down to earth by a long recital of facts."[27]

With that, Jackson launched into a full recapitulation of the Chicago riot, using direct quotes from Terminiello's testimony to show his intentions at the meeting. He read Terminiello's entire speech aloud, followed by selections from *Mein Kampf* and the writings of Joseph Goebbels to stress the similarity between the two. What transpired in Chicago evoked Weimar-era Germany where Nazi thugs began their rise to power by battling their Marxist foes in the streets. He who is master of the streets, said Jackson, quoting Hitler, "will some day be the master of the state."[28]

Terminiello, of course, "disclaims being a fascist," Jackson went on. "Doubtless many of the indoor audience were not consciously such. His speech, however, followed, with fidelity that is more than coincidental, the pattern of European fascist leaders." Appeals to freedom by fascists spouting propaganda was also a Nazi trick. The "invocation of constitutional liberties as part of the strategy for overthrowing them presents a dilemma to a free people which may not be soluble by constitutional logic alone," he warned ominously, and certainly not by clinging stubbornly to the "dogma of absolute freedom for irresponsible and provocative utterance."[29]

Had he stopped at this point, Jackson's dissent might have read like a Holocaust-tinged warning about the dangers of fascist antisemitism. Yet he was not done. As he continued, it became immediately obvious that he had *two* enemies in mind. Only one culprit was on trial, but the violence had two authors. Liberalism faced twin threats from the far right and the far left:

> This was not an isolated, spontaneous and unintended collision of political, racial or ideological adversaries. It was a local manifestation of a world-wide and standing conflict between two organized groups of revolutionary fanatics, each of which has imported to this country the strong-arm technique developed in the struggle by which their kind has devastated Europe. Increasingly, American cities have to cope with it. One faction organizes a mass meeting, the other organizes pickets to harass it; each organizes squads to counteract the others' pickets; parade is met with counterparade. Each of these mass demonstrations has the potentiality, and more than a few the purpose, of disorder and violence.

With such a "battle for the streets" raging in American society, the Court must not forget that "freedom of speech exists only under law and not independently of it." The only reason to curb that freedom was to prevent violence:

> It is the legal right of any American citizen to advocate peaceful adoption of fascism or communism, socialism, or capitalism. He may go far in expressing sentiments whether pro-semitic or anti-semitic, pro-negro or anti-negro, pro-Catholic or anti-Catholic. He

> is legally free to argue for some anti-American system of government to supersede by constitutional methods the one we have.

What the citizen may not do is utilize violence in a way that threatens the very foundations of the state:

> The choice is not between order and liberty. It is between liberty with order and anarchy without either. There is danger that, if the Court does not temper its doctrinaire logic with a little practical wisdom, it will convert the constitutional Bill of Rights into a suicide pact. I would affirm the conviction.[30]

Jackson's memorable closing phrase—an instant classic—captured the sense of a democracy blind to its own profound vulnerability to abuse at the hands of its enemies. In retrospect it is easy to see Jackson's fears of anarchy and revolution as an expression of Cold War liberal paranoia, a reactionary centrism that exaggerated the threats of the Left to justify its own moderate conservatism. Yet in denouncing the gap between theory and reality, Jackson voiced a realist, progressive sensibility that law must engage with the world around it. The law must take account of the true play of power in society. At the end of the day, there were real victims of violence who would pay the price for blind fealty to absolutist principle. He said as much in a private poem that he wrote out of frustration at the end of the case:

> If a special size street riot puts you flat on your back,
> Be philosophical with Douglas, Murphy, Rutledge, Reed, and Black;
> As you lie there bashed and bleeding, with your muscles badly hurt'n,
> Say a little prayer for Vinson, Jackson, Frankfurter, and Burton.[31]

EVERY ACT OF judgment tells a story about the law. *Terminiello v. Chicago* left America with many stories to choose from. Was it a victory for commonsense Americanism over communism, as Chicago's *Daily*

Tribune and *Daily News* blared? Or a revolutionary decision that imperiled democracy, in the estimation of the Atlanta *Constitution* and the Fresno *Bee*? A triumph for free speech, as the *Christian Century* averred? Or a devastating capitulation to "untrammeled hate" on par with the *Dred Scott* decision, in the words of the New York *Forverts*? The American media were as divided as the Supreme Court justices.[32]

So, too, was the public. For every person like Brooklyn schoolteacher Martin Wolfson, who thanked Justice Douglas for courageously ensuring "that our country is strong and our democracy sound," there was another like Manhattan attorney Louis Field. "I have been practicing law for twenty-three years," he wrote Douglas, "and I have never read a decision so utterly bogged down in platitudes, so utterly vicious in its implications of the triumph of evil as in the Terminiello case." Your lofty dictum about the "function of free speech" was "sheer nonsense."[33]

The ambiguity extended to opinions on how the Supreme Court had handled the subject of antisemitism in its deliberations. The lawyer Bessie Margolin, a former assistant solicitor general who had worked alongside Jackson at Nuremberg, heard in his dissent a profound epitaph for the slaughtered "six million Jews of Europe." By contrast, the Pennsylvania State University professor Jack Brumberg objected vociferously to the Court's whitewashing of antisemitism. He charged the Court with failing to recognize that antisemitism was not a generic form of bigotry but a specific attack on a vulnerable minority. Had Terminiello spoken of "atheistic, communistic Protestants," or "slimy, snaky, bedbuggy Protestants," he wrote, "that speech would not have produced a 'clear danger' because his head would knock on the stone wall of the majority. Attacking the Jewish minority group makes it a 'clear danger' . . . because the minority is a push-over, not a stone wall."[34]

Above all, the verdict prompted confusion. The law was supposed to fix the truth about hatred and set the rules of democracy. If free speech was a core American value, then the law should brook no vagueness about its limits. "Between them," complained *Time* magazine, the justices "managed to confuse further the complex line which defines the reasonable limits to freedom of speech." The *Bayonne Times* complained that even "with the best will in the world it is difficult to follow the reasoning of the United States Supreme Court on freedom of speech." The editors went on to complain, "Things were bad enough before, but last week's decision in the Terminiello case out of Chicago confounds confusion." Writing in the *Brooklyn Daily Eagle*, editor Robert Grannis confessed: "I'm confused . . . Where does free speech begin and where does it end? I want the higher-ups to tell me and the 5-to-4 decision just can't be the final answer."[35]

The lead characters in the legal battle were no less frustrated. In June, the Chicago appellate team took the rare step of lodging an emergency application for a rehearing by the Supreme Court. The Court declined the motion without comment, leaving legal observers bewildered and perplexed. Kalven criticized Douglas's weak argument, calling it a bait and switch. He had not determined the law in question to be unconstitutional, despite the rhetorical bluster. It seems obvious, Maslow concluded, that the Court simply wished to avoid taking a position on the entire issue. Even the ACLU was unsure of how to interpret the ruling. Publicly the group loudly claimed victory. In private, several leaders, among them Fraenkel, deemed the verdict disappointing and "confusing."[36]

The only person satisfied was Terminiello, who celebrated the decision as proof that "the Supreme Court is becoming more aware of Communist danger." He took the occasion to announce his retirement from the national stage. "I'm out of this mess now and I don't want to get it started again." Like everything else he said, Terminiello's disavowal of "this mess" was not true. Though he no longer sought the limelight, he continued to self-publish the odd pamphlet identifying Jews with a global conspiracy involving communism and the Illuminati against the Vatican. At the end of his life, he attempted to complete an autobiography to vindicate his view that he had been the victim of a Jewish plot. But the costs of professional bigotry, both economic and personal, had become too expensive for him to devote significant attention to it. In that sense, the litigation had succeeded in silencing hatred.[37]

The *Terminiello* decision guaranteed that the legal drama of antisemitism and the First Amendment was destined to continue into 1950s America. The case showed that antisemitism had become a testing ground on which America projected competing visions of its national identity at a moment when the meaning of liberalism was evolving rapidly. The Cold War introduced new moral and political challenges to America's self-image as a land of liberty. A liberalism premised on individual freedom and equal rights, yet maintained through racial and religious hierarchies, could no longer avoid reckoning with its contradictions. Even the Court was divided over their role in a society in flux. "There's not much use in a layman's attempting to make up his mind whether the present Supreme Court is predominantly 'liberal' or 'conservative,'" observed Clark Beache of the Associated Press about the *Terminiello* decision. Those political labels did not fit a changing Court—or a changing country.[38]

As with all law stories, the meaning of *Terminiello* would depend on the story that Americans would write for themselves in that uncertain moment of hope and fear. In that sense, the judicial cliff-hanger gave them the gift of a chance to reargue the case and so reimagine the future of free speech and minority equality.

5

A Postwar Pogrom

On Tuesday, November 8, 1949, Aaron Bindman threw a housewarming party that ended in a pogrom. Three weeks earlier, the thirty-two-year-old World War II veteran and labor organizer had moved his wife, Louise, and their two daughters into a new two-flat house on Peoria Street in Chicago's Englewood section, a working-class Irish Catholic neighborhood. That night the family hosted sixteen fellow union members of Local 208 of the International Longshore and Warehouse Union for dinner. Half were white, half were Black. The guest of honor was Yasuki Araki, a Japanese American labor leader visiting from Hawaii.[1]

By ten o'clock in the evening, a crowd of fifty to a hundred white men had gathered at the foot of the home's front steps. Rumors had spread that a Black family had moved into the house. Bindman, six foot one and slender with black hair and brown eyes, stepped outside onto his front porch to appeal for calm. His new neighbors would have none of it. "Let's get down to business," declared Frank Curtis, who lived two blocks away, "You have two children upstairs, don't you? If you want them to be O.K., you had better get those n—rs out of there and keep them out of there or we will burn down the building." As the guests fled, Araki himself emerged to address the crowd. We are all leaving, he explained, and you are misinformed. The new homeowner is white, not Black. That prompted another shout: "No he is not white, he is a Jew."[2]

Bindman summoned the police and demanded that they arrest his neighbor Curtis for threatening his family. At the local precinct, the desk sergeant refused to sign an arrest warrant. The next day Bindman went downtown to seek an audience with Mayor Martin Kennelly and Police Commissioner John Prendergast. Both men declined to see him. He returned home to find three hundred people massed on his doorstep. This time the mob had come for him. Despite the presence of a four-man police detail, the crowd began throwing rocks at the house. Ruffians shoved and beat passersby in the street. It was now a full-fledged riot. More police arrived, but no real effort was made to disperse the mob and no one was arrested.[3]

By Thursday night the mob had grown to roughly fifteen hundred people. They surrounded the house on all sides, and hurled bricks and rocks at the windows. Each time a window shattered the crowd cheered. Shouts rang out: "Lynch the Jews!" "Get that Jew bastard, n—r lover, lynch him!" "Burn the house!" "Let's go in and kill the Jews!" A rhythmic refrain started: "Let's start a race riot! Let's start a race riot!" A police line prevented access to the house, but every hour the mob rushed the cops, seeking to press their way in. The scene continued throughout the night as Bindman and his family cowered inside, his children quaking in terror.[4]

On Friday evening, Veterans Day, several thousand people massed in the streets around Bindman's house. Most reports suggested four thousand were present; some estimated as many as ten thousand. As night fell, the violence recommenced. Gangs of teenagers and men brandishing pistols surged through the neighborhood hunting for Blacks, Jews, "Commies," and college students. Bloodied victims crawled along the streets pursued by mobs; journalists and civil rights officials from the ADL and a liberal Catholic group were assaulted. On the main Englewood commercial strip, mobs ransacked Jewish-owned stores, beating the store owners who tried to prevent them. Hundreds of policemen stood by idly. Most of those arrested were victims, accused of starting violence. Spotting his neighbor in the crowd, one local Jewish man pleaded with him to stop his "Hitler-like" behavior. The response: "The only trouble with Hitler is that he didn't finish the job."[5]

As the situation devolved into open anarchy, Commissioner Prendergast ordered four hundred policemen dispatched to the neighborhood to restore order. They proved worse than useless. Some officers openly fraternized with the rioters, among whom were several off-duty policemen who lived on Bindman's block. Cops roughed up victims, treating them like criminals. One injured Jewish man was arrested along with three of his attackers. Placed in the same holding cell, they beat him a second time. Finally, on late Saturday evening, the fifth night, Prendergast issued an order to forcibly disperse the crowds. Rain and a temperature drop sapped the mob's energy. By Sunday morning the violence had ended.[6]

The Peoria Street pogrom has vanished from memory today. In its time, however, the riot shocked a city familiar with racial violence, sparking a strange sequel to the *Terminiello* case. The search for culprits eventually led to the arrest and conviction of Joseph Beauharnais, the leader of the city's newest white supremacist group, for violating the state law against group libel, and ultimately to the Supreme Court. Yet the riots and legal odyssey they prompted coincided with the rise of anti-communist paranoia, a panic that would result in new laws targeting suspected communists, curtailing immigration, and authorizing the government to expel political dissidents. Senator Joseph McCarthy was on the verge of mounting his terrifying political inquisition. From Hollywood to Washington, Cold War mania had begun to engulf America. Anti-communist authoritarianism refueled the myth of Judeo-Bolshevism. High Jewish visibility in left-wing politics transformed Jews into a symbol of the secret enemy hiding in plain sight.

Political panic intersected with growing racial strife. White rage at the prospect of ending segregation led to widespread rioting and violent terror against African Americans and their allies. At the very moment when long-standing barriers were falling in society, Jews found themselves recast as white impostors and racial mercenaries in a deepening struggle over equal rights. This antisemitism sharpened the dilemma for Jews navigating through an era of Cold War paranoia and racial struggle. Would banning hate speech advance the law's promise of equality? Or undermine individual freedom precisely when it was needed most by the victims of racism and demagoguery?

On the Sunday evening after the riot, Bindman answered a knock at the door to find the captain of the local precinct standing on his porch. The policeman had not come to check on his safety but to relay a message. In his hand he held the business card of Frank Burke, vice president of the Chicago City Bank and Trust Company. The bank was well known for its efforts to keep the neighborhood white through redlining, restrictive covenants, and rezoning the Englewood commercial strip. Why stay where you're not wanted? If Bindman agreed to leave the neighborhood, the bank would buy him out on very generous terms. Bindman took the card but declined the offer. "We'll fight it out here," he quipped, "rather than in some concentration camp later on."[7]

CHICAGO IN THE late 1940s was a city at war. The flood of arson, firebombings, and race riots across the city reached the level of "chronic urban guerrilla warfare." On occasion these eruptions swelled into major conflagrations. In the Airport Homes riot in 1946, Fernwood Park in 1947, and Park Manor in July 1949, white Chicagoans rioted to prevent African Americans from moving into their communities. Driving this violence was naked racism, compounded by a severe shortage of housing stock, the worst since the Great Chicago Fire of 1871.[8]

As African Americans, Mexican Americans, and others flocked to the city during World War II, they found themselves confined to overflowing neighborhoods. New Deal federal housing loans and the redlining practices of private banks had racialized real estate. In addition, up through World War II, over 80 percent of Chicago's housing supply was covered by restrictive covenants, legal agreements that prevented the sale or rental of "property to Negros, Jews, Orientals and others." The 1948 Supreme Court decision in *Shelley v. Kraemer* dealt the practices a serious blow, but in response, local Chicago communities organized white neighborhood associations to block home sales to "undesirables" through intimidation campaigns and physical violence. "Undesirables" was the word the local Catholic priest used in his Sunday sermon just before the Englewood riot, in which he urged his parishioners not to sell their homes to outsiders. When racism could no longer rely on the law, religion filled the vacuum.[9]

How undesirable were the Jews? In the postwar urban landscape, Jewish Chicagoans found themselves ambiguously positioned as both beneficiaries and victims of the racist backlash. In many cases, white Jews were grudgingly accepted by their Christian neighbors as the lesser evil when it came to demographic change. At other times, Jews faced rejection, including violence on occasion. A racist community might reluctantly tolerate a Jewish family's entry into the neighborhood only to turn hostile when issues of race and politics surfaced. "Let the Jews come in," declared one Englewood resident during the riot, "and the n—rs are right behind."[10]

Bindman's experience reflected that strange duality. At his service induction during World War II, the army clerk had recorded him as "white race," as opposed to "Negro, Oriental, Indian, or Filipino," but with "dark brown" complexion. His neighbors regarded him as white enough, until his left-wing politics and interracial associations followed his arrival. Then his whiteness vanished. The fact that Jews might be physically indistinguishable from other white Americans only made them more insidious. During the Englewood riot, roving mobs stopped passersby demanding to know their last names and Catholic parish. Young people with "Semitic-looking features" were assaulted, among them several non-Jews. One policeman assigned to quell the violence told a reporter that the victims deserved to be beaten because they were all communists. "How do you know they were communists?" the reporter inquired. "Because they were Jews," came the answer.[11]

Even in a city accustomed to race riots, Englewood shocked the Chicago civil rights community. It was not just the brutality on display or the police apathy but the fact that instead of Black homeowners, this time Jews were the targets. This is "the most violent outbreak of anti-Negro, anti-Semitic feeling in the recent history of Chicago," declared the Chicago ACLU, noting a "dangerous pattern" by which "an anti-negro demonstration took on an anti-communist complexion, concluded as an antisemitic riot." We have just witnessed, warned the Chicago ADL, "the extension on American soil—at this late date—of the Hitler propaganda falsely equating Jews with communists, a scapegoating of the negro minority, and a serious invasion of civil liberties."[12]

Worse than the riot was the stark silence from city leaders. Throughout the five days of violence, Mayor Kennelly refused to comment publicly. Two weeks later, he still had not issued a statement. When he finally spoke out, the mayor offered a mealymouthed proclamation calling for calm and blaming the unrest on "subversive groups." The local Jewish journalist Leo Lerner blasted the silence as patent hypocrisy:

> If the recent South Peoria Street race riots had taken place in Russia around 1900, the American newspapers would have blithely referred to them as pogroms. If they had taken place in Germany in 1938, they would have been called anti-Semitic demonstrations. If they had taken place in Egypt in 1947, they would have been called anti-Jewish riots. If they had taken place in Mississippi last week, they would have been called Ku Klux Klan activity. But because they took place on the South Side of Chicago, they are just incidents of no particular significance . . . a little sporting violence.[13]

The lack of condemnation was worse than hypocrisy, argued the American Jewish Congress's Rabbi Morton Berman. It was a complete moral failure on the part of city leadership. On December 1, he published a full-page open letter in the *Chicago Sun-Times*. "We had five days of street rioting on South Peoria Street," it read. "You, Mr. Mayor, have failed to take any forthright public position." The situation remained grave. "As long as anyone thinks violence is a useful tool in a racial or religious situation, every Chicagoan faces a real and personal danger."[14]

Aaron Bindman and his family were among those still in danger. For weeks afterward, he and his wife required police escorts to walk to and from the local streetcar stop. Another attempt was made to burn down his house. His children were bullied at school. He took to carrying a pistol when he left home. Police even installed wooden shacks on all four corners of his block, assigning a round-the-clock presence to watch the property. All this scrutiny was not just a reluctant concession to Bindman's family's personal safety—a courtesy virtually unimaginable to Black Chicagoans—it was also a visible form of political surveillance. The job of the police was to protect the city from Bindman as much as to protect him from his neighbors. For what no one wanted to say out loud was that Bindman was a communist.[15]

To ITS AMERICAN enemies, communism only ever meant one thing: a Moscow-directed revolutionary movement seeking to destroy liberal democracy and dismantle capitalism. To its adherents, American communism meant many things that changed over time: a global movement committed to replacing the inequities of modern capitalism with a just economic order; a covert revolutionary campaign in support of the Soviet Union; a utopian creed of universal equality and freedom from domination. For some Jews, the Soviet Union represented a powerful state committed to outlawing antisemitism and fighting fascism. In the late 1940s, Soviet communism's totalitarian crimes remained concealed behind the facade of a progressive state built on the ruins of an antisemitic Russian Empire. Awareness of Stalin's brutal 1948 antisemitic campaign, which killed many leading Jewish figures, was limited. Meanwhile, American far right ideologues continued to use anti-communism for spreading their own antisemitic propaganda.[16]

Though it began as an organization defending radicals and revolutionaries, the ACLU struggled to formulate a consistent position on American communism in the 1930s and 1940s. On the one hand, the core ideal of modern civil liberties consisted of the right to express any and all ideas short of violence without fear of government censorship or legal retribution. On the other, in the 1930s, ACLU leaders Roger Baldwin, Arthur Garfield Hays, and Morris Ernst led the organization into a liberal anti-communist position to the point of providing the FBI with secret access to their files even as they continued to defend individuals from unconstitutional violations and malicious government prosecution.[17]

In Chicago, that complex dynamic had caused the original split between the ACLU and the Chicago Civil Liberties Committee in the mid-1940s. It continued as the Cold War sparked a sweeping new round of anti-communist witch hunts. Trying to thread the needle, in 1949 the Chicago ACLU branch leaders publicly pledged to defend the civil liberties of individual communists and oppose loyalty oaths while behind the scenes they purged all suspected communists from their membership rolls. They also issued a stern warning against any communist attempts to subvert their organization or "the general civil liberties movement." Rumor and fear collided with principle and politics. The anti-communist crusade was potentially as destructive as the genuine threat of infiltration it sought to contain.[18]

Aaron Bindman represented a direct challenge to the ACLU's delicate balancing act. Born in Brooklyn to poor Polish immigrant parents, Bindman joined the American Communist Party while working in a warehouse during the Great Depression. Drawn to the message of universal equality, full employment, and anti-imperialism, he was never a militant revolutionary or a secret spy. His politics were those of a left-wing trade unionist who believed in Marxist socialism as a viable path to economic justice for American society and an urgent answer to the dangers of global fascism. After three years of college at the University of Illinois at Champaign-Urbana, Bindman entered the army in 1941 and served in the Pacific. Returning home he rose to become the secretary of the Chicago ILWU local, which represented more than twelve hundred workers.[19]

Bindman resigned from the Communist Party in 1947 after the passage of the Taft-Hartley Act requiring all union officials to swear an oath that they were not party members. Congress passed the law, overriding President Truman's veto; he had deemed it "a dangerous intrusion on free speech." The following year, the Mundt-Nixon Communist Control Bill, which would have required all members of the Communist Party to register with the attorney general as a prelude to arrest and deportation, passed overwhelmingly in the House of Representatives but died in the Senate Judiciary Committee.[20]

In this context, Bindman's communist associations colored the attitude of everyone involved in the aftermath of Englewood. One reason we know so little about the riot is that the major daily newspapers imposed a moratorium on press coverage. Bindman's own union's parent organization, the Congress of Industrial Organizations, refused to help him so long as he socialized with suspect elements. That was easier said than done. He had co-purchased the two-unit house with his friend Bill Sennett, who remained proudly identified as an ardent communist. The FBI stalked Bindman's wife, who worked as an occupational therapist at the Drexel Home for Aged Jews. He himself was trailed constantly by the police department's Red Squad. The police also declined to arrest local rioters perceived as rightly defending their neighborhood turf from outside agitators. As a result, the five nights of rioting involving thousands produced only fifty-four arrests, a quarter of whom turned out to be victims.[21]

At the first trial of men who had actually taken part in the violence, Judge Joseph McGarry acquitted one defendant and dismissed charges against two more. To call this "a race riot," he announced from the bench, was "a gross and unwarranted insult to the residents of this peaceful neighborhood" from which hail "some of the most eminent leaders in civic and social life of Chicago." There was no evidence, he claimed, to suggest an anti-Black or anti-Jewish character to the disturbance. This even though there had recently been a massive walkout by white students at Englewood High School protesting Black enrollment. The judge accused Bindman himself of perjury. All the violence stemmed from "a miserable conspiracy hatched" by a "vocal band of subversive agents, professional agitators and saboteurs," McGarry said, "for the purpose of discrediting the city government, the Police Department and the Court and the people who reside in this district."[22]

Was there a conspiracy behind the violence? Throughout the week of the riot, civil rights monitors reported seeing a tall, heavyset man with gray eyes, short black hair, and a trim mustache driving around the neighborhood in a brand-new black Cadillac. The mystery man materialized at key moments of violence, only to slink away again. He left behind flyers from a new organization, the White Circle League of America, dedicated to "ousting the Reds" from the country, "the complete separation of the Black and White races," and preserving the

"Rights of the White Race." Soon, the culprit was identified as Joseph Beauharnais, fifty-three, a newcomer to the roster of hate leaders.

Born Joseph Aloysius Harnois on Chicago's South Side in 1896 to a French Canadian father and Irish Catholic immigrant mother, Beauharnais served in World War I and then went on to a quiet existence as a salesman, barkeeper, and businessman selling novelties. During World War II he expanded a small leather goods business into a major company through selling leather-bound diaries to servicemen. After the war ended, he reinvented himself as Joseph Beauharnais, descendant of a French revolutionary and self-styled defender of "White racial pride" against the "dictatorial program" of civil rights. In the summer of 1949, as news broke of President Truman's plans for military desegregation, he penned an angry letter to Truman and Secretary of the Army Louis Johnson insisting that "the self-preservation of the White race demands total separation of the two races." The next month he spoke at a resident association meeting against housing desegregation in Park Manor, a Chicago neighborhood. His speech triggered a riot in which several African American homes were firebombed.[23]

The Englewood riot marked the official debut of the White Circle League. In the days after, Beauharnais flooded Chicago with handbills and pamphlets demanding city leaders halt communist-driven racial integration. Barring that, he warned, "the only weapon left to the White man is violence." He announced plans for an elite corps of "2,000 able-bodied White men" to assist the police in quelling race riots: a racist militia masquerading as citizen-deputies.[24]

Blacks formed the principal target for Beauharnais's hatred. Yet his racism was infused with a virulent strain of antisemitism. Jewish communists like Bindman were "non-Whites" who threatened the "preservation of the White race." There is "the nice type of Jew and then there is the small Communist type of Jew," he told a reporter after the riot. The nice type even included "many fine Jewish men and women in our organization," while the latter, represented by Bindman, the "typical small beady eyed . . . horned rimmed glasses type of Jewish Communist," secretly controlled America and plotted its ruin. Beauharnais's rhetoric was of a piece with his fatuous claim that he was not "anti-Negro or antisemitic," not "anti-anybody," only "pro-White." His attack on Bindman repeated some of the core tropes of American antisemitism: Jewish interracialists were replacing whites with Blacks; Judaism and communism were synonymous; Zionism was the true "power behind communism"; and race and religion fused together in a Christian white supremacy that sought to preserve "the White Gentile race."[25]

Beauharnais caught the immediate attention of Chicago civil rights groups. Within weeks of the riot, the ADL, the ACLU, and the Mayor's Commission on Human Relations had each dispatched undercover observers to White Circle League meetings. Yet there was no clear course of action. On the one hand, the perfect storm of antisemitism and anti-Black racism provided a pretext to unite minorities in the new push for civil rights. On the other, targeting Beauharnais would only risk bringing more attention to Bindman's communist ties. "Any liberal group concerned with preventing racial and religious disturbances can expect to be labeled 'subversive,'" remarked one Jewish leader, "with all the recrimination in this period of mass hysteria resulting from the Cold War." The ACLU continued to send undercover investigators to monitor the White Circle League, but it opted to take no action: "We believe it is better to ignore KKK'ism in Chicago at this point and exercise the silent treatment on Beauharnais."[26]

The ADL and the AJC shared this view, holding fast to the quarantine approach. The same month as the riot, the AJC's Solomon Fineberg published a new book, *Punishment Without Crime*, in which he condemned "the readiness of some Victimians to become furious whenever their group is defamed." To live "in a morbid atmosphere of anticipated 'martyrdom,' to expect to be treated unfairly by the members of other groups, to cultivate excessive resentment in oneself and in others," he warned, "is to promote one's own brand of inverted intolerance."[27]

Such stoic pronouncements concealed a deeper insecurity about the Judeo-communist conspiracy theory. Only months before, Mississippi congressman John Rankin had openly equated Jewish civil rights organizations with Stalinist communists, sponsoring a bill to criminalize membership in their groups. Fearful of such provocations, both the AJC and ADL had carried out internal purges, with the AJC announcing an alliance in 1949 with the archconservative All-American Conference to Combat Communism. When it came to Chicago, they reckoned that ignoring both Bindman and Beauharnais presented the best course of action.[28]

This view struck the leaders of the American Jewish Congress as dangerously misguided. It is obvious that "the Communist question here is a smokescreen to cover mob violence based primarily on racial and religious hatred," concluded Byron Miller, a former Truman administration lawyer who joined the organization as its chief Midwestern civil rights lawyer in 1947. The shocking "full-blown antisemitism" on display in Englewood demonstrated "even to the most unwilling observer that violent prejudice against Negroes is a direct danger to American Jews." We can ill afford to "wait until a Hitler has arrived in order to determine that the evils of hate mongering may be legally prevented." The question was how to respond.[29]

Two weeks after the attack, the Chicago Urban League's director, the African American attorney Sidney Williams, convened a meeting of representatives from 125 local labor, religious, and civil rights organizations to launch the Chicago Committee to End Mob Violence. The group held a daylong rally with speakers including Bindman and the labor activist Saul Alinsky. They urged city prosecutors to issue arrest warrants for the rioters and demanded that the mayor fire the police commissioner. They proposed impeachment for other city officials for negligence and malfeasance.[30]

Though they helped organize the event, the American Jewish Congress leaders led an informal coalition in a different direction. First, they demanded that the mayor issue a full statement setting the record straight about the riot. Then they launched a campaign, eventually successful, to secure police reforms involving new officer training and revised policies to prevent future riots. At the same time, they set about looking for ways to hold Beauharnais directly responsible and curb his activities. Soon two legal avenues crystallized. The Congress initiated a request to the state's attorney to revoke the White Circle League charter on grounds that it had violated its status and rights as a public charity. The other was to invoke the law of group libel.[31]

From the first revelation of Beauharnais's involvement, Congress leaders had contemplated taking legal action against him for racial and religious libel. In the months since *Terminiello*, they had continued to champion this idea by proposing state-level bills and a federal statute. Five identical bills had been introduced in the House of Representatives in the spring of 1948 and again in 1949 by a group of New York City Democrats and liberal Republicans. In Illinois, a group libel law already existed in the form of the 1917 statute banning publications that exposed "the citizens of any race, color, creed or religion to contempt, derision, or obloquy or which is productive of breach of the peace or riots." The punishment was a fine of between $50 and $200. The statute had not applied in the *Terminiello* case, but now it might apply to Beauharnais and his new racist campaign. Hence the Chicago trial offered a chance to test once and for all the constitutional validity of group libel.

In the first week of January 1950, an ad hoc group of leaders from the Congress, the CCLC, the Steel Workers Union, and two African American groups—the Cook County Bar Association of Black lawyers and the Civil Rights Congress, a left-wing rival of the NAACP—approached Cook County State's Attorney John Boyle to ask that he prosecute Beauharnais using the group libel law. Newly elected as part of the Democratic Party machine, Boyle was reluctant to cross city leaders. Both the mayor and the City Council worried that further attention would exacerbate racial tensions and give a platform to radical politics. They had no wish to see another Terminiello trial besmirch Chicago's good name. Boyle found support from the ACLU and ADL, both of which advised him against prosecution.[32]

Yet the Congress was determined to proceed. Together with the CCLC director Ira Latimer it hatched a plan to force the issue. On Friday evening, January 6, Latimer sent his son Ivon, a University of Chicago student, to attend a White Circle recruitment meeting. Beauharnais personally handed him a pamphlet calling on Chicago's white population to petition the mayor to oppose "the further encroachment, harassment, and invasion of White people, their property, neighborhoods and persons by the Negro." Our communities, the pamphlet warned, are at risk from the "rapes, robberies, knives, guns and marijuana of the negro" and must band together to avoid the degradation "of the White race and its natural laws by forced mongrelization." To prove that Beauharnais's pamphlet had been publicly distributed, a young Black man named Clifford McFarland made his way to Chicago's Loop the next morning, where he acquired the same pamphlet from a White Circle member standing on the corner of State and Madison Streets.[33]

This evidence was enough to convince a municipal court judge to issue an arrest warrant for Beauharnais. However, Boyle refused to budge. Finally, after weeks of pressure, he relented, but only to deploy a strategy to tank the case. He charged Beauharnais and then assigned the case to Albert Zemel, the most junior, least experienced member of his staff—and the sole Jew in an office full of Irish Catholics. Boyle assumed that Zemel would lose, and then liberal Chicago would not be able to claim that he had taken no action. Yet he had underestimated his young colleague. Zemel, the thirty-year-old son of Polish Jewish immigrants and son-in-law of prominent Reform Rabbi Solomon Goodman, had earned his law degree at DePaul University and knew the city's legal culture well. A brown-haired navy veteran with baby-faced good looks, Zemel was an active member of the local branch of the Jewish War Veterans of America and shared the organization's more confrontational approach to antisemites. He had already considered using the 1917 law against Beauharnais. Now came his chance.[34]

To mount his defense, Beauharnais turned to Terminiello's lawyer Maximilian St. George. In the preliminary hearings, St. George insisted on an all-Christian, all-white judge, jury, and prosecutor. He won on the first two counts. The case was removed from the docket of Judge Lewis Caplan and reassigned to none other than Judge Joseph McGarry. The selection provoked public outcry. McGarry's prior conduct had so outraged Chicago progressives that the Committee to End Mob Violence staged a mock citizens' trial of the justice for his "aiding and abetting mob violence" in the city of Chicago. "I was treated like a criminal for complaining against those who instigated the attack," Bindman had testified at the mock trial, "while the police fraternized with the guilty ones."[35]

Matters got worse when, during the jury selection, Judge McGarry acceded to St. George's request to disqualify two Jewish men and three Black women. Yet he did allow Zemel to remain on the case. Up for election later that year, the judge dared not cross Zemel's powerful boss, Boyle, and the Democratic Party machine. McGarry's forbearance on Zemel did little to boost hopes for a fair trial. Still, no one could predict what would happen on Tuesday, May 2, when the proceedings in *State of Illinois v. Joseph Beauharnais* began.[36]

IN 1732, AN anonymous handbill appeared in London alleging a brutal crime. The flyer accused a group of Portuguese Jews of burning a Jewish mother and her child to death as punishment for the woman's scandalous liaison with the child's Christian father. The publication reportedly led to mob attacks against Jews across the city. Jewish leaders demanded legal prosecution and the court assented. The publisher had inflamed public passions, "with a universal spirit of barbarity against a whole body of men," the judges wrote, wronging "the whole Jewish community" of London. In *King v. Osborne*, the judges found, essentially, that the entire community had been libeled.[37]

The crime of libel arose with the emergence of the printing press in English society. The dramatic expansion of newspapers and other print media in the 1600s gave rise to disputes about published statements that damaged individual reputations. *King v. Osborne* represented the very first case in which the crime of libel was applied to a group. Even as the judges found in favor of the Jewish plaintiffs, however, the extant court records left unclear whether the crime at issue was actually the incitement of physical violence against Jews via words or the spreading of malicious falsehoods that damaged their dignity. That ambiguity would haunt the legal concept all the way to modernity. Could words do harm without causing violence?[38]

"The right of giving the truth in evidence, in cases of libels, is all-important to the liberties of the people," Alexander Hamilton declared in 1804. Hamilton's comment captured the other key principle in libel law: A statement could not be libelous if proven to be true. "Truth is an ingredient in the eternal order of things," wrote Hamilton, and essential in the "judging of the quality of acts." For it allowed the law "to determine the intent" behind the offending statement. If a person could point to factual evidence as the source of their opinion, then they could justify that opinion as reasonable discourse. Though much contested in Hamilton's day, the focus on the intent of the author would become a hallmark of modern libel law. It suggested the liberal faith in human nature. Innocence equated with truth, malice with false motive. This emphasis on truth as defense also potentially undercut any group libel charge. If a bald assertion about a minority group proved true, how could it be said to be a libelous falsehood?[39]

That question dominated the three-day Beauharnais trial. Journalists and supporters of Bindman and Beauharnais packed the courtroom to watch the proceedings. After opening arguments, Zemel called both Ira Latimer and his son, along with Cliff McFarland, to establish the basic timeline of facts. Then the real action began. No one disputed Beauharnais's authorship. The question hinged on whether he had defamed Black Chicagoans by distributing his tract. To demonstrate the kind of people harmed by Beauharnais's actions, Zemel called a trio of eminent Black figures as expert witnesses. The renowned surgeon Ulysses Grant Dailey, police officer Captain Harry Deas, and Roosevelt College English professor Robert Crospey each represented a portrait of Black respectability and achievement. One by one, Zemel guided them through testimony about their storied careers and their experiences living in Chicago. Their profiles doubled as obvious refutations of the racist generalizations about Black poverty, drugs, and crime in Beauharnais's text.[40]

In response, St. George attempted the truth-as-defense strategy. The Illinois statute required that "In all prosecutions of libel, the truth, when published for good motives, and for justifiable ends, shall be a sufficient defense." His client was an honest political critic of racial integration, and the testimony of a few exceptional Blacks did not disguise the fact that the Black "invasion" and "mongrelization" of Chicago were objective descriptions of reality in the postwar city. In a clever move, he invoked the 1945 sociological study *Black Metropolis: A Study of Negro Life in a Northern City* by the African American scholars St. Clair Drake and Horace Cayton to prove that Black migration had transformed Chicago beyond recognition. Cross-examining the witnesses, St. George attempted to twist each man's words into support for his argument that "crime is rampant among the negroes." This proved a bridge too far even for Judge McGarry, who barred these inflammatory tactics across the board.[41]

On the third and final day of the trial, May 4, Beauharnais took the stand as the only defense witness. He insisted that his organization was not "anti-Negro," only pro-white. The purpose of the White Circle League of America, he told the jury, is "to maintain and safeguard the dignity, social edicts, customs, heritage, rights and ways of life of the White race in America." As he guided his client through his testimony, punctuated by Zemel's frequent objections, St. George tried to introduce more proof for Beauharnais's assertions. Having by now grown frustrated with the defense's antics, Judge McGarry sustained nearly all of Zemel's objections. This enraged Beauharnais. He had counted on the judge's support based on McGarry's exoneration of the Peoria Street rioters. Now he felt the judge and prosecutor were conspiring to clamp a muzzle on his face and violate his free speech rights. Just before resting his case, St. George tried one more tack. He offered to read official statistics about Black crime and white property values into the record. Judge McGarry rejected the information as "immaterial."[42]

At closing, Zemel declared that the White Circle League represented an "unlawful, un-American scheme." Beauharnais "is nothing but a racketeer who attacks every minority group," as evidenced by his un-American assault on jurors' race and religion. His only goal was "to make money for himself by stirring up hates and prejudices." St. George returned to his opening theme of the sanctity of the First Amendment, albeit with a heavy dose of racial and political innuendo. "We have always maintained that this is a white man's country, and in order to keep it that way, we must fight," he told the jury. "If we can't fight, we will have a totalitarian government, like in Russia. The principle in this case is freedom of speech and freedom of press only."[43]

The jury deliberated for only forty-five minutes before returning a guilty verdict. Beauharnais fumed. Judge McGarry announced the maximum penalty, $200. The jury, without Jews or Blacks, had no trouble finding the "hate-peddler guilty" of defamation, crowed one Jewish paper, while the African American *Chicago Defender* praised Zemel for his brilliant work. As for Beauharnais, he declared that the trial was a "travesty of justice," a conspiracy by the "un-American subversive, race-mixing elements" from "every special interest minority pressure group." An anonymous pamphlet entitled "The Vultures of Peoria Street" quickly appeared, which narrated the incident as proof positive of the anti-white, Judeo-communist conspiracy at hand.[44]

St. George immediately turned to the ACLU for assistance with an appeal. The Chicago branch leaders had closely followed the case and agreed that it was tailor-made for a constitutional challenge to the concept of group libel law. Once again they found themselves internally divided. Taking up St. George's challenge would allow the civil libertarians to defeat group libel once and for all. Yet why provide "a miserable race-baiter" more attention and support?[45]

Beauharnais's behavior after the trial only sharpened the dilemma. Along with his denunciations of the anti-white conspiracy that would "destroy our people and our country," he proclaimed that he would press on with plans to launch the White American Party. Though his White Circle membership remained small and his meetings drew only hundreds, not the thousands he promised, Beauharnais ratcheted up his rhetoric and provocations. He continued to stoke violence through rallies and mob actions across the city, including a courthouse melee in which he led his followers in mauling a Black news photographer, then beat and kicked the bailiff who tried to defend him.[46]

From the ACLU's perspective, Beauharnais was not just an unattractive client, he was also an antagonistic one. Even while St. George negotiated the appeal with the group, Beauharnais issued a statement blasting the ACLU as a "dangerous and subversive organization." Mortified, the Chicago branch attempted to negotiate a retraction in exchange for representing him. Beauharnais agreed, only to renege immediately, issuing a retraction that repeated the same charges in different form. A grueling series of internal debates ensued. The ACLU contemplated then abandoned the idea of filing a libel suit against Beauharnais. It went so far as to commission a pair of reports to argue the pro and con positions on taking his case.[47]

Finally, they reached an awkward compromise. The ACLU would support Beauharnais's appeal through an amicus brief at the Illinois Supreme Court level, and, if need be, at the U.S. Supreme Court. In the meantime, it would back efforts by the Illinois attorney general's office to revoke the White Circle League charter on grounds that the group's racial membership pledge and racist publications violated the Illinois state constitution's Bill of Rights and the Fourteenth Amendment.[48]

It was a clever gambit, for it allowed the ACLU to assert its commitment to protecting unpopular speech on First Amendment grounds while acting to advance civil rights through the Fourteenth Amendment. Yet defending a client while attacking his organization was also a problematic political move. In the end, the Illinois Supreme Court declined to accept the ACLU's amicus brief. That temporarily spared the libertarians the ordeal of watching as Beauharnais's lawyer turned the Bill of Rights into an argument for white supremacy.[49]

St. George's defense of his client at the Illinois Supreme Court centered on the claim that the state group libel law was unconstitutionally broad, hence a violation of the Fourteenth Amendment's guarantee of due process and a direct infringement on the First Amendment. If it were left in place, he wrote in his brief, "there could be no religious freedom; likewise there could be no political freedom." The judges should remember that the evil of racial integration could lead "in this country to a revolution such as occurred in Haiti where the negroes overthrew the whites and became supreme."[50]

St. George proudly cited the recent *Terminiello* case. If those antisemitic "highly inflammatory" statements were "protected by the constitution," surely the same must hold for Beauharnais's distribution of pamphlets, which featured "no riots, no crowds and, therefore, certainly nothing to show any danger of an immediate breach of the peace, riot, or substantive evil." There was no "clear and present danger" and no incitement to physical violence. "History is replete with examples wherein minorities of different races, colors, or creeds did become powerful and did take over the reins of government." What prevented such devastation in America was the "constitutional guarantee of free press." Should the Court uphold the conviction, "a minority group may become too powerful and our representative form of government will be lost."[51]

The argument failed to convince the justices of the Illinois Supreme Court. In January 1951 they affirmed the conviction. The statute in question was perfectly constitutional, wrote Chief Justice Joseph Fulton, neither too broad in scope nor too vague in wording. "Any ordinary person," he concluded, "could only conclude from the libelous character of the language that a clash and riot would eventually result between members of the White Circle League of America and the Negro race."[52]

Fulton's ruling underscored the strange career of Jewish civil rights in the postwar years. What had begun as an attack on the home of a Jewish communist ended with a conviction for segregationist pamphleteering. Antisemitism colored the entire affair; it even enveloped the trial itself. Yet the hatred that ended up criminalized was not antisemitism but anti-Black racism. The danger in question was defined as a clash between Black and white races. The pogrom on South Peoria Street receded to the background. In a liberal America divided by fears over communism yet sensitive to anti-Jewish stereotypes, Jewishness was best left unmentioned.

However, it was not only anxious liberals who played a part in the eclipse of antisemitism. The silence was also the product of a moment in which Jews fell once again ambiguously between Black and white America as the nation prepared for the battle over legal segregation. That fight would shape the course of Joseph Beauharnais's appeal against his hate speech conviction. Before he reached the United States Supreme Court, though, his path first ran through the Chicago suburb of Cicero—the site, in the summer of 1951, of the worst race riot in postwar American history.

6

Instrument of Democracy

In the Chicago suburb of Cicero, a mob of four thousand whites massed in front of a small three-story apartment building on the evening of Wednesday, July 11, 1951. They had come to block Harvey Clark Jr., a young Black navy veteran, his wife, Johnetta, and their two children from moving into their new home. As the crowd surged forward, they shouted, "Go! Go! Keep Cicero White!"—a slogan coined by Joseph Beauharnais. All day he had worked the scene, launching chants, passing out flyers and buttons. As darkness fell, rioters stormed the building. They ransacked the Clarks' apartment, torched their belongings, and set the entire structure on fire.[1]

The violence quickly escalated. The mob stoned the firefighters as they arrived and overturned police cars. Governor Adlai Stevenson called in the Illinois National Guard to restore order. It took the troops three days and a half mile of barbed wire to quell the riot. "It is sheer senseless destruction," remarked one official in the aftermath. "I have never seen anything like it since I saw fought-over war areas."[2]

While the riot still raged, the news broke that the ACLU had decided to handle Beauharnais's Supreme Court appeal. "If the right of free speech means anything at all," it announced, "it means freedom for the expression of opinions we hate as well as those with which we agree." The timing could not have been worse. Unlike other Chicago riots, Cicero drew national and even international attention. Seizing the moment, Beauharnais showed up at the Cicero courthouse three days after the ACLU's announcement to stage another unruly protest in defense of those arrested. Cicero proved that the time had come for racial revolution. "Awake, Chicagoland, awake," he announced, "your White man's glory is at stake."[3]

The ACLU's decision drew sharp criticism. "Exactly what, in the name of an all-merciful God, do you gentlemen think you are accomplishing in defending said Chicago moron?" wrote Isidor Shaffer, a New York City legal stenographer. "You'll strain at a gnat and swallow a camel. What price civil liberties if the happiness of Americans is destroyed?" This man has single-handedly terrorized the entire city of Chicago, complained the NAACP leader Walter White; how can you justify defending him? Patrick Malin, Roger Baldwin's successor at the ACLU, responded with sympathy and condescension. We recognize that this decision "may cause great harm even to the interests which we hold dear, such as equality for Negroes; but, in the forced choice between risks, we have always contended that the interests of American democracy—including the interests of Negroes and other minority groups—are on balance much better served by keeping that . . . kind of speech free." Then he accused the Black civil rights leader of placing minority needs before the common good: "This is one of those hard choices that people who believe in *all* civil liberties for *everybody* are frequently forced to make—in a conflict between free expression and respect for the human dignity of a minority group."[4]

When core rights conflict, law demands a choice. However much mid-century liberals might have imagined that choice as an agonizing contest between cherished values, their legal arguments ultimately came down to calculating risks and benefits. In the post–World War II era, shaped by battles against fascism and communism, civil liberties served as the primary defense against government tyranny. Civil rights—protecting minority groups from discrimination—ranked as an important but secondary concern. Indeed, the very fact that two different terms existed—civil rights and civil liberties—testified to how mid-century American liberalism treated individual freedom and minority equality as separate issues.[5]

Fear of communist infiltration and authoritarian control dominated all debates about expanding protections for minorities. Tellingly, the most persuasive liberal argument for ending segregation was not moral but strategic: Continuing racial discrimination gave the Soviet Union a powerful propaganda weapon against America.

In this political climate, advocates for group libel laws faced a steep challenge. They had to convince skeptics that restricting speech to protect minorities represented bold, necessary reform—not a dangerous legal experiment that could undermine the very freedoms America was fighting to preserve.

"Better caution before than tears later," warns the Yiddish proverb. For a people whose survival had depended on weighing risk, the postwar era brought American Jews to their own place of confusion. Judged by the standard of the Holocaust, or the tribulations of postwar Soviet and Middle Eastern Jews, American antisemitism seemed to pose significantly less danger. Yet who could predict where unchecked hatred might lead in a society gripped by Cold War fears and political extremism? After witnessing the Holocaust's horrors, how should American Jews measure risk?

The civil rights struggle they shared with Black Americans further complicated Jewish thinking about their place in society. In the minds of white supremacists, Jews and Blacks were linked—both targets in America's web of racial and religious prejudice. But legally, the two groups occupied different positions. A color line separated them that could not be ignored. As conflicts over desegregation intensified, Jews faced a strategic choice. Should they keep a low profile as an ethnic and religious minority, hiding behind their putative whiteness, or should they demand stronger group protections against targeted attacks? This uncertain Jewish calculus accompanied *Beauharnais v. Illinois* into the Supreme Court in the fall of 1951.

"CLEAR AND PRESENT danger depends upon whether the mischief of the repression is greater than the gravity of the evil, discounted by its improbability." These words came from *Dennis v. United States*, one of several cases from the years 1950 and 1951 through which the Supreme Court asserted a new test for balancing free speech against public harm. Danger was a function of how destructive the outcome would be and how likely it was to occur, weighed against the violation of an individual citizen's right to unfettered free speech. In *Dennis*, the Court voted 6–2 to sustain the conviction of eleven American Communist Party leaders accused of advocating the violent overthrow of the federal government by disseminating Marxist political pamphlets. The defendants claimed that they had merely advocated ideas, not endorsed revolutionary violence. Preaching communism was protected political speech. For the majority, however, the catastrophic potential outweighed the remoteness of any violent danger.[6]

Yet not all evils were created equal. In *Kunz v. New York*, the justices voted 8–1 to overturn the conviction of a conservative Baptist minister who held an illegal street rally at Manhattan's Columbus Circle after authorities denied him a permit due to his past inflammatory antisemitic and anti-Catholic remarks. The Court did not find evidence of danger that could justify prior restraint on speech. The lone dissent came from Justice Jackson, who argued that the virulent language in question could well lead to "evil acts." Alongside the danger of physical violence, he wrote, "fighting words" threatened a different kind of harm. Antisemitic chants strike like "missiles" at the minds of "Jews, many of whose families perished in the extermination furnaces of Dachau and Auschwitz." Was it not also "reasonable that the City protect the dignity of these persons against fanatics who take possession of its streets to hurl into its crowds defamatory epithets that hurt like rocks?"[7]

Jackson's reference to Dachau and Auschwitz was an early sign that the Nazi crimes had begun to leave their imprint on the American conception of hate speech. Yet his striking imagery blurred the line between physical danger and mental harm. In this case, the speech both augured future evil and triggered painful memories of past violence. That eloquent formulation was one of the clearest expressions of the harm hate speech posed to Jewish dignity. Still, words were not rocks, and Manhattan was not Auschwitz.

Such was the concern of law professor David Riesman. In the early 1940s, Riesman had been one of the first major thinkers to urge Americans to consider using group defamation to check the spread of antisemitism as part of the larger democratic response to totalitarianism. By 1951, however, he concluded that the totalitarian threat and its antisemitic offspring had passed. Now he worried instead that American Jews had turned legal vigilance into psychological neurosis. Too many Jews succumb to the temptation "to spend their lives as anti-anti-semites," he wrote in *Commentary* magazine. "We suspect that the vice crusader probably enjoys pornography. Perhaps the anti-anti-semite is fascinated by what he fights."

Riesman acknowledged that many "Jews, looking at the European experience, consciously or unconsciously feel that no dividing line separates an anti-Semitic remark from an extermination camp." In his eyes, this was a category error. Offensive language was not a form of persecution, much less a prelude to destruction. "Real action" meant violence of the kind witnessed in the Holocaust. Measured by that yardstick, American Jews had nothing to fear. "In the present context of American society," he wrote, "freedom of expression is one of the greatest safeguards for Jews and all other minorities subject to prejudice."[8]

Riesman offered a powerful critique of the distorting effects of trauma—and survivor guilt—among American Jews. Allergic to any trace of Jewish parochialism, he accused "militant" communal leaders of hijacking the Holocaust to ensure communal loyalty. His harsh words challenged Jews to differentiate between fear and discomfort when it came to offensive speech. Still, his cavalier dismissal of exaggerated Holocaust panic also trivialized antisemitic risk as irrelevant if it did not rise to that catastrophic level. In doing so, Riesman sidestepped the question of how the courts should measure danger.[9]

This approach anticipated the ACLU legal team's theory of the case. Beauharnais's defense was led by one of America's most eminent legal liberals, Alfred Albert. In his brief, Albert stressed that Beauharnais's views were as harmless as they were abhorrent. "There is something almost ludicrous in the spectacle of the full majesty of the law swooping down upon the bigot Beauharnais to punish him for his absurd utterances." Any risk paled in comparison to the threat of government repression. "Yesterday it was the freedom of twenty-five members of Jehovah's Witnesses, today it is Beauharnais's freedom; tomorrow it may be the freedom of a Negro to ask for a civil rights program because of the lynchings of a White man." Though he was active in Jewish civil rights, Albert left antisemitism conspicuously unmentioned. Published writings could never constitute a "clear and present danger." Nor, in the absence of a specific direct threat or "serious substantive evil," could Beauharnais's text be treated as anything remotely resembling "fighting words." The Illinois law under which Beauharnais had been convicted did not "regulate" speech for the purposes of public order or equal rights; it censored it.[10]

The risk of substantive evil formed precisely the heart of the State of Illinois's theory of the case. The state appellate work was handled by Zemel and Assistant State's Attorney General William Wines. In their filing, Wines and Zemel argued that it was the "substantive evil" of racial discrimination and its concomitant risk to the American public that justified the state law and its application to Beauharnais. "Totalitarian regimes arise from virulent racism," insisted the Illinois team, and though "the evil may be remote in time," the scale of its danger justified legal prevention. Even in written form, Beauharnais's claims fit both the "fighting words" and "clear and present danger" exceptions.[11]

The Illinois brief was effectively ghostwritten by the American Jewish Congress's Byron Miller, who seized on the *Dennis* standard as the quintessence of the entire group libel argument. "Sowing the seeds of racial hostilities creates such an enormous evil," he concluded, that "it is too late to wait until a Hitler has arrived in order" to turn to legal deterrence. In the end, Miller's invisible hand in the Illinois brief was the Congress's only contribution to the case. Over the objections of the Congress's civil rights team, the organization's leadership chose at the last minute not to enter the case with a separate amicus brief. Having yoked free speech to the measure of danger, Jewish liberals remained confused and divided over how to view the *Beauharnais* case. Better, they reasoned, to await the Supreme Court's decision.[12]

JOSEPH BEAUHARNAIS ARRIVED for his big day in Washington sporting an expensive new suit and a broad, defiant smile. Despite pleas of poverty, he let it be known that he had come by airplane. Making the rounds of the courtroom, Beauharnais warmly greeted his ACLU attorneys. Having spent two years denouncing the ACLU as a Jewish communist organization, he relished the fact that two young Jewish lawyers had been assigned to represent him.[13]

Albert began his oral argument with a lofty preamble about the need to protect "freedom for the expression of opinions we hate." His strategy, he had confided beforehand to colleagues, was to play on the Court's anti-communist bent. How can we allow a law so broad that an average citizen could be arrested merely for "calling Communism a criminal conspiracy"? Almost immediately, however, Justice Frankfurter interrupted. What if we *do* want to ban certain hateful expression? Regardless of the wording of the Illinois law, could *any* group libel law pass constitutional muster?

The justice returned repeatedly to that question. Each time, Albert waffled, trying to avoid a direct answer, which only provoked Frankfurter. He grew more and more angry until he was red in the face, pounding the table. Finally, Albert conceded that, yes, a constitutionally valid "group libel statute could be drawn up," provided there was a provision for "clear and present danger." "With that you undermine your whole case!" exclaimed Justice Black, jumping into the fray. Such laws would task judges with ruling on the legality of "social or political" statements. Seeking to steer the conversation onto a more favorable track for Albert, Black posed his own question: How could the First Amendment be reasonably understood to authorize the government to prevent "persons from expressing their views about other groups?"[14]

As Albert tried in vain to get a word in edgewise, Frankfurter and Black parried back and forth. Why must we say that "calling people derogatory names," should "be protected?" asked Frankfurter. "I thought the Constitution said something about 'equal protection of the law,'" cracked Black, to which Frankfurter responded sternly: "I thought the Fair Employment Practices Commission movement is recognition of the practical fact that further measures are needed to guarantee equal protection." The clash made for "as tense a day as I have ever seen in court," Albert recalled.[15]

At stake in the fight were two different views of the Constitution's handling of civil rights—and the role of courts in defending them. Black viewed individual freedom as under ever-present threat from government intrusion; Frankfurter worried that equal rights risked being sacrificed on the altar of libertarianism. Group libel laws would convert judges into political referees, Black insisted. On the contrary, Frankfurter argued, the greater danger was that judges exceed their authority and undermine racial and religious equality by imposing themselves on the democratic process. Civil rights expanded through laws made by legislatures not judicial fiat. The urgent need for racial justice demanded that judges acknowledge as much. As the two men fought, Albert and Levy quietly cheered for Black's position. He was "magnificent, cool and calm with a polite sarcasm that cut like the edge of an open knife," wrote Albert afterward. "It was some performance!" He thought their odds were good for a 5–4 victory, if not 6–3.[16]

Zemel watched all this unfold with a sense of wonder. He was shocked that his own case had reached the highest court in the land. Now he listened as Wines followed Frankfurter's lead to present his argument. The recent terrible events in Cicero were only the latest in a long line of disturbances in Illinois going all the way back to the 1908 Springfield Race Riots, in which white mobs attacked Black communities, and their Jewish neighbors, in the state capital, "perhaps as ghastly a holocaust of genocide as has ever occurred in the United States." It was precisely to prevent the "substantive evils" of race riots that the state legislature had written the law in question. Black again pushed back sharply. Why would such a law not apply equally to political parties in conflict? "I don't think the legislature intended to reach political parties," Wines responded. Pressing on that point, Jackson wondered aloud about the specific context of Chicago. "Can a political party be libeled in Chicago?" he asked. "You don't have riots between Democrats and Republicans?" Cutting in, Zemel quipped, "We don't have such problems there, Your Honor. In Chicago we have coalitions, not riots." The courtroom erupted in laughter.[17]

As the hearing wound down, Frankfurter added a last-minute request. Would the State of Illinois please provide a memorandum on the history of race riots in Illinois? "Add to that report," countered Black, "the record of political riots, labor riots, and religious riots." The dueling requests reflected the current salvos in the ongoing debate over which forms of speech—and which ideologies—posed a true danger to American society. In Black's eyes, a racist diatribe against integration was no more offensive than any other emotional speech in defense of a sensitive social or political question. Such matters should not justify limiting the most fundamental of civil rights. Frankfurter insisted that the unique evil of racial and religious hatred was different. Illinois's history of "race riots and interracial violence" would prove it.[18]

The dispute between Frankfurter and Black resumed three days later when the justices met in conference to review the case. It is high time for American law to accept the principle of group libel, Frankfurter announced to his colleagues. I have long been interested in this type of statute, he explained, citing the British 1937 law passed to handle the fascist leader Oswald Mosley. If a criminal libel exists against an individual, by logic it ought to apply to a "racial or religious group." We must extend "the law of libel to a group to protect its right against those who would like to liquidate the group," he stated starkly. Doing so would ensure that "law should be an instrument of democracy."[19]

Black vigorously disagreed. The speech in this instance was not even defamatory; it was political. Loathsome or not, he argued, "Beauharnais and his group were making a genuine effort to petition their elected representatives." States cannot "punish people for exercising First Amendment" rights. As for the argument about the evils of racism, the data on labor riots showed that left-wing labor activism was just as likely a source of social friction and deadly violence. The law's neutrality worked in everyone's favor. Any minority group that wished for such a law might find it used against them one day.[20]

The conference ended with a straw poll. Five justices voted to affirm the conviction—Frankfurter, Tom Clark, Sherman Minton, Jackson, and Fred Vinson—as against four who would reverse—Black, Harold Burton, Stanley Reed, and William Douglas. Frankfurter had narrowly prevailed.[21]

Five months later, that result became official. On April 28, 1952, the justices affirmed Beauharnais's conviction by the same slim 5–4 margin. Writing for the majority, Frankfurter explained the logic of the decision. Beauharnais's publication did not appear in a vacuum; it formed part of a long pattern of dangerous violence in American society. "In the face of this history and its frequent obbligato of extreme racial and religious propaganda," he wrote, "we would deny experience to say that the Illinois Legislature" cannot "curb false or malicious defamation of racial and religious groups, made in public places and by means calculated to have a powerful emotional impact on those to whom it was presented." Past precedent and present-day impact both mattered in determining the law's approach to hatred. Judges must not replace real-world moral reckoning with abstract reasoning.[22]

Equally important, Frankfurter insisted on the controlling relevance of the Fourteenth Amendment. Minority group dignity mattered in the pursuit of civil rights. It would be simply wrong for us to say that "speech concededly punishable when immediately directed at individuals cannot be outlawed if directed at groups with whose position and esteem in society the affiliated individual may be inextricably involved." To make this point, Frankfurter followed the path laid out by Alexander Pekelis and other progressive liberals of the 1940s who had called for analogizing civil rights to labor rights:

> Long ago this Court recognized that the economic rights of an individual may depend for the effectiveness of their enforcement on rights in the group, even though not formally corporate, to which he belongs . . . Such group-protection on behalf of the individual may, for all we know, be a need not confined to the part that a trade union plays in effectuating rights abstractly recognized as belonging to its members . . . a man's job and his educational opportunities and . . .

> dignity . . . may depend as much on the reputation of the racial and religious group to which he willy-nilly belongs, as on his own merits.[23]

We are not only individuals wandering through the world, Frankfurter reasoned. Our dignity, our security, and our life chances are affected by our collective identities and group attachments, which shape our concrete positions in society. Recognizing groups in law provided them a means to secure equal protection. Just as workers could band together to form legally recognized unions to address economic rights, so could members of minority groups exercise collective rights to prevent discrimination and harm. Nor was it a violation of liberalism; it was a more democratic version of liberalism, he argued, a means of making law into a true "instrument of democracy."

As for critics who worried that group libel laws would lead to censorship, Frankfurter dismissed this concern as no different from the risk of adverse outcomes inherent in all lawmaking. "That the legislative remedy might not in practice mitigate the evil, or might itself raise new problems, would only manifest once more the paradox of reform," he wrote. "It is the price to be paid for the trial-and-error inherent in legislative efforts to deal with obstinate social issues."[24]

Black deplored his colleagues' ruling. "This case is here because Illinois inflicted criminal punishment on Beauharnais for causing the distribution of leaflets in the city of Chicago," he wrote. "The conviction rests on the leaflet's contents, not on the time, manner or place of distribution." This was no "face-to-face" attack on an individual but one citizen's "genuine effort to petition their elected representatives." Political advocacy in defense of segregation was protected speech, plain and simple. Anything else was censorship, and "sugar-coating does not make the censorship less deadly." It was "startling and frightening" to see "state experimentation in curbing freedom of expression" just because "two or three naughty words" surfaced in a matter "of public concern."

To bolster his point, Black appended Beauharnais's leaflet to his dissent. "Whatever the danger, if any, in such public discussions," he continued, "it is a danger the founders deemed outweighed by the danger incident to the stifling of thought and speech." He likened Beauharnais to colonial Americans petitioning the king, and to the revolutionary drafters of the Declaration of Independence and the Bill of Rights. As for Beauharnais's critics, their unholy desires recalled the darkest chapters in human history, the "burning of books and even of the burning of witches."

Black's elevation of Beauharnais into a martyr for free speech was accompanied by a warning to minorities. The difficult national conversation on race might lead "both sides" to resort to inflammatory tactics. The law existed to protect mutual adversaries in an open fight. "Ironically enough, Beauharnais, convicted of crime in Chicago, would probably be given a hero's reception in many other localities, if not in some parts of Chicago itself. Moreover, the same kind of state law that makes Beauharnais a criminal for advocating segregation in Illinois can be utilized to send people to jail in other states for advocating equality and nonsegregation." To those "minority groups who hail this holding as their victory," they would do well to remember the ancient saying, "'Another such victory and I am undone.'"[25]

As expected, Black's libertarian ally Justice Douglas also took a dim view of Frankfurter's reasoning. "The First Amendment is couched in absolute terms—freedom of speech shall not be abridged," he wrote in his dissent. It therefore trumped the Fourteenth Amendment. In adopting "a constitutional interpretation which puts free speech under the legislative thumb," the Court had replaced the "free trade in ideas which the Framers of the Constitution visualized" with a "new orthodoxy—an orthodoxy that changes with the whims of the age or the day, an orthodoxy which the majority by solemn judgment proclaims to be essential to the safety, welfare, security, morality, or health of society."

Douglas's dissent offered an eloquent indictment of the perils of government speech regulation. Yet he could not quite make up his mind on what the law should be. In other parts of his dissent he displayed a notable openness to Frankfurter's argument about the unique dangers of antisemitic and racist speech. "Hitler and his Nazis showed how evil a conspiracy could be which was aimed at destroying a race by exposing it to contempt, derision, and obloquy," he wrote, and so "I would be willing to concede that such conduct directed at a race or group in this country could be made an indictable offense." There might well be instances of "clear and present danger" in which the government might curb "speech in order to prevent disaster." He believed those conditions simply did not obtain in the case of Beauharnais. Douglas closed with his own warning to minorities about the boomerang effect:

> Today a White man stands convicted for protesting in unseemly language against our decisions invalidating restrictive covenants. Tomorrow a negro will be hauled before a court for denouncing lynch law in heated terms. Farm laborers in the west who compete with field hands drifting up from Mexico; Whites who feel the pressure of Orientals; a minority which finds employment going to members of the dominant religious group—all of these are caught in the mesh of today's decision.[26]

Racial and religious conflict was an inevitable feature of modern democracy, suggested Douglas. Hatred was a rational response to economic competition. The task of law was to ensure free, fair relations between groups, not to repair entrenched structural inequities. The First Amendment represented the battlefield upon which the struggle over rights took place; it should not be mistaken for a weapon that any combatant might employ.[27]

The same pattern of ambivalence recurred in the most dramatic of all the dissents. At the December conference, Jackson had "unequivocally" insisted that the First Amendment was not absolute, positioning himself alongside Frankfurter in a reprise of their *Terminiello* position. If forty-some states had individual criminal libel laws, he suggested, then why not extend that principle to groups? Yet in the intervening months, even as Frankfurter won over Burton, Jackson wavered. The Illinois state law was valid, he reasoned, but the specific conviction in this instance was not. There was no "clear and present danger" in Beauharnais's publication. As for group libel, it remained theoretically viable:

> Group libel statutes represent a commendable desire to reduce sinister abuses of our freedoms of expression—abuses which I have had occasion to learn can tear apart a society, brutalize its dominant elements, and persecute, even to extermination, its minorities. While laws or prosecutions might not alleviate racial or sectarian hatreds and may even invest scoundrels with a specious martyrdom, I should be loath to foreclose the States from a considerable latitude of experimentation in this field. Such efforts, if properly applied, do not justify frenetic forebodings of crushed liberty.

To be sure, Jackson warned, there was a risk. "No group interest in any particular prosecution should forget that the shoe may be on the other foot in some prosecution tomorrow." Jackson's dissent was decidedly pragmatic. Group libel was neither a panacea nor a slippery slope to censorship. The essence of liberalism was about managing risk by distributing it equally across society. Ultimately, the possibility of violence remained a surer standard by which to judge harm. "One of the merits of the clear and present danger test is that the triers of fact would take into account the realities of race relations and any smoldering fires to be fanned into holocausts."[28]

On its face, the 5–4 decision in *Beauharnais* suggested a closely split Court torn over the boundaries of free speech. Yet when read closely, even the dissents amounted to a vindication of the majority's theory of the case. In that sense, the vote was 7–2 in acknowledgment that the Constitution allowed the government to ban hate speech. Five justices had affirmatively approved the Illinois law; six had indicated they would support a federal group libel law at least in theory; and seven would support redrawn state legislation. The path to group libel seemed viable if uncertain. But how would America respond?[29]

WHAT ARE YOU going to do about that "terrible decision," wrote an alarmed Gerald Smith to Roger Baldwin two weeks after the verdict. The ruling jeopardized his entire movement. I understand that the ACLU practices "antisemitism in reverse" by favoring Jews and Jewish lawyers,

Smith wrote, before pleading for their continued support: "I do know that it requires a philosophical Jew to defend my right of free speech." Baldwin replied defensively. There is no "pro-Semitism in framing our policies . . . Our Jewish board members and staff lean over backwards on that issue." In fact, he said, we have just taken the rare step of petitioning the Supreme Court for a rehearing in the *Beauharnais* case. That apperal is being "handled exclusively by Jewish lawyers and a Negro attorney acting for himself. They did so solely as a matter of principle in law and because it is a matter of policy."[30]

The "Negro attorney" to whom Baldwin referred was none other than Thurgood Marshall, the chief legal counsel of the NAACP. Marshall had crossed paths with Beauharnais in Cicero and he harbored no illusions about how dangerous the man was. Yet after the *Beauharnais* verdict, he took a personal leave from the NAACP to join the last-ditch ACLU effort. Group libel law "would more than likely boomerang against us and organizations of our type," he believed. In the hands of segregationists, such laws could squelch the civil rights movement.[31]

Marshall's decision to involve himself in the *Beauharnais* case signaled an overall shift in the larger NAACP strategy on civil rights litigation. Before the 1950s, NAACP lawyers focused less on tackling state-sponsored public segregation than on challenging broader private sector racism in American farms and factories. Their vision reflected an understanding of racism as the product of socioeconomic forces and legal structures, not simply the unfair treatment of an individual because of their skin color. That translated into defending the collective rights of Black workers rather than individual rights of victims of government discrimination. A focus on the evils of public segregation ignored how much racial inequality derived from the structure of the modern American economy built on the ruins of slavery.[32]

After World War II, however, Marshall and his colleagues narrowed their litigation focus to eliminating "separate but equal" institutions. In the era of the Cold War anti-communism, they calculated, it made more sense to stress individual freedom rather than any claims associated with collective rights of minorities or private enterprise. The evil of government discrimination became the quintessential racist expression and an un-American denial of individual rights. Group classifications had justified and upheld legal racism. Now ending racist laws would purge liberalism of all racism, rendering justice blind to group differences.[33]

The same logic flowed through Marshall's brief in *Beauharnais*. The Court had erred in ruling on the legality of group libel statutes, a constitutional question that was not explicitly raised in the lawsuit itself. As a result, all "political advocacy" now lies in danger from the "monumental" decision on libel, which would extend government control of individual freedom. The greatest danger in modern society was government discrimination against individuals on the basis of their ideas. Any speech restriction risked a slippery slope to state censorship.[34]

A strategic calculus also guided this logic. As civil rights leaders geared up for a wave of legal and political court battles related to racial equality, a libertarian First Amendment would reward more than it would subtract in this campaign. Staging public protests was crucial to challenging Jim Crow. In a climate in which McCarthyism targeted all manner of liberal groups with communist smears and government intimidation, curbing speech would hurt the civil rights movement's ability to advocate freely for its cause.[35]

However, on June 9, the Court declined the ACLU petition without comment. Group libel had officially become constitutionally valid. At the behest of the American Jewish Congress, four New York congressmen—Arthur Klein, Eugene Keogh, and Adam Clayton Powell Jr., all Democrats, and Jacob Javits, a liberal Republican—now moved to enshrine the decision in legislation, submitting a federal group libel bill to Congress. Introduced once before in 1949, the draft bill banned the use of postal services or interstate commerce for dissemination of material that defamed minority groups.[36]

In their press release, the congressmen—two Jews, one Irish Catholic, and one African American Baptist—made no mention of Beauharnais or Bindman. Instead, they framed the issue in terms of vandalism and domestic terror, referring to a recent spate of bombings in Florida "and desecrations of churches and synagogues in Pennsylvania and elsewhere." These events, they said in their joint statement, "are latter-day evidences of what libels of racial or religious groups are capable of bringing on in an American community." The law is not aimed at "honest people, regardless of how misguided" their view, but at "demagogues and dishonest purveyors of defamatory material."[37]

A small group of voices cheered the news of the Supreme Court decision and the draft bill. AJC leader Samuel Margoshes hailed the ruling as "a great victory in the war against bigotry" destined to "have a profound impact on group relations in America." It is high time, wrote the Minneapolis *American Jewish World*, for "the law to be brought up to the psychological and moral facts of life." We may "finally have a federal law that will declare antisemitism to be a crime in America," declared a columnist for the Yiddish-language *Tog*. The *Chicago Defender* also praised the decision as a welcome "legal and constitutional means to eliminate racial and religious poison from the bloodstream of our society."[38]

However, these scattered notes of approval were drowned out by a chorus of negative reactions. Newspapers ranging from the liberal *Washington Post* to the conservative *Chicago Tribune* lambasted the verdict as misguided censorship that defied "common sense." Thanks to this decision, "Beauharnais and his loathsome ilk are winning their fight," wrote the *Chicago Sun-Times*, "by forcing the enactment of measures which encroach bit by bit on the Bill of Rights as it affects all Americans." The African American *Pittsburgh Courier* cautioned its readers, "Our people should remember" that this ruling "may be a two-edged sword," supplying a weapon to "Negrophobes."[39]

Though the *Beauharnais* decision had come only three years after *Terminiello*, American society had changed. The ruling appeared smack in the midst of Senator Joseph McCarthy's anti-communist crusade. As the House Un-American Activities Committee pursued its investigations of communist influence in Hollywood and labor unions, the Wisconsin senator launched his own campaign to rid the federal government of hidden communists. The chilling spectacle of public inquisitions stoked fear in the hearts of even those Americans deeply concerned about communist threats.

American Jews had special reasons to fear McCarthyite anti-communism in mid-1952. Julius and Ethel Rosenberg, convicted of Soviet espionage, sat in prison awaiting execution. Both their supporters and detractors in the Jewish community feared the case would spark more antisemitism. But an even more proximate source of anxiety was the 1952 McCarran-Walter Act. Congress had undertaken the first fundamental revision of immigration and nationality law since the restrictive Johnson-Reed Act of 1924. The new draft law barred political "subversives" from entering the country and authorized the government to detain and deport naturalized citizens found to be engaged in "subversive" activity.[40]

Jewish leaders across the country reacted with open panic. "The bill, widely labeled 'America's first Nuremberg Law,' is clearly anti-Semitic," wrote the *Brooklyn Jewish Examiner*. "It bars entry to America to victims of Nazi brutality while it welcomes Nazis; it legalizes seizures and searches of non-citizens without court warrant and cancellation of citizenship of naturalized American citizens for petty reasons." Faced with this prospect, even some of the staunchest defenders of the *Beauharnais* effort wavered. "The real 'trouble-makers' are not the small-time racketeers and professional anti-Semites that once bedeviled American Jewry," declared *Sentinel* editor Jack Fishbein in June of that year. "They are the sinister forces at work in the Congress and other official bodies enacting their McCarran Acts, erecting their Concentration Camps, and preparing to deport hundreds of thousands of naturalized Jews."[41]

It was not only Jews whose views abruptly changed with McCarthyism. After initially hailing the *Beauharnais* decision, CCLC leader Ira Latimer soon shocked his allies by announcing his conversion to the cause of extreme anti-communism. He went on to initiate a purge within his organization, leading to its collapse, and then alleged a vast communist conspiracy extending across the entire Chicago legal community. Having flipped from progressive liberal to ultraconservative, Latimer launched the national right-to-work movement to crush the labor movement. He embraced antisemitism, and formed a close friendship with one of America's foremost white supremacist ideologues, the University of Illinois classics professor and John Birch Society leader Revilo Oliver.[42]

While Latimer busied himself with political self-reinvention, Aaron Bindman struggled to survive the aftermath of the riot. Throughout 1950 his family endured a string of vandalism attacks. A second arson attempt cost him his home. His insurer revoked his fire protection policy, leading his mortgage company to cancel his contract. On top of that, his neighbor sued him for false arrest and malicious prosecution. Then, in 1952, Bindman was publicly branded a communist traitor during HUAC satellite hearings in Chicago. In response, he pivoted from labor activism to civil rights, joining the Illinois leadership of the Civil Rights Congress and then the NAACP. He earned a PhD in sociology from the University of Illinois with a dissertation on Black civil rights protest. Bindman made little mention thereafter of his Jewish experiences, focusing instead on his allyship as a white American defending his fellow citizens.[43]

Bindman's transformation from victim of antisemitism to NAACP leader reflected a broader shift in how America viewed its Jews—and how they saw themselves. Younger Jews who flocked to the civil rights movement were increasingly identified not as a racialized minority, but as part of the white majority.

Several major changes drove this transformation. Jewish acculturation into white Christian America coincided with the broader deracialization of immigrant ethnic groups like the Irish and Italians. New civil rights laws provided dual benefits: protection from discrimination, which accelerated Jewish economic mobility into the middle class, and inclusion in a racial binary that coded them as white rather than as a targeted minority.[44]

Growing awareness of the Holocaust, though not as central to American consciousness as it would later become, dampened overt hostilities. This precipitous decline in antisemitic public opinion had perhaps the greatest effect on Jewish attitudes toward hate speech regulation. In spite of McCarthyism and the McCarran-Walter Act, the latest polling in 1952 suggested a dramatic weakening of antisemitic attitudes among the public. Many questioned whether enhanced group protection was still necessary if bigotry was losing traction in mainstream America.[45]

Proof of that came from no less a quarter than the sputtering career of Beauharnais. Accepting legal defeat, he returned to Chicago in the summer of 1952 and paid his court fine. Then he joined roughly two hundred radical right dissenters who gathered in Chicago that July on the sidelines of the Republican National Convention. Disgusted with the mainstream GOP as reflected in the two front-runner candidates, Robert Taft and Dwight Eisenhower, they pledged their support to General Douglas MacArthur. Yet their shadow convention collapsed over a dispute over the importance of antisemitism. One group, led by Beauharnais, insisted that as evil as Jews were, true conservatives should focus exclusively on preserving racial segregation. The other faction insisted that the "real issue" was "Jewish Communists" and the "secret government" running America and the world. The rift exposed the far right's own perplexity at where to slot Jews in a racial order defined by color. The episode confirmed to Jewish leaders that these sorts of professional bigots mattered less than the battle against legal discrimination.[46]

By the fall of 1952, the federal group libel bill died quickly in committee, failing to attract even a modicum of support. The state-level drafting of similar laws also petered out over the next two years, as civil rights groups turned their focus to desegregation. Even the Congress figures at the heart of the *Beauharnais* campaign questioned whether the fight against antisemitism warranted hate speech regulation. Many were now persuaded that antisemitic hatred, while still present, posed far less risk than other threats facing America. "McCarthyism, with its hideous power to enslave men's minds and to silence their voices," declared the Congress's Rabbi Morton Berman in 1954, is "an even more dangerous evil than anti-Semitism."[47]

Of all the changes of heart to take place in the wake of the *Beauharnais* decision, the most striking was that of Berman's colleague at the Congress, the lawyer Will Maslow. By 1954, the man who had long carried the torch for group libel now disavowed it. Maslow freely acknowledged the irony. If my opinion now is "contrary to the one I expressed several years ago, it means simply that I believe I was wrong then . . . in exaggerating the dangers." Enlarging American freedom would secure Jewish equality. Antisemitism no longer endangered America's Jews. Still, he held out one significant caveat: Should the situation change drastically, group libel remained a viable option. "If the day ever arises when antisemitic propaganda is disseminated on such a scale and under such auspices that it is a menace rather than an irritation," then the use of group libel legislation would be justified.[48]

Maslow's striking mea culpa reflected American liberalism's fundamental ambivalence about hate speech. Assuming that law and education eradicated large-scale discrimination, hateful words mattered less. Defaming a group was wrong, but not harmful enough to compromise individual free expression. Yet if the volume and tenor of such speech increased to the point where it posed a direct threat to society, then it could and should legitimately be targeted. Such a framing reduced harm to a problem of empirical measurement filtered through subjective experience. The need for the law was indexed directly to the perception of danger.

In truth, Maslow's ambivalence mirrored that of the Supreme Court decision itself; a plurality of its authors had effectively declared that group libel law was constitutional but inadvisable. Honesty required acknowledging its legal viability; prudence dictated that the option not be exercised. That left the question of hate speech in American law suspended between the optional and the necessary.[49]

The year 1953 marked the beginning of a new Supreme Court era with the appointment of California Governor Earl Warren as chief justice. The Warren Court dramatically expanded individual rights and ushered in desegregation. The First Amendment was central to the Court's work, including major cases involving libel law and press freedom. Yet when it came to one of the most significant First Amendment decisions, the Court maintained a studious silence. *Beauharnais* was never either explicitly overturned or reaffirmed. Instead, it lived on as a ghost in American law.[50]

Postwar liberalism promised to harmonize freedom and equality by making all individual citizens free and equal in the eyes of the law. Good speech would outweigh bad speech. Hatred would shrink to a private folly rather than a public menace. Yet lurking beneath the civil rights movement remained the problem of minority group equality. Did it suffice to ban discrimination to ensure equal protection under law? Or did some forms of hatred require special legal remedies? What would happen if and when an exceptional hatred returned with a vengeance?[51]

PART II

THE 1970s

7

Never Again

"Gentlemen, my name is Ted Frosch. I reside at 9131 Northridge Way in Skokie." The middle-aged man spoke evenly, with just the slightest hint of a Hungarian accent creeping in around his English vowels. "It came to my attention that on May the first, there is going to be a Nazi parade held in front of the Village Hall. As a Nazi survivor during the Second World War, I would like to know what you gentlemen are going to do about it."[1]

Everyone listening in the council chambers that late April 1977 evening knew to what he was referring. It had begun with the flyers. "We are coming!" screamed the text of the handbill emblazoned with an image of a swastika strangling a hook-nosed Jew. After years of battling "the Black Invasion of Southwest Chicago," the National Socialist Party of America announced, "We have decided to relocate in areas heavily populated by the real enemy—the Jews!" In just over a week, the Nazis would descend on the town of seventy thousand, roughly one in ten of whom was a Holocaust survivor.[2]

Frosch, born in Budapest, demanded answers. Tidy lectures about the First Amendment left him unmoved. Talk of an enhanced police presence missed the point. These people must be stopped before they come. "There is thousands of Jewish survivors of the Nazi Holocaust living here in Skokie and suburbs. We expect to show up at the Village Hall, and to tear these people apart if it is necessary," he warned. "We cannot, we *cannot* let it happen again, what happened during World War II. We *cannot* let these people just come into the midst [of] our village, in our community, and be dressed in Nazi uniforms and swastikas. We cannot let it happen again, sir."[3]

One by one, the survivors of Skokie lined up that night to echo the warning. As they spoke, the line between past and present dissolved. American antisemites mimicking Nazis were not just a simulacrum of evil; they were the very same ghouls reincarnated. For the sake of our sanity and our children's safety, you must act, former Auschwitz prisoner Fay Waldman testified. If not the government, the people would take matters into their own hands. "We might be the ones to break the law," she said, her Yiddish-accented voice vibrating with emotion, "all the wounds, and everything that we went through, will come and we might be the beast! Not them! And you will have to put us behind the bars."[4]

No single event better encapsulated the free speech debate in post-1960s America than Skokie. A sleepy Chicago suburb suddenly became the stage for a national drama of law and hatred. A passel of new Nazis gleefully claimed the mantle of the First Amendment, dutifully supported by their ACLU lawyers. At the behest of panicked, furious survivors, town leaders scrambled to block the march with a court order, and they rushed through a trio of municipal anti-hate-speech laws, citing *Beauharnais* as precedent. Still dissatisfied by these efforts, the town's survivors filed their own class action civil lawsuit alleging a new crime: menticide—the psychological equivalent of genocide. The sight of the swastika inspired such great fear and trauma that the mental harm inflicted equaled—or even outweighed—physical danger.

Over the course of the next year, these legal efforts sparked lengthy court battles, culminating in not one but two United States Supreme Court decisions in favor of free speech—and the Nazis. As all the legal options expired in the summer of 1978, hundreds of thousands of Americans—Jews and non-Jews—from across the country prepared to mass in Skokie in counterprotest. They were joined by planeloads of activists from Israel, among them Meir Kahane, the Orthodox rabbi and founder of the far right Jewish Defense League, who pledged his readiness to fight the Nazis with Jewish power. Chicago's Jewish socialists also mobilized with calls to "Smash the Nazis" in the name of antifascism. From across the world came offers of money and bullets.[5]

The show of unity masked the fact that Skokie fractured American liberalism. Half the ACLU's national membership resigned in protest. A great many of those resignations came from Jews angry with the organization's defense of bigotry in the name of freedom. Their anger stemmed from fear. Neo-Nazis had targeted Holocaust victims yet the law provided no protection. Fear bred a deeper cynicism about the larger tilt of civil rights in the 1970s. As affirmative action reshaped American society, Jews faced an unsettling paradox: They remained a vulnerable, racialized minority, yet new laws placed them on the white side of the color line.

Nothing better illustrated how antisemitism remained tethered to American racism than the fact that the National Socialist Party of America decided to strike Jewish Skokie only after a decade spent battling Black integration in Chicago. In the neo-Nazi imagination, Black Power was tied to "the real enemy," pseudo-white Jewish power. That obsession with Jewish racial identity would increasingly define the character of post-1960s white supremacy. This was especially evident in the life of the man who engineered the entire Skokie affair. Frank Collin's path to fame as America's leading antisemite began improbably enough with the story of his own Jewish father's escape from Nazi Germany.

ON THE NIGHT of November 9, 1938—Kristallnacht—Nazi brigades swept through German cities destroying Jewish homes, businesses, and synagogues. In the ensuing days, thousands of Jewish men arrested for "race defilement" and other crimes were sent to the Dachau concentration camp. Among the first prisoners to arrive was Max Simon Cohn, a twenty-five-year-old man from an Orthodox Jewish family in nearby Munich. Three months later he was released, and he quickly boarded a ship bound for New York, where an immigration clerk recorded his race as "Hebrew." Five years later, he became an American citizen. This time the papers listed a new name, "Max Frank Collin," and a new race, "White." They also mentioned his wife, a white Catholic woman named Virginia Hardyman, his profession as a slipcover manufacturer, and his infant son, born "Frank Joseph Cohn."[6]

Frank Collin was raised Catholic in a family of six in southwest Chicago. His father, Max, chose radical assimilation to solve his Jewish question. A name change and a new faith would leave no Jew left to hate. His actions led to a permanent break with his younger sister Ruth, the only other member of the family to survive. Young Frank grew obsessed with Nazism. He watched the 1956 NBC film *The Twisted Cross*, an early Holocaust documentary, and found himself transfixed by the images of Hitler and Nazi propaganda. One day he spied a white swastika painted on the wall near his elementary school, triggering "an emotional experience, a conversion" to a new radical faith.[7]

Collin was not alone in his fascination with Nazism. Across the early 1960s, the strange power of the swastika was spreading in American society. In the opening months of 1960, a shocking wave of vandal attacks dubbed the Swastika Epidemic swept across the world. In the United States, there were eight hundred reported instances of the Nazi symbol painted on synagogues and Jewish community centers. Some of this antisemitic vandalism could be traced to a new generation of white supremacist groups like the National States Rights Party, which in defense of segregation targeted both Jewish and Black communities with violence. The group was largely responsible for a wave of synagogue bombings across the South along with two attacks in Illinois, one of which targeted Anshe Emet, Chicago's largest Conservative synagogue.[8]

Above all, neo-Nazi culture derived from the American Nazi Party, a group founded by George Lincoln Rockwell. A former naval pilot and graphic artist, Rockwell led a series of radical right-wing organizations in the late 1950s, among them the National Committee to Free America of Jewish Domination. In 1960, he chose to rebrand his efforts with a Nazi theme, including uniforms, flags, and swastikas. "When I was in the advertising game," he explained, "we used to use nude women. Now I use the *Hakenkreuz* and stormtroopers. You use what brings them in."[9]

The shock imagery was accompanied by aggressive publicity stunts. Fanning out from the group's Arlington, Virginia, headquarters, Rockwell and his men picketed Jewish-owned stores in downtown Washington, DC, as well as movie theaters screening films about Israel or racial integration. Soon he began making trips to Chicago. There he found fertile ground among the city's poorer southwestern neighborhoods such as Gage Park and Marquette Park, where violent white resistance to residential integration continued.

It was not only white grievance but Black Power that shaped Rockwell's emerging ideology. In 1962, he attended a Nation of Islam rally in Chicago in the company of none other than Joseph Beauharnais, who had forged ties with the next generation of the far right. Born out of pan-Africanism, the Black Muslim sect espoused its creed of racial separatism as a radical answer to white racism. The two movements found a common enemy in Jews and their "parasitic" liberalism. The encounter led Rockwell to coin his own term, "White Power," the title of his 1967 manifesto.[10]

Collin secretly joined Rockwell's movement as a teenager. At Southern Illinois University in Carbondale, the clean-cut journalism major publicly styled himself a law-and-order conservative interested in free speech and principled dialogue. In February 1968, he invited Rockwell's successor, Matt Koehl, to speak on campus, after Rockwell had been shot to death by a disgruntled fellow Nazi several months earlier. Koehl's talk was interrupted by a mass walkout of Black students, leading to a scuffle with others in the audience. Over the next several weeks, as campus unrest mounted over Vietnam and civil rights, Collin tried bringing Koehl back for a public debate with the Black leader Stokely Carmichael. In letters to the campus newspaper, Collin decried "the howling throng of Negroes" under "Communist" control, yet he insisted that he cared most about open, honest dialogue in the spirit of free speech.[11]

That summer he came out as a Nazi. The swastika was the portal to total commitment. "Once you put that on your arm, you're dedicated," he remarked; "there's no turning back." He left college in the fall to set up the Midwest branch of the National Socialist White People's Party. Its headquarters was established in Marquette Park, the better to stoke more racial confrontation between Blacks and whites.[12]

In his new role, Collin roamed late 1960s Chicagoland speaking on college campuses, slowly building up a small but dedicated following of young white men. He was not a naturally charismatic leader. Short and slim with a slight paunch and thinning dark hair, he resembled Dustin Hoffman more than Adolf Hitler. His biting humor delivered in a clipped, nasal voice sounded more like a wisecracking provocateur than a fierce race warrior. Yet aggression coursed through his rhetoric, and his rallies ended in violence. His "Thirty Point Program" called for "the shooting on sight of all Black and anarchist rioters and looters" and the "liquidation of all Communists, pro-Communists, Zionists and other treasonous organizations."[13]

Jews, in his mind, were a separate race between white and Black, one that possessed massive "political and financial power." Collin accused them of "using the wild Negro masses to tear down civilized society and thereby clear the way for a race-mixed Communist America." Our goal is to rid "the United States of the Jewish element," Collin stressed, but he hastened to add that he did not propose physical extermination. "The way you smash Jewish power is actually not through violence," Collin insisted; "the way you do it is to expose it."[14]

Exposure was the same tactic adopted by the ADL when Collin first rose to prominence. In 1969 the group informed the FBI of his Jewish ancestry, which prompted Director J. Edgar Hoover to order an operation to discredit Collin. Agents from the Bureau's infamous COINTELPRO program, which targeted Black civil rights leaders and other designated enemies, chose antisemitism to fight antisemitism. They dispatched two anonymous letters to the NSWPP headquarters in Arlington revealing Collin's paternity. When nothing happened, they leaked the material to reporters, who rushed to interview Collin's father. He confirmed his biography and denounced his son's views. Yet Collin called a press conference to deny the reports. His father was lying. "If he was a Jew, I would certainly not have joined the Nazi Party. We are white-Aryan and under the Nuremberg laws in Germany if a man was even half Jew, he lost his citizenship." Nonetheless, the revelation prompted his colleagues to expel him from their ranks. His Chicago headquarters was firebombed. Undeterred, he launched a new organization, the National Socialist Party of America, and pressed on with his cause.[15]

In the first half of the 1970s, Collin staged more than forty White Power rallies and marches in and around Marquette Park. As they grew increasingly violent, the city finally refused to grant him a permit. The decision led Collin to enlist the ACLU's support. The group had represented Illinois neo-Nazi groups since the early 1960s. With their help, Collin sued, claiming his First Amendment rights had been violated by unconstitutional prior restraint. In 1972, the U.S. Court of Appeals for the Seventh Circuit found in his favor, ordering the Chicago Park District to issue him permits on demand for any location in the city. But by the fall of 1975, Chicago officials had had enough. They informed Collin that henceforth he would be required to obtain $150,000 worth of liability and property damage insurance before any future rally. The ACLU filed suit on his behalf once more.[16]

While the case progressed through the courts, Collin was enjoined from staging public protests in Chicago. Seeking a new outlet, he turned to the suburbs. In September 1976, he launched a massive leafleting campaign targeting the "Jew-ized suburbs." Last summer "we had thousands of people taking to the streets against blacks," he told a reporter. "Our goal is to get thousands of people to take to the streets of Skokie and Lincolnwood against the Jews."[17]

In October, Collin dispatched letters to Skokie, Lincolnwood, and several other towns, requesting permission to hold rallies in their public parks. Only Skokie replied. Following Chicago's lead, the Village Parks Department clerk informed Collin he would be eligible for a permit if he supplied an insurance bond of $350,000 against any possible damages. This answer prompted a change in plans. Rather than apply for a permit, Collin announced that on May 1 the National Socialist Party of America would stage a protest march on the sidewalk outside the Skokie town hall in defense of "White Free Speech."[18]

* * *

THE QUARTER CENTURY between the 1952 *Beauharnais* decision and the crisis of Skokie marked one of the most successful eras in modern Jewish history. Sociologists registered a precipitous drop in antisemitic attitudes. Jews flocked in growing numbers to universities, neighborhoods, and professions that had once excluded them. Indeed, some Jewish observers warned that America was *too* welcoming of its Jews. Acculturation and intermarriage might replace persecution as threats to Jewish collective survival.[19]

Much of that success originated in the landmark 1964 Civil Rights Act, which outlawed discrimination in employment and public accommodations on the basis of race, color, religion, sex, or national origin, and in federally funded education on the basis of race, color, and national origin. A parallel effort to separate religion and state also yielded new victories in the drive to remove government policies that privileged Christianity in public life.

Beyond its legal impact, the 1964 Civil Rights Act also symbolized the Black-Jewish partnership at the heart of the civil rights coalition. It was drafted in the Washington, DC, conference room of the Religious Action Center of Reform Judaism, which shared its offices with the Reverend Martin Luther King Jr.'s Southern Christian Leadership Conference. Yet the high-water mark of civil rights in the mid-1960s was followed almost immediately by a sharp crisis in Black-Jewish relations. Younger, more radical Black leaders questioned the paternalism of Jewish leaders and alleged Jewish economic complicity in the urban crisis. In the aftermath of the Six-Day War in 1967, the Black Panther Party and the Student Nonviolent Coordinating Committee adopted their anti-Zionist positions in a quest to forge international ties with global anticolonialism that further strained relations. Meanwhile, the 1968 fight over public education that pitted Jewish teachers and labor unions against local Black community leaders in Brownsville, New York, crystallized the rift.

Behind all these tensions lay thorny questions of race and power. "Negroes are anti-semitic because they're anti-white," argued the Black writer James Baldwin in an incendiary 1967 *New York Times Magazine* essay. African Americans harbored no intrinsic hatred toward Jews, he explained. They resented their symbolic status as a white minority whose traumatic past bore little relation to its present-day racial and economic privilege. Baldwin did not deny the horrors of Jewish history, including the Holocaust; he simply dismissed their relevance to the African American experience. "The Jewish travail occurred across the sea and America rescued him from the house of bondage, but America is the house of bondage for the Negro."

> In the American context, the most ironical thing about Negro anti-Semitism is that the Negro is really condemning the Jew for having become an American white man—for having become, in effect, a Christian. The Jew profits from his status in America, and he must expect Negroes to distrust him for it. The Jew does not realize that the credential he offers, the fact that he has been despised and slaughtered, does not increase the Negro's understanding. It increases the Negro's rage.

Whatever they had once been, whatever they still suffered, Baldwin suggested, Jews thrived in America because of their whiteness. Baldwin's deeper target was Christianity, which he held responsible for the sin of Western racism. Yet he lambasted Jewish liberalism as a mask for white privilege. In blaming the Jews for the hatred they suffered, Baldwin offered a conditional redemption. Jews could reject whiteness—and defeat antisemitism—by choosing de-assimilation. Ironically, one of the principal ways in which American Jews would do so after 1967 was through a broad embrace of Zionism, which Baldwin came to oppose virulently.[20]

Baldwin's splenetic words oversimplified a long, multifaceted story of partnership and intertwined vulnerability. Yet they captured several uncomfortable truths about the politics of antisemitism. The Holocaust could breed resentment as much as empathy among other victims of racism. Jews could be both perpetrators of injustice and victims of prejudice. Antisemitism extended across the political spectrum, even into the ranks of historical allies on the left. The rise of 1960s anti-colonial solidarities between Black America and Palestinians complicated the task of differentiating anti-Zionism from antisemitism. After the two Arab-Israeli wars of 1967 and 1973, Israel shifted—in image and in reality—from an embattled postcolonial state into a dominant military power ruling over a huge population of displaced and rightless Palestinians in the occupied West Bank and Gaza Strip. As ideological attacks on Israel increased in Soviet and Global South rhetoric, Israeli and diaspora Jewish leaders detected ever-blurring lines between anti-Zionism and antisemitism. The ADL's Arnold Forster and Benjamin Epstein popularized the idea of the demonization of Israel as a new form of traditional antisemitism in their 1974 book *The New Anti-Semitism*.[21]

Such rhetorical provocations deeply troubled the Jewish civil rights establishment, which spoke in increasingly bitter terms of the New Left's moral indifference and political abandonment of the Jews. The broader issue for Jewish civil rights activism, however, was that the definition of racism in the context of American society was undergoing a change, and with it the perceptions of antisemitism. In 1970, the educational psychologist Dr. Patricia Bidol-Padva pioneered the formula, "Racism equals prejudice plus power." Seeking to explain the persistence of racism, she theorized that members of the white majority failed to recognize their racial privilege vis-à-vis African Americans. That insight would prove central to the later emergence of sensitivity training and theories of white privilege. At the time, however, it served to register a growing dilemma for Jews who experienced their lives as a minority group yet inhabited the position of white Americans.[22]

Nowhere was this paradox more evident than in the Jewish responses to the rise of affirmative action. Begun in the Kennedy administration as a government hiring initiative to "ensure equal opportunity" for historically disadvantaged racial minorities, affirmative action grew during the late 1960s and early 1970s into a more expansive set of race- and gender-specific university admissions and hiring policies. Even as they benefited Jewish women, the policies proved divisive among Jewish liberals otherwise committed to the cause of racial equality. Granting group rights to certain minorities was viewed as a betrayal of the liberal principle of individual equality before the law.

Having fought in the 1940s and 1950s to overcome antisemitic admissions restrictions in higher education, Jewish civil rights leaders also struggled with the implications of affirmative action for Jewish identity and Jewish interests. As white Americans, read an internal 1972 American Jewish Congress report, we must support "measures that require us to pay part of the price to be paid by whites generally" in the drive for racial justice. "We must recognize a vital distinction between injury to Jews as Jews, and injury to Jews as part of the general white population." The ADL vehemently disagreed. "Reverse discrimination is inherently anti-semitic," they insisted, and "a direct threat to the security and the rights of America's Jews."[23]

The test of these positions came in 1974. That year the U.S. Supreme Court took up the case of *DeFunis v. Odegaard*, involving a Sephardic Jewish man who sued the University of Washington Law School over its affirmative action policies. All three major Jewish civil rights groups entered on his side. The American Jewish Congress and the American Jewish Committee sought nuanced positions, pledging support for minority advancement initiatives while attacking the use of formal racial quotas and preferential ranking systems as antithetical to meritocracy and liberal values. The ADL argued acerbically that affirmative action was anti-liberal and antisemitic. Given the "long history of discrimination against Jews by use of quotas, Jewish students should not be sacrificed on the altar of 'Black Progress.'"[24]

In the end, the Court evaded the question, ruling 5–4 that the case was moot on technical grounds. Yet the case crystallized the perception that civil rights law ignored Jewish equality—and that Jewish liberals had opted to work against their former Black allies. In 1977, just as the Skokie drama was breaking out, the Court again took up affirmative action in *Regents of the University of California v. Bakke.* That same year saw the first-ever federal government guidelines on how to define American racial groups for the purpose of census records and anti-discrimination law: White, Black, Native American, Asian / Pacific Islander, and Hispanic. Jews with origins in Europe were now considered formally white. A paradigmatic minority now officially found themselves recast as members of the white majority.[25]

All these developments reflected a changing definition of minority in American law and society—and prompted a spirit of cynicism among Jewish liberals about civil rights law more broadly. Some of that spirit would animate neoconservatism, a political movement that arose in the 1970s as an intellectual critique of progressive liberalism's supposed egalitarian excesses. It was in that context that the crisis of Skokie would balloon into a test case of liberalism's capacity—and willingness—to combat antisemitism.

On March 24, 1977, Skokie Mayor Al Smith convened a meeting with the rabbis of seven local synagogues to devise a collective response to Collin's plan. After twelve years in the role, the Catholic Democratic politician knew his local Jewish community well. He even regularly fundraised for the United Jewish Appeal's Israel Bonds campaign. Now Smith introduced two outside experts to explain the town's strategy. "The march is designed as a provocation," advised the ADL's Abbot Rosen, "and they would like nothing better than to have physical violence." Rosen had served as President Truman's first chief of the Civil Rights section of the Department of Justice, then gone on to helm the ADL's Chicago office. In that capacity he had worked on the *Beauharnais* case twenty-five years earlier; he saw no need to change course now. The quarantine strategy remained, in his view, the best way to handle hate-mongers.[26]

Rosen was also a longtime ACLU member, and his presence that evening vouched for the other guest speaker, David Hamlin, executive director of the ACLU's Illinois chapter. Freely acknowledging that Collin was his organization's client, he, too, recommended letting him conduct his event without interference. One by one the local rabbis and communal leaders lined up to endorse the plan devised jointly by the ACLU, the ADL, and town officials. A solution appeared at hand. What none of them anticipated was the reaction of the Skokie survivor community.[27]

Before World War II, Skokie had been known as "Little Germany," thanks to its German American population. The suburban town routinely hosted pro-Nazi Bund marches well into the 1940s. Change had not come easily. The first Black and Jewish families who arrived after the war faced housing discrimination and even violence. Public controversy flared in 1961 when Jewish residents challenged the placement of a Christian crèche in front of the Fire Department. Despite these problems, Jewish Skokie grew rapidly in the 1960s thanks to an interstate highway to Chicago and a large stock of new single-family homes. Skokie also became a magnet for Holocaust survivors. Roughly seven thousand of them lived there in 1977, where they clustered in a tight-knit subculture of their own within the larger population of forty thousand people, more than half of whom were Jewish.[28]

Among the first to challenge the quarantine approach was Erna Gans, fifty-four, who had escaped a Nazi death march at age twenty. Of medium height with brown curly hair and deep-set blue eyes, she hailed from Bielsko, in southern Poland, and had settled in Chicago with her husband after the war. "Why should we allow Nazis free access to the community?" she argued. Why should we let them "say those obscene words without being punished" and spout "their political philosophy against the right of Jews to live?" Gans had run for the Illinois State Senate in 1976 and headed the B'nai B'rith Janusz Korczak Lodge, an organization of local survivors. In the days after the March meeting, she emerged as a spokeswoman for the town's opposition, launching a grassroots group, Concerned Jewish Citizens. The Holocaust has taught that "inaction on the part of Jews with regard to anti-Semitism results in more blatant and vicious anti-Semitism," read one of their leaflets. It continued with a sharp rebuke: "Today in the Chicago area there are too many Jewish people including many of our leaders who . . . believe there is no danger or threat to our people, even from the Nazis who publicly proclaim our death sentences."[29]

As word of the controversy spread, new flyers appeared around town bearing a different message: "No Free Speech for Fascists." They were the work of a group of young Chicago Jewish socialists who had caught wind of Collin's plans. Within Skokie's Jewish community, opinions were divided as to what should be done. The one thing everyone agreed on was that they feared violence if the Nazis marched on May 1. Adding to the tension was Collin's campaign of intimidation. Jewish residents received menacing phone calls in the middle of the night reminding them of the upcoming march.[30]

Over the next few weeks, the mayor held fast to the ADL-ACLU plan at a series of community meetings. It is better to "pray for these poor misguided souls," he advised Jewish leaders, than to give them the attention they so desperately sought. Behind the scenes, however, dissent was mounting within his own administration. Skokie's chief corporation counsel Harvey Schwartz, who was Jewish, was convinced that no existing law could prevent the march. Yet the situation reminded his deputy Gil Gordon of the *Terminiello* and *Beauharnais* cases, which he had worked on as part of the American Jewish Congress back in the 1940s. Now he returned to the group libel principle. "I have never believed," he observed, that "to incite group hatred constitutes 'free speech' or 'freedom of ideas in the marketplace.'" Already in March, he had begun work on a plan to apply the *Beauharnais* decision to Skokie to stop the Nazi march. Finally, at the end of April, Mayor Smith sided with Gordon. It was time to go to court to stop the march.[31]

On Wednesday, April 27, Schwartz and Gordon filed a request for an injunction with the Cook County Circuit Court. In their brief, they argued that the march threatened the safety of Holocaust survivors and the public welfare. The swastika's display is "an incitement to violence" that poses a "grave and serious threat to the peace." The harm at hand justified prior restraint. The court should bar Collin from marching in the NSPA uniform, displaying the swastika, and/or distributing pamphlets "which incite or promote hatred against persons of Jewish faith or ancestry . . . or any faith or ancestry, race or religion."[32]

Going further, they introduced a novel claim. Displaying the swastika constituted "a symbolic assault" against the town's Jewish population. The idea of a "symbolic assault" echoed Justice Jackson's reference in *Kunz v. New York* to words flying like missiles at fearful Jews. Yet it represented a stark departure from existing law. Rather than classify speech as a potential cause of violence, now speech itself *was* violence.

The next afternoon, Judge Joseph Wosik presided over a hearing at the Cook County Circuit Courthouse in Skokie. Collin arrived with his ACLU lawyer, David Goldberger, a thirty-five-year-old Jewish Chicagoan and University of Chicago Law School graduate who prided himself on the fact that he defended all manner of extremists on both the right and the left. Goldberger, who sported dark muttonchops and a thick 1970s mustache, had represented Collin for the past three years. Also present were Mayor Smith and his two lawyers, and several Holocaust survivors and local Jewish leaders.

As the proceedings began, Goldberger moved for a peremptory dismissal. This is "a classic First Amendment case," he told Judge Wosik. There were simply no grounds to prevent Collin from marching on the sidewalk in his chosen dress and symbols. He reminded the court of the federal order allowing Collin to march in Chicago proper. Goldberger also cited *Terminiello* as precedent for allowing a speech even when it caused "public inconvenience, annoyance or unrest." He even referenced the recent Pentagon Papers case, in which the Supreme Court had refused to block *The New York Times* from publishing leaked national security documents about the Vietnam War. "If the injunction is issued," Goldberger summed up, "the Village of Skokie will be dancing on the grave of the First Amendment."[33]

Gordon pushed back. "I do not go along with esteemed counsel here on his free speech gig," he declared. "It is our position that the constitutional safeguards of the freedom of speech were intended to promote the dissemination of ideas in the marketplace," he explained, not to incite "hatred by reason of the skin, the color of people, where they came from. These are not ideas. These are obscenities." Swayed by Gordon's argument, Wosik allowed the case to proceed. One by one, town witnesses took the stand to testify to the great danger and likely violence between protesters and counterprotesters. Then came Skokie's star witness, Sol Goldstein.[34]

Born in the Lithuanian shtetl of Yurburg in 1914, Goldstein escaped from the Kovno ghetto and spent two years fighting with the underground partisans. Returning to his town after the war, he learned that his family had been buried alive. For three days the topsoil above their living grave churned as they lay dying slowly beneath the surface. In 1949 Goldstein settled in Chicago, where he became a prominent businessman and active philanthropist in the Chicago Jewish Federation. In 1977 he chaired the city's annual Israel Bonds drive. Then together with Erna Gans, he pushed aggressively to develop a formal counterprotest movement.[35]

Now, sitting in the courtroom, the sixty-four-year-old Goldstein fixed his gaze on Collin. Short and stocky with thick black hair and bushy eyebrows, he had the tough bearing of a survivor. In restrained but emotional testimony, he laid out what the antisemitic symbols meant to him. The sight of the swastika "reminds me of my closest family who were sent to death by this swastika, and it reminds me of the threat that I am not safe with my life. It reminds me that my children are not safe with their lives." If the Nazis showed up, bloodshed would inevitably follow. Their mere presence would overwhelm his self-control. "I don't intend to use any" violence, he testified, "but as a survivor I don't know if I can control myself."[36]

Goldstein's remarks led Goldberger to claim that Skokie was using a heckler's veto—just as in the *Terminiello* case—to attempt to restrict a speaker on account of his beliefs. To bolster his position, he brought Collin to the stand. The Nazi leader explained that he had no intention of inciting violence. He was a political leader who only wished to exercise his First Amendment rights. Under Gordon's questioning, he conceded that his views aligned perfectly with those of Hitler as stated in *Mein Kampf*. That admission proved determinative for Judge Wosik.[37]

We must defend speech that we detest, the judge declared, but even Voltaire never faced this kind of situation. The Holocaust was "the worst atrocity ever," and the confrontation between survivors and a self-professed Nazi in Skokie was "unique in the history of the United States and indeed in the history of the world." To force Holocaust survivors to relive those memories would be to commit a grievous crime. To risk any violence would be unconscionable. He barred Collin from marching on Sunday, May 1. Echoing Jackson's *Terminiello* dissent, Wosik pronounced, "Our democracy was not created to maintain the instruments of its own destruction."[38]

The Thursday afternoon injunction triggered a dizzying cat-and-mouse sequence. Late on April 29, Friday afternoon, just before the onset of the Jewish Sabbath, Collin announced a change of plan. Rather than appear on Sunday, May 1, as proscribed, he would show up the day before, Saturday, April 30. The march would go on. That news sent Schwartz and Gordon scrambling to find a judge willing to emend the court order. On Saturday morning, a different local judge agreed to extend the injunction to cover all possible dates pending final judicial review. When Collin's four-car caravan from Chicago drew up to the Skokie exit from the I-94 freeway, he found it blocked by police officers brandishing the revised court order. Collin turned around and retreated to Chicago, temporarily defeated.[39]

But no one had thought to tell the rest of Skokie. Some one thousand people massed outside the town hall for hours that Saturday afternoon, waiting for confrontation. They had come at the behest of Gans and Goldstein, who called "on every Jew" to show up to stop the "Nazi menace" and remember "the six million martyrs." Their signs bore the names of death camps—Buchenwald, Auschwitz, Dachau—along with slogans such as "Never Again" and "Smash the Nazis." We will "create conditions," Goldstein told the crowd, that "will prevent a repetition of the Holocaust."[40]

Watching the survivors, some of them "in almost a catatonic state—petrified-shaking-crying," proved revelatory for Schwartz. Having been skeptical about the constitutionality of the injunction he had just sought, he now changed his mind. "What I realized at that moment was that what we were facing had nothing to do with the First Amendment," he recalled. "When someone wants to come marching into your town, with the announced intention to kill you, there was hardly anything left to discuss." Just the act of marching would be "more like a physical assault than an exchange of ideas."[41]

On Monday, May 2, the Village Board of Trustees met to take steps to make the injunction more permanent. They passed three new legal ordinances devised by Schwartz and Gordon, laws intended to prevent any future appearance by Collin. Ordinance #994 required demonstrations of more than fifty people to possess $350,000 worth of insurance coverage for damage and liability. It also banned events likely to "create an imminent danger of a substantial breach of the peace, riot or similar disorder" or "portray criminality, depravity or lack of virtue in, or incite violence, hatred, abuse or hostility toward a person or group of persons by reason of reference to religious, racial, ethnic, national or regional affiliation." This language of group defamation directly echoed the 1917 state law cited in *Beauharnais*. The same language appeared in Ordinance #995, which prohibited distributing "materials which promote and incite group hatred." Ordinance #996 prohibited demonstrations with "military-style uniforms." Faced with the specter of antisemitic hatred, Skokie had returned to *Beauharnais*. But was it still valid constitutional law?[42]

"AS THE WHOLE world knows by now," began the 1960 full-page advertisement in *The New York Times*, "thousands of Southern Negro students are engaged in widespread non-violent demonstrations in positive affirmation of the right to live in human dignity as guaranteed by the U.S. Constitution and the Bill of Rights." In Montgomery, Alabama, this peaceful protest has been "met by an unprecedented wave of terror" from the local police. Out of this seemingly straightforward statement, sponsored by the Committee to Defend Martin Luther King and the Struggle for Freedom in the South and signed by over sixty prominent liberals, grew the most important First Amendment libel case in American history.[43]

Though the advertisement did not mention him by name, Montgomery police commissioner Lester Sullivan successfully sued *The New York Times* for $500,000 in libel damages for injuring his reputation as a public official. The implications for both the civil rights movement and the media were chilling. If libel laws could be deployed so casually to squelch the publication of fact-based statements, then libel law would become a cudgel in the hands of state officials. In March 1964, however, the Supreme Court overturned the verdict, ruling 9–0 in favor of the newspaper. Public debate must remain "uninhibited, robust, and wide-open," wrote Justice William Brennan, and that "may well include vehement, caustic, and sometimes unpleasantly sharp attacks on government and public officials."[44]

New York Times Company v. Sullivan transformed libel law, not only narrowing the right to sue news media and other publishers for libel but also more generally shrinking the role of defamation in American law. In its wake, the leading First Amendment scholar Harry Kalven Jr., who had advised on *Terminiello*, predicted that the story of group libel in American law had ended. An unrestricted First Amendment had become an indispensable instrument of African American emancipation. More broadly, the 1964 *Sullivan* decision formed part of a series of cases, chief among them *Brandenburg v. Ohio* (1969) and *Cohen v. California* (1971), that further reshaped the definition of "clear and present danger" and "fighting words," raising the threshold for banning offensive speech on grounds of public order. In *Brandenburg*, for instance, after an Ohio Ku Klux Klansman challenged his conspiracy conviction for advocating violence against Jews and Blacks, the Court shrunk the definition of "clear and present danger" to "imminent lawless action." Thereafter, the government would have to prove deliberate intent *and* direct likelihood of violent outcome to preempt or punish speech-related activity.[45]

The assumption behind all these rulings was that the dangers of government censorship still far outweighed the risk of any harm produced by words. The marketplace of ideas would ultimately solve the problem of hateful speech. The less state speech regulation, the better for all. How, then, should society handle hate speech? Moral outrage would substitute for legal sanction. The bigot could freely speak their mind, and society would respond with rhetorical denunciation.

The move to public shaming was perfectly illustrated by the fortunes of the Illinois group libel statute on which *Beauharnais* had been based. In 1961 the state legislature overhauled its criminal code and in the process repealed the 1917 law. Yet hate speech remained enshrined in state law as a kind of shadow statute: "To promote the dignity of the individual," read the 1970 revised Illinois Constitution, "communications that portray criminality, depravity or lack of virtue in or that incite violence, hatred, abuse or hostility toward any group of persons in this State by reason of or by reference to religious, racial, ethnic or national affiliation are condemned." *Beauharnais* lived on in symbolic form as a nonlegal ideal. This curious compromise again encapsulated American liberalism's ambivalent approach to hate speech. The government called out the evil in hate speech while disempowering itself to combat it. Hate speech was serious enough to denounce, but not serious enough to proscribe.[46]

IN EARLY JUNE, the ACLU filed suit in Illinois state court to overturn Judge Wosik's original injunction barring the march. In *National Socialist Party of America v. Skokie*, it challenged the ban as wholly unconstitutional. With proper police planning and a pledge from Collin to march without chanting slogans, there was no evidence of "clear and present danger" or "fighting words." Yet the Illinois appellate court declined to hear the case on an expedited basis. In response, the ACLU filed an emergency petition with the U.S. Supreme Court. On June 14 the Court issued a per curiam opinion on a 6–3 vote that the Illinois courts must either hold a hearing on the merits of the ACLU petition or immediately lift the injunction.[47]

While *National Socialist Party of America v. Skokie* worked its way through the Illinois court system, a second, highly unusual lawsuit surfaced. It began when Judge Abraham Marovitz of the U.S. District Court for the Northern District of Illinois called several Chicago law firms seeking lawyers to work pro bono on a campaign to halt the march without compromising the First Amendment. He found his man in Jerome Torshen, a successful litigator with strong Democratic Party ties. Torshen was also one of several Chicago-area ADL members dissatisfied with their leadership's quarantine approach. They soon hit upon a new strategy. Why not a civil tort suit on behalf of Skokie's Holocaust survivors?

Psychological harm had grown increasingly cognizable in American tort law. The concept of "Intentional Infliction of Emotional Distress" had been codified in the Second Restatement of the Law of Torts in 1965 as a new civil offense: "One who by extreme and outrageous conduct intentionally or recklessly causes severe emotional distress to another is subject to liability." Did this not comport with Skokie's own assertion of Collin's planned "psychic assault"? They quickly settled on Sol Goldstein as their lead plaintiff.[48]

In late June, Torshen and a group of lawyers from five major Chicago law firms sued for a "preliminary and permanent injunction" to prevent the march on grounds that Collin's actions would amount to a tortious injury to Goldstein and other Holocaust survivors. If the Nazis marched in Skokie, they would cause psychic trauma to the plaintiffs. The "direct and proximate . . . presence of persons bearing the symbols and insignia of the Nazi party marching in or through their home community" would "recall the Holocaust which the survivors experienced and will impose on them severe and extreme emotional distress."[49]

To validate this claim, Torshen submitted expert testimony from Dr. Lawrence Freedman, a University of Chicago forensic psychiatrist renowned for his pioneering studies on the psychology of political violence. "The traumatized individual remains sensitized and vulnerable to signs and symbols" associated with "profound trauma," Freedman asserted. The parade with "swastikas, Nazi-like uniforms and the marching of men in para-military style could inflict serious recurrences of the psychic assault previously suffered by these people." There was even a name for this kind of crime, "menticide," the mental equivalent of genocide, a recently coined term for extreme "psychological assault."[50]

American law had long recognized equality as connected to dignity. Some of the main evidence for the disparate impact of "separate but equal" doctrine in *Brown* had been psychological studies of the negative effect of prejudice on Black schoolchildren. Now it was the memory of past trauma on elderly Jewish survivors. "Their fear is unimaginable," Rabbi Lawrence Montrose, the "unofficial chaplain" of Skokie's survivors, told *The New York Times*. "They still wake up screaming at night sometimes—after 30 years . . . And now they think these guys are here to finish Hitler's job for him." Even the ADL's Abbot Rosen now reversed himself. "I am of the liberal Left and I am a First Amendment person," he explained, but a march through a town of survivors represented "an intentional specific assault," akin to holding a rally in front of paraplegics at a Veterans Administration hospital to demand that they should all be euthanized.[51]

The ACLU was flabbergasted by the "revolutionary" approach of the Goldstein lawsuit. They were also furious that their ADL allies had abandoned them. "Do you know what this case comes down to?" a disgusted David Goldberger told one interviewer, "The people in Skokie think they have a constitutional right not to be insulted." Worse still in his mind were his opponents' legal tactics. Torshen's team placed their case under the auspices of the Public Affairs Committee of the Jewish United Fund, the Jewish philanthropic umbrella organization for the region, lending it a quasi-communal dimension. Jewish Chicago was now effectively a party to a lawsuit against the ACLU.[52]

In his motion to dismiss the case, Goldberger argued that the lawsuit opened a slippery slope for all First Amendment cases involving hate speech. If accepted, even a screening of a movie or TV show in Skokie that depicted Nazi persecution of Jews might be preemptively banned. Arguing on grounds of emotional distress was a Pandora's box. Other private groups might employ the same approach to shutter offensive speech for subjective reasons. Even segregationists could insist on banning Black civil rights marches on grounds that they, too, proved to be "emotionally disturbing." Above all, the supposed injury was not even real; it was merely a form of "speculative harm." Besides, there was a simple solution to avoid the harm: stay home.[53]

In search of a precedent, both the Skokie legal team and the ADL-affiliated lawyers behind the menticide case turned back to *Beauharnais*. Technically, the decision still stood. Whether published or spoken, words could harm. Malicious hatred would inevitably trigger physical violence between Jews and Nazis. The ADL lawsuit took this proposition one step further. Mental pain was not merely a violation of human dignity; it was a physical assault on minority minds—and a violation of equal protection.

As the battle over Skokie intensified, the lines blurred between physical danger and mental anguish. The link to the Holocaust endowed antisemitism with an aura of uniqueness far beyond religious bigotry or racial hatred. No one involved in Skokie believed that the Holocaust was going to repeat itself in suburban Illinois that summer. Yet the hatred in question appeared so immense, the emotional harm so painful, as to invert the classic distinction between words and actions. "Just as the Constitution does not preserve the right of the Nazis to physically assault the Holocaust survivors in Skokie," wrote Judge Wosik, "so should it not license them to perpetrate an infinitely more serious assault upon their sensibilities." The Nazi swastika was "infinitely more" dangerous than a street riot, because it represented "the symbolic equivalent of a public call to 'Kill all Jews.'" In this reasoning, sticks and stones were *less* dangerous than hurtful words. That logic collapsed the distinction between street-level physical danger and mass atrocity.[54]

The intensity of these arguments all but guaranteed that one or more of the Skokie cases would make their way to the Supreme Court for constitutional review. But such a process could take weeks, if not months. In the meantime, Collin continued to threaten an appearance in Skokie with or without a permit. More controversy worked in his favor, drawing increasing media attention. Reporters began arriving at his Chicago headquarters seeking insight into his plans. The American public also began to take notice of the bizarre, gripping legal drama playing out in the heartland. Letters from across the country poured into the Skokie mayor's office with offers of support. Jewish leaders also began to grasp that something unprecedented was taking place. A new situation might require a radically new approach to antisemitism. Apart from all the court proceedings, was it time to confront the Nazis directly in the streets?

8

Holocaust Traumas

At noon on Monday, July 4, 1977, a crowd of two thousand protesters massed in front of the Village of Skokie Town Hall. Word had spread that Frank Collin would once again try to march that day in defiance of the law. This time it was not only survivors and other local Jews who showed up to protest. Rabbis stood side by side with Christian clergy sporting yellow star armbands in an act of solidarity. Black civil rights leaders from Chicago's South Side mingled with white steelworkers, Latino activists, and Vietnam veterans. Trotskyite Anti-Zionists held aloft signs protesting fascism next to people waving Israeli and American flags. Despite the sweltering 95-degree heat and the helicopters buzzing overhead, the mood remained relaxed, even upbeat. On the two hundred and first anniversary of the birth of the United States, Americans appeared united against hate.[1]

Amid the sea of T-shirts and bell-bottoms, the grim-faced young men of the Jewish Defense League stood out conspicuously. Marching single file, they were dressed in military-style uniforms, black boots, and helmets emblazoned with a clenched fist inside a Star of David. Some carried baseball bats, others clubs or metal pipes. "There will be no Nazis marching in Skokie, police or no police," JDL leader Rabbi Meir Kahane, the far right Jewish extremist, shouted through a bullhorn to the five hundred people who had drifted over from the main rally to hear him speak in the parking lot of the Jewish Community Center. The horrors of the Holocaust justified blocking the Nazis by any means necessary, he maintained, including violence. Then Kahane led the crowd in a call-and-response chant of the slogan he had made famous: "Never Again." In his view, Holocaust memory demanded vigilante justice.[2]

Skokie Jewish leaders were furious that Kahane had showed up that day. His anti-liberal philosophy fetishized Jewish power and demonized Palestinians. His militant slogan of self-defense—"For Every Jew a .22"—suggested that only force could stop hate, even if it meant destroying ethics and generating still more hate in the process. Throughout the 1970s, JDL had conducted a deadly bombing campaign targeting Soviet and Arab diplomatic institutions across the United States. Kahane had recently completed a year's sentence in U.S. federal prison for manufacturing explosives.[3]

Most American Jews recoiled from Kahane's dark, dystopian vision of Jewish history and shunned his extremist views on Israel and Palestine. Yet many voiced similar disillusionment with liberal pieties about free speech in the face of unparalleled evil. "Where in the hell is it in the Constitution that says they can march on the Fourth of July?" complained Skokie's Democratic congressman Abner Mikva. A longtime ACLU member and civil liberties lawyer, Mikva had famously defended both the Jewish comedian Lenny Bruce and *Playboy* magazine on obscenity charges. But to his mind the Holocaust was simply different. "In a real sense, we are all survivors of Nazism," Mikva explained, "and the Nazi symbols of hate and destruction recall a nightmare that millions of other Americans share."[4]

The view was echoed by Reverend C. H. Turner, who had driven up from Chicago's South Side to rally with Kahane. Turner had spent years leading the city's Dr. Martin Luther King Jr. Movement against housing discrimination and opposing Nazi marches in Marquette Park. Now, standing next to Kahane, a man who had launched his career by race-baiting Black civil rights leaders, Turner spoke as if he, too, were a Jew. For the sake of "our forefathers who died in the Nazi concentration camps," he told the raucous, cheering audience, "the Nazis must go." As the crowd joined in his chant, he urged them on. "Louder. The Nazis must go!"[5]

July 4, 1977, was the day that the Holocaust became an American story. Now anyone might imagine themself as Hitler's victim and everyone could denounce antisemitism. By casting themselves as the descendants of the Nazis, down to the swastika armband and flag, and targeting Hitler's victims, Collin's troupe let all Americans visualize themselves as Holocaust survivors. In a 1970s America struggling profoundly with racial divisions and the aftershocks of the Vietnam War, the Holocaust beckoned as the quintessence of un-American evil. The worst hatred of all came from far outside the frame of American history; the original sin had been committed long ago and far away, and the prime victims were elderly refugees from another country's shameful past. This reincarnated enemy, against which Americans had once fought, presented a compelling symbol around which to rally in defense of national virtue.[6]

It was an exceptional hatred, one that demanded an exceptional response. Yet the law seemed not only powerless but complicit in the conflict at hand, having only temporarily blocked the Skokie march. "I'm not the only one who wonders at the hasty leap to the tried-and-true formula of 'freedom of speech equals democracy equals justice equals Mom and apple pie and God Bless America,'" declared Erna Gans. Fellow survivor Harold Zissman, sixty-seven, echoed her cynicism. I am for "freedom of speech," said the former Soviet partisan fighter, but there is no "justice in these laws." In a telling slip, Zissman invoked the "Second Amendment of Free Speech," which he defined as the right to oppose with force anyone who would make "me re-live the agony one more time."[7]

That day remained peaceful for the simplest of reasons. No Nazis showed up to march. Once again, Collin aborted his plans at the last minute. Half posturing coward, half cunning strategist, he teased his opponents as he waited for the multiple court cases to reach a resolution. Even in his absence, however, Collin had unleashed something that would not soon disappear. Skokie had escalated into a national symbol of a universally condemnable hatred in a country adrift. As the conflict in Skokie dragged on that summer, it revealed an America as unified in their opposition to antisemitism as they were divided over law's role in ending it.

"THE SUPREME LAW of the Land," as the U.S. Constitution names itself, is the object of near-religious veneration for Americans. The ideal of a law-bound republic that can weather all storms and redeem its own sins by returning time and again to its unchanging legal charter is a mainstay of American thought. In the twentieth century it developed into an ideology that the political scholar Judith Shklar termed "legalism." Throughout an era of global wars and economic depression, Americans of all kinds came to believe that constitutional law offered an enduring exit from the divisive conflicts that had destroyed other great societies. Law transmuted ethics and politics into objective rules untainted by prejudice or factional interest. When properly executed by responsible judges and lawyers, constitutional law turned enemies into opponents, power struggles into negotiations, and violence into debate. If Americans followed the rules, justice would prevail without mass upheaval and violent destruction.[8]

The high-water mark of legalism came in the era of the Warren Supreme Court (1953–1969), a bench full of liberals who used the power of judicial review to decisively expand civil liberties, reduce press censorship, curb obscenity laws, affirm racial equality, establish reproductive freedom, and generally promote individual rights, especially free speech. Yet the decade from the late 1960s to the late 1970s shook many Americans' faith in law's capacity to transcend politics. Bloody social protests, urban riots, and political assassinations suggested a society spinning perilously out of control. Presidential corruption and discoveries of domestic espionage by the CIA and FBI rocked public confidence. Revelations about government malfeasance in the Vietnam War exposed national leaders who acted with impunity and gross deception. Each of these dramas provoked fears that law was no match for surging chaos and societal disruption.

"Our problem," wrote Yale Law School professor Alexander Bickel in his posthumously published 1975 classic *The Morality of Consent*, "is the totalitarian tendency of the democratic faith." A heterodox liberal, Bickel worked on *Brown v. Board of Education* as a young clerk to Justice Felix Frankfurter yet criticized affirmative action, co-authoring the ADL's amicus brief in the *DeFunis* case against the University of Washington Law School. He defended *The New York Times* for its publication of the Pentagon Papers yet worried that a libertarian First Amendment could lead to utter ruin. "There is such a thing as verbal violence, a kind of cursing, assaultive speech that amounts to almost physical aggression, bullying that is no less punishing because it is simulated." Bickel's critique threatened to collapse the distinction between word and action. Neo-Nazi "advocacy of genocide" was a case in point. Such speech did not just activate passions that might prove dangerous; it reshaped the rules of reality:

> This sort of speech constitutes an assault. More, and equally important, it may create a climate, an environment in which conduct and actions that were not possible before become possible . . . To listen to something on the assumption of the speaker's right to say it is to legitimate it . . . Where nothing is unspeakable, nothing is undoable.[9]

Bickel did not live to see Skokie. However, his skepticism about liberalism's laissez-faire attitude toward extremist speech anticipated a rising sentiment in the legal world of the late 1970s. On both the left and the right, legal thinkers began to question whether the judicial liberalism of the postwar period, with its steady expansion of freedom of expression, represented an error. Bickel's disciples on the right pointed to Skokie as a symptom of a larger problem of liberal democracy's abandonment of morality. The conservative jurist Robert Bork, a Presbyterian convert to Catholicism, blamed a progressive "legal order" that failed to make essential moral judgements about good and evil. It was a gross error for lawyers to claim that, as he put it, "Nazi ideology is constitutionally indistinguishable from republican belief."[10]

Bork's views were echoed by the Jewish political scientist Hadley Arkes, who seized on the ACLU's Skokie position as evidence that law had lost its primal connection to morality. What the courts have done is not libertarian but "anti-libertarian," he insisted. By refusing to exercise legal judgment on the moral content of the Nazi speech, the courts lend credence to the cynical belief "that the law is merely a polite form in which the force of the many may govern the few." Arkes went on to make Skokie—and *Beauharnais*—a centerpiece of his 1981 book *The Philosopher in the City: The Moral Dimensions of Urban Politics*, where he launched a conservative assault on what he saw as liberalism's moral relativism.[11]

These kinds of critiques echoed modern conservatism's indictment of liberalism for its secularism and value neutrality on moral questions. These fears were sparked by radical protest of the kind seen in campus anti-war demonstrations and 1960s urban riots, which, conservatives felt, represented a decadent society on the path to self-destruction. In this context, unlimited free speech marked the end of virtue, and tolerating Nazis showed the Left's amoralism at its worst. Brushing off its own antisemitic elements, particularly within the evangelical Christian community, the conservative right now blamed Skokie on the totalitarian left.[12]

Yet the sight of Nazis threatening Jews also troubled the progressive left. The situation laid bare "the inherent limitations of the First Amendment under bourgeois democracy," declared the National Lawyers Guild in a public statement. Its authors, among them the radical Black activist Fania Davis, sister of Angela Davis, questioned the larger relevance of law to racial justice. While constitutionally protected free speech is tactically useful "for helping to build progressive movements" to fight against white supremacist groups, she and her colleagues wrote, "the primary and major arena in this struggle is political-economic, not legal." Law was a necessary evil.[13]

Similarly, the pioneering critical legal theory scholar Richard Delgado would invoke Skokie in his pathbreaking 1982 study of hate speech, "Words That Wound." Following precisely the logic of Goldstein's menticide lawsuit, he proposed a new "tort for racial slurs" that would allow private citizens to sue in civil court for group defamation. Such a law could "protect the interests of personality and equal citizenship that are part of our highest political traditions and moral values . . . thereby affirming the right of all citizens to lead their lives free from attacks on their dignity and psychological integrity." Delgado's work went on to inspire the entire movement of critical legal studies and critical race theory.[14]

That both the conservative right and the progressive left could reach the same conclusion about the First Amendment with regard to Skokie suggested a common dissatisfaction with the reigning civil liberties model. Conservatives might demonize social change and progressives might idealize it, but both objected to what they saw as the rigid formalism that had overtaken First Amendment law. Each wing disputed the claim that physical violence must remain the boundary for state action against hate speech. Though they drew different conclusions about the legal solutions to America's ills, conservatives and progressives found themselves alarmed by the gap between law and justice on display in Skokie.

They were joined in this view by some centrists. Among them was the University of Chicago constitutional scholar and former Frankfurter clerk Philip Kurland, who had taught Goldberger. A leading liberal, Kurland had advised the Chicago City Parks Department in the original lawsuit blocking Collin's march. He also co-authored the ADL *DeFunis* brief with his old friend Bickel. Now, Kurland insisted that *Beauharnais* was a viable precedent for curbing antisemitic speech. Let us discard the platitudes about freedom "for the thought we hate," he told a University of Chicago Hillel audience. We are dealing, he said, not with mere libel, but public welfare and basic equality. The free speech fanatics were misguided utopians. "How many times does the Constitution command that this bloody, depraved credo of Aryan supremacy has to be brought to the marketplace of ideas before it is deemed bested by 'a truth'?"[15]

In between these two poles were other centrist liberals who opposed restricting free speech. Some viewed taking fire from both sides as confirmation of the correctness of their stance. Tolerating the Nazis was simply the "small price" to "pay for the privilege of living in a non-authoritarian society," wrote the editors of *The New Repub-*

lic, contrasting America favorably with Eastern Europe. Here "the police are used to protect minorities—no matter how offensive to the majority—rather than to harass and intimidate them." Writing in *The Nation*, the University of Wisconsin political philosopher Carl Cohen insisted that a libertarian model of free speech was a bulwark against authoritarianism from the right and the left. He blasted Skokie's resuscitation of the "group libel" argument as a slippery slope to government censorship. Geoffrey Stone, also a University of Chicago First Amendment scholar and Kurland's colleague, dismissed "group defamation" as "a relic of a bygone era." For these liberals, individual civil liberties remained the cornerstone of American democracy.[16]

As the professors debated, many Jewish civil rights leaders admitted to feelings of confusion and ambivalence. "We have a dilemma as Jews within the American liberal tradition," declared Rabbi Arthur Hertzberg of the American Jewish Congress. When free speech and equal protection for Jews clashed baldly, which should prevail? The tension was exacerbated by the news that summer that the Supreme Court would once again take up the divisive question of affirmative action with the much-awaited sequel to *DeFunis*, the *Bakke* case, in which a white applicant to the University of California medical school claimed preferential admissions policies for minorities were unconsitutional. For many Jewish civil rights leaders, regardless of their stance on affirmative action, the juxtaposition of Black and Jewish experiences revealed a frustrating asymmetry. Affirmative action provided African Americans with group-based protections against discrimination, but Jews lacked similar collective legal remedies when facing direct civil rights threats. This dilemma of having to choose between defending individual freedom and protecting Jewish civil rights led many Jewish liberals to redirect their anger toward a new target: the lawyers defending the Nazis.[17]

"Dear Brother Goldberger," the letter began. "Being a fellow Jew, I believe we might discuss the Nazi Party and its well-known attitude towards Jews (extermination of same)." The letter writer, the Chicago playwright and journalist Seymour Heller, had proudly praised the ACLU in the 1960s when it defended Collin's mentor, George Lincoln Rockwell. Now he professed astonishment and outrage at Goldberger's defense of Collin. What "evenhandedness" and "legal equanimity" you exercise! "If you had been a Jewish lawyer in Germany, long before they carted you to Auschwitz perhaps you might have fought for the Nazi right to march and demonstrate as you do now." You are not preserving "democracy, but idiocy." "Why did Jewish lawyers rush to defend the Nazis," asked Elie Wiesel in a similar vein, "and not the Jewish survivors in Skokie, Illinois?" Such Jews betrayed their people.[18]

The first two months of the Skokie saga triggered an enormous wave of resignations from the ACLU, including a conspicuous number of Jewish members who made no secret of the reason for their departure. As the numbers spiked into the thousands, staff worried that the organization's financial future was in doubt.[19]

Along with the anger from the rank and file, Chicago ACLU leaders found themselves the target of both the far left and the far right. The JDL and the Marxist-Leninist International Committee Against Racism staged separate sit-ins at their downtown Chicago offices. The protests were worrying, especially given the JDL's documented propensity for terrorist violence.

The depth of animosity, especially from his fellow Jews, caught Goldberger completely unprepared. In his innocence, he assumed his critics would understand the principled commitment to free speech for all. He even offered to help Skokie Jews with the legal permits for a counterprotest of his client. What was more liberal than to defend the rights of both parties in an ideological conflict? For his naivete, Goldberger was accused of colluding with evil and labeled a "neo-Nazi." Friends and family turned on him. One relative threatened to kill his client. Anonymous callers threatened to murder him. Goldberger's own rabbi denounced him from the pulpit as he sat in synagogue.[20]

Undeterred, Goldberger crisscrossed the Chicago region in the summer of 1977, making scores of appearances at synagogues to rally supporters and engage critics. "Who better than a Jew knows the real meaning and importance of our First Amendment?" Goldberger told his audiences. "Who better than a Jew knows whose rights will disappear in a second, if we permit the disappearance of some other group's rights first?" Demonizing defense lawyers, he patiently explained, betrayed a profound misunderstanding of the legal system and a dangerous ignorance of the sacred right to counsel for the accused. History's "ultimate victims" must resist the impulse to deny rights to their fellow citizens, or else we can "say Kaddish for the First Amendment."[21]

While Goldberger fought these skirmishes on the local level, ACLU national director Aryeh Neier mounted a broader campaign in defense of the organization. Born in Berlin in 1937, he had escaped two years later with his family and settled in New York City. Neier was no stranger to controversy. Soon after he assumed the directorship, a leaked trove of FBI documents exposed the depth of the ACLU's earlier cooperation with the government on domestic surveillance of progressive political activists. Critics charged that the most famous American civil liberties group served as one large government informant. Neier fought back and worked to repair the group's reputation, including among its own disillusioned membership. Now Skokie threatened to renew the crisis.[22]

Unsympathetic to the ACLU's critics, Neier felt that American Jews had overreacted to the threat. These would-be Nazis were a miserable, pathetic little bunch, "not something to take seriously." Jews had lost perspective on the actual dangers involved and the reality of constitutional law. A clear distinction must be made between extreme speech and violent incitement. Even the letters he received telling him that he "should have died in a Nazi death camp are also protected by the concept of freedom of speech," Neier argued. "They are not specific threats of bodily harm." Neier did not dismiss antisemitism completely. Behind his cavalier dismissal of Jewish fears about neo-Nazism lay a deeply rooted conviction that the greatest dangers to Jews always stemmed from government, not society:

> Because we Jews are uniquely vulnerable, I believe we can win only brief respite from persecution in a society in which encounters are settled by power. As a Jew, therefore, concerned with my own

survival and the survival of the Jews—the two being inextricably linked—I want restraints placed on power.

Thus Jews had a particular vested interest in defending Nazi rights. Neier held a strikingly pessimistic, Holocaust-tinged view of Jewish history: Jews would never escape anti-Jewish hatred. Their best strategy was to limit the state's capacity to harm its citizens, since that power could easily be turned against Jews. Free speech rights served as a crucial check on government power, which was the true threat to society. "To defend myself, I must restrain power with freedom, even if the temporary beneficiaries are the enemies of freedom." The best way to protect American democracy from its avowed enemies was to defend them.[23]

As the public relations crisis worsened, Neier sought a new strategy. If Jews were the organization's loudest critics, the ACLU needed to secure Jewish expressions of support. At his behest, both Reform Judaism's Union of American Hebrew Congregations and the National Council of Jewish Women issued statements in support of the ACLU position. The leading Reform rabbi Balfour Brickner called on Jews to resist the pull of "strong emotions," and maintain their historic commitment to fighting for civil rights, including a robust defense of free speech. In August, Neier issued an open letter signed by sixty prominent American Jews, including lawyers, journalists, and public figures such as writers Nat Hentoff and Studs Terkel, and Columbia law professor Ruth Bader Ginsburg, a former ACLU staff lawyer. "We loathe the Nazis and are disgusted by all that they stand for," read the statement. "But as Americans, and especially as Jews, we recognize the paramount importance of preserving the rights of free expression." All Jews should remember that the ACLU had "fought and won many battles to protect the rights of Jews and other minorities." The First Amendment was the best bulwark against Jewish insecurity and discrimination in America.[24]

Of these signatories, it was Nat Hentoff who offered the most powerful—and revealing—defense of the ACLU's position. "Keeping the First Amendment intact," wrote the *Village Voice* columnist, is "the best defense against waking up one morning and hearing on a loudspeaker that all Jews must assemble in Times Square—or its equivalent in other cities—within an hour." Hentoff's comments were more than a rhetorical flourish. "I have had that fantasy since I was a boy in rampantly anti-Semitic Boston," he added, and "I do not entirely believe it to be, necessarily, forever fantasy." Even as he downplayed the specific neo-Nazi threat in Skokie, Hentoff expressed genuine fear that the Holocaust might recur in America. He was not alone. Shared Holocaust trauma played a decisive role in the emotional reactions that summer, even among native-born American Jews.[25]

Skokie marked a turning point. Before the mid-1970s, most Americans knew little about the Holocaust and thought about it even less. Indeed, the word "Holocaust" itself was rarely used to describe the Nazi genocide of the Jews. Despite breakthrough cultural moments such as the publication of *The Diary of Anne Frank* (1947) and Elie Wiesel's *Night* (1960), Holocaust memory was largely restricted to the Jewish community. Museums did not yet exist, public memorials were few and far between, and Holocaust history was not taught in high schools or universities. Only in the middle of that decade did the mass murder of Jews begin to come into focus as a catastrophic event separate from the broader crimes of fascism. In 1975, the historian Lucy Dawidowicz published her bestselling account, *The War Against the Jews*, in which she argued that Hitler's antisemitic campaign comprised a distinct war of its own within the Second World War. The year before, the scholar and survivor Dr. Yaffa Eliach established the first Center for Holocaust Studies in New York. The first Holocaust educational initiatives emerged in public schools around the country in 1977. The same year, New York's Cathedral of St. John the Divine hosted its first interfaith Holocaust memorial service, while in Washington, the Carter administration floated the idea of a "U.S. memorial to the victims of the Holocaust."[26]

This surge in Holocaust memory culture during the late 1970s arose from the same factors driving the growing awareness of international human rights. In a moment of national confusion and political malaise, Americans longed for moral absolutes beyond the treacherous realm of politics. Skeptical about their government's direction after Vietnam and

Watergate, an anxious public discovered in the Holocaust a resounding story of good and evil. This was evident in the flood of phone messages and letters directed at ACLU offices and Skokie's town hall. The story was so elemental—Nazi villains, Jewish victims—that it supported all manner of meanings. Person after person voiced outrage that neo-Nazis dared insult the memory of U.S. soldiers who died fighting to save the Jews. For some, Skokie absolved Americans of their national sins and recast their country as history's redeemer. Others spoke in Christian terms as a battle between godless hate and Christlike love. For the secular-minded, Skokie offered a drama of humanist universalism. Since Nazi hate targeted so many groups—Blacks, Jews, Asians, Latinos, women, gays, progressives—opposing it became a focal point for liberal unity.[27]

These visions reflected a common belief that the Holocaust served as a moral touchstone for the nation's conscience. Its importance was self-evident to all involved, even as they disputed its meaning. To the ACLU's Jewish lawyers, the Holocaust taught the need to check government power, even if that meant permitting hate speech. To their Jewish critics, the ACLU's defense of Jew hatred in the name of democracy revealed the bankruptcy of American liberalism. Long after Skokie faded from the headlines, this divide endured, reflecting the Holocaust's profound yet contested place in American life.

Three days after the July 4 protest, the court battles resumed. The ACLU appealed Judge Wosik's original injunction barring the march to the Illinois State Appellate Court in *National Socialist Party of America v. Skokie*. The justices returned with a compromise. The Nazis must be allowed to march in uniform with their messages, but without the swastika. The display of the swastika "will incite large numbers of Skokie residents to violence and retaliations." Ever since *Terminiello*, the Illinois justices noted, it has remained unclear "whether anti-Semitic or other similar derogatory statements may be considered as fighting words when intentionally delivered to and heard by the reviled party." While they found the status of hate speech as "fighting words," ambiguous symbols were clearly not. The swastika is "a personal affront to every member of the Jewish faith in remembering the nearly consummated genocide of their people committed within memory," and hence the visual equivalent of "fighting words." The mere display of the swastika in front of any citizen, Jewish or not, amounted to harmful incitement to violence.[28]

Most Jewish legal observers hailed the court's ruling as a victory. "The Nazis are emasculated without their swastika and will not march under this condition," predicted the ADL's Abbot Rosen. Even should they attempt to do so, he added, the Goldstein menticide lawsuit would also block the march without any "interference with free speech." That case had been scheduled for a late August trial. Until then, Collin was required by the court to give Goldstein seven days' notice if he intended to appear in Skokie. There was cautious reason to believe that the whole situation might blow over.[29]

But the ACLU rejected the court's compromise and prepared to fight on every possible front. In August, Goldberger launched a three-pronged attack. First, the ACLU appealed to the Illinois Supreme Court in the original injunction case, *National Socialist Party of America v. Skokie*. While the court agreed to review the case, it let the revised injunction remain in place during deliberations. When Goldberger filed an emergency petition asking the U.S. Supreme Court to lift the injunction, Justice John Paul Stevens, serving as circuit justice for the Seventh Circuit, denied the request.

At the same time, the ACLU lodged another appeal in the Goldstein menticide lawsuit. Goldberger hoped to get the case dismissed on constitutional grounds before trial. That appeal led to procedural delays lasting the remainder of 1977.[30]

Not content with these two interventions, the ACLU also launched a third, completely new lawsuit in August. In *Collin v. Smith*, Goldberger filed suit in federal court on Collin's behalf, challenging the three Skokie ordinances that blocked his appearance. At issue were the insurance requirement, the ban on military uniforms, and the prohibition on the swastika and other hateful expressions. This case would produce the only trial in the entire Skokie drama after the initial April 1977 proceeding, and it would revive the specter of *Beauharnais* and group libel.

On December 2, the Skokie and ACLU teams met for a bench trial in the *Collin v. Smith* case in the Chicago federal courtroom of Judge Bernard Decker, a Republican appointee of John F. Kennedy. As before, Goldberger argued that the First Amendment trumped any other legal claims. Skokie's three laws were patently unconstitutional. The insurance requirement constituted an unfair prior restraint on speech. The prohibition on military uniforms had already been struck down by the Illinois court. All that remained, Goldberger claimed, was the swastika ban. The law rested on *Beauharnais*, which he argued was defunct. Though never explicitly overturned, *Beauharnais* had been rendered obsolete by *Brandenburg* and *Sullivan*. *Brandenburg* effectively legalized hate speech, while *Sullivan* radically shrank the scope of libel law. Abusive rhetoric did not automatically constitute incitement to violence, nor could a mere symbol like the swastika qualify as "fighting words." No antisemitic symbol could by itself overpower rational citizens. Ultimately, Goldberger contended, Skokie residents could choose how to interpret the messages, or whether to encounter them at all.[31]

Skokie counsel Harvey Schwartz and Gil Gordon doubled down on the harm of group libel. They began by calling their star witness, Sol Goldstein. He repeated his testimony about the devastating impact of seeing swastikas. On cross-examination, however, Goldstein made damaging concessions: He had voluntarily attended other Collin rallies in Chicago that summer, where he saw swastikas on display. His home library even contained books with swastika photographs. How then, Goldberger demanded, could he claim these symbols were so uniquely harmful? Goldstein dismissed the premise. Context mattered. A big-city rally or a printed history book was hardly the same as an invasion of the streets of his home community. To see the swastika displayed publicly in Skokie would mean "death after torture" for him and his fellow survivors.

Alongside Goldstein, the Skokie legal team made a bold tactical move to reinforce their case. They called four witnesses representing different ethnic and racial groups harmed by hate speech. Ross Harano, former president of the Japanese American Citizens League, had been born in an internment camp in California during World

War II. He testified about the profound impact of racial slurs on himself and his children. Similar testimony came from Carmelo Rodriguez, a Latino youth social worker, and Thaddeus Kowalski of the Polish American Congress, who insisted that "Polish" jokes could cause real "psychological trauma." The message was clear: Antisemitism was part of a larger pattern of hate speech that harmed all kinds of Americans. Skokie offered an easy rallying point.[32]

Unfortunately, Skokie's argument linking antisemitism with color-based racism and other prejudices was undermined by the controversial testimony of the town's expert witness Professor David Gutmann, chief of psychology at Northwestern Medical School. He testified that Nazi demonstrations would cause survivors "significant psychological harm." For them, he argued, the logical boundary "between insult and blow, between epithet and murder breaks down" in such situations. Such "nice distinctions" between word and action are "the luxury of those who laugh at scars because they never felt a wound." According to Gutmann, antisemitism's unique history placed anti-Jewish hate speech in a category of its own:

> Jews have even more reason than blacks to disregard the usual distinction between word and deed when the word in question is an anti-semitic epithet. The Jews have known persecution in all times in virtually all lands . . . What would be paranoia for others is sober realism for Jews . . . The words of any Nazi to any Jew have, by definition lost the usual intent and limitation of words: they are symbolic continuations of the Holocaust, literal perceptions of the climate of the Holocaust, and preparations for a new Holocaust . . .

Going even further, he insisted that physical and mental harm were one and the same:

> The boundary between insulting words and murderous deeds is insubstantial, nonexistent. The word "fire!" intentionally uttered in a crowded theater does not there have the power to inflict deadly burns; but such words can bring about mass death just as surely as

> the fire to which it refers. The same equation holds true for the otherwise neutral word "Jew!" when uttered by the Nazi. In Jewish ears that word can cause anguish, rage, intolerable anxiety as much as any knife aimed at a Jewish child.[33]

Gutmann's testimony stretched the concept of psychological harm to hyperbolic extremes. If potential Jewish victims could not differentiate between knife threats and epithets, then the only way to protect Jews under law was to ban any negative utterance whatsoever, at least from self-professed antisemites. Goldberger moved to disqualify Gutmann's testimony, arguing the psychologist was too partisan and emotional. As evidence, he submitted a crude letter Gutmann had written to the ACLU: "The Nazis wet dream about murder while you legislate them into the new version of Martin Luther King."[34]

Gutmann was not the only witness the ACLU sought to discredit. In its filing, the ACLU argued that all the witnesses were motivated by "strong personal biases" and a desire "to further the interests of their particular minority group." Gordon vociferously rejected this accusation of special pleading. Using law to seek relief from harm, he countered, was the very definition of equal protection. Civil rights law rested on the premise that individual dignity and security for minorities depended on the group's welfare and status.[35]

After more than six months of legal wrangling, early 1978 brought swift and momentous decisions in all three cases. In late January, the Illinois Supreme Court struck down the original Skokie town injunction, *Skokie v. NSPA*, and at the same time dismissed the *Goldstein* lawsuit. We "reluctantly conclude that the display of the swastika cannot be enjoined under the fighting-words exception to free speech," wrote the judges, "nor can anticipation of a hostile audience justify the prior restraint." The ACLU had won the first two cases. Then, on February 23, 1978, Judge Bernard Decker issued his ruling in the third case, *Collin v. Smith,* striking down all three ordinances enacted in Skokie.[36]

"*Terminiello* and its progeny establish that there is a constitutional right to incite unrest, dissatisfactions and even anger with social conditions," Decker wrote. "The distinction between inciting anger with social conditions and hatred of the person or group perceived to be responsible for that condition is impossible to draw with the requisite clarity and depends to a great extent upon the frame of mind of the listener." Hatred lay in the eye of the beholder. It was beyond the courts to parse the subjective experience of discrimination. Even if they wished to rely on *Beauharnais*, he explained, its status was fundamentally ambiguous. On the one hand, the decision was over a quarter century old and incompatible with more recent rulings; on the other, the Supreme Court had never explicitly overruled it. As such, the district court must reach its own independent decision. In this case, there simply did not seem to be enough evidence of "inherently likely" violent injury to the rights of Skokie Jews to meet even the *Beauharnais* standard.[37]

The three defeats in rapid succession appeared to clear the way for Collin to finally mount his march. Claiming victory, he announced the date: Thursday, April 20, 1978, what would have been Hitler's ninety-ninth birthday. That was soon replaced with a new one: Saturday, April 22, the first night of Passover. Both dates passed without incident, however, as Skokie's lawyers secured a forty-five-day stay of the Decker decision while the Seventh Circuit Court of Appeals considered their appeal.[38]

If there was a silver lining in Decker's ruling from Skokie's perspective, it was his admission that the *Beauharnais* precedent might still be valid. That inspired the Skokie Jewish coalition to revive the original 1917 state law. On April 14, at their behest, a group of Democratic state senators proposed a pair of group libel bills in the Illinois legislature. The first bill criminalized the "public display of racial hatred" or "criminal group defamation" as a Class A misdemeanor, establishing a right for any affected party to seek a preemptive injunction. The second bill prohibited "parades and demonstrations by groups which arouse reasonable apprehensions" of the use or display of "physical force in promoting any political object," while also banning "the use of symbols having associations with political violence" or "quasi-military uniforms." "Reasonability" was to be defined by the judge's consideration of "the racial or ethnic character of the community." Having discarded Illinois's group libel law only fifteen years before, legislators now retrieved it as a tool to face a new generation of antisemites.[39]

The Carroll and Nimrod bills, named for their sponsors, were unanimously endorsed by the Illinois Senate Judiciary Committee on May 2. They sailed through the full Senate chamber two weeks later. Despite legal skepticism from many quarters over the constitutionality of such statutes, they won strong vocal support from several prominent legal figures, including Philip Kurland, Victor Rosenblum of Northwestern Law School and the local ADL, and Joel Sprayregen, former general counsel of the Illinois ACLU. As May drew to a close, the bills passed to the Illinois House for review. Meanwhile, all eyes turned back to the courts, where Skokie's appeal of the city's three statutes was pending. A ruling there might affect the prospects of the new state legislation.[40]

On May 22, 1978, a three-judge panel of the Seventh Circuit affirmed Judge Decker's decision. With "repugnance" and "extreme regret," wrote Judge Wilbur Pell, a Nixon appointee, we conclude that the Skokie lawyers have not proven that physical violence is either likely or inevitable. As for the town's group libel argument that the march was "a substantive evil that it has a right to prohibit: the infliction of psychic trauma on resident Holocaust survivors," that might pass legal muster if the survivors were "a captive audience" or threatened in "the privacy of the home." However, the government could not simply "declare the entire Village, at all times, a privacy zone that may be sanitized from the offensiveness of Nazi ideology and symbols."[41]

In a long partial dissent, Judge Robert Sprecher, a fellow Nixon appointee, registered his unease over the exceptional nature of the case. All three courts involved, including his own, had felt "the need to apologize for" their decisions. In the face of such an extraordinary scenario, the courts should not rush to squeeze the facts into stock legal formulas. "Unique First Amendment controversies," he wrote, "require an attempt to consider unique approaches." The "unique amalgam of complex First Amendment concepts" and the situation of "uniformed Hitlerian Nazis" demonstrating in a town of Jewish survivors mandated closer legal scrutiny than his colleagues had offered. He professed sympathy with the group libel claim but suggested that the burden of proof had not (yet) been met.[42]

In his dissent, Sprecher noted one other "unique" factor present in Skokie. In contrast to decades past, American Jews were now much more inclined "to confront threatened oppression with active resistance and aggressive retaliation." Jewish quietism had been replaced with a muscular response, and the law should take notice. Sprecher's observation spoke to a new political reality. No longer did Jews adhere to the "silent treatment" approach to combating extremist provocateurs. Self-defense meant legal offense. When the law failed to provide a solution, Jews looked to advance one of their own. What linked a radical extremist like Meir Kahane to a Holocaust survivor like Erna Gans was a shared conviction that Jewish dignity demanded acts of resistance to antisemitic oppression. Justice required confrontation. Just as the African American freedom struggle shifted in the late 1960s from strategic nonviolence to aggressive action "by any means necessary," in Malcolm X's famous phrase, Skokie revealed a Jewish America itching for its fight.

9

Symbol of the World

"I will ask the Four Questions, and I invite everyone who believes in America to join in the response." Paul Newman's voice booms out across Chicago's Soldier Field stadium. After the parade of Holocaust survivors toting banners with the names of their former concentration camps, after the Hebrew memorial prayers and the speech by the president of the United States, Skokie Day culminates in a call-and-response liturgy between the Hollywood actor and the hundred thousand people clutching candles in the dark. "What makes this country different from any other country in the world?" Newman asks. "What makes America different is that sacred right—I repeat—*sacred right* for the other son of a bitch to be dead wrong!"[1]

"Skokie Day" never happened, despite the detailed, vivid script. Neither did "First Amendment Day," "National Call to Conscience Day," or "Human Dignity and Brotherhood Week." In the first half of 1978, a stream of proposals ranging from the earnest to the absurd flowed into Skokie's town offices and national Jewish organizations. Let all American Christians wear Star of David armbands for a day. Skokie ought to erect a model concentration camp across the street from the town hall, complete with prisoners dressed in camp uniforms. Bring in the Chicago Symphony Orchestra to play "America the Beautiful" and a medley of Israeli folk songs. Invite Bob Hope, Bob Dylan, and Reverend Billy Graham to headline a star-studded festival. Or, in the inimitable suggestion of one Bud Laing of Sherwood, Oregon, force the Nazis to conduct their march along a town road covered with farm manure.[2]

Even if the Nazis won the right to speak, they would still lose in the marketplace of ideas. Moral condemnation would replace legal prevention. A superior message armed with a bigger megaphone would drown out the competition. Patriotic symbols would counteract swastikas. Above all, counterprotest would defeat hate speech.

Politics depends on monopolizing the public voice. Leaders speak for the people; voters delegate their voice through voting. In American democracy, where no single centralized body formally represents Jews before the law, Jewish political leadership derives its authority from voluntary membership in private organizations. Over the course of the postwar decades, even as they competed against one another, national Jewish communal organizations coalesced into an informal establishment that assumed the right to speak—or remain silent—in the name of American Jews.

Skokie challenged that authority. It was one thing to support legal challenges in court against antisemites, and quite another to stage large-scale political protests. Such proposals ran directly against the entrenched "quarantine" position of every major American Jewish organization. The volume of Jewish rage—and the moral authority of Holocaust survivors—forced a reckoning with the political demands of the Jewish public. Silence was no longer an option.

As the court battles reached their end in the late spring of 1978, communal leaders confronted a Jewish America no longer willing to seek permission to speak out against antisemitism. The memory of the Holocaust spurred a demand for public action. Protecting dignity required asserting Jewish identity directly in the face of bigots. With or without Paul Newman's stage direction, Jews were ready to raise their voices in protest.

* * *

For Sol Goldstein there was never a question of whether or not to organize a counterprotest against the Nazis. From the outset, he urged Chicago's Jewish officials to develop a plan in the event that the court maneuvers failed. In mid-February 1978, he finally got his chance. After the recent string of court defeats, Goldstein received approval from the Chicago Jewish Federation to set up the Committee on Individual Liberty and Jewish Security. As its name suggested, the group consciously sought to hold the First and Fourteenth Amendments together in a single Jewish frame of self-defense and civil liberties. "This march has become an issue for all Americans," Goldstein announced in a press release, and the public was ready to unite behind the Jewish community. "There are many people in this country who remember that in addition to the six million Jews slaughtered during the Holocaust five million Christian civilians were exterminated and 190,000 American soldiers lost their lives fighting the Nazi war machine."[3]

Anticipating an April march, Goldstein's committee appointed Eugene DuBow, Midwest AJC official, as the coordinator for what was dubbed the Skokie Project. DuBow set about designing a massive public event that would showcase American pluralism in solidarity against hate. A broad array of religious, veterans, and civil rights groups signed on, among them the Chicago Catholic Women, the National Conference of Christians and Jews, the Chinese American Civic Council, the United Auto Workers, the Teamsters, the AFL-CIO, and the Italian American War Veterans.[4]

Yet even as support broadened and deepened, the leaders of national Jewish organizations eyed these plans with worry. Mass protest violated the tried-and-true communal strategy for handling antisemitic agitation. The terms of the internal debate were neatly reflected in the struggles of AJC board chairman Maynard Wishner, a former civil rights lawyer and financial executive who also served as vice chair of the Chicago Jewish Federation. "We do live in strange times with anomalies," he told his colleagues at the May AJC board meeting. Polling suggests that "prejudice against Jews as individuals is at an all-time low," while "attacks upon us as a group have become totally acceptable." Jews had found enormous acceptance and success in America, yet remained a ripe target for extremism. How, then, should danger be measured and self-defense mounted?

Wishner spoke for a generation whose sensibilities had been molded by the moderate reformist ethos of the 1940s and 1950s. As a young civil rights lawyer, he had been present on Peoria Street in 1949 when Beauharnais's incitement led to the attack on Aaron Bindman's home. He had witnessed decades of violence in Chicago and elsewhere, while struggling for racial justice. Those years had proven that free speech worked in favor of Jewish rights, whereas counterprotest proved counterproductive. But the times had changed, and Jewish political sensibilities with them. "Never Again" used to be the slogan of Meir Kahane and his militant extremism, he remarked, yet now the words resonated deeply "in the hearts and minds of all of us." In a country galvanized by the protest movements of the 1960s, the rise of Black Power, and the Jewish campaign on behalf of Soviet Jewry, many Jews—young and old—no longer believed in the old tactics:

> We, the inventors and advocates of the quarantine treatment as the most effective Jewish response to agitators, now confront the possibility that with changing times, changing media, yesterday's solutions may not be adequate for the problems and issues of today. Even if we have the capability to sit down and coldly, rationally determine the soundest, most effective response, we do not have the capability of imposing those judgments on a heterogeneous, anxious, and distressed community.

We have reached a "historic moment" that calls for a new approach, Wishner asserted: "loud and clear and visible" protest. Still, opinion remained divided. When it came time for the ballot on whether to lend official support to the counterprotest, the AJC leaders voted in favor by the slim margin of 118–108.[5]

It was not only principle that held communal leaders back from endorsing a public counterprotest. By far the biggest concern was the likelihood of violence. Frank Collin maintained that he and his men would march peacefully in defense of their rights but warned that if we are "physically attacked, we will fight with a ruthlessness as terrifying as it will be thorough." On the Jewish side, there were also people spoiling for a fight. They included the JDL, the Illinois Jewish War Veterans of America, and some local Jewish socialist activists and individual Holocaust survivors. Of these militants, the Chicago JDL branch's rhetoric caused the most alarm. Though they claimed to have broken with Kahane, the local JDL had spent years brawling with Nazis on the streets of Chicago. That spring they upped the ante with a call for "young, tough, black people to go with us to Skokie" to fight Nazis. Plans were made to charter a jumbo jet to fly in several hundred protesters from California. Some commentators cheered the prospect. Let the Nazis march but without police protection, suggested Chicago columnist Mike Royko. A good beating at the hands of the "angry crowds in Skokie" would serve as the best form of justice, in his view.[6]

The most decisive communal vote on whether to support protest in Skokie took place in late April at the governing assembly of the NCRAC, the national federation of Jewish public affairs councils. But the result was an awkward 12–12 tie. Rather than break the tie with his vote, Chairman Ben Chernov proposed a new resolution: Chicago Jews should protest if they so chose but should stay far away from the site of any "Nazi provocations," and other Jewish communities should not send people to join them in Skokie. The Chicago federation reacted with fury at this "gratuitous slap" in the face. It was Sol Goldstein who brokered the eventual compromise: Jewish communities around the country were invited to send small "symbolic delegations" to Skokie.[7]

Meanwhile, the American public's interest in Skokie was growing by leaps and bounds. A key factor was the NBC television broadcast *The Holocaust*, a nine-and-a-half-hour miniseries that aired across five nights from April 16 to 20. An estimated 120 million Americans—more than 50 percent of the national population—tuned in. "Finally people are recognizing the importance of knowledge, and what happened during the Holocaust," remarked Erna Gans. "And instead of silence they're talking about it, learning about it, and maybe will have a lesson from history, instead of forgetting about history." Though lambasted by experts for its saccharine depiction of victims and maudlin storytelling, the television show catapulted the Holocaust into the center of American consciousness as never before. It even popularized the term "the Holocaust." Thanks in large part to the miniseries, "the Holocaust" began to function as shorthand for the face of ultimate evil.[8]

In the wake of the broadcast, the roster of protest participants grew to include several senators and congressmen from across the country. Among the notable figures were Reverend Jesse Jackson, German Consul General Dr. Egon Raster, AFL-CIO head William Lee, and progressive evangelical leader Dr. Ronald Sider, who all announced their intentions to come. President Jimmy Carter voiced his support for the march and pledged to send State Department human rights czar Patricia Derian. Messages of solidarity poured in from Canada and Europe. In Israel, plans were made for a charter flight to ferry in protesters.[9]

Local figures also prepared their responses. In mid-April, the town sponsored a Holocaust Remembrance Week, which featured an interfaith Jewish-Protestant-Catholic "Service of Solidarity and Remembrance" held at Niles West Township High School. The National Conference of Christians and Jews sent a batch of yellow Star of David armbands for the occasion to be worn as a "badge of honor," to mimic what "King Christian of Denmark did in 1943," based on a popular myth that he led his people in donning the armbands so the Nazis could not distinguish Jews from other Danes.[10]

In their own search for symbols, the Skokie Project organizers braided together Holocaust remembrance and American patriotism. Though the exact date of Collin's march remained unknown, they formalized a plan for a counterprotest officially sponsored by the Chicago Jewish Federation. The event would commence with a rally at the Niles West Township High School stadium. "The Star-Spangled Banner" and "America the Beautiful" were on the program, along with the Pledge of Allegiance. Then the crowd would hear a roster of short speeches from President Carter's emissary, Illinois Governor Jim Thompson, Mayor Smith, Chicago Jewish communal representatives, and Christian and Jewish clergy. Two Hebrew mourning prayers would be chanted and a set of shofar blasts would signal the commencement of the march, which was to follow a route that avoided close contact with the Nazi demonstration. A Holocaust Remembrance Week would follow with new educational initiatives.[11]

On May 23, the day after the Seventh Circuit finally handed down its decision, Collin issued a press release with the subject line "How to Stop the Nazi March in Skokie." If the town and state pledged to abandon all future legal efforts to block his appearances *and* the Chicago Park District abolished its insurance requirements for public rallies, Collin promised to cancel his Skokie plans and return to his original protest site on the South Side. Collin knew there was little chance that his opponents would agree to his terms. Still, he portrayed himself as a loyal citizen standing up for the rights of all Americans against the threat of government tyranny. Mayor Smith rejected the offer out of hand. The Skokie Jewish leadership concurred. "We cannot in good conscience permit the pain of the Jewish community to be transferred to other targets of Nazi hatred," Goldstein declared. Solving Jewish Skokie's problem at the expense of the African American community in Marquette Park was unacceptable, morally and politically.[12]

On May 25, Skokie issued two permits: one for Collin and his group of seventy-five people to march in front of the Village Hall, and the other for the massive counterprotest. In exactly one month's time, on Sunday, June 25, the "Battle of Skokie," as some were now calling it, would finally take place.

Even as the countdown began, Skokie's lawyers tried one last Hail Mary to the U.S. Supreme Court. On Monday, June 5, Schwartz and Gordon filed a motion for an emergency stay of the Seventh Circuit's decision and a petition for certiorari, asking the Court to hear the three ordinances case. That move presented national Jewish leaders with yet another dilemma. Should they add their own voices to the eleventh-hour legal maneuver with amicus briefs?

"THE NATIONAL AND international attention which this case has attracted does not result from sensationalism or morbid curiosity," wrote Schwartz and Gordon in their Supreme Court filing, but from the "heightened consciousness and perception of American Jews as a result of the Nazi

Holocaust and the juxtaposition of their 14th Amendment rights against the 1st Amendment rights of the American National Socialist (Nazi) Party." None of the precedents and analogies applied to this case fit. This was not the equivalent of political protest against the Vietnam War (*Cohen v. California*) or government censorship of the press (*New York Times Co. v. Sullivan*). It was not about using criminal syndicalist laws to punish an extremist group (*Brandenburg v. Ohio*) or even prior restraint because of a heckler's veto (*Terminiello v. Chicago*). The one precedent that most directly applied to Skokie was the only case that had never been overruled: *Beauharnais v. Illinois.*[13]

Invoking *Beauharnais*, the Skokie lawyers quoted Justice Frankfurter's opinion to the effect that restricting bigoted speech was not the same thing as political censorship. We wholeheartedly accept "that all ideas should compete in the marketplace," they wrote, but this "does not mean that the marketplace itself should be unregulated for the public good." The Nazi "racial taunt is not an idea but a blow . . . totally lacking in social content." Such speech "deserves no more protection in the marketplace of ideas than would a nationwide TV broadcast advertising a false miracle cancer drug." They closed by quoting Justice Jackson's dissent from *Kunz v. New York* in which he castigated his colleagues for requiring a community to help a bigot play with racial and religious explosives in the public streets. "The plaintiff Collin would play with the same explosives in the streets of Skokie, Illinois."[14]

It fell once again to Justice John Paul Stevens to handle the Skokie petition. The Chicago native had previously ruled against Skokie in his capacity as circuit justice. Anticipating a major case at hand, on Friday, June 9, he ordered the Court's legal officer to prepare a background report and called his colleagues into conference the following Monday afternoon for a discussion.[15]

The Burger Court dated to 1969, when Warren Burger succeeded Earl Warren as chief justice, and included four men added by Presidents Nixon and Ford to increase the conservative contingent—Burger, Lewis Powell (1972), William Rehnquist (1972), and Stevens (1975). Although the Court did further separate church and state in *Lemon v. Kurtzman* (1971), it tacked right on many issues, including school desegregation, obscenity, and immigration. Most immediately relevant was the 1974 case *Gertz v. Robert Welch, Inc.*, in which a Jewish Chicago lawyer sued the antisemitic far right John Birch Society for defamation. There, the Court lessened the burden of proof for private individuals alleging libel. Where it would go on Skokie was anyone's guess.[16]

The prospect of the Supreme Court's taking up the case divided the three major Jewish civil rights organizations. Where some wished to resurrect *Beauharnais*, others favored the ACLU position. After much internal debate, the American Jewish Congress decided on a compromise. Should the Court proceed, they would support Skokie's ban on the swastika and Nazi uniforms as symbolic "fighting words." They summed up their position neatly: "March, Yes; Swastikas, Uniforms, No." The ADL took the same tack. For its part, the AJC simply could not decide. Its antisemitism czar, Solomon Fineberg, came out of retirement to decry the "hysteria" about Skokie. His successor, Milton Ellerin, asserted that there was no real neo-Nazi threat. In the end, the board prepared two different resolutions—one in support of Skokie, the other against—and asked local chapters to vote to reach a final decision.[17]

All the debate turned out to be for naught. On June 12, one week after the Skokie brief was filed, the Supreme Court denied the request for an emergency stay by a 7–2 vote. The two dissents came from Justices Harry Blackmun and William Rehnquist. However, the Court held the petition for certiorari over to consider for the fall term. The case remained live, but in the meantime the march would go on.

As THE NEWS broke, panic set in. On Tuesday, June 13, Mayor Smith was rushed to the Evanston hospital with a heart attack. The next day, the Illinois House of Representatives took up a final vote on the new state laws paralleling the Skokie ordinances. Already approved by the Senate, the bills faced opposition in the House Judiciary Committee during a marathon session the week before. Erna Gans was one of a string of Holocaust survivors and other advocates who testified in support of them. "To us, the swastika is the symbol which united the murderers of the world," she said. "We're not talking about abstract ideas," added former ACLU lawyer Joel Sprayregen. "We're talking about genocide." University of Chicago Professor Geoffrey Stone spoke against these views, pointing out the likely constitutional problems with the laws. He was joined by ACLU chief Aryeh Neier, who summed up his position crudely: "Let's defend an occasional Nazi. That's the price of our constitutional system." Like the eleventh-hour court appeal, the legislative effort failed. On June 14, the full House chamber voted to defeat the two bills. There was no longer any law to block the march.[18]

Tensions mounted as Sunday, June 25, approached. Preparations were made for a mass presence of state police and Illinois National Guard, extra jail cells, and a mobile field hospital with emergency blood supplies. President Carter telegrammed Sol Goldstein to voice his "complete solidarity" with "those citizens of Skokie and Chicago who will gather . . . in a peaceful demonstration of their abhorrence of Nazism." The Justice Department dispatched a special team of Community Relations Service officials tasked with keeping the two protests apart.[19]

On Wednesday, June 21, came another surprising twist: A federal judge struck down Chicago's ban on Collin's marching in Marquette Park, the original grievance that had prompted his pivot to Skokie. Collin had now won on all fronts. Both Skokie and Chicago lay open before him. At a Thursday evening press conference at his headquarters, he declared total victory. Then he announced that he had finished with Skokie. "The whole Skokie issue was pure agitation on our part to force the system to restore our rights to free speech," he explained. There would be no march there. Instead, he would march the day before on Saturday, June 24, at Federal Plaza in Chicago, followed by a Sunday, July 9, march in Marquette Park.[20]

Why did Collin change his mind? Most Jewish leaders believed they had successfully deterred him with threats that the massive counterprotest would dwarf his small group in Skokie. Violence certainly loomed. On the same day as Collin's press conference, a young Jewish man was arrested for plotting to firebomb his office. Others thought

Collin canceled Skokie because he had achieved all his goals. He had won a legal victory, inspired panic in the Jewish community, and seized the world's attention. The town remained hostage to his whims. As he warned reporters, "The moment I suspect that our rights are again being abridged, that we will no longer have free access to public parks, that is the very moment that I will reschedule a public demonstration in Skokie. Cancellation of this one march does not mean that I forgo all future demonstrations in Skokie."[21]

On June 24, Collin's small band of twenty-some men marched under heavy police escort in Federal Plaza in Chicago. Despite the absence of any official counterdemonstration, they were met by three thousand protesters. Ironically, the police had escorted them to and from their rally in a paddy wagon via an underground garage. As she stood behind the police line, staring at an actual swastika for the first time since World War II, Erna Gans screamed in anger at Collin's men. "Why don't you come here?" With her fists clenched, she spoiled for a fight. Then she turned her attention to the police: "Why don't you let us come at them?" After ten minutes, it was over. No arrests were made, no injuries reported. In a broader sense, Skokie had ended without a clear winner.[22]

Collin and a small group of followers held their long-awaited return to Marquette Park some two weeks later, on Sunday, July 9. They once again faced a large group of two thousand diverse counterprotesters: Jewish leftists, JDL militants, Maoist communists, and Black civil rights activists. Scores of Orthodox Jews from neighboring synagogues showed up as well. The local white population turned their ire against the Black and Jewish counterprotesters, shouting, "Go back to Skokie, kikes," and "Gas them, gas them!" Despite the volatile situation, a massive police presence kept the situation from escalating. The day ended without significant violence.[23]

As disturbing as it was, the July 9 march proved to be the beginning of the end for Collin. He announced more rallies in Chicago suburbs and threatened to return to Skokie if blocked. He staged an unsuccessful run for the Chicago City Council. Yet internal rivalries and personal demons soon consumed him. In 1980, Collin was arrested on child molestation charges and subsequently imprisoned for several years. His organization collapsed in his absence. Upon release, he reinvented himself as Frank Joseph, a New Age conspiracy theorist, writing popular books about the Knights Templar's secret ties to ancient America and the lost civilization of Atlantis. Collin ceded neo-Nazism to an emerging new generation of white supremacist groups. The saga of Skokie had ended.

The legal coda to Skokie occurred in the fall of 1978, when the Supreme Court considered the two cases that were still outstanding. Although the Court had refused to halt the march, it had held over Skokie's petition for certiorari in the matter of the three ordinances. Goldstein's attorneys also lodged a final appeal of his menticide suit. In October 1978, the Supreme Court declined to hear either case. On the Skokie ordinances, Justices Harry Blackmun and Byron White dissented. *Beauharnais* had never been "overruled or formally limited in any way," they wrote, and Skokie "affords the Court an opportunity to consider whether . . . there is no limit whatsoever to the exercise of free speech." Hate speech "just might fall into the same category as one's 'right' to cry 'fire' in a crowded theater, for 'the character of every act depends upon the circumstances in which it is done.'" Those few lines summarized a century of Supreme Court opinions on free speech to reveal a simple truth: American law had not yet resolved the question of hate speech.[24]

Or perhaps it had. In the eyes of the ACLU's David Goldberger, Skokie proved the greatness of the American system. "Free speech," he told a visiting French journalist, "is what makes us different from any other democracy in the world." The real issue at Skokie was not the Nazis, horrible as they were, but the preservation of the core principles of American democracy. Defending Nazis, Goldberger wrote in a fundraising appeal to Jewish members, was painful but necessary work. Doing so allowed the ACLU also to serve as America's "watchdog and enforcer of the Bill of Rights." Of the six thousand cases it handled—defending the rights of Black civil rights activists, fighting book bans, protecting the rights of mentally disabled persons and women who had abortions, and generally checking government power—only six, or one-tenth of one percent, resembled Skokie. Yet those six must be defended in order to preserve the rest.[25]

Goldberger's missive was intended to address a real problem. In the aftermath of Skokie, the ACLU remained financially crippled by the wave of membership resignations. Despite identifying with liberal causes, many Jewish supporters felt that free speech now came at the expense of their civil rights. The idea "that Jewish security is best served by vigorous defense of free speech," wrote one AJC official, "was simply not convincing to most American Jews when faced with the threat of Nazis goosestepping through the streets of the United States." When *Commentary* magazine polled fifty-two prominent Jewish intellectuals about the state of liberalism several months after Skokie, only two mentioned free speech, and then only to criticize blind fealty to it.[26]

Undeterred, Goldberger and other ACLU leaders insisted that the defense of free speech was a Jewish interest. Minorities needed rights protection most of all. Free speech was also a Jewish value. To prove his point, Goldberger closed his fundraising appeal with a provocative gesture. You "have identified yourself as a part of the 'saving remnant' of our own time," he wrote, so we ask you "not just to support ACLU but to save it." The phrase "saving remnant" stemmed from the biblical book of Isaiah, where it referred to God's chosen few who would survive a terrible ordeal to carry on the divine mission to humanity. After the war, it had been adopted to refer to Holocaust survivors in displaced persons camps. Now, Goldberger invoked it to suggest Jewish civil libertarians had passed through their own moment of destruction. Their task was no less than to redeem American liberalism by holding fast to the law.[27]

The ACLU campaign succeeded brilliantly. Through 1979, the organization gained forty thousand new members and replenished its coffers. Skokie became a defining symbol of American civil liberties—proof of the necessity and wisdom of defending freedom for thoughts we despise and for those who despise us.

* * *

"THE WHOLE WORLD looks upon us, the whole world," declared Sol Goldstein at one point in the final days of the Skokie saga, and we "will not disappoint humanity." He then quoted from the *Ethics of the Fathers*, an ancient text of rabbinic Judaism: "The book lies open, and the hand still writes." God would record the events and pass judgment on people's deeds, the original text implied. Goldstein took it to mean something different: History remained still to be written; the future was open. We must fulfill our two "sacred" obligations: to remember the "six million Jews" and to achieve "a free society where there is no room for killing, for hatred." We may lose in court, but "we are winning now as the world is being educated to the dangers of the Nazis." That will make Skokie into "a symbol of the world."[28]

Goldstein's speech evoked a new purpose for Skokie as a national history lesson. The crisis could transform Holocaust remembrance into an antidote to hate speech. Hatred began with ignorance, tolerance with knowledge. The best response to bigotry was to demonstrate where it ultimately led. Teaching the Holocaust would provide moral edification. The shock of absolute evil would stimulate the ethical imagination.

The Skokie survivor community carried this message into a campaign to establish an Illinois Holocaust Museum in their town. Leading the effort was Gans, who also spearheaded a successful drive to make Illinois the first state in the country to require Holocaust education in public schools. She later made Holocaust remembrance and education central to her tenure as the first female president of the B'nai B'rith organization. Gans took pride that "Skokie woke up the conscience of humanity." Yet her commitment to Holocaust education did not diminish her disappointment in the law or her desire to change it. "One can easily distinguish between marching for freedom and equality, and marching for genocide," she insisted. Gans gathered six hundred thousand signatures on a petition to create a new federal law banning racial and religious defamation. Free speech is important, she explained, but we must "protect our society from neo-Nazism and from ideologies that preach hate and promote hate symbols."[29]

Gans's words captured the puzzle of Skokie. For all the talk of

Nazism, the greatest danger was not mass murder on American soil, but a loathsome assault on the dignity and psychological well-being of Jewish survivors of European genocide. Even as the monstrous symbolism provoked moral outrage, the arguments for removing First Amendment protection for the march oscillated between two distinct claims: that the speech violated the civil rights of the potential victims and that it would incite violence. Though related, these remained fundamentally different in law, one seeking protection from physical danger, the other from harm to dignity. The small scale and bizarre nature of the threat tempered perceptions of its power. However violent their ideology, these antisemites seemed more like historical reenactors from another country's past than a genuine menace.

The best proof of that seemingly harmless hate came in Hollywood's treatment of Skokie in the 1980 comedy film *The Blues Brothers.* The plot centers on two white Chicago blues musicians, Elwood and Jake Blues, played by *Saturday Night Live* stars Dan Aykroyd and John Belushi, who race against time to save the inner-city Catholic orphanage in which they grew up from government foreclosure for unpaid back taxes. Driving through rural Illinois, they come across an American Nazi rally on a bridge, where the police are holding back an angry scrum of anti-Nazi counterprotesters. "White men! White women! The swastika is calling you," says the party leader into a megaphone. "The Jew is using the Black to muscle against you."

Stuck in traffic, Elwood and Jake ask the police officer what's causing the holdup. "Those bums won their court case so they're marching today," he explains. "I hate Illinois Nazis," Jake responds. Elwood proceeds to drive their car directly into the rally, sending the goons leaping off the bridge into a nearby stream. The anti-Nazi crowd cheers. The Nazi leader fumes. He and his men spend the rest of the film chasing the duo. At the end, the Nazi leader plunges to his death after driving off an unfinished freeway.

The Illinois Nazis are violent. They are antisemitic. They are also pathetic and comical. Their own absurdity proves their undoing. America can afford to tolerate them because despite their bluster they harm only themselves. This image of antisemitism, as a unique but harmless hatred, would be Skokie's other legacy in the American imagination. The ultimate danger, the Holocaust, was clear but not present in American society as the 1970s drew to a close. Truly dangerous antisemitism belonged to another time and place. Yet the book of history lay open, its next chapters still to be written.

PART III

2017–2025

10

Jews Will Not Replace Us

"They came from the south end of the Lawn. It almost looked like a river of . . . flames." Peering through the peephole of the door to her dorm room on the historic quad, University of Virginia senior Diane D'Costa pressed her face close, her black curly ringlets brushing the door as her warm, dark eyes widened in terror watching two endless lines of men with torches trudge in pairs directly past her door. Their "angry, guttural" rhythmic chants were chilling: "Blood and soil," "White lives matter," "You will not replace us," and "Jews will not replace us." As the marchers traversed the quad toward the Rotunda, more men emerged from the shadows, swelling their ranks. Some wore Nazi and white supremacist symbols, others dressed in the alt-right uniform of khakis and white polo shirts.[1]

It was just after nine o'clock on the evening of Friday, August 11, 2017. Earlier that day, D'Costa—a Jewish and Latina woman from Maryland and vice president of the Class of 2018—had moved into her senior-year Lawn room. One of fifty-four historic residences in Jefferson's original Academical Village, these coveted dorms were awarded annually to top student leaders as one of the university's highest honors. Now what should have been her prize had become a trap.

D'Costa raced around the room, frantically seeking protection. She yanked the blinds shut, locked the door, then tore off her ring, which bore the words of the Shema prayer, and hamsa necklace. Spotting a painting with Israeli flags, she wrenched it from the wall, "but there was no way to remove the physical indicators from my body. Everything about who I am felt like a threat." Her chest constricted. Her ears rang. "I was kind of in shock of what was happening," she recalled. "It was the most traumatized I ever felt as a Jewish person. I was scared for my life. I thought that I was going to die if people knew who I was."[2]

Then came a knock. It was Wendy Baucom, the dean's wife, who lived in the faculty pavilion next door. She had come to whisk D'Costa to safety. For ten minutes, D'Costa huddled on Baucom's second-story balcony, stupefied by the scene below. Then she fled through a back entrance and down an alley to a friend's waiting car. "It was like I was fleeing my house . . . I have memories of my family telling me stories of my great-grandmother fleeing Poland. And it felt like fleeing my home from Nazis, but on the Lawn."[3]

Reaching the northern end of the Lawn, the men climbed the stairs flanking the Rotunda, then descended the rear steps onto the wide plaza below. As they marched, they barked a low one-word chant—the surname of Dylann Roof, who murdered nine African Americans at a Charleston church in 2015, transformed into an animalistic call. On the plaza, the marchers reached their destination: a statue of UVA's founder, Thomas Jefferson.

A small band of students there had formed a human chain around the monument, clutching a homemade banner that read "UVA Students Act Against White Supremacy." The mob encircled them. They jabbed and swiped with their flaming torches, taking turns rushing the student line, seeking a pretext to attack. The students bowed their heads to avoid eye contact, chanting "Black lives matter."

While chaos unfolded on the plaza, Charlottesville's clergy gathered a block away at St. Paul's Church for an interfaith service. Despite security concerns, the atmosphere inside remained spirited and positive. Rabbis Tom Gutherz and Rachel Schmelkin of Congregation Beth Israel, the town's synagogue, led the assembly in a Hebrew song about redeeming the world through love. As the service concluded, police ordered everyone to shelter in place. The situation across the street had turned dangerous.[4]

Just after 10 p.m., scuffles erupted at the statue's base. Protesters lunged at the students, grabbing for their banner and hurling lit torches at them. March co-organizer Chris Cantwell, a burly, bald-headed New Hampshire native, pepper-sprayed local trans activist Emily Gorcenski. Fistfights broke out across the plaza. Throughout the violence, Charlottesville and university police stood by, ordered not to intervene—the event was deemed a political rally protected by the First Amendment. The alt-right had broken no laws.

Yet the students feared for their lives. Dean of students Allen Groves pushed through the mob to offer them safe passage. A flaming torch struck his arm. Finally, after ten minutes that felt like an eternity, police declared an emergency and ordered everyone to disperse.[5]

Diane D'Costa did not sleep that night. By morning, she was back in her childhood bedroom in Maryland, "violently scribbling" in her notebook. I was "trying to shake the images that refused to leave my brain. I needed them out. I needed them gone," she recalled. "The things I saw, heard, and felt on August 11, 2017, no human being should ever have to experience . . . No one should ever feel like they will die if they are seen because of who they are."[6]

In Charlottesville, America's unending struggle over race and power found its newest battlefield. The euphoria of the post–Cold War years had dissolved into millennial dread—endless war, terror, economic ruin. A Black president's historic ascent had given way to an aging white demagogue trafficking in racial grievance and conspiracy theories. This new populism cloaked itself in the rhetoric of free expression while demanding its opponents be silenced. Its disciples cast progressive sanctimony as state censorship, blind to their own doctrinal rigidity. What passed for libertarian principle was in fact permission for hatred.

Charlottesville heralded a dark turn in American antisemitism as well. Merely a year earlier, a prominent political scientist had proclaimed, based on ADL data, that "anti-semitism has virtually disappeared in the United States." Arguably, he wrote, "it is far easier to be Jewish than to be a member of any other minority in American society."

One August weekend shattered such complacency. It presaged an era of anti-Jewish violence that would be marked by attacks of a magnitude unprecedented in American history.[7]

The shock brought not only fear but profound bewilderment. In the era of Black Lives Matter, why target Jews? D'Costa was among many who felt this jarring dissonance. "I saw a mass of people carrying lit torches chanting 'Jews will not replace us,' and I was very confused as to why they were there. The Robert E. Lee statue is why I heard they were coming. And I don't know what Jews have to do with Robert E. Lee."[8]

Robert "Azzmador" Ray had the answer. As the burly, bearded Texan stumbled away from the scene Friday night, wiping pepper spray from his eyes, he declared to a reporter standing nearby that it was time to end "Jewish control of America." The "ovens are gonna be a lot hotter than this fucking pepper spray." The reporter asked, "What about the blacks?" Without missing a beat, Ray spat out his response. "They can go back or whatever. They don't run anything."[9]

THE THREE DECADES between Skokie and Charlottesville witnessed profound shifts in American free speech jurisprudence. The Supreme Court wrestled with flag desecration, pornography, corporate political expression, and religious bigotry. Federal courts weighed campus speech codes against constitutional principles and struggled to regulate the nascent internet. Yet the period's most consequential legal innovation lay not in any First Amendment ruling but in the birth of a new criminal category. In the wake of Skokie, American law pivoted from trying to police hate speech to prosecuting hate crimes.

In 1981, the ADL introduced a model hate crimes bill for states and cities across the United States. There are some "bias crimes" whose harm "cannot be measured solely in terms of property damage assessments or physical injuries," wrote ADL staff attorney Steven Freeman. "Such crimes have a special emotional and physical impact that extends beyond the original victim" and they "damage the very fabric of our society." The ADL recommended adding two new criminal offenses to American law codes: "institutional vandalism," defined as the desecration of religious buildings, schools, and religious community centers, and "ethnic intimidation," the targeting of a victim on the basis of "race, color, religion, or national origin." The draft statute did not criminalize hatred by itself but added penalty enhancements to preexisting crimes.[10]

The new legislation swept across America in the early 1980s, as cities and states embraced variations of the ADL's model statute. Some laws prohibited the desecration of religious institutions; others criminalized vandalism employing "symbols of racial or religious hatred" to intimidate. Congress, sensing the political moment, began crafting federal hate crimes legislation.[11]

The ADL's proposal arose in response to an alarming surge in antisemitic crimes nationwide. When the organization launched its annual audit in 1979, tracking incidents state by state, the numbers climbed precipitously: 120 in 1979, 377 in 1980, 974 in 1981. This wave encompassed swastikas, anti-Jewish graffiti, firebombings, and physical assaults on a scale unseen in decades. Yet Jewish civil rights leaders diverged sharply over what these statistics meant. While ADL experts saw something sinister—"a pervasive and deep-rooted antisemitism which has lain dormant for the past 20 or 30 years"—the crimes consisted largely of minor property vandalism, often committed by teenagers. In 1982, over 80 percent of arrests involved youth under twenty. Even within the Jewish communal establishment, skeptics questioned whether this constituted a genuine "epidemic."[12]

Still, two developments sparked support for hate crimes legislation. First came a resurgent wave of white nationalist and neo-Nazi groups; the Ku Klux Klan had reemerged on the national stage with swelling ranks and renewed militancy. More disturbing still was the proliferation of domestic terror groups—Posse Comitatus, Aryan Nations, the Order—that melded anti-government extremism with antisemitic ideology. Their violent campaign soon followed: attacks on federal agents and Jewish targets, including the 1984 assassination of Denver radio host Alan Berg.[13]

Beyond these immediate threats, the ADL's proposal gained momentum from a broader cultural shift in American law. The legal system had gradually come to prioritize the victim's experience and the psychological impact of crime. Reflecting this shift, the ADL's draft statute proposed allowing bias crime victims to sue for damages, including "emotional distress." Justice now demanded that law acknowledge the wounds inflicted on the victim's psyche.[14]

The legislation appeared during a particularly hostile moment for civil rights. The Reagan administration arrived in 1981 determined to dismantle federal civil rights programs that conservatives viewed with open contempt. The fact that the ADL's proposals found champions among gay and lesbian activists and liberal organizations—Alabama's Southern Poverty Law Center, Virginia's National Anti-Klan Network—only deepened conservative suspicion. Yet hate crimes laws garnered unexpected bipartisan support, buoyed by a crusade on the right: the victims' rights movement. Reacting against the 1960s expansion of criminal defendants' due process protections, conservatives argued that victims deserved equal consideration. By 1982, Reagan's Presidential Task Force on Victims of Crime was proposing a constitutional amendment for victims' rights, declaring that crime's "psychological scars are perhaps the hardest to bear."[15]

Hate crimes legislation offered an elegant resolution: It preserved victims' dignity while leaving speech untouched. Words and ideas remained beyond the reach of the law, but criminal acts motivated by bias could face enhanced penalties.

This approach gained traction even as some progressive civil rights lawyers in the late 1980s flirted with reviving group libel. Critical legal and feminist scholars popularized the phrase "hate speech," while universities experimented with campus speech codes. Federal courts, however, rejected even the most modest attempts to rethink First Amendment law. Ultimately, hate crimes legislation became central to American jurisprudence while "hate speech" remained merely a term of moral condemnation.

Yet this new framework still failed to resolve Skokie's central dilemma. Were not swastika graffiti, burning crosses, even acts of harassment fundamentally forms of expression? Where, precisely, did protected hate speech end and punishable hate crime begin?[16]

In the early 1990s, the Rehnquist Court—which had taken shape after William Rehnquist's elevation to chief justice in 1986 and shifted decidedly rightward with Reagan and Bush appointees—offered contradictory guidance. In *R.A.V. v. City of St. Paul* (1992), the justices unanimously struck down a Minnesota municipal ordinance banning burning crosses and Nazi swastikas when used to provoke "anger, alarm or resentment in others on the basis of race, color, creed, religion or gender." Five justices, led by Justice Antonin Scalia, deemed the law an impermissible form of "viewpoint discrimination," while the others concurred with the opinion on different grounds. Then the following year, in *Wisconsin v. Mitchell*, the same Court unanimously upheld a state hate crime law against a First Amendment challenge. This judicial ambivalence persisted for a decade, until *Virginia v. Black* forced the Court to confront cross burning directly.[17]

In 1952, Virginia had enacted an anti-Klan statute criminalizing cross burnings, public noose displays, and masked gatherings. Following a wave of swastika vandalism in the early 1980s, the legislature expanded the law in 1983, making Virginia among the first states to classify defacing religious buildings with swastikas as a felony. Two decades later, the ACLU challenged a series of cross burning convictions before the Supreme Court.[18]

At oral argument, ACLU attorney Rodney Smolla, a prominent Virginia law professor, contended that burning crosses or flags, painting swastikas or even Stars of David on buildings—all constituted protected expressions of religious or political belief. Any prohibition, he argued, amounted to unconstitutional content and viewpoint discrimination.[19]

Virginia's state solicitor, William Hurd, countered that the law targeted unlawful intimidation, not speech. This statute "protects a very important freedom, freedom from fear, and it does so without compromising freedom of speech," he told the Court. "Surely, for all the reasons why we can ban threats of bodily harm, 100 times over we can ban this exceedingly virulent weapon of fear." If hate crimes laws did not violate the First Amendment, then neither should laws banning unlawful intimidation.[20]

"Cross burning is a form of assaultative speech designed to induce fear in others, not any particular viewpoint or message," declared the ADL. They were joined by the American Jewish Committee, the Zionist women's group Hadassah, the NAACP, and the American-Arab Anti-Discrimination Committee, among others, in an amicus brief likening both burning crosses and swastika displays to "fighting words." By contrast, the Thomas Jefferson Center for the Protection of Free Expression, headed by former University of Virginia President Robert O'Neil, was among those who insisted that all free speech was imperiled by the law in question.[21]

In a fractured decision riddled with partial dissents, the justices struck down the specific law while affirming the constitutional principle behind such laws. Writing for the plurality, Justice Sandra Day O'Connor articulated a nuanced distinction. States could "ban cross burning carried out with the intent to intimidate," but only when it constituted "true threats"—"those forms of intimidation that are most likely to inspire fear of bodily harm." Such "a particular form of assaultive speech or intimidating conduct" possessed "no social value," O'Connor declared, and states retained "the power to regulate the broader class of intimidating or threatening speech intended to induce serious fear in others."[22]

The Court had circled back to Jackson's reasoning in *Terminiello* and Frankfurter's logic in *Beauharnais*, with echoes of Skokie. When deployed threateningly, certain symbols lost their constitutional protection. Hateful acts employing them could be prosecuted. While no symbol by itself could be banned, the law could criminalize expressive acts based on their impact on victims—provided that intent was established.

Virginia's legislature responded by rewriting its statute to avoid regulating content. The revised code, stripped of any reference to crosses, established a felony punishable by up to five years in prison for burning any object on public or private property so as "to place another person in reasonable fear or apprehension of death or bodily injury." For fifteen years, this provision lay dormant—rarely invoked, largely forgotten.[23]

Then, in the spring of 2017, white supremacists arrived in Charlottesville bearing flaming tiki torches.

On Saturday morning, May 13, 2017, a hundred people assembled at McGuffey Park in downtown Charlottesville. Uniformed in khaki pants and white polo shirts, the men, joined by a handful of women, formed two columns and marched eastward on Jefferson Street to a drumbeat, Confederate flags and hate-filled placards aloft. The procession skirted Lee Park, where the town's annual Festival of Cultures was underway, then passed First United Methodist Church. On its steps stood a pair of newlyweds. "Have lots of babies!" someone bellowed at the white couple, drawing cheers from the ranks.[24]

They passed Congregation Beth Israel, where a bar mitzvah was taking place. Joshua Zimmerman, a recent college graduate, exited the building wearing his kippah to investigate the commotion and was met with a torrent of antisemitic slurs. The marchers finally reached Jackson Park at the historic courthouse, where Confederate General Thomas Stonewall Jackson's bronze figure sat astride his horse atop a neoclassical pedestal. As the crowd gathered, a series of speeches inaugurated what would become Charlottesville's "summer of hate." First to the podium: Richard Spencer, the far right's ascendant provocateur. The thirty-nine-year-old, tall with a medium build, sported his signature undercut—sides and back closely cropped with longer brown hair on top, slicked back. Raising a bullhorn, he announced to the crowd, "I'm here to take part in this great celebration of our heritage, and to say 'no' to the city of Charlottesville." The city had recently voted to remove the Confederate statue of Robert E. Lee.[25]

Spencer descended from Dallas wealth—a WASP scion who followed a predictable path from prep school to UVA, then earned his master's degree at Chicago before pursuing a doctorate in modern European history at Duke. In 2006, he abandoned academia for journalism and activism. After he was dismissed from a job at *American Conservative* magazine for his radical views, he founded his own journal and revived the National Policy Institute, a far right think tank in Alexandria, Virginia. From this perch, he labored to repackage white nationalism for mainstream consumption.[26]

Dispensing with garish uniforms and overt talk of violence, Spencer's alt-right movement peddled pseudointellectual theories about racial demography and Western civilizational decline. The movement surged onto the internet with a wave of trolls and extremist websites. Platforms like Twitter and Discord were soon suffused with offensive racist humor that blurred the line between taboo talk and dark fantasy, armchair bluster and real-world action. Online trolls reveled in unmasking Jewish enemies by appending triple parentheses ((())) to their names. Irony became their weapon, offense their objective.

Donald Trump's victory in the fall of 2016 proved a watershed for Spencer's movement. The populist candidate who peddled racist "birther" conspiracies about Barack Obama and conjured visions of migrant invasions electrified the alt-right. Days after the election, Spencer addressed followers in downtown Washington, culminating in a chilling exhortation: "Hail Trump! Hail our people! Hail victory!" The words, deliberate echoes of Nazi tributes to Hitler, drew Nazi salutes from the crowd. The movement had found its moment; now it needed a cause to ignite broader white rage. The campaign against Confederate monuments provided the perfect spark.[27]

Charlottesville had erected its Jackson monument in 1921, followed by Lee in 1924—part of the Lost Cause mythology then sprouting across the South. Their unveiling coincided with the revival of the Ku Klux Klan in Charlottesville. The Klan issued an open call in the pages of the town's *Daily Progress* newspaper for "native-born, white Americans" willing to pledge loyalty to "Christian Religion," "Free Speech," and "Liberty and White Supremacy." In 1924, the state also passed its Racial Integrity and Sterilization Acts, which enshrined white supremacy and eugenics in Virginia law. The former law banned interracial marriage and classified as white a person who had "no trace whatsoever of any blood other than Caucasian." The latter law, which became a model for other states, mandated sexual sterilization for "mental defectives" deemed to have "hereditary forms of insanity that are recurrent, idiocy, imbecility, feeble-mindedness or epilepsy."[28]

Nearly a century later, Lee's and Jackson's monuments remained affixed to the landscape of a Southern college town riddled with contradictions. The small city, dubbed Brooklyn on the Blue Ridge, was a progressive enclave popular with artists, musicians, and other bourgeois bohemians. Luxury horse farms owned by millionaires sat not far from pockets of rural poverty. Meanwhile, the town's small urban core struggled with racial disparities and police brutality.

Charlottesville's identity was also deeply intertwined with Thomas Jefferson's dual legacy as a visionary architect of American democracy and an all too ordinary exponent of American racism. His Monticello estate, a UNESCO World Heritage Site, played host every year to a Fourth of July citizenship oath ceremony for new citizens. Yet the site's leadership had only recently begun acknowledging uncomfortable truths about Jefferson's slaveholding and his sexual relationship with the young enslaved woman Sally Hemings.

In 2016 a petition was submitted to the city council by a local African American high school student, Zyahna Bryant, calling for the removal of the Lee statue because of its ties to the Confederacy and racism. In February 2017, after much rancorous debate, the council voted to take it down. This decision prompted a lawsuit by the Sons of Confederate Veterans—and a campaign by a "pro-white, free speech" activist, Jason Kessler. A 2009 University of Virginia graduate, Kessler had drifted steadily from the liberal left to the far right, becoming a local agitator who claimed to expose reverse racism. Connecting with Spencer, the two men organized the May rally, which became the genesis of the much larger Unite the Right event in August.[29]

At the park that May afternoon, speakers included Mike Peinovich, the host of the *Daily Shoah* podcast, who warned that removing the statues was only the beginning. Soon it will be "a hate crime to show pride in your people, pride in your race." Spencer then returned for the event's finale. As plumes of green and gray smoke from flares rose into the sky, he began to shout. "I don't want to live in a world of equality. I want to live in a world of beauty. I want to live in a world of gods and heroes like Robert E. Lee and Stonewall Jackson. I want to live in a world of the white men who created our civilization." As the applause erupted, Spencer reached his crescendo: "We will not be replaced from this park. We will not be replaced from this world. Whites have a future. We have a future of power, of beauty, of expression . . . and we will seize it."[30]

That evening, Spencer and Kessler led another rally after dark, this time at Lee Park. The marchers came bearing flaming tiki torches. As they marched in pairs around the Lee monument, they chanted "Blood and soil," "Russia is our friend," and "We will not be replaced." The Charlottesville police showed up, found a single counterprotester, and declined to take action. When queried, local officials explained that their hands were tied by the law. A spokesperson stated, "While we prefer protesters get permits like any other event, such assemblies are protected by the First Amendment." No one had thought to consult the law books for the torch burning statute.[31]

Spencer posted a photo of himself later that night, clad in a black shirt with an olive drab blazer, clutching a torch and staring into the camera with a hint of a smirk on his face. He captioned it "#torchlight." It was a wholly "peaceful demonstration," he told the media. The torches were but a theatrical gesture and a nod to the medieval past. At a drunken house party the same evening, meanwhile, he joined in a lusty rendition of "Tomorrow Belongs to Me," the song from the musical *Cabaret* that had been adapted for *The Man in the High Castle*, an alternate history television show depicting a Nazi-occupied America. That was followed by a chant of "Sieg heil!" with Nazi salutes.[32]

Thrilled by the success of their enterprise, Spencer and Kessler began planning a sequel event: Operation Unite the Right Charlottesville 2.0. The time had come to forge a national movement. "We're raising an army, my liege," Kessler playfully told Spencer in a private online chat group, "for free speech, but the cracking of skulls if it comes to it." Various extremists and groups signed on, creating a who's who of the American far right, among them radio shock-jock Chris Cantwell; *Daily Stormer* website founder Andrew Anglin; Nathan Damigo, leader of Identity Evropa; and Jeff Schoep of the Aryan Nationalist Alliance.[33]

Unite the Right encompassed a broad and sprawling ideological spectrum. Some preached white racial populism, others neo-Confederate nationalism; still others fantasized about a global race war. Many hailed Trump and the Republicans as saviors, while some dismissed both government and president as already compromised. What bound these disparate factions together was a doctrine of racial supremacy and their shared fixation on an enemy they believed remained unvanquished. "When the Jews took over our society and turned it into a kiked-out living hell, they marked their achievement by declaring a 'Summer of Love,'" wrote Anglin of their plans. "They took everything away from us. That age is ending now. We are taking back our birthright. This summer, a Black Sun will pass over America," he predicted, invoking an obscure Nazi symbol. "I am declaring the summer of 2017 the Summer of Hate."[34]

EVERY AGE FORGES its antisemitic mythologies anew. Ancient libels of Jewish conspiracy persist, but each era recasts them in the vernacular of its own anxieties. Societies transmute their fears into anti-Jewish fictions.

As Holocaust memory became central to Western democracy's identity in the late twentieth century, Holocaust denial emerged as the primary anti-liberal countermyth. Within Black America, amid the urban crises of the 1980s and 1990s—poverty, crime, despair—the Nation of Islam peddled fantasies of Jewish responsibility for slavery, drugs, and disease. Even Protestant evangelical Zionism harbored currents of apocalyptic conspiracy. It combined support for the State of Israel with images of secular Jews as both globalist elites and agents of the Antichrist destroying the world through progressive values, global finance, and the pursuit of one-world government.

In a twentieth-century Middle East convulsed by colonialism, revolution, and autocracy, humiliated by Israeli victories in 1948 and 1967, and enraged by Palestinian suffering, Arab nationalists and Islamists spun elaborate theories of Jewish world domination. Hamas's 1988 charter epitomized this paranoia, warning that Jews, "with their money," had orchestrated the French and Russian Revolutions, destroyed the Caliphate, ignited both world wars, and seized "control of the world media, news agencies, [and] the press." Citing *The Protocols of the Elders of Zion*, the Hamas charter claimed that Jews commanded the globe through the United Nations, the Freemasons, and Rotary Clubs. This conspiratorial antisemitism would metastasize throughout Islamist ideology following 9/11, the American wars in Afghanistan and Iraq, and the Second Intifada.

In 2011, the French ultrarightist author Renaud Camus published *The Great Replacement*, in which he claimed Muslim immigrants were destroying French civilization. Camus's theory quickly spread across far right circles in Europe and the United States, fusing with a long-standing antisemitic trope of Jewish replacement. Behind the non-white hordes lay the hidden hand of Jewish power, often epitomized by the Hungarian-born Holocaust survivor and financier George Soros. By supposedly financing immigration and encouraging interracialism, liberal Jews were engineering the demographic replacement of Christian white America. This "great replacement" amounted to a secret campaign to achieve "white genocide."[35]

Like other antisemitic conspiracy theories, replacement theory mixed contemporary fears with old tropes of malevolent, secretive Jewish power. Ancient Christians had propagated myths of Jews as religious impostors who compromised the true faith; modern racists likened Jews to racial pretenders whose white skin only made them more dangerous. Ancient Christians had dreamed of a world without Jews; modern white supremacists embraced a messianic vision of defeating their eternal enemy once and for all. Such was the power of the myth that it even overtook the most elemental American hatred. "Yes, the South has a 'black' problem," declared Unite the Right leader Dr. Michael Hill of the neo-Confederate League of the South. "But our biggest problem—and one even Christian members within our own ranks refuse (or fear) to acknowledge—is the 'Jewry' problem. Indeed, organized Jewry has been at the root of most of the South's troubles for the past 100 years."[36]

Replacement theory took hold just as America was confronting white supremacy anew. After the killing of Trayvon Martin in Florida in 2012, followed by the police killings of Michael Brown in Ferguson and Eric Garner in New York in 2014, Black Lives Matter emerged as a decentralized national movement. This loose activist network advanced a progressive anti-racism that fused calls for racial empowerment with demands for police reform. Black Lives Matter popularized concepts of white privilege and systemic racism, arguing that racial hierarchy was encoded in America's fundamental structures. These critiques ignited fierce, intense, and vital debates about how the past haunts the present and how best to pursue racial justice.

Black Lives Matter's power lay in its simplicity, which also proved to be its vulnerability. The movement's framework of white supremacy as a color-based hierarchy rooted in slavery captured an essential truth about the persistence of racism in the country. Yet this ideological rigidity reduced race to pigmentation, essentializing difference and flattening the complexities of racism. While the movement sometimes expanded to embrace other non-white and indigenous peoples as fellow victims, its equation of white supremacy with white skin obscured the distinct role of antisemitism in America's imagination of power and otherness. The men who descended on Charlottesville came thirsting for battle with Black Lives Matter, yet they spoke obsessively of annihilating their ultimate enemy, the Jews.

SPENCER AND KESSLER's plans for Charlottesville 2.0 were preempted by another racist gathering—a small Klan rally on Saturday, July 8, 2017. That afternoon, sixty marchers, among them Klan members from North Carolina, descended on Justice Park (formerly Jackson Park) bearing signs proclaiming "Communism = Judaism," "Jews are Satan's children," and other antisemitic and anti-Black vitriol.

Unlike the May rally, however, this time the white supremacist rally faced massive resistance. Weeks earlier, Charlottesville's newly formed Black Lives Matter chapter had pledged to provide "community defense," vowing to protect Black bodies from police violence and repel "racists who wanted to invade and take over" the city. More than fifteen hundred people answered their call, chanting "Black lives matter" and "No cops, no KKK, no racist USA."

When the rally ended, chaos exploded. Counterprotesters trailed Klan members to their parking garage, blocking their way. Police in riot gear, wielding automatic weapons, deployed tear gas against the crowd, violating their own use-of-force protocols. Twenty-three arrests followed in the melee.[37]

The July rally ignited local fury, directed not only at the Klan but also at police and city officials. Public rage centered on Mayor Michael Signer, who would become a target for both the racist right and progressive left. A forty-four-year-old white progressive with a Berkeley doctorate, Signer had arrived in Charlottesville with national Democratic ambitions. Though elected to the city council and appointed mayor by his colleagues, his role remained largely ceremonial—Charlottesville's council-manager system vested real power in a professional city administrator. The ambitious politician compensated by courting media attention. After Trump's inauguration, he staged a downtown press conference denouncing the "Muslim ban," and anointing Charlottesville the "capital of the resistance." The city, he told the large crowd, was the "ancestral home of America's deepest principles of religious toleration," and would lead the fight against "religious intolerance and bigotry."[38]

Signer's "resistance" speech also marked one of his first public acknowledgments of his Jewishness. Childhood encounters with antisemitism had driven him toward what he termed "an assimilationist and somewhat self-denying" relationship with his identity. In 2017, passing as an assumed Christian white man still felt safer than being openly Jewish in the South. Over the following months, antisemitic emails and death threats flooded his inbox. One cartoon depicted Robert E. Lee executing him in a gas chamber, a Star of David pinned to his lapel. Other attacks linked him to his African American vice mayor, Wes Bellamy—a rising political star dogged by a history of inflammatory racial, sexist, and homophobic tweets.[39]

In the run-up to the July rally, Signer had turned to the ADL for counsel, and adopted its classic quarantine strategy. "Don't Take the Bait," he urged locals in a Facebook post, encouraging the public "to ignore this ridiculous sideshow and to focus instead on celebrating the values of diversity and tolerance" at a cultural festival scheduled for the same day. The message resonated with some parts of the Charlottesville community, but many local activists reacted with anger. Signer already had one strike against him: He had voted against removing the Lee statue, arguing in city meetings that it was better to contextualize difficult history than to erase it. His July plea to ignore the Klan was heard as an expression of white privilege and liberal condescension in the face of racist danger.[40]

When Signer declared a victory for "both the First Amendment and public safety" after the rally, his comments triggered an even larger backlash. The progressive National Lawyers Guild, the ACLU, and the libertarian Rutherford Institute penned a joint open letter criticizing the "outsized and militaristic governmental response" to peaceful counterprotesters. They decried the "highly militarized law enforcement presence who, prior to any clear and present danger of violence, descended on the scene dressed in riot gear, driving armored vehicles, and carrying weapons typically used only in war zones."[41]

Outrage was compounded by another revelation. City police had visited local activists' homes before the weekend seeking information about counterprotest plans. Though intended for de-escalation, these tactics struck activists as bald intimidation. Black free speech was suppressed while Klan speech was protected by the police.[42]

Throughout late July and early August, these tensions prompted intense debates over free speech, race, and protest that would shape the city's response to Unite the Right. Yet a deafening silence surrounded antisemitism. Despite the death threats targeting Signer as a Jew, some anti-racists condemned him as no better than the Klan. Signer maintained that the white supremacists represented "a last gasp of the bigotry that this country has systematically overcome"—a claim local Black activists dismissed as liberal fantasy, blind to the structural racism Black Lives Matter sought to expose. His appeals to civility and free speech drew accusations from Black intellectuals that he fetishized the First Amendment to amplify racists while silencing anti-racists. "Reactionary voices," argued the author Marc Mazique, had deliberately muddled the meaning of free speech by "reinforcing a system where the voices of those with greater social power—white folks, male-identified folks, straight folks, etc.—are able to maintain that power over those with less power."[43]

The city council meetings over which Signer presided grew ever more heated and confrontational. African American activist Nikuyah Walker, who would succeed Signer as mayor, accused him and a colleague of being "the same kind of white people who closed schools after *Brown v. Board of Education* instead of forcing integration." At least you are "open about the fact that you are overseers," she added. Worse still, in the eyes of some, Signer's talk of antisemitism displaced attention from anti-Black racism. In the struggle over racial justice, there was only one difference worth considering. That dynamic was neatly expressed in a banner unfurled at one city council meeting: "Black Lives Matter. Fuck White Supremacy."[44]

Rachel Schmelkin also felt this dissonance. Born and raised in Cincinnati, the junior rabbi—twenty-eight years old, newly married, short with long brown curly hair and a warm, broad smile—had come to Charlottesville fresh from rabbinical school. She immersed herself in interfaith work through the Clergy Collective, a liberal coalition formed after the Charleston church massacre. She joined a second, more radical group—Congregate Charlottesville, founded by Christian ministers Seth Wispelwey and Brittany Caine-Conley—committed to direct action and nonviolent physical resistance. Together with Black Lives Matter, they also formed Solidarity Cville, a "community defense network of Charlottesville activists acting in solidarity with communities of color locally and globally to fight all forms of white supremacy."[45]

Schmelkin embraced this mission, declaring in one sermon that white Jews must recognize they could "be both oppressed (as Jews who experience antisemitism) and oppressors (as whites who benefit from the color of our skin)." Yet she found herself disturbed when fellow Charlottesville clergy dismissed Jewish vulnerability outright, citing factors such as Jewish wealth.[46]

The dissonance intensified when Reverend Osagyefo Sekou arrived in July. The African American minister, who had led Ferguson protests, came to train activists in peaceful resistance. Throughout the sessions, Sekou explicitly linked anti-racism to Palestinian liberation. When Schmelkin, a progressive Jew who opposed the Israeli occupation, objected to the repeated obsessive focus on Zionism as irrelevant and counterproductive, colleagues justified it by claiming without proof that Charlottesville police used Israeli-manufactured tear gas. For Schmelkin, this first brush with what she termed "antisemitism on the left" proved jarring. But August's looming rally left no time for reckoning.[47]

EVER SINCE OLIVER Wendell Holmes Jr. invoked the analogy of "shouting 'fire' in a crowded theater," American constitutional law has allowed restrictions on speech based on time, place, and manner. In the years after Skokie, the Supreme Court formalized this approach with a three-prong test, requiring that any restriction be "content-neutral," be "narrowly tailored" to serve significant governmental interests, and preserve "ample alternative channels of communication."[48]

Despite the equivocal ruling in *Virginia v. Black*, the libertarian emphasis on speakers' rights dominated the Court through the 2010s. In *Citizens United v. Federal Election Commission* (2010), the Court narrowly ruled that political spending is a form of protected speech, granting corporations First Amendment rights. In *Snyder v. Phelps* (2011), the family of fallen marine Matthew Snyder sued the Westboro Baptist Church for defamation, civil conspiracy, and intentional infliction of emotional distress. The lawsuit challenged the church's practice of picketing military funerals with viciously homophobic messages, blaming service members' deaths on America's tolerance of sin. The justices ultimately ruled 8–1 in favor of the church's right to protest. American jurisprudence had embraced a libertarian absolutism that elevated free speech above nearly all competing values. This doctrine would prove central to the legal battles preceding Unite the Right, and the question of whether speech could be halted to prevent violence.[49]

The August Charlottesville chapter began with Kessler's permit application for a "free speech rally in support of the Lee monument" scheduled for ten o'clock on the morning of Saturday, August 12. He estimated four hundred participants. His intentions were peaceful, Kessler stressed—merely to challenge the double standard that allowed every group except white people, America's "indigenous" founders, to defend their rights.[50]

Like far right ideologues before him, Kessler preached discipline while hinting loudly at the necessity of violence. His enemies included not only Black Lives Matter but Antifa, the decentralized anti-fascist network that had appeared in 2016 to combat right-wing authoritarianism. Though most adherents practiced nonviolence, a radical fringe embraced anarchist ideology and physical confrontation with fascists. Throughout spring and summer 2017, clashes between the far right and Antifa in Berkeley, Portland, and Pikeville, Kentucky, sparked talk among the alt-right of a "Summer of Rage" culminating in the "Battle of Charlottesville."

Kessler, Spencer, and other Unite the Right organizers set up a secret Discord server to coordinate plans for Charlottesville on which they plotted for the "violent battle" they hoped and prayed would come. They gleefully discussed how to outfit their side with "helmets, shields, and body armor" and arm themselves with dual-use weapons. They encouraged attendees to bring "signposts, shields, and other 'self-defense implements,' which could be transformed from 'free speech tools into self-defense weapons should things turn ugly.'" Let Antifa throw the first punch, then they would respond with overwhelming force.[51]

Even without knowledge of these clandestine plans, Charlottesville officials grew anxious as August approached. "If you want to defend the South and Western civilization from the Jew and his dark-skinned allies, be at Charlottesville on 12 August," Michael Hill tweeted on July 24. Andrew Anglin of the *Daily Stormer* promised: "August 12, 2017 is going to be a shot heard around the world. Next stop: Charlottesville, VA. Final stop: Auschwitz." Yet city attorneys maintained that banning the rally based on such rhetoric—or even on potential clashes between extremists—would violate the First Amendment. Without specific evidence of violent intent, just relocating the event from downtown would likely fail in court.[52]

That calculus changed on Monday, August 7, when the ADL issued a press release noting that the Unite the Right event would likely be the "largest public rally by white supremacists in 10 to 15 years." The violent rally in Pikeville had drawn 125 white supremacists; Charlottesville might draw closer to four thousand. The same day, Charlottesville officials notified Kessler that the risk of violence and disorder was too great. If he did not agree to relocate, his permit would be canceled.[53]

Kessler responded with a lawsuit. The Virginia ACLU and the Rutherford Institute took his case—a decision that fractured the civil liberties community. Rodney Smolla, who had argued *Virginia v. Black* for the ACLU, refused to participate. "I won't be a fig leaf for Nazis," declared ACLU Virginia board member Waldo Jaquith, resigning via Twitter. "Don't defend Nazis to allow them to kill people." The rally's true purpose, he explained, was "to draw an audience of opponents who they could violently assault." Unlike in Skokie, Jewish organizations remained conspicuously silent. Only the ADL spoke, repeating its July advisory to avoid staging any counterprotest: "Don't take the bait."[54]

On Friday afternoon, August 11, U.S. District Court Judge Glen Conrad heard oral arguments at an emergency hearing in the federal courthouse in Charlottesville. "This is a clear case of content-based discrimination," ACLU lawyer Victor Glasberg told the court. As proof of the city's bias against his client, he referenced Signer's "resistance" speech, along with a more recent denunciation by the mayor of the "racist and bigoted" rally. "This is an issue of public safety," countered city attorney Craig Brown. The projected crowd size far outstripped police capacity, dramatically increasing the likelihood of public disorder. Comments Kessler had made about "white genocide" and intending to march with or without a permit were threats. Yet Brown could not provide specific evidence of an organized plan for disorder or violence. So, at eight o'clock on Friday evening, the judge issued his ruling: The Saturday rally must proceed as planned.[55]

Ironically, evidence for the city's claim existed—it simply never reached the city lawyers in time. Already in July, Virginia State Police intelligence analysts had gotten wind of a planned Friday night event and prepared a report that reached local police and the University Police Department. For reasons that remained unexplained, no one informed the university administration. Meanwhile, a cluster of progressive activists had penetrated the Unite the Right Discord server. Mistrustful of Signer and the police, however, they declined to share information that might have convinced the court to halt or move the rally. On Friday afternoon, the same hackers also learned of the torchlit march planned for that night at UVA. Relayed to university authorities at 3:00 p.m., it still failed to elicit a response. The authorities ended up treating the Friday night march as a political rally rather than a violent incursion.[56]

Still, the primary cause of the ensuing violence was the actions of the Unite the Right rally organizers. Determined to stage spectacle and sow chaos, they deliberately concealed the nature of the Friday night event until the last possible minute. Their decision to attack student counterprotesters surrounding the Jefferson statue demonstrated their thirst for violence. This was compounded by the university's failure to utilize its own law against open-flame devices on university property.

Nor did anyone recognize that the state law against torch intimidation provided grounds to shut down the event. The law designed to prevent such violence was forgotten, hiding in plain sight. Had it been remembered, the deadly weekend might have ended then and there.[57]

Alan Zimmerman, fifty-nine-year-old congregation president, stood outside the synagogue on Saturday morning surveying the armed men across East Jefferson Street. A private security guard stood by his side while forty congregants prayed inside. As Zimmerman watched, three men in camouflage fatigues bearing semiautomatic rifles took up position on the sidewalk opposite the synagogue building. Had they come to target the Jews or defend them? It was unclear.[58]

Jewish leaders had spent weeks before Charlottesville 2.0 begging the police to assign dedicated security to the synagogue. The march organizers' rhetoric was terrifying, and word of the synagogue's proximity to the Lee statue had circulated online. "We felt like nobody was paying attention," recalled Schmelkin. "It felt like the Charlottesville police department did not understand that the groups that were coming really, really hate Jews, and that we could be a target." On Friday afternoon, the CBI staff had renewed their plea for a police detail one last time. No officer was dispatched.[59]

Left to fend for themselves, the synagogue hired their own security for the day. Services were moved to an earlier time. After receiving an overnight bomb threat, congregants relocated all but one of the Torah scrolls to a secure location. Rabbi Gutherz would spend the day monitoring the situation. Schmelkin attended a clergy sunrise service, but chose not to join the counterprotest at the park, fearing for her personal safety. Instead, she participated in a rotation of clergy maintaining a spiritual vigil at the local Methodist church overlooking Emancipation Park (the renamed Lee Park).[60]

The local activist community also came out in large numbers on Saturday morning. UVA students and members of the Showing Up for Racial Justice collective gathered at McGuffey Park to play drums and sing. A handful of Christian ministers and rabbis came from across the country, including Dr. Cornel West and Rabbi Mordechai Liebling, a cofounder of T'ruah: The Rabbinic Call for Human Rights. Some progressive Jewish activists affiliated with the anti-occupation group IfNotNow were also present. Meanwhile, established Jewish organizations chose not to organize any public response.[61]

While some more militant Antifa protesters were present, they represented only a small fraction of the counterprotesters, vastly outnumbered by peaceful demonstrators and moderate groups. The Redneck Revolt troupe, a ragtag band of anti-racist Southerners who espoused armed self-defense against white supremacists, did show up and appointed themselves guards for the counterprotesters' staging area. The streets also filled with many local Charlottesville residents, drawn by equal parts curiosity and conviction, most of whom simply wanted to stand against hate in their community.[62]

At 9:42 a.m., well before their permitted start time, the first Unite the Right contingent entered Emancipation Park. Led by Identity Evropa's Elliott Kline and bearing the movement's flags, they chanted "You will not replace us" as they crossed the park. More protesters streamed in. Some sported Spencer's preppy uniform—khakis and polos, as if dressed for Saturday golf. Others came equipped for battle: Norse symbols, Confederate and Nazi flags, improvised weapons of PVC pipe and Plexiglas shields. Chris Cantwell arrived with an arsenal—three pistols, two semiautomatic rifles, and a knife.[63]

Then there were the signs and banners. "Jewish Media going down," "ZOG" [Zionist Occupied Government]. "Jewish privilege," "White genocide." Robert "Azzmador" Ray's sign read "Gas the kikes, race war now!" As protesters passed the synagogue, many shouted "Sieg heil" and other antisemitic slogans and chants.[64]

The first signs of disorder broke out at ten o'clock just outside the northeast corner of the park. Unite the Right had refused police escort into the park, leading to chaotic scenes of confrontation with counterprotesters ringing the site. Soon fights broke out on Market Street, near the park's front entrance. As they trudged forward, protesters positioned their flagstaffs as lances, ready to jab at the faces of their opponents who tried to block their path.[65]

Among the police, chaos reigned. Charlottesville officers and state troopers operated on different radio channels with no coordination between commanders. Confusion pervaded every aspect—staging, tactics, riot gear deployment. Many officers lacked basic crowd control equipment. Most damaging was that police had orders to remain behind barricades except in case of "the most serious physical confrontations." The passive approach ignored the crucial fact that Unite the Right leaders intended to provoke confrontation. Detective Tony Newberry grasped this immediately. After speaking with a rally organizer that morning, he turned to his partner: "They do not plan on this going well."[66]

At 11:22 a.m., Andrew Anglin posted a photo of the Unite the Right protesters on Twitter with a caption: "We have an army. This is the beginning of a war." All-out violence had commenced. Beatings proliferated. Law enforcement hadn't vanished from Charlottesville's streets—it had simply abdicated.

At the synagogue, services ended early. Alan Zimmerman and Rabbi Gutherz spirited away the remaining Torah scroll. Then a neo-Nazi entered the courtyard and drew a gun. As congregants fled inside, self-identified Antifa rushed from the neighboring lot, wielding sticks to defend the worshippers and expel the intruder.[67]

At 11:30 a.m., Police Chief Al Thomas declared an unlawful assembly. Police began dispersing rallygoers, but they directed them toward counterprotesters, igniting fresh violence. At noon, Virginia Governor Terry McAuliffe declared a state of emergency. Within ten minutes, the park emptied, but violence trailed the dispersing crowds. A rallygoer punched a counterprotester. Corey Long, a local Black man, sprayed flames from an aerosol can at passing marchers. Richard Wilson Preston, a Baltimore Klan leader, responded by drawing his pistol and firing at Long's feet. State troopers twenty feet away stood idle. Miraculously, no one was shot, although a group of white men set upon a Black man, DeAndre Harris, savagely beating him.

The Unite the Right groups reassembled at McIntire Park, one mile away, where they staged an impromptu rally with a speech from America's leading Klansman David Duke. Spencer crowed to his followers about their "moral victory." The law—and the ACLU—were on their side. The story was not over: "We are going to make Charlottesville the center of the universe." Spencer mocked Signer's name, asking the crowd how to pronounce it. They replied, "Jew! Jew! Jew!"[68]

Meanwhile, three friends—Heather Heyer, Marcus Martin, and Marissa Blair—were walking down a side street from the downtown mall when they heard an engine roar. The crowded street included UVA students Natalie Romero, Devin Willis, and Sophie Schechtman, whose weekend had begun counterprotesting Jefferson's statue the previous night. Before anyone could react, a gray Dodge Challenger plowed into them. The driver, James Alex Fields Jr., had traveled from Ohio to march with Vanguard America. Bodies flew—Romero, Martin, and Schechtman among them. Fields reversed at high speed, backing up for blocks before police stopped him a mile away.

Thirty people lay injured. Heather Heyer was dead. The death toll climbed later that day due to a terrible accident. A state police helicopter responding to a bomb threat crashed, killing troopers Jay Cullen and Berke Bates—another emblem of order consumed by chaos.[69]

For Charlottesville's Jews, the terror was not over. At 3 p.m., a tweet announced plans to gather at the synagogue "to torch these Jewish monsters." Gutherz rushed to check the building. No one came.[70]

The Unite the Right organizers reconvened that evening at a house party to celebrate their victory. In a secretly recorded video, Spencer vowed to return. "We are coming back here like a hundred fucking times," he screamed. "Like this is never over. I win! They fucking lose!" As he raged, his inadequacy was laid bare.

> I am so fucking mad at these people. They don't do this to fucking me. We are going to fucking ritualistically humiliate them . . . Little fucking kikes. They get ruled by people like me. Little fucking octoroons . . . my ancestors fucking enslaved those little pieces of fucking shit. I rule the fucking world. Those pieces of fucking shit get ruled by people like me. They look up and see a face like mine looking down at them. That's how the fucking world works. We are going to destroy this fucking town.[71]

* * *

DIANE D'COSTA WAS correct. Time and space collapsed in Charlottesville. The German 1930s came to twenty-first-century Virginia, European racism grafted onto its American cousin. A riot planned on cloud servers sprang from fantasies of reversing the past. Charlottesville marked a transformed America. The bigotry on display was both sickeningly familiar and terrifyingly new. Hate marched gleefully. Law abandoned order. History had lurched off script.

11

Privileged Hatred

"I thought I should put out a comment as to what's going on in Charlottesville," President Donald Trump told the small press gaggle gathered at the Trump National Golf Club in Bedminster, New Jersey, shortly after three o'clock on Saturday, August 12. "We condemn in the strongest possible terms this egregious display of hatred, bigotry, and violence on many sides, on many sides."[1]

Those three words of moral equivocation set the country on a course of strife. A chorus of condemnation from both left and right erupted over the president's evasion. Seeking damage control, the White House hastily issued a second statement in his name: "Racism is evil. And those who cause violence in its name are criminals and thugs, including the KKK, neo-Nazis, white supremacists, and other hate groups that are repugnant to everything we hold dear as Americans." The White House announced a federal civil rights investigation into the planning of the car attack.[2]

Yet the following Tuesday, the president returned to his original position. "What about the alt-left that came charging at the, as you say, the alt-right?" he asked reporters at Trump Tower in Manhattan. "Do they have any semblance of guilt?" The "fake news" media maligned the Unite the Right protesters. "You had some very bad people in that group, but you also had people that were very fine people, on both sides."[3]

The president's relapse renewed the outrage. Even some fellow Republicans decried the obvious dereliction. "Call evil by its name," declared Utah Senator Orrin Hatch. "My brother didn't give his life fighting Hitler for Nazi ideas." "The #WhiteSupremacy groups will see being assigned only 50% of blame as a win," tweeted Florida Senator Marco Rubio. The president must "describe events in #Charlottesville for what they are, a terror attack by #whitesupremacists."[4]

Naming is an act of power. Words confer dignity or impose harm. Speech registers moral judgment and silence erases. But doublespeak inflicts its own injury on truth. Trump's verbal wink acknowledged hatred only to rationalize it. Each subsequent statement of clarification followed by disavowal only worsened the offense. The yawning chasm between official rhetoric and underlying reality suggested the real message: Liberalism was but a game that the most powerful man in the world refused to play.

Charlottesville marked a new chapter in the story of American antisemitism. The violence was so shocking that even the ACLU announced it would no longer defend white supremacist groups who "carry weapons and are intent on committing violence." It was followed by extreme acts of hatred and violence, including Pittsburgh's 2018 Tree of Life synagogue shooting, the worst episode of anti-Jewish mass violence in American history. Antisemitic conspiracy theories seeped into the political mainstream. The violent spectacle set a dangerous precedent, emboldening extremists and paving the way for the January 6, 2021, insurrection. [5]

Charlottesville also ushered in a new era of politicizing antisemitism. Even as the events of August 2017 revealed the dangers of white supremacy, America struggled to agree on the meaning of that phrase. That disagreement extended to the definition of antisemitism as well, and to its relationship to racism, a tension immediately evident at the University of Virginia in the aftermath of Unite the Right.

On Sunday, August 13, the university's president, Teresa Sullivan, issued a statement on the weekend's events. "As a public institution, we value diversity, inclusion and mutual respect," it read. "The views of many of the groups who converged on Charlottesville are in direct contradiction with this. There were racist, anti-immigrant, homophobic, and misogynistic chants. Such rhetoric is not intended to bring us together; it is intended to drive us apart." The statement went on to disclaim responsibility for the conflagration. As a public institution, the university was required to follow state and federal law regarding the First Amendment rights to free speech, peaceable assembly, and "the public's right to access open spaces." The police had intervened only "once physical altercations among the protesters began to escalate."[6]

The statement made no mention of the fact that the altercations consisted of students squaring off against armed men. More strikingly, it omitted antisemitism. The conspicuous silence highlighted a painful truth: The hatred at the heart of the crisis could not even be named.

> To hurt the Negro and avoid the Jew
> Is the curriculum. In mid-September
> The entering boys, identified by hats,
> Wander in a maze of mannered brick
>   Where boxwood and magnolia brood
>   And columns with imperious stance
>   Like rows of ante-bellum girls
>   Eye them, outlanders.

THE POET KARL Shapiro spent only one semester at the University of Virginia, in the fall of 1932. It was enough to inspire the future Pulitzer Prize winner and U.S. poet laureate to write his famous 1940 poem "University," which harshly skewers the genteel Southern university for its proud traditions of hatred.[7]

Shapiro's verse captured the way in which the university's provincial chauvinism belied its stated ideals of freedom and equality. The vaunted "academical village," designed for students and professors to live as equals alongside one another in an Edenic community, existed only because of wealth gained through plantation slavery; the

Republican ideal of virtuous student self-governance coexisted with segregation.

Within that cocoon of Southern racism, Jews occupied a peculiar place of privileged tolerance and demonstrable exclusion. A school famous for its religious ecumenicalism shunned the fortunate few admitted to its ranks. In Shapiro's day, Jewish students were physically quarantined from Christians, required to live in Jewish-only dorm suites. "Poise is a club," wrote Shapiro in the poem, suggesting the double entendre: an elite preserve and a potential weapon. Perhaps, he asked in a companion poem entitled "Jefferson," the dark forces within the "school of freedom" emanated from its founder, the "noble lord" himself?[8]

"This institution will be based on the illimitable freedom of the human mind," wrote Jefferson in 1820, a year after the university's establishment. "For here we are not afraid to follow truth wherever it may lead, nor to tolerate any error so long as reason is left free to combat it." That powerful Enlightenment vision was to set the new school on an exalted path of universal liberty and unfettered inquiry. Yet the man behind the Declaration of Independence could not follow his own words to their most obvious conclusion. The same pen that wrote of "illimitable freedom" and following "truth wherever it may lead" also wrote of Black Americans as biologically inferior by nature, invoking "the real distinctions which nature has made" to justify enslaving those whose labor built his university. Jefferson decried slavery as a "moral depravity" even as he designed his academical village to be maintained by it—reason left free to combat every error except the one that sustained his world.[9]

Contradictions also marked Jefferson's relationship to Jews and Judaism. The author of Virginia's 1786 *Statute for Religious Freedom* condemned the fact that a people whose religion formed "the parent and bases of all those of Christendom" was "singled out by all of them for persecution and oppression." He proudly declared that the University of Virginia would "set the example of ceasing to violate the rights of conscience by any injunctions on the different sects respecting their religion." Unlike Harvard, Yale, and William and Mary, Virginia was to have no Christian church at its center, but instead a library housed in a rotunda inspired by the Roman Pantheon—knowledge, not doctrine, as the institution's sacred heart.[10]

Even as Jefferson championed religious liberty in principle, however, his private writings revealed a darker current of thinking about Jews. He disparaged Jewish beliefs as morally corrupt products of "a bloodthirsty race, as cruel and remorseless" as their vengeful Old Testament God, and he lambasted Jewish tribalism and misanthropy. Whereas he saw the seeds of universal reason in Christianity, he treated Judaism as an ancient relic in need of moral repair in line with the anti-Jewish tropes of Christian supersessionism. In this respect, Jefferson was not unlike his Enlightenment contemporaries, including the philosopher Immanuel Kant, who counted Jews among his friends and envisioned a single ethical standard for all humanity while calling for the "euthanasia of Judaism" in order to achieve a truly "pure moral religion."[11]

The tension between universal reason and human hierarchy passed into the culture of the University of Virginia. Its long tradition of scientific racism began with the third professor appointed to the faculty in 1837, Dr. James L. Cabell, a pioneering American physician and public health expert who invented antiseptic surgery and modern sanitation. As a hugely influential faculty leader, he also invoked Lamarckian evolution to defend both slavery and Christian salvation. He and his colleagues transformed the university from a secular institution to a nonsectarian one—by which they meant generically Christian, including all Protestant and Catholic denominations, rather than genuinely inclusive of non-Christian faiths. A Christian chaplain was appointed annually, and Cabell helped persuade his colleagues to build a chapel on the grounds to correct Jefferson's error and counter the spirit of "paganism." Over five decades, Cabell instructed the sons of white Protestant planter aristocrats in the ways of Southern honor and tradition.[12]

That blend of race and religion led to intense hostility toward Jewish students and faculty. In 1841, the legendary mathematician James Joseph Sylvester arrived from England to become the first Jewish professor appointed at any American university. He lasted only four months, resigning after experiencing physical threats and anti-Jewish slurs. It would be another eighty years before another Jewish professor was hired.[13]

The Civil War opened a new window of acceptance for a generation of native-born Southern Jews willing to embrace the Confederate cause. Among them was Gratz Cohen of Savannah, the university's first Jewish student. He enrolled in 1862 but did not live to graduate, dying on the battlefield at age twenty. In his wake followed a limited number of Southern Jewish students who embraced the ideology of white supremacy and the Lost Cause. That investment in whiteness was captured in Moses Ezekiel's 1910 *Thomas Jefferson* statue at the Rotunda, which included allegorical figures of "Liberty, Justice, Human Freedom, and Religious Freedom," the last illustrated through a list of various divine names, including "God-Jehovah," Brahma, Ra, Allah, and Zeus.[14]

As the twentieth century dawned, however, white supremacy redefined itself with a focus on Anglo-Saxonism and a newly rigid, legalized racial hierarchy in which Jews in the South were recast as non-white. Cabell's handpicked successor, Professor Paul Barringer, who served as the university's de facto president from 1895 to 1903, championed the pseudoscientific theory of white "pure Saxon blood" as the foundation for a new American racial myth. This came at the same moment as the rise of the one-drop rule that defined racial Blackness in terms of an immutable characteristic that overrode whiteness. Thanks to Barringer's efforts, the school grew into a major center for the racial eugenics movement. He and his peers grudgingly accepted Jews as a "dusky, primitive" subset of inferior whites in a WASP-led order in which Blacks remained explicitly excluded and reviled.[15]

In the 1920s and 1930s, the prominent professors Ivey Foreman Lewis and Harvey Jordan helped develop Virginia's sterilization policies and racial purity laws. First as dean of students and then dean of arts and sciences from 1946 to 1953, Lewis worried nearly as much about Jewish racial "clannishness" and immorality as he did about Black inferiority. Until the 1950s, he tracked applicants in terms of three categories: "Virginians, non-Virginians, and Hebrews," and he promoted admissions quotas to restrict Jewish enrollment. This policy mirrored the antisemitic quotas common at elite universities before 1950.[16]

The situation began to change after World War II as the university slowly grew from a Southern bastion into a national institution. The GI Bill expanded higher education access, enabling a new generation of students to enter elite universities in unprecedented numbers. Virginia particularly attracted Jewish men from across the country who were still rejected by elite northeastern schools. A handful of new Jewish faculty also arrived in the early postwar years, among them the first Jewish law professor, Mortimer Caplin, a beloved figure at the school who led the effort to admit Gregory Swanson, the first African American student, in 1950.

Still, the spirit of the Old Confederacy lived on. Football games featured the Confederate flag and the band's version of "Dixie." The newly opened Hillel House for Jewish students faced antisemitic backlash after it hosted civil rights meetings beginning in 1945. After *Brown v. Board of Education*, the NAACP selected Charlottesville as one of the communities where it would work to implement school integration. The town responded by launching a campaign of "massive resistance," in which white families boycotted public schools in protest. Noted segregationist John Kasper blamed local Jews and communists for conspiring with "Nigras" to dismantle "white-organized Christian civilization" and "destroy the Anglo-Saxon in Charlottesville." A rash of antisemitic vandalism in the town and at the university in 1960 prompted the city council to pass the first municipal law in Virginia banning the defacement of religious buildings, a precursor to the 1983 state law.[17]

The late 1960s heralded a new era as civil rights and anti-war protests rocked the university. The school's student population tripled in size from 1960 to 1975, in part as a result of the admission of women from 1970. Black enrollment rose across the first half of that decade, reaching five hundred students, accounting for just over 3 percent of all students. Even as a younger generation of professors brought liberal sensibilities to the university and Black students led racial justice campaigns, the old ways persisted. The fraternity system, the heart of the school's social world, remained segregated by race and religion. In 1975 the school made national headlines when it was revealed that the president and some 150 other professors and administrators belonged to the

Farmington Country Club, which excluded Black and Jewish members and guests.[18]

Jewish life in Charlottesville and at UVA began to grow in tandem during the 1980s and 1990s. Congregation Beth Israel, the oldest continuously running synagogue in Virginia, hired its first full-time rabbi in 1979 and grew into a community of hundreds of families with a thriving preschool. By the 2000s the university featured a renewed Hillel program, a Chabad House, and a significant Jewish studies program. Jewish students flocked to the school from across the country, drawn by its academic reputation and vibrant Jewish community. By 2017 the law school that had once barred women now had a Jewish woman as its dean.

Despite these changes, Jewish students and faculty still inhabited a Christian-dominated culture, experiencing ongoing neglect and occasional overt antisemitic acts. The school touted its inclusiveness yet deferred to Christianity at every turn. On Friday nights the football team prayed with their own personal Christian chaplain. Jewish women reported widespread gendered antisemitism throughout the fraternity and sorority system. These slights and erasures were only the visible expressions of what many privately described as a deeper dynamic of quiet sidelining. "What was always so challenging at UVA for me was the sense that being Jewish, and in particular being an observant Jew, made one an outsider, a problem," recalled Professor Vanessa Ochs, rabbi and founder of the UVA Jewish studies program. The exclusion was subtle but unmistakable, yet those who made "any effort to name it aloud" risked being dismissed as paranoid.[19]

None of these indignities matched the African American experience at UVA, which ranged from patterns of discrimination to cases of police brutality. Decades after integration, racism continued to roil UVA in profound ways. To address ongoing problems of racial inequality, the university launched its Office of Diversity and Equity in 2005. In 2013 the President's Commission on Slavery and the University began to identify and memorialize sites of slave life and labor, including newly uncovered Black cemeteries located just steps from the new South Lawn humanities building. The eugenics tradition finally began to be openly addressed with the renaming of buildings that had been dedicated to the leading racist professors.[20]

What was missing from this process was any reckoning with the function of antisemitism in the creation and maintenance of white supremacy. In this regard, UVA was symptomatic of a larger trend at the time at universities and beyond. The point was powerfully made in a landmark essay, "Skin in the Game," by the leading African American civil rights activist Eric Ward, published in June 2017. Years of studying white racial extremists had led Ward to a key realization about race and religion in America. Far from being a special case, antisemitism was "integral to the architecture of American racism." Precisely because of their white skin and Jewish religion, Jews were ascribed the status of "the absolute other, the driving force of white dispossession." Ward cautioned against dismissing antisemitism as ancillary to the struggle for Black equality and freedom. On the contrary, this "particular and potent form of racism" is "so central to White supremacy," he wrote, that Black people will "not win our freedom without tearing it down."[21]

Ward's words spoke to the University of Virginia's incomplete reckoning with white supremacy. The Unite the Right rally offered a moment to reexamine the entangled histories of racism and antisemitism together. Instead, antisemitism was once again passed over in silence.

ON WEDNESDAY EVENING, August 16, four days after the Unite the Right rally, several thousand students and community members gathered to march across the Lawn with candles. When they reached the steps of the Rotunda, they held up their lights as they joined in song. The strains of Black spirituals and the unofficial UVA anthem, "The Good Ole Song," carried hopefully into the night.

Leading the procession was Truman Brody-Boyd, a third-year student from Williamsburg, Virginia. Tall and athletic, with short black hair, the champion handball player was visibly Jewish, wearing a yarmulke. Brody-Boyd had experienced firsthand the terror of white supremacists invading Grounds (the UVA moniker for the core campus area surrounding the Academical Village). In his role as a resident adviser, he had spent the weekend helping frightened freshmen move in and find safety. Now he walked side by side with two Black student leaders, Bryanna Miller and Wes Gobar, in what felt to him like a "true moment of unity." Fittingly for a school steeped in a culture of student self-governance and leadership, these three undergraduates led the way at the rally, embodying a powerful repudiation of the hatred that had swept across the same space days earlier.[22]

The following Monday brought another rally, the March to Reclaim Our Grounds, which focused on concrete repair. Brody-Boyd joined several hundred students who marched to the Jefferson statue. The marchers carried the banner from the counterprotest on Friday, August 11, with some of the injured at the lead. Once there, the activists unveiled a ten-point list of steps for how to respond to white supremacy at the school.

The roster of demands centered on uprooting the university's legacies of slavery and segregation. It called for boosting the number of African American undergraduates from just over 6 percent to nearly 20 percent to match the state demographics and hiring more faculty from groups that were "underrepresented." They insisted that "UVA's historical landscape must be balanced." To do so required the removal of Confederate plaques on the Rotunda, the renaming of buildings "named after prominent white supremacists, eugenicists, or slaveholders," and the recontextualization of the Jefferson statue to explain its role "as an emblem of white supremacy." The activists made no mention of antisemitism or the historical Jewish marginalization at the university [23]

The student silence on antisemitism mirrored the university administration's reluctance to address the issue. Faculty in the Jewish studies program felt the official silence most acutely. We were targeted in the August attack, recalled Ochs, and yet we received no "public acknowledgment" or assistance afterward. Overwhelmed by caring for traumatized students and colleagues while teaching to the moment, they received no help. "We just got silence, and that silence from the university persisted, no matter what we requested." Even as we support programs to combat racism, homophobia, and anti-immigrant sentiments," lamented her colleague Gabriel Finder, we "stand alone when it comes to denouncing antisemitism." The bitter irony cut deep: A university community that recognized many forms of hatred ignored one that had long helped construct the hierarchies it sought to dismantle.[24]

Brody-Boyd, who became the Jewish student representative to the March to Reclaim Our Grounds coalition, reported the same experience. Students waited in vain for President Sullivan to appear at one of Hillel's weekly Friday night Shabbat dinners. Among his fellow activists, he recalled that "the virulent, aggressive, violent antisemitism of the day was very quickly drowned out by the racist overtures and the anti-Black hate that was going on as well." While he supported the demands for institutional reforms, Brody-Boyd grew tired of reminding his peers at meeting after meeting that Jewish students had fled the Lawn in terror just weeks before.[25]

Awkward conversations soon yielded to outright conflict. In November, the Jewish Leadership Council, Hillel's student self-governance body, applied to join the Minority Rights Coalition, the umbrella group for all minority student communities. Despite its charter's commitment to representing all minority groups and "creating a university community that truly embraces diversity in all its forms," MRC leadership balked at admitting the JLC. The problem was the JLC's affiliation with Hoos for Israel, a pro-Israel educational organization. Already on edge from the Trump administration's travel ban, Muslim students within the MRC had experienced Islamophobic incidents, including alt-right hate flyers posted on the September 11 anniversary. They saw pro-Israel advocacy as threatening.[26]

Many MRC leaders were also deeply committed to the Palestinian cause, viewing it as part of building anti-racist coalitions among communities of color. They believed diversity should be judged by power dynamics, not mere inclusion. "UVA must, without hesitation, name and denounce white supremacy in all of its insidious forms," MRC Vice President for Advocacy Raiya Al-Nsour declared after the March to Reclaim Our Grounds. True diversity required considering how race, gender, religion, and other factors intersected with power, both locally and globally. Oppression was structural; opposing it was a yes-or-no proposition. By these standards, affiliation with a pro-Israel group represented political support for an unjust regime, placing the Jewish student community on the wrong side of a global justice issue.[27]

The JLC countered that most of its constituent organizations were apolitical; even Hoos for Israel avoided specific ideologies, focusing on "open dialogue about tough topics," given the Jewish community's diverse views on Israel. Moreover, the group's president was Brody-Boyd himself, a recognized progressive leader on minority issues. "They knew my values in every way possible," he recalled, and they still said, "'You're not a minority . . . because we don't find some part of you acceptable.' That was really, really hurtful."[28]

The dispute fundamentally centered on competing definitions of solidarity. Jewish student leaders argued that their Israel engagement was no different from other member groups' heritage advocacy—after all, the Muslim Student Association regularly organized Palestine- and Kashmir-related cultural and charity events. For these students, internal Jewish debates over Zionist politics took a back seat to a basic moral commitment to Israel. Singling out a Jewish group, especially during a moment of profound vulnerability, struck them as a clear double standard.

MRC representatives, however, viewed claims of apolitical Israel engagement as disingenuous; any pro-Israel orientation was inherently political and therefore incompatible with the coalition's mission. Jewish students countered by charging MRC leaders with failing to recognize antisemitism as part of the very structural racism they opposed. These blind spots on both sides prevented any meaningful understanding.[29]

Days before the vote on the JLC's membership bid, an incident on campus brought the tension behind the scenes out into the open. On February 22, the UVA Hillel, Hoos for Israel, and CavPac, the local AIPAC affiliate, co-sponsored an event billed as Building Bridges, which brought four Israel Defense Force reserve soldiers to Grounds in the spirit of "open dialogue about the complex issues facing our students." Despite the fact that the tour's sponsor was an aggressively partisan Israeli organization, Reservists on Duty, the organizers promised that the event would provide an unrestricted opportunity for the speakers to respond to "tough questions from the University community." We felt then, recalled Brody-

Boyd, "that it's better to have these conversations in the same room, right? Instead of a tweet war, or a statement war, or an awkward passing by in between classes, or, like, two tables across from each other on the South Lawn." They proposed dialogue about points of division.[30]

In one sense, the event succeeded. Student leaders from the Black Student Alliance and Muslim Student Association showed up for over two hours of frank, difficult conversation about the Israeli-Palestinian conflict. They questioned the speakers—three Jewish Israelis and one Druze Israeli—about their military service and Palestinian rights. Fifteen minutes in, however, a group of protesters entered the room waving Palestinian and anarchist flags. Wielding a megaphone, they chanted in call and response, "Fight the power, turn the tide, end Israeli apartheid." Brody-Boyd stood up and invited them to stay and engage in dialogue. He was told, "We will not dialogue with racists." It took a call to the campus police to get the group to leave the building. Outside, they continued their chants for the duration of the meeting.[31]

What followed offered a preview of the disputes that would consume American campuses in the aftermath of October 7, 2023. Brody-Boyd found the protest offensive and discriminatory. Other Jewish students likened it to verbal assault. "I felt very threatened," explained sophomore Ben Borenstein. "It was probably the most afraid that I've been in a situation at U.Va." This is the same "anti-Israel hate movement" that I experienced as an undergraduate at Berkeley, wrote law student Baruch Nutovic. These activists are "trying to drive a wedge between Jews and other minorities, suggesting that Jews are not a minority group."[32]

Dean of students Allen Groves issued his own strong denunciation, siding with the Jewish student groups. "Freedom of expression, freedom of association, and freedom of religion are all critical tenets of our diverse community of scholars," he wrote in an email to all undergraduates. But we must "reject the 'heckler's veto' of shouting down those with whom we may disagree." The aggressive interruption violated the free speech rights of the organizers—and university rules—and such protest "runs counter to our important shared values of respect and intellectual inquiry, and should be firmly rejected."[33]

Palestinian students and their supporters were equally adamant that pro-Palestinian activists had the right to protest a racist propaganda event. "The real threat to academic freedom," wrote Students for Peace and Justice in Palestine, "is not students and community members exercising their right to peacefully protest a public meeting, but rather those who would acquiesce to its destruction elsewhere in the name of a false objectivity." They acknowledged that "many students in attendance felt threatened" but countered by asking "Mr. Groves, the Brody Center, and the student body to consider how the Palestinian population of UVA might feel when IDF members are on grounds." For them, the presence of Israeli soldiers on campus constituted its own form of threat—one that justified their disruption as legitimate protest rather than suppression of speech.[34]

A similarly hostile response to Groves's statement came from a collection of student groups led by the Graduate Student Coalition for Liberation, including the Young Democratic Socialists of America and UVA Students United Against White Supremacy, the same organization that had counterprotested the torchlit march on Friday, August 11. "Your letter presented a certain group of students robbing another group of students of their right to free speech, categorically demoting protest below a vague idea of engagement. However, we believe that protest is a form of political engagement." They went on to explain that the charge of antisemitism, as they perceived it, was woefully misplaced and slanderous. "As a multi-racial, multi-ethnic, and multi-denominational group that includes pro-Palestine Jewish and non-Jewish people alike," they wrote, "we sympathize, and many of us empathize, with the fear that many Jewish students feel after the horrific events of this past summer." But not all Jewish people support the Israeli occupation, "and we find your subtle equation of anti-semitism and pro-Palestinian rights to be morally reprehensible."[35]

To the JLC leaders, free speech meant open dialogue, not hostile intimidation bordering on hate speech. The tactics and rhetoric were offensive and discriminatory, causing Jewish students fear. To the pro-Palestinian advocates, who included Jewish victims of the August 12 car attack, free speech was being selectively defined on political grounds.

The perceived insinuation of antisemitism—though not specifically made by the dean or the Hillel leaders—amounted to a gross libel. Their position was summed up by reference to a sign displayed at the event by one of the protesters: "Anti-colonial, not anti-semitic, solidarity with Palestine." Moreover, the claim that the event was an apolitical discussion rang false, given that it involved foreign soldiers and a pro-Israel political advocacy organization.[36]

A week after the event, the MRC leadership voted against JLC membership. "The MRC fully affirms that Jewish students at UVA comprise an underrepresented minority community that faces real threats of discrimination and that deserves coalitional support," they wrote. Yet the Hoos for Israel affiliation left MRC members feeling "concerned and unsettled." The MRC proposed various alternative arrangements to equal membership amounting to an honorary status or a carve-out to avoid the Hoos for Israel affiliation.[37]

The decision angered Jewish student leaders. "To be Jewish, on this campus and in this country," wrote the JLC in response, "is to be a minority population." Now we are being asked to accept unequal status and lesser respect compared to "other minority populations." While acknowledging the controversy and deep impact on all sides of the Israeli-Palestinian conflict, they insisted "we cannot and will not apologize for our right to support a Jewish homeland." To these students, the Israel litmus test felt discriminatory. Aware of the sensitivity, the MRC leaders privately pleaded with Brody-Boyd and other Jewish students. "Please do not say that this was antisemitism," he recalled being told repeatedly. After much internal debate, they chose not to file a formal complaint, opting for strategic diplomacy instead.[38]

Yet silence had its limits. "I am appalled," Diane D'Costa wrote in the *Cavalier Daily*. "As both a person of color and a Jewish student, I've lived with microaggressions, stereotypes and discrimination my entire life, yet with the trauma of this fall I've never felt more acutely aware of and threatened because of my identity." The decision to deny a Jewish group membership because of its "openly Pro-Israel stance" not only violated the student organization's own bylaws but also mocked the very principles of diversity and dialogue. “Today, Jewish students at the University are in a hard place—the same organization that aims to advocate for minority students and diversity does not value their identity and contribution enough to allow them full membership.”[39]

From an overlooked component of the campus response to white supremacy, Jews had finally entered the center of the frame. In Charlottesville, as in the rest of the country, that entrance would prompt a showdown over the very definition of antisemitism—and its place in the question of Israel/Palestine.[40]

As long as there has been Zionism there has been anti-Zionism, and for just as long debates have flourished about anti-Zionism's relationship to antisemitism. Early anti-Zionists, Jewish and non-Jewish, opposed Zionism for a variety of reasons, both political and theological, pragmatic and philosophical, none of which were necessarily antisemitic. Yet if anti-Zionism was never—and still is not—an intrinsically antisemitic position, it also has always encompassed more than mere opposition to Zionism's tenets and practices. Rather, anti-Zionism emerged from a constellation of political and religious movements—from ultra-Orthodox Judaism to Palestinian nationalism to Bolshevik socialism—each of which defined itself, in part, by opposing the Jewish nationalist project as its ideological other.[41]

Anti-Zionism, along with Zionism, also evolved across the twentieth and twenty-first centuries in response to the forces of history. After 1917, Jewish and non-Jewish anti-Zionists opposed the British Mandate as an unjust violation of the Palestinian right to national self-determination. Paradoxically, while the Soviet Union became the first state to officially ban antisemitism, it simultaneously developed a coded language in which “Zionist” served as a thinly veiled slur for the imagined Jewish enemies of the communist regime. Plucked out of its context in the contest for Palestine, “Zionist” expanded across both the global left and right, and within the Muslim and Arab Middle East, as a convenient antisemitic euphemism for “Jew.”

The creation of the State of Israel in 1948 and the Palestinian Nakba profoundly exacerbated tensions in the Middle East and beyond, infusing anti-Zionism with the quality of pan-Arab ideology against an enemy state allied with the European colonial powers. The same moment also unleashed a new phenomenon of antisemitic proxy attacks that collapsed the distinction between Jews and Israel, particularly in Arab and Muslim states where some Jews were stigmatized as a potential fifth column or virtual citizens of Israel unless they explicitly renounced any ties to Zionism. In the decades that followed, this pattern transformed synagogues and Jewish institutions around the globe into targets for antisemitic violence regardless of their ties to the State of Israel.

As the international human rights movement spread in the 1950s and 1960s, it focused attention on the plight of Palestinian refugees and Israeli treatment of its Arab citizens. This new human rights arena also became a political battleground where Israel and its allies clashed with Arab and Soviet representatives over the boundary between anti-Zionism and antisemitism. In the context of the Cold War and decolonization, Soviet and Arab diplomats mixed legitimate criticism with antisemitic rhetoric couched as principled anti-Zionism, while often asserting their steadfast opposition to antisemitism. In response, Israel and Jewish groups often dismissed all human rights concerns as veiled antisemitism. Israel's critics also invoked Nazi comparisons, a pattern that began in the Cold War, and the more they did so, the more even liberal Jewish organizations retreated from engaging with Palestinian grievances—each side's excesses reinforcing the other's intransigence.[42]

This pattern only intensified after the 1967 Six-Day War. Israel defeated several combined Arab state armies and then pressed on to conquer the West Bank, Gaza, and East Jerusalem. That brought 1.5 million stateless Palestinians under its rule, compounding the dispossession of 1948. In the absence of peace negotiations, Israel's occupation—originally characterized by Israeli authorities as temporary—gradually became permanent. This indefinite occupation, which denied Palestinians both Israeli citizenship and national self-determination, generated profound ethical and political challenges for Jews worldwide. It also coincided with a pattern of terrorist attacks by some Palestinian militant groups against both diaspora Jews and Israeli civilians.

During the 1970s, the UN Decade for the Elimination of Racism, a global campaign linked Zionism to South African racial apartheid, culminating in the 1975 UN General Assembly resolution GA 3379 declaring "Zionism is a form of racism and racial discrimination." The "Zionism is racism" resolution came to be a litmus test in the debates over anti-Zionism and antisemitism. To the Palestinian world and its supporters in the global human rights community, the assertion marked a clear expression of anti-colonial resistance and opposition to racism, given the ongoing Israeli negation of Palestinian nationhood and two-tiered legal system for Jews and non-Jews in the Occupied Territories.[43]

To pro-Israel critics, "Zionism is racism" represented a perverse example of antisemitic logic and bias overtaking the United Nations. Inverting the moral compass, Jewish victims had been recast as the oppressors, and their liberation movement slandered as the quintessence of hatred. Jewish civil rights groups increasingly argued that anti-Zionism on the global left had evolved into a "new antisemitism," demonizing the State of Israel with the same tropes once applied to Jews. In 1990, the American Jewish Committee declared that anti-Zionism was merely "sophisticated antisemitism" by another name. The following year the UN General Assembly voted to revoke the 1975 resolution.[44]

The year 2001 marked a turning point in the evolution of antisemitism and anti-Zionism. Against the backdrop of the collapsed Oslo Accords and the Second Intifada, the UN World Conference Against Racism, Racial Discrimination, Xenophobia and Related Intolerance was convened in Durban, South Africa, in late August and early September. Some American and Israeli participants reported widespread antisemitic rhetoric and hostility culminating in the renewal of the Zionism-as-racism argument. In their view, the global movement against racism had become fundamentally antisemitic.

Palestinian activists rejected this charge, heralding the Durban Conference as a breakthrough in mobilizing global civil society in support of Palestinian rights. The event paved the way for the Palestinian Boycott, Divestment, Sanctions movement, which aimed to use a nonviolent academic, cultural, and economic campaign similar to the anti-apartheid campaign to end the Israeli occupation, secure the Palestinian right of return, and achieve equal rights for Palestinian citizens of Israel. By rejecting normalization of the Israeli regime, BDS organizers openly sought to delegitimize Israel and Zionism, but insisted that their intentions were wholly free of antisemitism. Many Jewish leaders dismissed that rhetoric as a ruse by which BDS activists camouflaged their campaign to eradicate Israel.

The September 11 terror attacks occurred just three days after the Durban conference ended, transforming American society and its relationship to Muslims and the Muslim world. In the years that followed, both Islamophobia and global antisemitism intensified dramatically. High-profile terror attacks around the world coincided with a significant uptick in documented incidents throughout Europe. In response to this surge—particularly incidents stemming from Middle East–related hostilities—the European Union launched an initiative to develop an informal definition of antisemitism that would help law enforcement better recognize and categorize antisemitic crimes.[45]

In 2016, the International Holocaust Remembrance Alliance, an intergovernmental taskforce, adopted the Working Definition of Antisemitism as a nonlegally binding standard: "Antisemitism is a certain perception of Jews, which may be expressed as hatred toward Jews. Rhetorical and physical manifestations of antisemitism are directed toward Jewish or non-Jewish individuals and/or their property, toward Jewish community institutions and religious facilities."

That terse, elliptical formulation was accompanied by a short list of examples that focused heavily on anti-Israel beliefs and statements, among them "the targeting of the state of Israel, conceived as a Jewish collectivity" through "denying the Jewish people their right to self-determination, e.g., by claiming that the existence of a State of Israel is a racist endeavor" and comparing "contemporary Israeli policy to that of the Nazis," and using "symbols and images associated with classic antisemitism . . . to characterize Israel or Israelis."[46]

Crucially, the IHRA definition also said that "applying double standards" to Israel "by requiring of it a behavior not expected or demanded of any other democratic nation" constituted antisemitism. However, the definition included a major caveat: that "criticism of Israel similar to that leveled against any other country cannot be regarded as antisemitic." That qualifier meant that in theory the definition of antisemitism still depended on context.[47]

At the same time, 9/11 marked a shift to a conservative jurisprudence of anti-antisemitism. In 2004, the Bush administration lawyer Kenneth Marcus introduced a new policy for the Office of Civil Rights at the Department of Education. To protect Jewish students from antisemitism masked as political speech, henceforth, Title VI of the Civil Rights Act of 1964, which prohibited discrimination in federally funded schools and universities, would be applied to cases of "anti-Zionism as racism." Marcus had long championed a move of American Jews and Blacks to the Republican Party and chaired the Washington, DC, chapter of a Republican pro-Israel PAC. He had attacked affirmative action in higher education as an unconstitutional legacy of historical anti-Jewish quotas. Now he proposed to offer Jewish students more protection from discrimination, particularly hate speech, through using civil rights laws.[48]

Marcus's key strategy was to argue that Title VI of the 1964 Civil Rights Act could protect Jewish students from campus antisemitism. Title VI requires universities receiving federal funding to prevent discrimination based on "race, color, or national origin," but notably exempts religion from its protections. To work around this limitation, Marcus argued that Jews should be considered both a racialized group and a national origin group. As he explained: "Jewish students are protected from discrimination based on their ethnic or ancestral background. This is because Jewish students are targeted not only based on their actual religious practices or on tenets of the Jewish religion, but also for their perceived ethnic, racial, or ancestral identity."[49]

Marcus's move flipped the conservative position from opposing antidiscrimination law as a violation of the First Amendment, an intrusion of government regulation on business, and an exacerbation of racial divisions into embracing it, albeit highly selectively. More striking, his model relied on the progressive theories associated with feminist and intersectional legal scholarship. To Marcus, this new approach was a way to offer equal protection and stop "anti-Semitic harassment" without violating the First Amendment. "Although federal anti-discrimination law is a rather blunt instrument for addressing such matters," he explained, "it can be an effective one when properly utilized."[50]

In response, several civil rights groups, among them the Southern Poverty Law Center, the Lawyers' Committee for Human Rights, the NAACP, and the American-Arab Anti-Discrimination Committee, denounced Marcus for hijacking anti-discrimination law to chill free speech. Notably, only one Jewish group, the progressive National Council of Jewish Women, joined this chorus of critique. The AJC and ADL abstained from entering the debate, while the American Jewish Congress and the Zionist Organization of America, an ultra-conservative body, endorsed the change. That same year, the ZOA filed the first, unsuccessful Title VI complaint on behalf of a student.[51]

To his critics, Marcus pointed out that this was no different from analogous issues that arose "in race, ethnicity, sex, or disability cases." Any claim of harassment triggered the same problem of civil rights clashing with free expression. The only difference in the case of antisemitism was the willful refusal of critics to acknowledge it, which he took as evidence of a thinly concealed antisemitic character. "Those who would defend the recent outbreak of campus anti-Semitism" on free speech grounds "are rather like the man who shouts, 'First Amendment!' in a burning building."[52]

These initiatives would largely lie dormant during the remainder of the Bush administration and the eight years of the Obama presidency. Marcus spent that time writing two books on the subject and creating the Louis Brandeis Center for Human Rights to drive litigation related to anti-Zionism as racism. In October 2017 he returned to his former government role as assistant secretary of education for civil rights and head of the Department of Education's Office of Civil Rights. That year, the ADL reported its single largest annual increase in antisemitic incidents since 1979. Roughly 10 percent occurred on college campuses, a nearly 90 percent increase from the year before.

The vast majority of these incidents—which were self-reported by victims and relied in many cases on victims' perceptions of antisemitic intent—involved harassment or property vandalism. Only a small fraction involved physical violence.[53]

The pattern changed dramatically in October 2018 when a white supremacist attacked Pittsburgh's Tree of Life synagogue, killing eleven people and injuring several others. The gunman was motivated by antisemitic "replacement theory." Six months later, in April 2019, another deadly shooting targeted the Chabad synagogue in Poway, California.

The Trump White House was repeatedly accused of using antisemitic tropes and refusing to disavow support from far right groups. Months before the Charlottesville attack, Trump drew strong criticism from Jewish organizations for a presidential statement on International Holocaust Remembrance Day that neglected to mention Jewish victims. The policy response to the two synagogue shootings finally came in December 2019, when Trump issued his "Executive Order on Combating Anti-Semitism." The order, however, concentrated almost exclusively on combating left-wing anti-Zionist activism on college campuses rather than addressing far right violence. The text reaffirmed Title VI's policy relevance and mandated government use of the IHRA working definition."[54]

Widespread indignation ensued, from both liberal and progressive quarters of Jewish America. Kenneth Stern, a principal drafter of the IHRA definition, denounced the move as a political weaponization of antisemitism. "If you think this isn't about suppressing political speech, contemplate a parallel," he wrote. "There's no definition of anti-black racism that has the force of law when evaluating a Title VI case. If you were to craft one, would you include opposition to affirmative action? Opposing removal of Confederate statues?"[55]

Stern's examples were not incidental. They reflected a liberal American Jewish vision of civil rights in which Blacks and Jews remained allied as two classic minorities who shared a common struggle against white supremacy. However, both conservatives and progressives had begun to separate racism from antisemitism in their approaches to racial justice. Marcus argued that the new legal policies would end the double standard by which left-wing antisemitic speech received more tolerance than hate speech targeting other campus minorities. Yet conservative doctrine of anti-antisemitism exceptionalized antisemitism under the guise of treating it equally.

Meanwhile, progressive anti-racists focused on white supremacy as the root evil requiring eradication from American life. But their framework, which reduced racism to a color binary, relegated antisemitism to an ancillary prejudice. Some went further, too, likening Zionism to a form of white supremacy. The consequences of divergent approaches would soon become apparent, beginning in Virginia.

IN MID-SEPTEMBER 2020, Hira Azher, a Pakistani American student and founder of a Muslim organization, posted a sign on her Lawn room door that read "Fuck UVA. UVA Operating Cost—KKKOPS-Genocide-Slavery-Disability-Black—Brown Life." The sign signified her righteous anger. "It is undeniable that white supremacy and settler-colonialism are foundational to the University of Virginia," she explained in a *Cavalier Daily* op-ed, and "the University and the Lawn have always been, and will continue to function as, a space for whiteness in which I will never be fully welcomed." The same held true when "any Black person, Indigenous person or person of color enters Grounds."[56]

Azher's defiant act of protest prompted Bert Ellis, a 1975 UVA graduate, to show up at her door armed with a small razor blade to remove the profanity from her sign. Ellis felt the sign desecrated the Lawn. He was equally offended by "how many very radical liberal signs were posted on doors" on other Lawn rooms. He confronted Azher in a brief conversation, before university employees asked him to leave.[57]

Ellis, a white Christian man, had his own complicated history with free speech. In the mid-1970s, he had stirred controversy by blocking a gay speaker from campus while inviting William Shockley—a 1974 Nobel Prize–winning physicist turned white nationalist—to debate his views on eugenics during Black Culture Week. Now he grew enraged that the political activism of minority students was undermining the stature of the school.[58]

The confrontation sparked enormous controversy. UVA's new president, Jim Ryan—a law professor and a popular figure with students and alumni alike—defended Azher's right to free expression. "The profanity on the sign is offensive and, in many ways, disheartening," he explained, but "to remove this sign because of its content would run afoul of the Constitution and our own commitment to protecting free speech." Under pressure from many alumni, he issued new regulations on lawn signs, attempting to balance free expression with the decorum expected of a UNESCO World Heritage Site.[59]

Ryan's compromise position pleased no one. In a conversation with him that Azher secretly taped and released, she resisted his framing the controversy around free speech as "a disservice to all the pain and suffering that students, especially that I, have faced, and other students from marginalized identities have faced." Azher tried to steer the conversation "beyond free speech" toward a concrete if far-ranging set of demands about racial reckoning, disability access, and COVID-19 response, and more equitable policies toward employees and Black Charlottesville. In fact, the university had appointed a blue-ribbon panel to rethink how it approached diversity and commemorated race and slavery on its physical landscape. A new DEI initiative was underway.[60]

Azher's call to "move beyond free speech" prompted the Student Council to pass a resolution echoing the demand. They endorsed the March to Reclaim Our Grounds proposals, alongside additional labor and disability reforms. While affirming support for "free speech and protest"—particularly regarding lawn signs like Azher's—the council demanded "immediate action" and "meaningful change" on institutional issues.[61]

Simultanously, the Student Council passed a separate resolution condemning a professor who made an insensitive joke that mocked cultural stereotypes. They called for penalties against faculty members who engage in "racist actions or statements." The contradiction between championing free expression in one resolution while calling for speech-based penalties in another went unaddressed.[62]

Mirroring this selective approach from the opposite direction, Bert Ellis pledged his commitment to free speech while arguing for an exception regarding the Lawn, citing its status as both the symbolic heart of the university and a UNESCO World Heritage Site. He launched an alumni group, the Jefferson Council, dedicated to defending the honor of Thomas Jefferson's legacy and restoring what he saw as political balance to the university. Ellis was joined by Jewish alumnus Joel Gardner, who graduated from the college in 1970 and the law school in 1974. Gardner similarly criticized what he called the "divisive politicization of the Grounds," which he attributed to "the social justice diversity and inclusion agenda based on race, ethnicity and gender."[63]

A Jew from New York City, Gardner had cherished his undergraduate days and wistfully recalled the venerable college traditions. He brushed past his experience of antisemitism and dismissed the concept of "systemic racism" as a myth—as well as any ties between racism and antisemitism. He lambasted progressive anti-racism as an ideological threat to "academic freedom," "diversity of thought," and "freedom of speech." Gardner opposed "group identity" based on "racial, ethnic and gender identification," yet he remained an ardent Zionist active in fundraising for the Israeli army. He championed unfiltered free speech while simultaneously insisting that BDS advocacy should be banned as illegal antisemitic discrimination.[64]

Gardner's contradictions were most apparent regarding antisemitism itself. He derided minority students' "grievance and victimization culture," while asserting that UVA had a "longstanding antisemitism problem" and that "the Jewish people have been the most oppressed people in world history." He complained that anti-racists failed to recognize Jews as an oppressed group needing protection, yet criticized the university for accommodating other minority groups seeking identical recognition and safeguards. In essence, Gardner—like many conservative anti-antisemites—was torn between incompatible positions: that civil rights protection had gone too far in balkanizing America and that such efforts simply had not extended far enough to include Jews.[65]

Gardner was correct about one thing. The university administration did not grasp how to handle antisemitism. When one of the main alumni supporters of the Jewish studies program wrote to Provost Elizabeth Magill that year to request a meeting about support for the department, he got no reply. Despite perceptions of Jewish power, Jewish alumni and Jewish studies faculty felt voiceless and disempowered four years after 2017. A faculty program devoted to studying the causes and legacies of August 11–12, 2017, notably omitted any mention of antisemitism. When Jewish studies offered to appoint a faculty representative to the Dean's Council on DEI, the proposal was dismissed as unnecessary—ignoring the possibility that scholars of Judaism might have uniquely relevant insights and personal vulnerabilities. The DEI office's pattern of oversight continued: They failed to acknowledge a complaint about scheduling an inclusion workshop on Yom Kippur, offered no assistance to Jewish faculty who faced harassment during a campaign to block an Israel-related photography exhibition and artistic residency, and took no action following a student council election in which Jewish students reported antisemitic behavior by a candidate.[66]

The wounds of Charlottesville were reopened with the events of January 6, 2021. President Joe Biden had cited President Trump's "both sides" comment as the inspiration for his decision to launch a campaign. Now on the day Congress met to certify Biden's victory, Trump held a rally promoting conspiracy theories of election fraud. The frontal assault on the core institution of American democracy drew directly on the logic and rhetoric of the Unite the Right rally, right down to the assumption that the First Amendment licensed rioting. It also manifested strains of racism and antisemitism, including the infamous "Camp Auschwitz" T-shirt and the appeal of a "Great Revolution" against a Jewish-controlled government. Biden would later release the first-ever U.S. National Strategy to Counter Antisemitism, but violence and conspiratorial thinking had already invaded American political discourse, energized by antisemitic undercurrents.[67]

Following the January 6, 2021, insurrection, UVA President Ryan announced a new plan to strengthen democracy. As part of that effort, in the spring of 2021, Ryan launched two new initiatives: a Committee on Free Expression and Free Inquiry, composed of faculty, students, and alumni, including Joel Gardner, and a Naming and Memorials Committee. Speech and space would be considered in parallel, Ryan explained, as the university charted a way forward in this perilous moment of American democracy. "We are working to give voice to our commitment as an educational institution to the free and open exchange of ideas," he declared, "and to grapple with the complexities of our university's history and the names that we honor."[68]

On May 6, as the semester was winding down, Ryan joined students to celebrate free speech and civil discourse at the historic Beta Bridge on Rugby Road. For generations, students had painted messages advertising charitable fundraisers, parties, sporting events, and political causes on the low-slung stone bridge spanning the block connecting a stretch of academic buildings to the residential area that houses the fraternities and sororities. By tradition, the messages are left for a minimum of twenty-four hours before being painted over. The May 6 event left two messages: "There is common ground on our grounds," and "#hashitout."[69]

Days later, fighting broke out between Hamas and Israel. An Arab student group responded by painting "Free Palestine" and "End the Occupation" on the bridge. Before the traditional twenty-four hours had passed, Jewish students painted over the slogans with "Peace for Israel." When the Arab students attempted to repaint, their work was vandalized—presumably by the same Jewish students.[70]

The war of words moved online. Hoos for Israel called for honest dialogue while accusing pro-Palestinian advocates of spreading "misinformation" and "hatred." Students for Peace and Justice in Palestine rejected the very premise of a "conflict with two sides," declaring there could be no dialogue about "ongoing, escalating genocide and ethnic cleansing of Palestinians by Zionist forces." Some thirty student groups co-signed their statement calling for revolutionary struggle to decolonize and liberate Palestine. They ranged from the Bengali Student Association to the Young Democratic Socialists to the Society of Hispanic Professional Engineers. Notably, the list included the organization that claimed to represent all minority communities at the university, the Minority Rights Coalition.[71]

* * *

On June 21, 2021, President Ryan announced the UVA Statement on Free Expression and Free Inquiry with great fanfare. "All views, beliefs, and perspectives deserve to be articulated and heard free from interference," he asserted. "The University must not stifle protected expression, permit others to obstruct or shut down such expression, or regulate the tone or content of responses that stop short of interfering with others' speech or violating the law." He took care to note that "time, place, and manner" regulations remained in effect.

The statement went on to lionize free speech and the university's connection to the First Amendment through Jefferson and Madison. "At the same time," he noted, "the University has not always fulfilled its aspirations, exploiting enslaved laborers and excluding Black Americans, women, and groups and viewpoints disfavored by the majority." Once again, Jews did not make the list.[72]

But the deeper flaw in the UVA statement was its failure to reconcile two competing ideals: free speech as an unlimited enterprise, and the promise of equality and respect. The four years since Charlottesville had revealed a campus where virtually everyone felt aggrieved by the speech climate. Dueling grievances emerged: Jewish students cited intimidation from anti-Zionist activism that limited their expression, while Palestinian and Muslim students pointed to bias against their viewpoints and safety concerns. All professed commitment to free speech, even those cynical about its promises. Yet all called for limits on hate speech.

Ryan's statement fell short of the moment. It provided no road map for how a university might embrace both freedom and equality, no sense of how these foundational promises of American democracy might complement rather than compete. At the university Jefferson designed to pursue truth without compromise, the founding contradictions endured, unresolved and perhaps unresolvable.

12

Trial Without End

"This case is a case about violence and intimidation that was planned for months and culminated in a tragic and violent weekend, August 11th and 12th of 2017, right here in Charlottesville, Virginia." Plaintiff's attorney Karen Dunn stood at the lectern in the courtroom for the U.S. District Court for the Western District of Virginia on a cold Thursday morning in late October 2021. Small in stature, with tightly cropped brown curls, the former federal prosecutor and associate White House counsel searched out the eyes of the COVID-masked jurors to her right as she laid out her opening argument in *Elizabeth Sines, et al. v. Jason Kessler, et al.* "The nine victims sitting here today seek justice and accountability for 'physical, emotional, and monetary harm' suffered as a result of the defendants' actions, and 'they believe the truth about what happened in Charlottesville must be told.'"[1]

More than a hundred different trials resulted from the events of A11/12, as locals referred to that weekend. The State of Virginia convicted Ohio man James Alex Fields Jr. for the car-ramming murder of Heather Heyer and assault of other victims. He received multiple life sentences. Four white men went to prison for the vicious beating of DeAndre Harris. Chris Cantwell pleaded guilty to assault and battery for using pepper spray on Friday night. Scores of other court cases dealt with the continued fallout over the Confederate statues.[2]

Yet none of these matched *Sines v. Kessler* in sheer drama or historical import. Dunn co-led an all-star legal team together with Roberta Kaplan, famous for defending gay marriage in the 2013 landmark U.S. Supreme Court case *United States v. Windsor* and representing E. Jean Carroll in her defamation lawsuit against Donald Trump. The blond-haired Kaplan brought a street fighter's swagger to the courtroom that earned her the sobriquet "force of nature." After the Trump Justice Department decided not to prosecute the Unite the Right leaders, the lawyers launched a civil lawsuit against the men who had planned the rally, their organizations, and Fields. All stood trial together for the injuries they had inflicted on peaceful counterprotesters.

Sines v. Kessler represented an audacious act of legal creativity on a grand scale. Four years of planning produced a weeks-long trial involving nine plaintiffs, twenty-four defendants, thirty-six witnesses, and five terabytes of digital evidence. It was a mammoth undertaking involving massive security to handle multiple death threats, further complicated by the ongoing pandemic.

The lawsuit combined a variety of violations of state and federal hate crimes laws, including harassment, tortious assault and battery, and intentional infliction of emotional distress. Most imaginatively, the lawsuit employed an 1871 federal anti–Ku Klux Klan law to stop twenty-first-century white supremacy. In the end, however, the entire effort boiled down to one question: Had the organizers of the 2017 Unite the Right rally engaged in a civil conspiracy to commit racially motivated violence? Or had they simply exercised their First Amendment rights?

Don't be fooled, Dunn warned the jury as she continued her opening argument. This lawsuit is not about free speech. Our clients do not claim that the defendants' words caused the violence. Rather, their words were used to organize violence, and those same words now prove their intentions and motivations. "Our case is about the planning, execution, and celebration of racially motivated violence."[3]

"Our case is entirely this," countered defense attorney James Kolenich. "Rhetoric, language, is protected." The Cincinnati, Ohio, lawyer, who boasted that he took the case "to oppose Jewish influence in society," represented Jason Kessler, Nathan Damigo, and Damigo's organization, Identity Evropa. There was no diabolical plot before Charlottesville, Kolenich argued. My clients planned "a political rally." Their self-defense preparations against Antifa and offensive humor online hardly amounted to a hate crime. It was the government's duty to protect their free speech rights, and the government had failed in that responsibility.[4]

Other defense lawyers made the same assertion. Edward ReBrook, a decorated Iraq War U.S. Army veteran, argued that his clients, Jeff Schoep and the National Socialist Movement, were not even present at the Friday night torch rally or the moment when Fields carried out his car attack. "Can people that weren't even around be blamed for the actions of another?"[5]

Lurking beneath the denials of conspiracy was a darker insinuation about the real conspiracy at hand. ReBrook denounced the "New York" lawyers who "come down here to Virginia and whittle away at the First Amendment for the purposes of vengeance." Chris Cantwell, who represented himself, put it more plainly, invoking an old antisemitic canard, "They cry out in pain as they strike you."[6]

Another antisemitic trope surfaced in the opening argument of Richard Spencer, who also chose to defend himself. He launched into a long-winded disquisition on Old Testament vengeance and Israelite "scapegoating." This case is "actually about something much bigger" than the law, he announced grandiosely. "It's about justice itself."[7]

"Mr. Spencer, I hate to interrupt you," interrupted Judge Norman Moon, an octogenarian federal judge from southern Virginia appointed by President Bill Clinton. "We're not sending a message here," he patiently explained over Spencer's whine about his right to present the "big picture." The jury's job is strictly to judge the facts and apply the law, Moon declared. "The evidence and the law is what should control the decision, not the bigger picture."[8]

The Charlottesville proceedings represented an ambitious wager on the part of the plaintiffs' lawyers: that a major trial could not only deliver justice but fix truth in an age of lies. Where false equivalencies rationalized extremist violence—where hatred masqueraded as harmless hyperbole—a civil rights trial would clarify the boundaries between free speech and unlawful conduct. It would restore the moral luster and authority of law itself.

That wager risked an adverse outcome. A win for the defense would bolster their legitimacy. A loss might play into their narrative of free speech martyrdom. Even the trial itself might be diverted into a platform on which white supremacists could air their ideas and impugn the law.

Last to speak on the first day was attorney Joshua Smith, who represented David Matthew Parrott, Matthew Heimbach, and the Traditionalist Worker Party. Born Daniel Joshua Nusbaum, the Cornell Law graduate had publicly renounced his Jewishness—and his gayness—to embrace white supremacy. He became notorious during the trial for slipping the word "kike" into his remarks to try to desensitize the jury.

Smith's breathless, rambling opening statement was more akin to a dorm room debate speech than a coherent legal argument. It culminated in the same thinly veiled slur as his colleagues. The true conspiracy here lies with one group seeking "to use the courts to crush the other group because" they "can't actually take away their First Amendment rights." That drew a hasty reprimand from Judge Moon. "Well, Mr. Smith, I just don't know where you were when we have had the arguments this afternoon," he said. "Just don't do that."[9]

The brief exchange illuminated the fundamental tension at the heart of the proceedings. The plaintiffs' counsel aimed to document the verbal hatred motivating the violent conspiracy. Free speech was not on trial, only the hateful men who had willfully harmed peaceful counterprotesters—and who were hiding behind free speech. The defense attorneys sought to flip the script, casting the defendants as free speech heroes. Their clients were being judged not for their actions but their words. They were the ultimate victims; the counterprotesters were only the public face of radical leftist aggression. In the courtroom were their Jewish overlords, who were hiding behind civil rights.

The early appearance of antisemitism—a mythical theory of evil power—foreshadowed how the trial would transcend questions of fact or free speech. Over the coming weeks, the courtroom was destined to become a battleground, a referendum on whether law wielded power or power wielded law.

* * *

A BASIC DIVIDING line within the American justice system centers on the distinction between criminal and civil law. Under criminal law, the government prosecutes gross infractions that harm the state and the public interest. The chief penalty for wrongdoing is physical imprisonment, the loss of personal liberty. Civil law typically governs private disputes between individuals or organizations involving property or damages. Punishment often takes the form of monetary compensation from one party to another.

In the aftermath of Skokie, however, a new trend emerged in American law: private civil rights lawsuits by victims of racist violence. In 1980, the Southern Poverty Law Center, an Alabama public interest firm founded by three men—lawyer Morris Dees, a white Protestant, his Jewish colleague Joseph Levin Jr., and Black civil rights legend Julian Bond—launched a pioneering class action lawsuit against the Invisible Empire of the Knights of the Ku Klux Klan for assaulting peaceful civil rights marchers in Decatur, Alabama. They won a large monetary award of damages that bankrupted the group.[10]

Four years later, two young Jewish lawyers from Washington, DC, Kevin Lipson and Irvin Shapell, adopted the same tactic against a posse of eight neo-Nazi men convicted of vandalizing a local synagogue with swastikas and other antisemitic graffiti. Frustrated by the passivity of Jewish civil rights groups at Skokie, Lipson explained, we went "looking for something creative and noble to do to vindicate the rights of Jews." The duo persuaded the synagogue leaders and members, many of them Holocaust survivors traumatized by the attack, to sue the vandals.[11]

To make their case in *Shaare Tefila Congregation v. Cobb*, Lipson and Shapell turned to the 1866 and 1871 Civil Rights Acts, the latter known as the Ku Klux Klan Act, which allowed private citizens to sue other citizens for damages for civil rights violations. Codified as federal law sections 1981, 1982, and 1985(3), the laws were created to protect African Americans from white racial terror and violence by guaranteeing "the full and equal benefit of all laws and proceedings for the security of persons and property as is enjoyed by white citizens." We came up with a theory, said Lipson, "that because Nazi ideology identifies Jews as a race that they should be protected by the race statute." It did not matter if Jews in 1980s American society were treated as a religious minority, with the vast majority of European-descended Jews technically classified as white by law. The crime was motivated by racial prejudice because the criminals believed Jews were non-white.[12]

The first judge to hear the case rejected the argument, reasoning that the law could not apply since both parties were white. A 2–1 federal appeals court split led to the Supreme Court in 1986. The ADL, the American Jewish Committee, the Lawyers Committee for Civil Rights, the NAACP, and two Holocaust survivor groups all joined in an amicus brief in support of the synagogue. While they rejected "the notion that Jews should be classified as members of a distinct 'race,'" they wrote, "the statute must be construed to cover acts of racism directed towards Jews." The 1866 law was plainly intended "to protect any group which a defendant regards as different from and inferior to white citizens."[13]

The Rehnquist Court agreed. In a unanimous ruling, the justices ruled that the law could be applied to Jews. "The question before us is not whether Jews are considered to be a separate race by today's standards," wrote Chief Justice Rehnquist, but whether at the time of the statute's adoption, "Jews constituted a group of people that Congress intended to protect."[14]

Shaare Tefila contained a valuable insight about the dynamics of racialization. Racism is prejudice based on perception and social structure, not immutable characteristics like skin color or physiognomy. In fact, during oral arguments, Justice Thurgood Marshall raised the question of whether his own father, who looked "white, with blond hair and blue eyes," had cause to sue for race discrimination under the law. The defense attorney replied in the negative. "Oh, but he did," declared Marshall. "He was a Negro," despite his physical appearance. He proceeded to pose the question of whether Black Jews who faced antisemitic persecution would have a cause of action under the law. When the lawyer insisted that they could not, Marshall lost his patience. "Death to the Jew! That's what the swastikas mean."[15]

Shaare Tefila opened the door to a potential new avenue of civil rights protection, and not only for Jews. In a twist, the Court paired the *Shaare Tefila* case with a similar lawsuit, *Saint Francis College v. Al-Khazraji*, in which an Iraqi-born Muslim college professor fired from a Christian college sued alleging racial discrimination. The same logic applied to Arab Americans, a group technically classified as white under American law. Just as with antisemitism, anti-Arab bias could be considered a form of racial discrimination.[16]

The twin victories of the Jewish congregation and the Arab Muslim professor suggested a way forward for the law to recognize the complex parallels and interconnections between color-based racism and antisemitism, Islamophobia, and anti-Arab racism. Amid the intensifying Middle East conflict during the First Intifada, it was a striking sight to see Jewish and Arab and Muslim groups joined together as allies in the American civil rights struggle.[17]

The dual cases also represented an early example of the legal theory of intersectionality in practice. Developed by critical legal scholars like Kimberlé Crenshaw, the theory held that anti-discrimination law needed to recognize certain kinds of overlapping identities that fell between the cracks of the categories used to define discrimination. A Black female student could face both racism and sexism, multiplying the effect of each in a way that a simple claim of discrimination on the basis of race or sex would fail to capture. As *Shaare Tefila* and *Al-Khazraji* demonstrated, Jews and Arabs were perfect candidates for this legal understanding, since they could face both racial and religious discrimination, often intertwined in a single species of hatred, even if it did not fit any of the conventional categories.[18]

Ironically, however, the main use of the new ruling would come not from Jewish progressive lawyers but in the form of a Jewish conservative legal strategy of applying Title VI to anti-Zionist speech. While establishment Jewish civil rights groups declined to take advantage of the Supreme Court decision to expand anti-discrimination protection, Kenneth Marcus cited the decision in 2004 in developing his new theory of Title VI; he invoked *Shaare Tefila* to show how the law could be applied to racialized religious minority groups, among them Jews, Sikhs, Muslims, and Arabs. Other minorities were slow to adopt Title VI for battling discrimination, in part because before 2023 it had little enforcement power. The few successful cases resulted only in consent agreements in which schools enhanced anti-bias trainings.[19]

In theory, Marcus's approach did not single out antisemitism. It even covered Jews who identified as members of a Jewish national group but rejected Zionism. However, in practice it severed antisemitism from other forms of discrimination, leading to an obsessive focus on left-wing antisemitism that frequently collapsed legitimate anti-Zionist speech into antisemitism with little legal or intellectual rigor.

Sines v. Kessler sought to do the opposite—to reconnect antisemitism to anti-Black racism in the realm of civil rights law, an inherently liberal project that was supported by liberal backers. To fund the lawsuit, Kaplan and Dunn partnered with Amy Spitalnick, a veteran Democratic communications professional who had worked for the New York attorney general and J Street, a liberal Zionist lobby promoting the two-state solution. They created a nonprofit organization, Integrity First for America, and recruited Hillary Clinton to help fundraise. From the outset, the lawsuit was intended to promote a bipartisan struggle against antisemitism and to recognize it as interconnected with other forms of hatred.[20]

THAT DELICATE TASK was reflected in the quest to build a plaintiff class that reflected the range of victims affected by the violence in Charlottesville. Their original plaintiff roster included eleven victims who alleged "a conspiracy . . . to hurt black and Jewish individuals, and their supporters, because of their race at the August 11th and 12th events." That language mirrored the 1866 statute, which included "white supporters" as victims of racial discrimination. The lawsuit characterized the defendants' motivations as an interconnected web of "racist, anti-Semitic, sexist, homophobic, and xenophobic ideologies."[21]

Of the eleven victims, three were white and Christian: Elizabeth Sines, a UVA Law student; Reverend Seth Wispelwey, of the Congregate Charlottesville clergy group; and UVA library employee Tyler Magill. Three were African American: Marcus Martin, a local landscaper; Marissa Blair, a paralegal; and Devin Willis, a UVA undergraduate. One was Mexican American: April Muñiz, a pharmaceutical researcher. They were joined by four other plaintiffs, all of them members of Congregation Beth Israel—Dr. Hannah Pearce, a retired dermatologist, sisters Rebecca and Sophie Schechtman, and their mother, Lisa Draine, an events planner. Rebecca had grown up in Charlottesville and gone on to law school at NYU. Her sister Sophie had been a UVA undergraduate at the time of the attack; she had counterprotested at the Rotunda on Friday night and suffered two broken legs in Saturday's car ramming. Though Draine was Catholic, she had raised her daughters as Jews together with their Jewish father.

Draine and her daughters chose to appear as Jane Does, citing safety concerns. By January 2018, the three women had withdrawn from the case after James Fields's attorney demanded they reveal their identity—a risk they deemed too dangerous. Their concerns were well founded: one of the defendants, Michael Tubbs, had already served four years in prison for stealing military weapons as part of a plot to bomb Jewish- and Black-owned businesses in Florida. They, along with Magill (who suffered a stroke after being hit by a Unite the Right protester), were replaced by Chelsea Alvarado, a Latina social worker; Thomas Baker, a white conservation biologist; and UVA student Natalie Romero, a Colombian American. The two students, Romero and Willis, had protested with Schechtman on Friday night, and Romero suffered severe injuries from the car ramming on Saturday.[22]

With the departure of the Schechtman sisters, only Hannah Pearce remained as a Jewish plaintiff. On the Saturday morning of the rally, she had gone to check on the synagogue following the overnight bomb threat. Outside on the street, a protester noticed the Star of David on her necklace and T-shirt. "Oh good," he shouted, "they're marking themselves for us, so it's easy to find them." Someone hurled an object that struck her—a bag of urine, she discovered, though in that terrifying moment she had feared for her life.[23]

Still, Judge Moon appeared indifferent, if not oblivious, to Pearce's claims of antisemitic harm aligned with legal precedent. He deemed her injuries insufficient, though they were no less serious than those of other plaintiffs, such as Sines. More broadly, Moon appeared unable to grasp the racialized component of antisemitism in Pearce's case, and he dismissed her claims that her right to use of property had been violated since the synagogue had not been physically damaged. As a result, Moon dropped Pearce from the lawsuit.[24]

This absence produced a number of striking contradictions. A coalition of racist antisemites and their attorneys faced off against victims who were mostly people of color. Those victims were represented by a conspicuously Jewish legal team—besides Kaplan, Dunn, and their partner Spitalnick, they included lawyers Jonah Levine, Michael Bloch, and Yotam Barkai.[25]

The ironies were unmistakable: Jewish victims had been excluded from the trial, yet Jewishness permeated the proceedings as a focal point for the racial animus and antisemitic subtext running under the surface. Jewish attorneys defended victims of racism while themselves facing hatred in the courtroom. These dynamics reflected the complex and often ambiguous position of antisemitism within America's broader struggle with racial hatred.

"I JUST HEARD loudness," recalled Natalie Romero, "almost like thunder, like the world was—the earth was growling." The petite, dark-haired young woman breathed heavily, steadying herself on the witness stand on the trial's second day as she recounted the horror of the Friday evening torch rally. The sky above her had blazed with flames, a sea of bodies surging toward her. A spray of mace filled her eyes and a burning torch landed at her feet. "It just felt like war," the student and Army ROTC cadet told the court. As the ring of fire closed in on her, she pressed herself against the cold marble of the Jefferson statue, praying. This must be what it felt like when women were burned at the stake, Romero thought at the time.[26]

In the end, it was not fire but steel that nearly killed her. On Saturday afternoon, as Romero walked away from the chaos of the scene downtown, Fields slammed his car into her, fracturing her skull and leaving her with multiple other injuries.

One by one the victims took the stand over the course of the trial's opening week to narrate their stories. Marcus Martin described throwing his fiancée, Marissa Blair, out of the path of the car. The force of its impact shattered his body, leaving his sneaker embedded in the car's grille. Thomas Baker described the severity of his life-changing injuries from being directly hit by the car. Others, like Wispelwey and Sines, spoke of psychological trauma.

Seeking to address the glaring absence of Jewish plaintiffs in a trial about antisemitism, Kaplan called Diane D'Costa to testify as a non-party witness. Though intended to provide the missing Jewish voice, her testimony instead amplified the trial's central paradox: D'Costa could recount her harrowing experience of fear and flight, but, as a mere witness rather than a plaintiff, she had no legal standing to advance a claim. Her presence underscored rather than resolved the irony of a trial about antisemitism with no Jewish victims of record.

In their cross-examinations, the defendants' lawyers tried to shift blame for the violence onto poor policing. They also hunted for evidence of direct ties between the plaintiffs and Antifa or Black Lives Matter. Most of all, though, they insisted that their words and beliefs bore no relation to the harms suffered by the plaintiffs. "If the plaintiffs could sue us for hate speech, they would," argued Chris Cantwell. "Since they cannot, they're suing us for a nonexistent conspiracy. They are trying to squeeze size 12 hate speech into size 5 conspiracy heels."[27]

Despite Cantwell's quip, the law was not in his favor. "A conspiracy," as Judge Moon told the jury at the outset, "is a kind of unlawful partnership in which each member becomes the agent of every other member." It did not matter if some of the conspirators' objectives were legal. Or if there was no formal agreement or open discussion of a plan. They need not all know all the details or even one another's identities. All that was required was a finding that a "preponderance of the evidence" pointed to "a mutual understanding, either spoken or unspoken, between the conspirators to commit at least one unlawful act." In addition, evidence of a conspiracy can come not only through discussions before or during an act, but also after it occurs, through the celebration or ratification of the act's intent.[28]

As the trial progressed, Kaplan and Dunn brought an avalanche of evidence pointing to that mutual understanding. Decrypted chat threads, unlocked cell phones, leaked videos, and other data dumps exposed the defendants' private machinations in lurid detail. Little framing was needed to show the extent of their desire to inflict harm on their racial enemies. Still, the meaning of those messages and violent fantasies became the essence of the case. Were they just chat room hyperbole? Or deadly serious planning? Was gassing Jews a preposterous adolescent boast? Or a murder plot?

The sociologist Peter Simi, an expert witness, was assigned the task of answering those questions. He testified about the alt-right's strategy of frontstage and backstage communications. In public-facing contexts, they used deliberately provocative language while maintaining their fealty to civil liberties and peaceful protest. Behind closed doors they unveiled their true hatred and plans for incitement and violence. In this way, they trod the line of plausible deniability.

Blurring the line between reality and fiction was both a recruitment strategy and a legal technique. Simi cited the *Daily Stormer*'s style guide, which counseled contributors to avoid illegally promoting violence on the internet while normalizing violence as the eventual outcome. "Most people are not comfortable with material that comes across as vitriolic, ranting and unironic hatred," wrote defendant Andrew Anglin. Hence ironic humor was essential for rhetoric. "Generally, when using racial slurs, it should come across as half-joking—like a racist joke that everyone laughs at because it's true . . . The unindoctrinated should not be able to tell if we are joking or not."[29]

To further decode the language, the plaintiffs introduced testimony by Samantha Froelich, a former girlfriend of defendant Matthew Heimbach. "Communist" and "globalist" both meant "Jewish person," she explained. "These are dog whistles that you would use in everyday conversation to see if someone was on the same wavelength as you." Another dog whistle was "Zionist," she added; "well, that's not really a dog whistle, that's really out there." Her comment once again captured the doubleness of anti-Zionism. In some cases, it can take the form of principled opposition to Zionism, while in others "Zionist" serves as an antisemitic shorthand for "Jew."[30]

It was a comment on the Holocaust that proved the most shocking moment of the trial. "Welcome to the alt-right," Froelich recalled being told as a new recruit to the movement, "where the Holocaust never happened, and we want it to happen again." Here was irony stretched to the point of absurdity. Where was truth in a world where commitment to stable reality was abandoned?[31]

On the trial's eighth day, Dr. Deborah Lipstadt, the foremost Holocaust denial expert and at the time the Biden administration's Special Envoy to Monitor and Combat Global Antisemitism, was called to the stand. Her task was to explain the history of antisemitism and its connection to white supremacy. Twenty years earlier, Lipstadt had endured her own legal ordeal, after the British Holocaust denier David Irving sued her for personal defamation. Now she squared off against a new generation of antisemites who had built their ideologies around a slippery mixture of Holocaust denial and celebration.[32]

In pretrial filings, Chris Cantwell had opposed her appearance, dismissing it as another instance of the plot against white people: "Lipstadt's purpose here is to tell the jury that refusing to enter the verdict in the Plaintiffs' favor is the moral equivalent of genocide against the 'Jewish people.'" In reality, he added, "the entire purpose" of our "peaceful political protest was to oppose the physical and cultural genocide that extremists such as Lipstadt have been carrying out against America's white working-class population . . . whose lands are being stolen from them as we speak."[33]

Now confronting her on the stand, Cantwell took his cross-examination in a different direction. He began by asking her to read his post from July 15, 2017, in which he wrote, "America will never be free until the last kike is strangled with the entrails of the last male Democrat." Then he pivoted to a debate about stereotypes and humor.

"In the course of your study of antisemitism," he asked, "did you come across any jokes that were just jokes?"

"I don't know what you mean by 'just jokes,'" Lipstadt replied sharply.

"Well, it seems to me that the implication that you're drawing is that when people in these posts that you're looking at . . . you're saying that there is some kind of intent, a desire to destroy the Jewish people," he asked wryly, but what if it's all an "innocent antisemitic joke"?

Cantwell pressed on, trying to paint her as a scold: "If somebody was going to make a joke about the Jewish people, would the Holocaust be an easy target?"

Lipstadt's response was unforgiving: "I find it hard to imagine that using a genocide which killed six million people, irrespective of their religion, their identity, their nationality, a topic for jokes."[34]

In refusing to dignify Cantwell's obfuscations, Lipstadt did yeoman's service for the historical profession. Yet her performance also confirmed the futility of arguing with antisemites. Just as Sartre had once observed, the antisemite likes to "play with discourse . . . discredit the seriousness of their interlocutors." Turning deliberate paradox into an operating principle challenged the law's drive for clarity and precision. In the context of the courtroom, it served the defendants' aim of sowing doubt and confusion about their intentions.[35]

More broadly, though, Cantwell's challenge pointed to the underlying antisemitic trial strategy. Every victim was a pawn, every expert witness an agent of Jewish conspiracy. The trial amounted to an inversion of power. "Looking at the actual social situation in the United States today," wrote Cantwell in a court motion, the Ku Klux Klan Act should be "more appropriately used against antifa and members of the woke progressive left to protect white working people and their supporters than it is used to protect the antifa domestic terror organization." As proof, he argued, one only needs to "look over to the plaintiffs' table to see how the power structure has lined up to protect the violence of the plaintiffs." Cantwell contrasted his miserable poverty and weakness with the "army of Jewish lawyers with an eight-figure budget" who "bully us in court and defame us in the press and on social media platforms we have all been banned from."[36]

Much like the rally itself, where the marchers chanted "Jews will not replace us," Jews were an invisible enemy operating behind the scenes to disempower white Christian America. Manipulating Black and Brown hordes, as well as transgender bodies, Muslims, Asians, and all manner of other inferior enemies, the Jews were waging war against the white man. In this antisemitic imagination, the authority of law was weaponized against white freedom. The Jews were a symbol of supreme power—even the law lay in their hands, making the defendants not misjudged men but martyrs to justice.

The moment evoked Shakespeare's *The Merchant of Venice*, where Shylock demands in court his pound of flesh from his debtor Antonio, declaring, "I crave the law." Bassanio pleads with Portia to prioritize justice over law through Christian mercy: "Wrest once the law to your authority. / To do a great right, do a little wrong, / And curb this cruel devil of his will." Yet ironically, here the antisemites—like Shakespeare's Christians—wielded law as a weapon against Jews, then condemned that same law as cruel and harsh when Jews sought its protection.

America largely forgot about the Charlottesville trial while it was happening. Federal courtrooms prohibit cameras. Without trial footage, cable television networks quickly lost interest. Better visuals and simpler story lines came from two sensational murder trials taking place elsewhere at the time. In Kenosha, Wisconsin, the white teenager Kyle Rittenhouse was on trial for shooting three men during a racially charged 2020 riot. In Brunswick, Georgia, three white men were on trial for the 2020 murder of a young Black man, Ahmaud Arbery, killed while jogging. These murder trials overshadowed civil litigation stemming from a four-year-old riot.

Charlottesville also forgot about its trial. Local progressive activists stayed home, enforcing a public silence of their own. Most days the plaza in front of the courthouse was empty. At day's end, as the winter night took over, Rabbi Tom Gutherz kept a solitary vigil outside the courthouse. His lonely act of witness stood in damning contrast to a town and a nation that preferred to look away.[37]

A mile down the road, UVA students remained consumed with the debate over free speech and racism. While the trial was happening, Young Americans for Freedom, a hard-right conservative student organization, held a symposium, "In Defense of Mr. Jefferson," with *National Review* editor Rich Lowry and Texas Republican congressman Chip Roy, both UVA alumni. The event sought to defend Jefferson's reputation against charges of racism. It prompted a letter-writing campaign against its "racist" revisionism, and an expletive-laced attack on the student group appeared on the Beta Bridge. That drew a retort from the Young Americans that their free speech was under attack. No one mentioned the trial.[38]

Elsewhere in the state, attention focused on the final days of a gubernatorial election that pitted former Democratic Governor Terry McAuliffe, who had held office in 2017, against newcomer Glenn Youngkin, a wealthy Republican financier. Youngkin had positioned himself as a Trump-friendly moderate conservative, a suburban "soccer dad" who could heal partisan divides. Yet on the campaign trail he stoked moral panic about public schools and demonized transgender students. He also vowed to ban abortion. Despite his "bedrock" commitment to free speech, he pledged to ban "critical race theory," beginning with the work of African American author Toni Morrison.[39]

Virginia Democrats accused Youngkin of racist dog whistles and "repeated use of antisemitic tropes," including the "antisemitic conspiracy theory" about the hidden hand of George Soros in funding a stealth progressive takeover of local school boards. His opponent McAuliffe had rushed out a widely criticized book about Charlottesville in which he cast himself as a heroic anti-Trump figure. He worked hard to tie Youngkin to Trump.[40]

While the trial was underway, Youngkin visited Charlottesville for a campaign rally. In a bizarre stunt, activists from the anti-Trump Republican Lincoln Project showed up dressed as white supremacists with tiki torches. The performance drew universal condemnation. Imitating the very racists at whose hands people in town had suffered injury and death was worse than poor taste. But lost in the noise was a legitimate critique: Why had Youngkin not taken the opportunity to more forcefully denounce white supremacy?[41]

Youngkin brushed off charges of bigotry while pointedly avoiding mention of the trial. Rather than seize the moment to reject the far right as extremists incompatible with conservative values, he chose silence. Instead, he pivoted to accuse Vice President Kamala Harris of fostering anti-Jewish hatred and touted his plan for a Virginia Antisemitism Commission. "Virginia and America must always stand with our Jewish friends and Israeli allies against the tide of hate and discrimination," he declared, positioning himself in contrast to the Democrats.[42]

This move exemplified the emerging conservative playbook: Even as Youngkin denounced anti-racism as a corruption of liberal ideals that threatened free speech, he championed a selective fight against antisemitism. The real threat to Jews came not from white supremacists but from anti-Zionism on college campuses. Accusations about Christian nationalism or Republican ties to the far right were merely smears and distractions. The true danger facing American Jews, he claimed, lay elsewhere.

On November 2, 2021, Youngkin was elected governor. He immediately pledged "to really stand up on university campuses for both free speech but also for respect." The meaning of that pledge became clear on his first day in office, as he issued a bevy of executive orders. Executive Order #1 banned "critical race theory and its progeny" of "inherently divisive concepts" in K–12 public education, defined as "any ideas in violation of Title IV and Title VI of the Civil Rights Act of 1964." In the name of countering structural racism, white privilege, and affirmative action, Youngkin outlawed any discussion of them.

This hyperbolic assault on the teaching of American history turned anti-discrimination law into a cudgel to suppress critical discussion of racism's historical legacies or present-day differential impact. Another Youngkin executive order redirected his Diversity, Equity, and Inclusion office to a new focus on "the promotion of diverse free speech and inclusive civil discourse, and a role in promoting the honest and complete teaching of history." Youngkin insisted on free speech even as he promoted strict limits on it and issued a nakedly political demand for ideological balance. To helm the office, he turned to the same Charlottesville school superintendent, Dr. Rosa Atkins, who had passed over antisemitism in silence in the aftermath of August 11/12.[43]

Executive Order #8 fulfilled Youngkin's campaign pledge to create a commission addressing the "intolerable rise in antisemitism." Notably absent was any mention of Charlottesville or white supremacy;

instead, Youngkin called for adopting the IHRA definition of antisemitism, with its sweeping approach to labeling anti-Zionist critique of Israel as antisemitic. He also declared his opposition to "any effort to bring the BDS philosophy or actions into Virginia." This proposal was so vaguely worded and broadly defined that it would likely chill free speech while failing to distinguish legitimate political criticism from actual discrimination.[44]

A year later, when this state Commission to Combat Antisemitism issued its final report, Charlottesville was barely mentioned. It earned two paragraphs out of 13,000 words. The report cited a "former president" who "met recently with two notorious anti-Semites." The oblique reference was to Trump's Mar-a-Lago meeting with live-streamer and Groypers leader Nick Fuentes and antisemitic rapper Kanye "Ye" West. Yet Trump was not named because in the words of commission member Bruce Hoffman, "we didn't want it to be partisan." Nor did he and his colleagues note that Fuentes had attended the 2017 Unite the Right rally. The report went on to urge the passage of a state law that would criminalize doing business with anyone who supported the BDS movement on grounds that this would "isolate, delegitimize, and destroy Israel as a Jewish state through economic means."[45]

Youngkin's avoidance of Charlottesville foreshadowed the conservative legal playbook for the coming years. Aggressive efforts to combat antisemitism would take the form of a near-exclusive focus on left-wing varieties arising out of the Israeli-Palestinian conflict. Meanwhile, white supremacy, Christian nationalism, and far right antisemitism were either downplayed or distorted. Soon enough, anti-antisemitism would be weaponized to criminalize pro-Palestinian advocacy. Jewish rights became a tool to silence broader political dissent. To do that, conservatives first had to pry antisemitism away from racism, exceptionalizing it in guise of acting on it—the very opposite of the *Sines v. Kessler* approach. Youngkin's silence on Charlottesville was telling. In the eyes of the Right, only antisemitism from the Left deserved attention—a portent of the politicized reception that the trial would receive.[46]

* * *

"MEMBERS OF THE jury, now you've heard all the evidence in the case," Judge Moon began, and your task is "to apply the rules of law, so given, to the facts as you find them from the evidence in the case." It was late November, just days before Thanksgiving. Before closing arguments began, the judge patiently outlined the jury instructions, beginning with an exhortation to suspend "prejudice, sympathy, guesswork, or speculation" in their deliberations.[47]

Moon proceeded to tackle the First Amendment question head-on. While the "abstract advocacy of lawlessness or mere advocacy of use of force is protected speech," he said, planning a conspiracy is "not protected by the First Amendment."[48]

Kaplan picked up on that theme in her closing argument, stressing that neither ideas nor speech were on trial. "The First Amendment does not protect acts of violence," she declared. "It does not protect planning for violence." The First Amendment provides no defense to breaking the law or engaging in a conspiracy to do so. Nor could claiming that the violence was political, rather than racial, hold water. "When defendants say 'Communist,'" she told the jury, "what they mean is 'Jew.' And the defendants refer to all of their enemies, all of their perceived enemies of the white race, interchangeably, as Communists, as Antifa, as Jews, as kikes."[49]

In her closing, Dunn reminded the jury of the core elements of a conspiracy—agreement, foreseeability, overt action, and damage. She zeroed in on a text exchange between Cantwell and Spencer: "I'm willing to risk a lot for our cause, including violence and incarceration. Many in my audience would follow me there, too, but I want to coordinate and make sure it's worth it to our cause."[50]

"Ladies and gentlemen," Dunn continued, "this has every element in this one message: Racially motivated violence and coordination. And Mr. Spencer responds, 'It's worth it, at least for me.'"[51]

Dunn went on to review all the discussions among the organizers about running over counterprotesters with cars and their open threats to use cars as weapons. After examining the plans for violence and the execution of it, she briefly cited several moments afterward in which the plaintiffs celebrated their achievement, a clear criterion for conspiracy.

Dunn read aloud Cantwell's tweet: "If you think the alt-right is insignificant, you might want to ask the bleeding commie filth we sent to the morgue and hospitals how insignificant we are."[52]

AGAINST THE MOUNTAIN of evidence of their clients' culpability, the defense attorneys all denied the charges and cried witch hunt. Their clients' views were on trial, not their actions, and those actions fell short of conspiracy. Cantwell used his closing argument to painstakingly review videos of the Friday night torch rally frame by frame, trying once again to show an organized Antifa plot to attack and entrap him. He ended by screaming, "This whole case is a lie."[53]

Defense attorney Kolenich suggested that the alt-right and Antifa were akin to rival softball teams, both spoiling for a good old-fashioned brawl. Even if they had come expecting fistfights and street scuffles, even if they had *wanted* violence, no one on his team could have foreseen or agreed to a car-ramming attack.

Smith cast his clients as political dissidents unaffiliated with the Unite the Right leadership. They had not even been physically present during the Friday night rally or on Saturday at the site of the attack. To make his point, he invoked their ideology. If you want to know the real reason they went to the rally, he explained, then watch this video. He spent the rest of his time playing a YouTube video about the "white genocide" organized by "the international Jewish system." In attempting to exonerate his clients, he had instead demonstrated precisely the antisemitic conspiracy thinking at the heart of the plaintiffs' case.[54]

In his own closing, Spencer tried to return to his opening monologue about justice. He contrasted the biblical scapegoat cast out into the wilderness to die under Mosaic law with the Newtonian ideal of truly rational justice. Ancient vengeful tribalism had been superseded by high-minded universal reason. Then, he pivoted to Jesus, asking, "What made Jesus a radical, an extremist? What got him executed? What made him an object of hatred by his own community?"[55]

Judge Moon again cut him off. Spencer grew angry and demanded the right to use poetic license to make his point. Moon refused, admonishing him to stick to the case and the law at hand. "But it's within my right," whined Spencer again, "to give people the big picture. If I can't do it now, when can I do it?"[56]

Spencer's ignorance of courtroom procedure was plainly evident. But so too was his deeper purpose: to shatter the trial's formal constraints, expose what he saw as the Jewish materialistic interests lurking behind the plaintiffs, and recast himself as a free speech martyr. Beyond the rituals of procedure lay his real target—the Jewishness of the law itself.

DELIBERATIONS BEGAN ON Friday, November 19, and resumed the following Monday. By the afternoon of the next day came word that the jury had reached its decision. As the verdicts rolled in, audible gasps greeted the announcement of the damage awards: over $26 million total, $2 million in compensatory damages and a historic $24 million in punitive damages.

Yet the wrinkles were immediately obvious. The jury had deadlocked on the two federal conspiracy charges, resulting in "no verdict," while finding liability on state-level claims, including conspiracy to violate civil rights, hate crimes harassment, tortious assault and battery, and intentional infliction of emotional distress. Why had they found the defendants liable for racially motivated violence under state law but not federal law?

When it came to compensatory damages—money for actual harms suffered—they awarded $2 million to individual plaintiffs, along with the rest as punitive damages, intended to punish outrageous conduct and deter other offenders. These funds were disbursed in varying amounts, evidently based on the severity of physical injuries suffered.

Since the jury members were anonymous, their reasoning remained unknown. Perhaps the split federal-state verdicts reflected compromise based on internal disagreements. Perhaps the jury believed federal claims warranted a higher level of proof. Or perhaps they wished to send a message—or they simply wanted to go home for Thanksgiving.

What the jurors didn't know was that the punitive damages awarded would prove merely symbolic. Virginia state law caps punitive damages at $350,000 per case and mandates that juries should not be informed of this limit beforehand. Judge Moon would eventually trim the verdict down to $350,000 per plaintiff, while leaving in place the compensatory damages.[57]

In the press room, the court reporters pondered what the verdicts meant for the larger story. "What's the point?" asked one journalist. "Spencer has no money." "But it will place a black mark on him," answered another after a pause. "It will also bankrupt these groups." Similar verdicts in the past had shut down organizations like the Aryan Nation. "These guys are all screwed," chimed in another reporter, "but they've mainstreamed it successfully."

Both predictions proved prescient. Spencer's specific alt-right movement never recovered from its 2017 zenith. Leaders scattered, their followings evaporated. Andrew Anglin and Robert "Azzmador" Ray had fled before the trial began—Ray died in hiding in 2024, while Anglin remained a fugitive. Spencer and Cantwell filed appeals that went nowhere; the Unite the Right movement was finished. At the same time, their core ideology—redemptive violence wedded to replacement theory—endured. The internet persists as a rage factory where racists self-radicalize in digital echo chambers. Six months after the verdict, an eighteen-year-old white supremacist live streamed his assault on a Buffalo grocery store, murdering ten African Americans. His manifesto rehearsed familiar conspiracies: white genocide engineered by shadowy Jewish power, Black violence as its instrument.

Meanwhile, these conspiracy theories migrated from the margins to mainstream conservative discourse. Throughout 2021 and 2022, replacement theory became a staple of Tucker Carlson's Fox News commentary. The same ideological currents found institutional expression in the second Trump administration, in immigration policies championed by the likes of White House Deputy Chief of Staff Stephen Miller, border czar Tom Homan, and Secretary of Homeland Security Kristi Noem.

Newer figures who emerged from Unite the Right's ranks have been able to operate with relative impunity. Nick Fuentes, a Boston University freshman at the time of his participation in Charlottesville, later launched his America First movement—a toxic blend of Holocaust denial, antisemitic dual loyalty accusations, and Christian nationalist ideology. Enrique Tarrio, a former Florida state director of Latinos for Trump, attended the Charlottesville rally and went on to steer the Proud Boys toward escalating political violence that culminated in the January 6, 2021, Capitol attack. Though convicted of seditious conspiracy and other federal charges, he received a presidential pardon from Trump.

Another Charlottesville veteran, Vanguard America member Thomas Rousseau, seized control of the organization in the aftermath and rebranded it as Patriot Front, continuing to orchestrate violent demonstrations nationwide. In 2024, Virginia issued a felony warrant for Rousseau on charges of "burning an object to intimidate" during the August 11 torchlight rally—part of a belated wave of hate crimes prosecutions.

These prosecutions, launched in 2023 by James Hingeley, the new Commonwealth's attorney for Albemarle County, which includes Charlottesville, yielded eleven convictions. At the conclusion of the final trial, Hingeley declared the effort successful in delivering justice to lawbreakers while clarifying that prosecuting every rioter was never the goal. "Free speech in our country means that you can say terrible, hateful things and still not commit a crime."[58]

"THE MOST OBVIOUS way" to handle hate speech without violating the First Amendment, Supreme Court Justice Elena Kagan argued in a seminal 1993 essay, "is to regulate not speech, but conduct." Hate crimes laws aim to do precisely this, yet they offer an incomplete remedy. While such laws avoid viewpoint discrimination, they fail to deliver complete justice because they focus on the offender's motive rather than the victim's actual harm.[59]

Seeking to bridge the gap between the libertarian and egalitarian wings of First Amendment jurisprudence, Kagan called for a "purely pragmatic approach to regulating hate speech" in American law through increased reliance on "hate torts." As she wrote, "Communities should be able not only to impose enhanced criminal sanctions on the perpetrators of hate crimes, but also to provide special tort-based or other civil remedies for their victims." Though she diplomatically sidestepped whether this formulation constituted group libel in new guise, her proposal illuminated how civil litigation might achieve justice where criminal law falls short.[60]

In many respects, the Charlottesville trial realized Kagan's vision of "hate torts." When criminal law offered no other remedy for hatred, civil law beckoned with its promise of financial justice. In a capitalist America, the power of the purse would achieve a proportionate, rational resolution.

This strategy has grown more effective as society has increasingly financialized in recent decades. Social media platforms, political movements, universities, and hate groups now operate within a single network of banks and financial institutions, making economic pressure more potent—even in the era of cryptocurrency. Suing neo-Nazis for their actions held clear appeal. Harms could be proven and legally recognized, moral responsibility assigned to the architects of hateful violence, and consequences imposed without putting hate speech itself on trial.

Still, *Sines v. Kessler* revealed the inherent limitations of hate torts as instruments of justice. Civil litigation calculates harm in terms of individual material injury, not collective dignity or the broader terror inflicted on vulnerable communities. While tort law provides concrete remedies, it fundamentally reframes victims and perpetrators as competing parties in an economic dispute. Public welfare becomes subordinated to this rivalry between private interests.[61]

The very language of civil law reinforces this clinical approach: "liability" replaces "guilt" and "preponderance of evidence" supplants "beyond a reasonable doubt," shifting justice into a register of probability and causation rather than moral condemnation. Harm may be proven and quantified, but the resulting accountability remains necessarily incomplete.

This inherent incompleteness becomes even more troubling when considering the moral power of any civil trial. That power—the capacity to establish truth and educate the public—depends, even more than in criminal proceedings, on the narrative society constructs around the trial. Framed as a contest between private interests rather than moral judgment, a civil trial's ultimate meaning remains hostage to history's verdict.

On Monday evening, December 6, 2021, the Charlottesville City Council held a hearing on the fate of the Robert E. Lee monument. Years of court fights had succeeded in establishing that the city possessed the right to remove it. Now came the question of how to dispose of the eleven-hundred-pound bronze statue. The winning proposal came from Dr. Andrea Douglas and the city's Jefferson School African American Heritage Center. They proposed to melt it down and use the ingots to create a new public artwork for Charlottesville in an initiative to be called "Swords into Ploughshares." An act of imagination would transform a stark symbol of hatred into a radically new kind of historical memorial.[62]

Among those who spoke that night in support of "Swords into Ploughshares" was former plaintiff Lisa Draine. "For four years I've driven by the Lee statue reliving that awful weekend that my family and our community endured," she said, and it was now time to "correct the harms of the past four hundred years that our Black citizens have endured. As long as the Lee statue remains intact, the harm persists."[63]

Draine's testimony was a powerful reminder that the story of antisemitism in Charlottesville remained intertwined with a deeper, wider history of racism. Her words were echoed by Rabbi Gutherz, who also endorsed melting down the statue. Charlottesville has "forced us to think again about the stories we have been telling ourselves," he wrote in an open letter to his congregation—both in terms of "our belief in a kind of 'American exceptionalism' as regards Jewish history" and about "the kind of security we came to feel we were entitled to, even as violence against other racial and religious minorities continued to be an ongoing feature of our current moment."[64]

Gutherz was calling for Jews to reckon more directly with American antisemitism: how it persists largely unacknowledged and how its connections to other forms of racism are routinely ignored by Jews and non-Jews alike. The myths of exceptionalism needed dismantling: the myth that antisemitism hardly matters in America, that it exists apart from other hatreds, and that American history itself is exempt from such patterns. Only by abandoning these illusions could Jews reclaim their place in the common struggle for justice.

"Swords into Ploughshares" takes its title from the book of Isaiah. There, the biblical prophet speaks of a future era of peace among nations, when the people "shall beat their swords into plowshares, and their spears into pruning hooks. Nation shall not lift up sword against nation, neither shall they learn war anymore."[65]

Less commonly remembered is the verse's opening line, "And God shall judge among the nations, and shall rebuke many people." America's reconstruction depends on both the hard task of historical reckoning and the hopeful art of spiritual renewal. The vision of peaceful harmony does not substitute for legal justice but complements it. In a nation of many peoples, the law must face the hatreds that divide us.

Afterword

In the summer of 2022, UVA President Jim Ryan asked me a question no university leader had raised in my sixteen years there: What should we do about antisemitism and free speech?

As director of the Jewish Studies Program, I had requested this meeting to discuss the campus climate. I urged him to address antisemitism without isolating it from other hatreds, to link free speech to equal rights, and to engage the Israeli-Palestinian conflict through teaching and dialogue before it erupted on campus.

Why open such a contentious topic? he asked.

Because silence breeds mistrust and emboldens those who act in bad faith, I replied. Antisemitism has become a pressing political concern. While public scrutiny centers on Governor Youngkin's executive order regarding race, his plans targeting antisemitism have quietly positioned higher education in the line of fire.

Ryan dismissed this as a pet issue for a fringe group of Trump-aligned Republicans.

Antisemitism has surprising reach and political traction, I countered. The time to reckon with it is now, before the next crisis.

He took what I said under advisement. We never had occasion to speak again.

* * *

On October 7, 2023, Hamas fighters breached Israel's southern border, killing 1,200 people, committing acts of sexual violence, and abducting 250 hostages into Gaza. Israel responded with airstrikes and ground operations that, some two years later, had killed more than 65,000 Palestinians, displaced millions, and destroyed much of Gaza's infrastructure. Both sides have evidently violated international law—Hamas with its targeting of civilians and Israel with its disproportionate use of force and weaponization of food and aid. The scale of Palestinian death and suffering constitutes a humanitarian and moral catastrophe that no diplomatic accord or legal process can undo.

Within weeks of October 7, Americans divided into warring camps. At a November 2023 march in support of Palestine in Washington, DC, the Charlottesville sisters Sophie and Rebecca Schectman protested not only Israel's military offensive but Zionism itself. Back in 2017 "we had to stand up and be present in the streets" to oppose white supremacy, Rebecca explained. "And it's the same thing right now" with Zionism, which she equated with the alt-right's white supremacy. "I think particularly as Jews, we have to call out violence, apartheid, and genocide happening in the name of Jews."[1]

Meanwhile, at UVA, Israeli American freshman Matan Goldstein draped himself in an Israeli flag and walked to the Rotunda to "bear witness" to "the single most catastrophic act of antisemitic terrorism since the Holocaust." He chose the day of a pro-Palestinian walkout. His counterprotest sparked confrontations in which he was shoved and harassed. He later experienced bullying and death threats. Goldstein sued President Ryan and the university for civil rights violations, claiming the campus had become a hateful, hostile environment for Jewish students.[2]

These responses—Schectman's anti-Zionist activism and Goldstein's lawsuit—laid bare the fissures running through American Jewish life. Schectman, a civil rights lawyer, condemned the practice of invoking antisemitism to suppress criticism of Israel. Goldstein, by contrast, argued that permitting pro-Hamas speech and student organizations he likened to Hamas "sleeper cells" was unlawful. The university's response revealed a double standard, he alleged, when compared to its handling of anti-Black racism.[3]

As Palestinian casualties multiplied and hostages suffered in Gaza, antisemitism shifted from a peripheral matter to a defining fault line in American politics. Universities were caught in a vise: safeguard protest and free expression while addressing the fears of Jewish, Muslim, Israeli, and Palestinian students—each group experiencing real harassment, each group complaining of being silenced. A congressional hearing in November 2023 involving the presidents of Harvard, MIT, and the University of Pennsylvania (the latter formerly the provost of UVA) crystallized the moment. The pained exchanges over antisemitism and free speech on campus exposed both liberal evasiveness and conservative opportunism: university presidents who stumbled over how context shapes speech and cynical Republicans who exploited their failure.

By spring 2024, Gaza protest encampments had spread nationwide. Debates over slogans like "From the river to the sea" devolved into absolutist positions—civil rights versus free speech—with no recognition of Justice Oliver Wendell Holmes Jr.'s axiom that words take their meaning from context. Phrases spoken without antisemitic intent could land with antisemitic force; by the same token, not every anti-Zionist expression was a hate crime.[4]

By sidestepping antisemitism, American universities never mastered the balance between free expression and equal protection. When October 7 thrust the Middle East into campus quads, they found themselves in possession of legal frameworks with no common language for using them. Years of avoiding the subject of antisemitism left university leaders struggling to frame a coherent narrative for how protest and debate vis-à-vis the Israeli-Palestinian conflict should take place. Moral collapse followed: crude binaries of oppressor and liberator, terror supporter and anti-war protester. On many campuses, hastily assembled committees divided affected populations into parallel Jewish and Muslim camps, treating student communities like political constituencies while ignoring the actual dynamics of antisemitism, Islamophobia, and anti-Palestinian racism. No space remained to mourn all victims or hold multiple truths. The unresolved tensions on display in Charlottesville had hardened into national paralysis.

In July 2024, I was contacted by Gregory Brown, a UVA alumnus representing Matan Goldstein in his lawsuit against UVA. While I sympathized with concerns about UVA's handling of antisemitism, the case troubled me. In his public remarks, Goldstein had sharply criticized Jewish campus leaders, accusing them of moral cowardice. The lawsuit was encouraged by the Jefferson Council, the alumni group whose representatives had minimized the 2017 torchlight march and leveled baseless antisemitism charges against former colleagues. Brown's brief painted all pro-Gaza protesters as terrorist accomplices, claimed to speak for every Jewish student, and alleged that UVA sympathized with Hamas over its own Jewish community. I declined to participate.[5]

Six months later, Goldstein settled. Gregory Brown joined the second Trump administration as deputy head of the DOJ's Civil Rights Division, where he led efforts to defund universities over antisemitism and DEI. Among his targets was UVA. By summer 2025, President Ryan was forced to resign.

Trump's second term delivered the cruelest irony: abusing Jewish fear to dismantle higher education. Without due process or court findings, the administration froze university funding, withdrew support for scientific research, and detained and deported foreign students for statements about Israel. Constitutional protections collapsed.

What claimed to be the largest legal reckoning with antisemitism in American history doubled as its supreme trivialization—transforming a real problem into a political cudgel against universities, Palestinians, Muslims, and immigrants. And only supposed left-wing antisemitism counted; Christian nationalists and other antisemites were excused because of their support for Israel. The result was lawless legalism:

justice by fiat that trapped American Jews in an impossible bind. Who would call out the weaponization of campus antisemitism and risk being accused of downplaying hatred? Who would acknowledge the fears of both Jewish and Palestinian students and face condemnation from both sides for relativism?

This pseudo-justice—policies that claimed to combat antisemitism while eroding everyone's freedom—amounted to an assault on education and democracy. Liberal silence created a vacuum that antiliberal populists filled with their campaign to "defend the Jews." This cynical politicization drained antisemitism of meaning while exalting it as an exceptional form of hatred. Rather than broadening legal protections, these measures appeared to privilege one group above all others, further blurring the line between law and politics.

As WE HAVE seen, law's struggle with antisemitism in America long predates October 7. What, then, should we make of the history presented in this book? It allows for two readings.

The first reading finds familiar patterns. Antisemitism moves in cycles. It flares in times of national crisis, when America wrestles with race and religion, when civil rights hang in the balance. In these moments, it resurges as a populist myth of power, before cresting and receding. The Jewish abandonment of group libel law during McCarthyism teaches a clear lesson: Antisemitic speech poses less danger than authoritarianism itself. The imperative is to defend free speech to preserve liberalism.

The second reading argues that we have missed past chances to combat a substantive evil. The law permits far more regulation than we have attempted under the First Amendment. We arrived at this dangerous juncture by refusing to curb hate speech, allowing hatred to infiltrate mainstream politics, and permitting social media to destroy privacy. We separated free speech from civil rights, making it harder to distinguish between political grievance and material harm. This reading's lesson is to seize this moment to revise liberalism for the world we actually inhabit.

Both readings are true. Antisemitism is neither eternal virus nor genetic fate; it is a human-made myth about race, religion, and power.

We must historicize rather than pathologize it—understanding how it emerges when the very categories of minority and majority shift beneath our feet.

To craft principled and effective law, we must treat antisemitism as neither exception nor abstraction. While antisemitism has distinctive features, it cannot be severed from the struggle against other hatreds. We err when we collapse all hatreds into one, and when we isolate each as incomparable. Though antisemitism defies conventional categories of racism and religious prejudice, we must integrate it into our legal framework, preserving its distinctiveness while weaving it into the larger fabric of equality. Only then can we build remedies worthy of this moment and a liberalism worth defending.

How, then, do we secure equal protection without sliding into censorship? How do we create both freedom and equality without forging tools that can be turned to intimidate others?

What we need is not slogans about free speech but durable safeguards that protect rights and empower pluralism. Efforts to curb legitimate speech in the name of combating antisemitism are both wrong and disingenuous. Those who borrow the machinery of illiberalism will live to regret the harm done to their neighbors—and their democracy. One injury cannot be healed by inflicting another.

Yet illiberal authoritarianism will not be defeated by nostalgic invocations of lost golden eras of free speech, nor by tallying hypocrisies on right or left. Politicization is a symptom, not a disease. Empty rhetoric about the virtues of free speech is not, ultimately, a true defense of free speech. Nor are privatized media empires that promise liberation while binding expression to algorithms and oligarchs. The marketplace of ideas is no laissez-faire bazaar, but a public institution shaped by law.

There is no clean escape from the tension between free speech and group equality—nor should there be. These interdependent goods are bound together in the American democratic project. Personal freedom requires collective welfare; free expression nurtures pluralism; dissent depends on equal protection.

The First Amendment may be first, but it is not the only amendment. We need a pluralist liberalism that honors difference without fetishizing it, backed by laws that protect free speech not through absolutism, but by preventing its abuse.

Could we envision a constitutional prohibition on hate speech, as earlier generations once dared to imagine? Though our present libertarian speech culture appears hostile to such possibilities, we inhabit an era where the impossible has repeatedly become inevitable. For generations, constitutional scholars held as gospel that free speech protections could never extend to corporations—until in 2010 the Supreme Court's *Citizens United* decision shattered that certainty. *Roe v. Wade* stood as settled precedent for half a century—until it didn't. These seismic shifts remind us that constitutional law remains an open field of interpretation, forever in flux despite originalism's pretensions to fixity.[6]

As for the reflexive warning that touching the First Amendment invites tyranny, this claim has been exposed as unfounded by recent events. Illiberal regimes need no constitutional amendments; they simply invoke national security to gut rights at will.

Even without going so far as to resurrect group libel laws, however, we can craft protections that safeguard dignity and prevent genuine harm while avoiding the muzzling of dissent. In an age when a single online falsehood can obliterate a reputation in moments, why surrender the regulation of online hate speech entirely to private actors while shielding platforms from liability? When hatred flows seamlessly from screen to street, why not strengthen privacy laws to recognize doxxing as the hate crime it often is? When public protest proves vital yet hazardous, why not adopt anti-masking laws that strip anonymity from both agitators and authorities alike?

We have watched both free speech and censorship become political weapons. We have witnessed stumbles and overcorrections, mounting cynicism and exhaustion. What we have yet to do is imagine and build something better.

The path forward depends on both our current legal architecture and the future we dare to envision. This history offers not a road map but a reservoir of ideas and experiments—some promising, others cautionary. We must draw from this well not to re-create the past, but to forge a future where freedom and equality strengthen rather than undermine each other. Law must tame politics; it is up to us to design the framework for doing so.

NEARLY FIFTY YEARS ago, in the crisis at Skokie, Sol Goldstein reached for a rabbinic line: "The book lies open, the hand still writes." As we saw, he lifted it from its original context—where every deed is recorded in the divine ledger and justice will come—and transformed it into a civic summons. America, he suggested, is an unfinished manuscript; the future is still to be written by this generation and the ones to come.

A few lines earlier in the same ancient text, the rabbis offer a paradox: "Everything is foreseen, yet freedom of choice is granted." If our fate is known, what room is left for choice? As we reckon with antisemitism's long past and America's uncertain future, that tension presses hard. How do we honor history's weight without surrendering our power to build a more just tomorrow? The persistence of antisemitism and law's limits in taming the damage words inflict can tempt us toward resignation. This drama of hatred began before us and will not end with a single statute, election, or war. How, then, do we act with clarity and resolve?

The ancients felt that tension and refused both fatalism and pious passivity. They continued: "And the world is judged with goodness." They held faith in both divine judgment and human freedom to remake the world. Choices carry consequences, which are the price of freedom.

History, too, sits in judgment as we read the past from the vantage point of the present. In either case, the charge remains: We must choose—and choose wisely—how we shape our laws and press the claims of justice.

NOTES

INTRODUCTION

1. *Commonwealth of Virginia v. Jacob Dix*, Albemarle Circuit Court (June 6, 2024), Trial Transcript (hereafter Dix Transcript).
2. "Message from the University of Virginia," August 12, 2017, news.virginia.edu; University of Virginia, August 2017 Archive, august2017.lib.virginia.edu (hereafter UVAA), Peter Blake, "August 17, 2017, email from Executive Director of State Council of Higher Education in Virginia (SCHEV) to UVA President"; Charlottesville Public Schools Convocation Speech of Dr. Rosa Atkins, August 15, 2017.
3. Donald J. Trump, "Remarks on Infrastructure and an Exchange with Reporters in New York City," August 15, 2017, The American Presidency Project, www.presidency.ucsb.edu.

CHAPTER 1: SOMEONE ELSE'S SKIN

1. Native American girls were also relegated to the Miss Sepia America contest, also known as the Miss Bronze America pageant, though a native Miss Oklahoma competed in the Miss America 1941 contest. Puerto Rican and indigenous Hawaiian contestants were admitted to the Miss America pageant in 1948. "Beauties on Parade at Atlantic City," *Philadelphia Inquirer*, September 5, 1945; Susan Dworkin, *Miss America, 1945: Bess Myerson and the Year That Changed Our Lives* (Newmarket Press, 1987), 88; "Miss Sepia Philadelphia Given Crown," *Atlanta Daily World*, July 10, 1945; Nelson Johnson, *The Northside: African Americans and the Creation of Atlantic City* (Plexus Publications, 2010), 43; Bryant Simon, *Boardwalk of Dreams: Atlantic City and the Fate of Urban America* (Oxford University Press, 2004).

2. "Leyb Meyerson, foter fun der sheynhayt-kenigin, dertseylt vegen zayn tokhter un ir svivve in di sholem aleykhem hayzer," *Der Tog*, September 11, 1945; Dworkin, *Miss America*, 68–69.
3. Dworkin, *Miss America*, 93–94.
4. When a reporter for a Yiddish daily interviewed her father hours after her win, he stressed his daughter's commitment to education (and her exceptional grades) and her passion for "Jewish and social causes." "Leyb Meyerson"; Penelope Armstrong, "Tall Girl with a Flute," *Philadelphia Inquirer*, October 14, 1945; William Frank, "The Man About Town," *Wilmington News Journal*, November 5, 1945.
5. The sole Jewish corporate underwriter, Henry Harteveldt, owner of the Harvel Watch Company, threatened to go public if Myerson were surreptitiously disqualified. "'Miss America' May Hail from N.Y.C.," *Chester Times*, September 7, 1945; "Beauty Queen of AAF Veterans," *Lowell Sun*, September 6, 1945; Dworkin, *Miss America*, 93–94, 145, 148; Jennifer Preston, *Queen Bess: The Unauthorized Biography of Bess Myerson* (Contemporary Books, 1990), 31, 124.
6. David Schwartz, "The Beauty of America," *Wisconsin Jewish Chronicle*, October 5, 1945.
7. Dorothy Kilgallen, "Voice of Broadway," *Bangor Daily News*, September 25, 1945; "Veterans' Choice Wins 'Miss America' Title, Scholarship," *Buffalo Evening News*, September 10, 1945; Dworkin, *Miss America*, 171; "Miss America to Be Feature of Victory Loan Parade," *Wilmington Morning News*, October 31, 1945; "Idishe mis amerike aplodirt in senat," *Der Tog*, November 10, 1945. On Myerson's physical appearance and the aesthetics of Jewish whiteness, see Sarah Banet-Weiser, *The Most Beautiful Girl in the World: Beauty Pageants and National Identity* (University of California Press, 1999), 161–66.
8. Dworkin, *Miss America*, 178–80.
9. Preston, *Queen Bess*, 40.
10. Dworkin, *Miss America*, 189.
11. "America has no history of anti-Semitism," wrote Anti-Defamation League founder Sigmund Livingston in 1944, unironically. "It is a late import from Europe, where it was the poisonous aftergrowth in the jungles of religious fanaticism and superstition." Sigmund Livingston, *Must Men Hate?* (Harper & Brothers, 1944), xii.
12. Morris Schappes, ed., *A Documentary History of the Jews in the United States: 1654–1875* (Schocken Books, 1952), 1–2.
13. Arthur Wetsteijn, "Colonies of Concord: Religious Escapism and Experimentation in Dutch Overseas Expansion, ca. 1650–1700," in Joke Spaans and Jetze Touber, eds., *Enlightened Religion from Confessional Churches to Polite Piety in the Dutch Republic* (Brill, 2019), 107–8; Naomi Cohen, *Jews in Christian America: The Pursuit of Religious Equality* (Oxford University Press, 1987), 15.
14. Leonard Dinnerstein, *Antisemitism in America* (Oxford University Press, 1994), 8.
15. David Nirenberg, *Anti-Judaism: The Western Tradition* (W. W. Norton and Company, 2013); Jean-Frédéric Schaub, *Race Is About Politics* (Princeton University Press, 2019); Magda Teter, *Christian Supremacy: Reckoning with the Roots of Antisemitism and Racism* (Princeton University Press, 2023), 16–44.

16. Nancy Shoemaker, "How Indians Got to Be Red," *American Historical Review* 102:3 (June 1987): 625–44; Teter, *Christian Supremacy*, 45–78.
17. On the small but important phenomenon of multiracial Jews, see Laura Leibman, *Once We Were Slaves: The Extraordinary Journey of a Multiracial Jewish Family* (Oxford University Press, 2021) and Shari Rabin, *The Jewish South: An American History* (Princeton University Press, 2025), 66–67.
18. Jaap Jacobs, *New Netherland: A Dutch Colony in Seventeenth-Century America* (Brill, 2005), 373–79; Evan Haefeli, *New Netherland and the Dutch Origins of American Religious Liberty* (University of Pennsylvania Press, 2012), 115–22; Schappes, *Documentary History*, 4-5.
19. Jacob Rader Marcus, ed., *The Jew in the American World* (Wayne State University Press, 1996), 32.
20. Roger Williams, *The Bloody Tenent Yet More Bloody* (London, 1652), 149; Cohen, *Jews in Christian America*, 17–18.
21. Antony Polonsky, *The Jews in Poland and Russia*, vol. 1 (Littman Library of Jewish Civilization, 2010), 29; Christhard Hoffmann, Werner Bergmann, and Helmut Walser Smith, eds., *Exclusionary Violence: Antisemitic Riots in Modern German History* (University of Michigan Press, 2010).
22. Frederic Jaher, *A Scapegoat in the New Wilderness: The Origins and Rise of Anti-Semitism in America* (Harvard University Press, 1996), 130.
23. Schappes, *Documentary History*, 80–81. For a critical reappraisal of the origins and meaning of this letter, see John Dixon, "Rethinking American Jewish Emancipation: New Views on George Washington's Newport Letter," *American Jewish History* 107:4 (2023): 731–56.
24. "All Christian sects enjoy in America an entire liberty," wrote France's ambassador to the United States in 1786, but "the Jews have the exercise of their religion only." The Protestant architects of American religious freedom conceive of religion itself as anything other than a private, individual experience centered on personal beliefs and internal devotion. This post-Reformation model of religion—a word that did not even exist in the Hebrew language—ill fitted the Jewish tradition's blend of divine laws, separate calendar, customs, and ethno-spiritual culture that governed every aspect of Jewish existence. Jaher, *Scapegoat*, 168; Leora Batnitzky, *How Judaism Became a Religion* (Princeton University Press, 2011); Hasia Diner, *A Time for Gathering: The Second Migration, 1820–1880* (Johns Hopkins University Press, 1995), 131–32.
25. In the few instances when nineteenth-century Jews challenged these laws in court, judges typically ruled that Sunday laws merely constituted an exercise of police powers to maintain morality and public order, with no punitive impact on Jews. Many such laws technically remain in force. Kyle Volk, *Moral Minorities and the Making of American Democracy* (Oxford University Press, 2014), 45–65; Morton Borden, *Jews, Turks, Infidels* (University of North Carolina Press, 2011), 111–15, 142; Cohen, *Jews in Christian America*, 48; Teter, *Christian Supremacy*, 128–40; Sarah Barringer Gordon, "The First Disestablishment: Limits on Church Power and Property Before the Civil War," *University of Pennsylvania Law Review* 162:2 (2014): 307–72.

26. Women and indentured servants were de facto excluded as well. Jared Goldstein, "How the Constitution Became Christian," *Hastings Law Journal* 68:2 (2017): 259–308; Borden, *Jews, Turks, Infidels*, 25, 109.
27. By contrast, African Americans were legally barred from serving in the federal military until the Emancipation Proclamation and served thereafter only in segregated units.
28. Eric Eisner, "'Hebrews in Favor of the South': Jews, Race, and the North Carolina State Convention of 1861–1862," *Southern Jewish History* 24 (2021): 1–47; Rabin, *The Jewish South*, 100–16.
29. Because of its depiction of a restless, heroic Jewish nation in exile, Ezekiel's biographer Samantha Baskind terms *Israel* "one of the earliest statements on modern Zionism in sculptural form." Abby Schwartz, *Artistic Expressions of Faith in Judaism, Christianity, and Islam* (Taft Museum, 1997), 10; Samantha Baskind, *Moses Jacob Ezekiel: Jewish, Confederate, Expatriate Sculptor* (Penn State University Press, 2025), 78–79.
30. Simon Wolf, *The Presidents I Have Known from 1860–1918* (Byron S. Adams, 1918), 89; Baskind, *Moses Jacob Ezekiel*, 14–36. During World War II, the United States Treasury featured "Religious Liberty" in a nationwide advertising campaign for war bonds. "Our defenders of faith must have planes, cannon, shot and thousands of other items" to win the war for "religious liberty," read one 1945 newspaper advertisement. "Religious Liberty," *Warren Times-Mirror*, April 27, 1945.
31. Wilhelm Marr, *Der Judenspiegel* (Hamburg, 1862), 41–42, 51; Moshe Zimmerman, *Wilhelm Marr: The Patriarch of Antisemitism* (Oxford University Press, 1986), 48, 84–85.
32. Wilhelm Marr, *Der Sieg des Judenthums über das Germanenthum vom nicht confessionellen Standpunkt aus betrachtet* (Bern, 1879), 29–31; Wilhelm Marr, *Goldene Ratten und rothe Mäuse* (Chemnitz, 1880), 6.
33. "A Sensation at Saratoga: New Rules for the Grand Union," *New York Times*, June 19, 1877.
34. *Coney Island and the Jews* (New York, 1879), 20–21; "No Objections to 'White Jew,'" *The White Jew*, August 9, 1879; Dinnerstein, *Antisemitism*, 40; Teter, *Christian Supremacy*, 198–205. See also Britt Tevis, "'Jews Not Admitted': Anti-Semitism, Civil Rights, and Public Accommodation Laws," *Journal of American History* 107:4 (March 2021): 847–70.
35. Already in 1876, the Supreme Court had ruled in *United States v. Cruikshank* that the Fourteenth Amendment could not prohibit private discrimination or apply federal civil rights laws to state governments. *United States v. Cruikshank*, 92 U.S. 542 (1876); *The Civil Rights Cases*, 109 U.S. 3 (1883).
36. J. C. Levenson, "The Etiology of Israel Adams: The Onset, Waning, and Relevance of Henry Adams's Anti-Semitism," *New Literary History* 25:3 (Summer 1994): 583.
37. Deborah Dash Moore, *B'nai B'rith and the Challenge of Ethnic Leadership* (State University of New York Press, 1984), 103.
38. Mark Twain, "Concerning the Jews," *Harper's New Monthly Magazine* (June 1899): 528, 535.

39. Joel Perlmann, *America Classifies the Immigrants: From Ellis Island to the 2020 Census* (Harvard University Press, 2018), 22, 92–93, 100; Katherine Benton-Cohen, *Inventing the Immigration Problem: The Dillingham Commission and Its Legacy* (Harvard University Press, 2018), 89–103.
40. Founding Charter, *B'nai B'rith News*, October 1913, 1. On the early origins of the ADL, see Joseph Kirman, "Major Programs of the B'nai B'rith Anti-Defamation League: 1945–1965," PhD diss., New York University, 1967, 51–61.
41. Moore, *B'nai B'rith*, 105; "Founding Charter," *B'nai B'rith News*, October 1913; *Report of the Anti-Defamation League* (San Francisco, 1915), 5; *Report of the Anti-Defamation League of B'nai B'rith* (Chicago, 1920), 14; Kirman, "Major Programs," 73–74.
42. A similar impulse led Adolph Ochs, the Jewish publisher of *The New York Times*, to write at the behest of the ADL to daily newspaper editors across the country in 1913, requesting they refrain from using the word "Jew" as a noun or verb, and only when absolutely necessary as an adjective. Moore, *B'nai B'rith*, 105, 111; Evan Schultz, "Group Rights, American Jews, and the Failure of Group Libel Law, 1913–1952," *Brooklyn Law Review* 66:1 (September 2000): 71–144; Jeffrey Gurock, "The 1913 New York State Civil Rights Act," *AJS Review* 1 (1976): 96.
43. Kirman, "Major Programs," 78.
44. Leo Ribuffo, "Henry Ford and *The International Jew*," *American Jewish History* 69:4 (June 1980): 465–69; "President Wilson Heads Protest Against Anti-Semitism," *Bridgeport Telegram*, January 17, 1921; Neil Baldwin, *Henry Ford and the Jews: The Mass Production of Hate* (Public Affairs, 2001), 147–48; Victoria Saker Woeste, *Henry Ford's War on Jews and the Legal Battle Against Hate Speech* (Stanford University Press, 2012).
45. Laura Weinrib, *The Taming of Free Speech: America's Civil Liberties Compromise* (Harvard University Press, 2019).
46. For an important study questioning the conventional wisdom about this metaphor, see Vincent Blasi, "Holmes and the Marketplace of Ideas," *Supreme Court Review* (2004): 1–46.
47. "There is no law than can kill bigotry, hatred, prejudice and the evils that grow out of human ignorance and frailty," countered Mayor James Curley, "but the arm of the law is long enough and its hand heavy enough to reach both scoundrel and fool when they undertake to translate their evil passions into actions dangerous to the public weal." Harvard University, Zechariah Chafee Jr. Papers, Box 30, Folders 20–22, James Curley to John Codman, October 4, 1923, and ACLU to James Curley, October 11, 1923; Samuel Walker, *In Defense of American Liberties: A History of the ACLU* (Oxford University Press, 1995), 61; Shawn Lynch, "'In Defense of True Americanism': The Civil Liberties Union of Massachusetts and Radical Free Speech, 1915–1945," PhD diss., Boston College, 2006, 40–44.
48. *Whitney v. California*, 274 U.S. 357 (1927).
49. Kirman, "Major Programs," 96; Baldwin, *Henry Ford*, 306–7; Leo Ribuffo, *The Old Christian Right: The Protestant Far Right from the Great Depression to the Cold War* (Temple University Press, 1983), 128–77.

50. Dinnerstein, *Antisemitism*, 131; Nathan Belth, *A Promise to Keep: A Narrative of the American Encounter with Anti-Semitism* (Times Books, 1979), 151, 156.
51. New York University, Jewish Labor Committee Papers (hereafter JLC), Box 270, Folder 4, Memorandum, June 10, 1943.
52. Much of this violence was ignored in the mainstream press. One exception was the coverage in the liberal tabloid *PM*. See, for example, "Chicago Police Stopped Attacks on Jews," *PM*, January 3, 1945.
53. Ben Harris, "Jewish Quotas in Clinical Psychology? The *Journal of Clinical Psychology* and the Scandal of 1945," *Review of General Psychology* 13:3 (2009): 252–61; JLC, Box 270, Folder 42, Anti-Defamation League Memorandum, August 2, 1945.
54. "Horner Approval Still in Dispute," *New York Times*, February 11, 1945.
55. "22 protsent fun oysgefregte amerikaner soldaten heysen gut hitlers shekhites oyf yiden," *Forverts*, January 25, 1946; Belth, *Promise*, 151.
56. Dworkin, *Miss America*, 191–94.
57. National Archives and Records Administration (hereafter NARA), RG65, 100-367944, FBI Memorandum, February 3, 1950.
58. NARA, RG 65, HQ 100–530; ADL Memorandum, June 15, 1945.
59. YIVO Institute for Jewish Research Archive, American Jewish Committee Records (hereafter YIVO AJC), RG 347.17.10, Box 1, Folder 1, "Combatting Anti-Semitism Through Public Information and Education," May 28, 1946; Interview with Benjamin Epstein in Oscar Cohen and Stanley Wexler, eds., *"Not the Work of a Day": Anti-Defamation League of B'nai B'rith Oral Memoirs* (Anti-Defamation League, 1989), vol. 1, ii–iii, vii, 93–95.
60. Wendy Wall, *Inventing the "American Way": The Politics of Consensus from the New Deal to the Civil Rights Movement* (Oxford University Press, 2008); Stuart Svonkin, *Jews Against Prejudice: American Jews and the Fight for Civil Liberties* (Columbia University Press, 1997).
61. Earl Conrad, "Miss America Is Beauty + Brains," *Chicago Defender*, January 19, 1946; *Report of the Anti-Defamation League of B'nai B'rith* (Anti-Defamation League, 1946), 10–12; "Miss America Packs 'Em In for Lectures," *Los Angeles Times*, April 28, 1946; Dworkin, *Miss America*, 196.
62. Myerson's Chicago visit was organized by a new friend, Martha Glaser (later Gleicher), who was the special assistant to the Chicago mayor charged with fighting racism and antisemitism in the city. "Miss America in City," *Chicago Tribune*, February 26, 1946; "You Can't Be Beautiful and Hate," *Boston Globe*, March 17, 1946; University of Pittsburgh, Erroll Garner Archive, Martha Glaser Papers, www.digital.library.pitt.edu, Memos by Martha Gleicher, January 18, May 10, and November 18, 1946.
63. "Miss America Packs 'Em In for Lectures"; "'Miss America' Urges Interrace Cooperation," *Chicago Defender*, June 1, 1946; "'Miss America' Turns Lecturer," *Fort-Myers News Press*, April 21, 1946; Conrad, "Miss America."
64. "'Miss America' Turns Lecturer"; Bess Myerson, "Miss America Speaks to Young America," *Jewish Veteran* (April 1946): 4–5.

65. "Luncheon Speaker," *Chicago Tribune*, June 4, 1946; "Lead Fight Against Bigotry," *Wisconsin Jewish Chronicle*, June 21, 1946; "Miss America of '45 in Comic Portrays Fight for Tolerance," *Detroit Jewish News*, September 20, 1946; "A Real Miss America," *New Heroic Comics* 41:1 (March 1947); L. Malkes, "Di sheyne meydlakh vos vern oysgeklibn yeden yor als 'Mis Amerike,'" *Forverts*, September 20, 1946.

CHAPTER 2: A RIOT IN CHICAGO

1. Norman Stoken, "They'll Hear from Judge Heller," *The Sentinel*, February 12, 1946; G. L. K. Smith, "Red Mobsters Attack America First Rally," *Cross and Flag* (March 1946): 719.
2. "Khuligan Dzherald Smit git zikh iber dem politsay," *Forverts* (Chicago edition), February 9, 1946; "Order G.L.K.'s Arrest After Riot at Rally," *Chicago Daily Times*, February 8, 1946.
3. "Khuligan Dzherald Smit"; "Clashes Mark Gerald Smith Rally," *Chicago Tribune*, February 8, 1946; Jack Fishbein, "The Editor Views the News," *The Sentinel*, February 7, 1946.
4. "Terminiello Invades Philly; Hits Zionists; FDR, Truman Called 'Tools,'" *Jewish Post*, January 25, 1946.
5. Alan Brinkley, *Voices of Protest: Huey Long, Father Coughlin, and the Great Depression* (Vintage, 1982), 17; Gerald L. K. Smith, "This Is Nationalism," *Cross and Flag* (February 1946): 708; Supreme Court of the United States, Transcript of Record: Arthur Terminiello, Petitioner, vs. City of Chicago, 1948 (hereafter Terminiello Transcript).
6. Smith, "This Is Nationalism."
7. Terminiello Transcript.
8. University of Notre Dame, Arthur Terminiello Papers (hereafter ATP), CTRM 1/08, Terminiello Draft Memoir; Edward Euelenberg, "Jury Finds Terminiello Guilty; Diatribes Against Jews Read to Court," *Jewish Post*, April 5, 1946; Terminiello Transcript.
9. *Report of the Anti-Defamation League of B'nai B'rith* (Anti-Defamation League, 1947), 10; American Jewish Historical Society, American Jewish Congress Papers (hereafter AJCP), I-77, Box 13, Folder 1, American Jewish Congress Annual Report, May 28, 1946.
10. YIVO AJC, RG 347.17.12, Box 151, Folder 10–1, Edward Jelenko, "Arthur W. Terminiello" (March 4, 1946); ATP, CTRM 1/01, Terminiello Draft Memoir; "Communications," *The Heights*, April 5, 1927; H. Sylvester, "Dynamite in Alabama," *Commonweal* 28 (Summer 1938): 573–74; *Greenville Advocate*, February 28, 1936; Michael Williams, "Gospel by Gas: Priest Uses Modern Trailer Spreading Faith in Southern Alabama," *Literary Digest* (March 13, 1937): 36–37.
11. David S. Bovée, *The Church and the Land: The National Catholic Rural Life Conference and American Society, 1923–2007* (Catholic University Press, 2010); ATP, CTRM 1/01, Terminiello Draft Memoir; Sylvester, "Dynamite"; Arthur Terminiello, "A Co-Operative Village," *Boston College Alumni News* (February 1942):

14; Luigi G. Ligutti and John C. Rawe, *Rural Roads to Security; America's Third Struggle for Freedom* (Bruce Publishing Company, 1940), 331–32; Samuel Myers, "Consumers' Cooperation: A Plan for the Negro," PhD diss., Boston University, 1942, 94–95; Arthur Terminiello, "Christocracy—The New Order," *St. Teresa Village News*, October 1941.

12. On Terminiello's impact on Jewish Alabama, see Dan Puckett, *In the Shadow of Hitler: Alabama's Jews, the Second World War, and the Holocaust* (University of Alabama Press, 2014), 190–95; Jelenko, "Terminiello"; ATP, CTRM 1/01, Terminiello Draft Memoir.
13. Mark Newman, *Desegregating Dixie: The Catholic Church in the South and Desegregation, 1945–1992* (University of Mississippi Press, 2018), 31; University of Michigan, Gerald Smith Papers (hereafter GSP), Box 17, A. Terminiello to G. L. K. Smith, January 25, 1947; "Terminiello Invades Philly"; ATP, CTRM 1/01, CTRM 1/05, CTRM 1/10, and CTRM 1/14, Terminiello Draft Memoir; "Can It Rise Above Its Source," *Roanoke Rapids Herald*, January 10, 1946; University of Texas, Arlington, George W. Armstrong Papers (hereafter GAP), Box 148, Folder 29, A. Terminiello to G. Armstrong, October 29, 1945; "The World Plot Unfolds," *Birmingham News*, November 29, 1945; "Priest Blames Leftist Smear for His Ouster," *Chicago Tribune*, November 25, 1945; G. L. K. Smith, "Editorial Briefs," *Cross and Flag* 4:10 (January 1946): 686; YIVO AJC, RG 347.17.12, Box 151, Folder 2, ADL Memo, December 7, 1945 and J. Proskauer and T. J. Toolen correspondence, March 22–October 31, 1945.
14. Jelenko, "Terminiello"; ATP, CTRM 1/01, Terminiello Draft Memoir; GSP, Box 14, G. L. K. Smith to R. Baldwin, January 15, 1945.
15. ATP, CTRM 1/08 and CTRM 1/13, Terminiello Draft Memoir.
16. ATP, CTRM 1/13, Terminiello Draft Memoir.
17. ATP, CTRM 1/8, Terminiello Draft Memoir.
18. ATP, CTRM 1/01, Terminiello Draft Memoir; "Khuligan Dzherald Smit."
19. "Clashes Mark Gerald Smith Rally."
20. Chicago History Museum, Ira Latimer Papers (hereafter ILP), Box 4, CCLC Minutes, 1945; "Chicago Police Stopped Attacks on Jews," *PM*, January 3, 1945.
21. Kermit Small and Van Allen Bradley Jr., "Chicago, the Munich of America," *American Mercury* (November 1943): 544.
22. A graduate of Ohio State University, where he wrote an MA thesis on Black nationalism, Latimer taught at a missionary college in China and then at LeMoyne College, an African American school in Memphis, Tennessee, before relocating to Chicago. "West Side Calls Community Conference to Combat Anti-Semitism," *The Sentinel*, December 2, 1943; "Community Conference Will Outline Methods to Combat Anti-Semitism," *The Sentinel*, January 13, 1944; "Illinois U. Winks at Racism," *Civil Liberties News* 1:6 (September 21, 1945): 2; Ira Latimer, "Free-Religion Trial Opens in Champaign," *Civil Liberties News*, 1:7 (September 14, 1945); 1; ILP, Box 6, I. Latimer to *Chicago Tribune*, September 1, 1948; Ira Latimer, "Political Potentialities of the American Negro: A Natural

History of American Negro Nationalism, or 'Race Consciousness,'" MA thesis, Ohio State University, 1932.

23. ILP, Box 4, CCLC Minutes, 1944.
24. ILP, Box 4, E. Ryerson III to I. Latimer, February 27, 1944.
25. "Letters to the Editor," *The Sentinel*, February 28, 1946.
26. For his part, Smith made a distinction between Baldwin and "his Jew lawyers." GSP, Box 19, G. L. K. Smith to M. St. George, April 24, 1946; Princeton University, ACLU Papers (hereafter PU ACLU), vol. 2619, R. Baldwin to G. Leonard, April 11, 1944.
27. ILP, Box 6, Draft Memo, March 23, 1948; "Civil Liberties . . . For Whites Only?" *Chicago Defender*, January 27, 1945; PU ACLU, vol. 2619, G. L. K. Smith to R. Baldwin, March 15, 1944, and *ACLU Bulletin* 1123, April 17, 1944; ILP, Box 4, CCLC Minutes, 1944; University of Chicago, ACLU Papers (Illinois Division) (hereafter UC ACLU), Box 41, Folder 3, ACLU Executive Committee Minutes, 1945–1946; ILP, Box 6, Letter to the Editor, September 1, 1946, *Chicago Tribune*, and from I. Latimer to E. Allen, n.d.; Laura Weinrib, "Law, History, and the Interwar ACLU's Jewish Lawyers," in Jacob Katz Cogan and Kenneth Mack, eds., *Between and Across: Legal History Without Boundaries* (Oxford University Press, 2024), 269–88.
28. UC ACLU, Box 77, Folder 4, R. Baldwin to Chicago ACLU, April 20, 1945, and L. Despres to H. Jack, February 6, 1946; YIVO AJC, RG 347.17.12, Box 151, Folder 10–1, Memo from Arnold Forster to ADL Regional Offices, March 7, 1946; "Current Comment," *Jewish Post*, February 22, 1946; *Report of the Anti-Defamation League* (1947), 10.
29. S. Anhil Fineberg, "Can Anti-Semitism Be Outlawed?" *Contemporary Jewish Record* 6 (December 1943): 619–31; JLC, Box 271, Folder 36, Solomon Fineberg, "Gerald L. K. Smith," November 20, 1945; American Jewish Archives (hereafter AJA), Solomon A. Fineberg Collection, MS-149, Box 3, File 5, S. Anhil Fineberg, "Gerald L. K. Smith" (August 1972). See also Solomon Fineberg, *Overcoming Antisemitism* (Harper & Brothers, 1943).
30. Jack Fishbein, "Disastrous 'Shah Shah' Policy Must End," *The Sentinel*, February 14, 1946; Avrum Tapper, "Tips for Tap," *The Sentinel*, March 7, 1946.
31. Municipal Code of Chicago, 1939 §193–1.
32. The committee also hired the legal stenographer to preserve a transcript as possible evidence. "Current Comment"; Edward Durchshlag, Letter to the Editor, *Jewish Post*, March 15, 1946; "Civil Liberties Street Meeting Permit Refused," *Chicago Tribune*, February 7, 1946; Jack Fishbein, "The Editor Views the News," *The Sentinel*, February 7, 1946; Jack Fishbein, "The Significance of the T. Verdict!" *The Sentinel*, April 11, 1946; ILP, Box 5, CCLC Minutes, 1946; "Judge Samuel Heller Appeals to Rabbi Stephen S. Wise," *The Sentinel*, June 17, 1943; Interview with Charles Heller, May 12, 2020.
33. On his stationery, Terminiello printed two mottoes, one in English and one in Latin. The English text read, "United for the cause of freedom of speech, the

press, religion and assembly," along with Benjamin Franklin's aphorism, "Those who would give up essential liberty to purchase a little temporary safety deserve neither liberty nor safety." The Latin phrase stemmed from ancient Christianity associated with Eusebius and Constantine: *In hoc signo vinces*, or "In this sign you shall conquer." GWA, Box 146, A. Terminiello to G. Armstrong, October 29, 1945; ILP, Box 4, G. L. K. Smith to CCLC, March 13, 1945; ATP, CTRM 1/01, Terminiello Draft Memoir.

34. Smith, "This Is Nationalism," 708; ATP, CTRM 1/01, Terminiello Draft Memoir.
35. Stoken, "They'll Hear from Judge Heller."
36. "12 of 15 Seized at G. L. K. Smith Meeting Freed," *Chicago Tribune*, March 12, 1946; "Clashes Mark Gerald Smith Rally"; Edward Euelenberg, "Jury Finds Terminiello Guilty," *Jewish Post*, April 5, 1946; Robert Birchman, "1,500 Chicago Workers Picket G.L.K. Smith's Fascist Meeting," *The Militant*, February 16, 1946.
37. ATP, CTRM 1/01, Terminiello Draft Memoir.
38. ATP, CTRM 1/01 and CTRM 1/08, Terminiello Draft Memoir; Terminiello Transcript, 53; "Clashes Mark Gerald Smith Rally"; "G.L.K. Smith in New Booking—By Police," *Cleveland Plain Dealer*, February 9, 1946.
39. ATP, CTRM 1/09, Press Release, February 7, 1946, and Terminiello Draft Memoir; "Gerald Smith and Followers Win Jury Trial," *Chicago Tribune*, February 14, 1946.
40. Stoken, "They'll Hear from Judge Heller."

CHAPTER 3: FIGHTING WORDS

1. Ira Latimer, "The Fight Against Anti-Semitism," *The Sentinel*, April 11, 1946; S. Regensburg, "Shtodt-Regiruing fongt on dzhuri-protses gegen khuligan Smit un zayne adyutanten," *Forverts* (Chicago edition), March 28, 1946.
2. Praised for its exposure of the menacing fascist forces in American society, the 1944 trial also drew questions about the wisdom and legality of the Smith Act, a 1940 law passed by Congress in response to wartime fears about traitorous subversives who might import Nazism to the U.S. Maximilian St. George and Lawrence Dennis, *A Trial on Trial: The Great Sedition Trial of 1944* (National Civil Rights Committee, 1946), 4, 12, 60–61, 69; "Date Set for Trial for Smith, Others," *Jewish Post*, February 22, 1946; S. Regensburg, "Khuligan Dzherald K. Smit un zayne adyutanten velen krigen a dzhury trayel; veren bashuldigt in hetsen un rayoten," *Forverts* (Chicago edition), February 14, 1946.
3. His second chair, Harry Iseberg, was Jewish, as was city attorney Barnett Hodes. It would be another forty years before the Supreme Court banned race as a factor in jury selection in *Batson v. Kentucky* (1986). Religion is still not uniformly banned from consideration in peremptory challenge during voir dire. See Brian Bornstein and Monica Miller, *God in the Courtroom: Religion's Role at Trial* (Oxford University Press, 2009), 15–38. "A. A. Pantelis," *Chicago Bar Record* 44:1 (October 1962): 40; Edward Dunne, *Illinois, The Heart of the Nation* (Lewis, 1933), vol. 4, 264–65; Regensburg, "Shtodt-Regiruing fongt"; GSP, Box 18, C. Dilling to G. L. K. Smith, March 20, 1946.

4. Parallel state charges for instigating a riot were deferred until after the city prosecution was complete. Regensburg, "Shtodt-Regirung fongt"; Municipal Code of Chicago, 1939, §19.
5. Regensburg, "Shtodt-Regiruing fongt."
6. "Anti-Semitism does not fall within the category of ideas protected by the right of free opinion. Indeed, it is something quite other than an idea," Sartre concluded, and for that reason "I refuse to characterize as opinion a doctrine that is aimed directly at particular persons and that seeks to suppress their rights or to exterminate them." Jean-Paul Sartre, *Anti-Semite and Jew*, trans. George Becker (Schocken, 1995), 6, 13; GSP, Box 19, A. Terminiello to G. L. K. Smith, April 10, 1946.
7. Alexander Pekelis, "Full Equality in a Free Society," in Alexander Pekelis, *Law and Social Action—Selected Essays*, ed. Milton Konvitz (Cornell University Press, 1950), 225–26, 230.
8. James Loeffler and Yosef Malka, "An Act of Dignity: Alexander Pekelis and the Jewish Legal Realist Tradition," in Reut Paz, Ann-Kathrin Steger, and Anna Pingen, eds., *Seeing Antisemitism Through Law: High Promises or Indeterminacies?* (Göttingen, forthcoming); AJCP, Box 600, Folder 33, Will Maslow, "Alexander H. Pekelis—Some Personal Recollections."
9. The American Jewish Congress pressed the same argument in the 1950 U.S. Supreme Court case *Sweatt v. Painter* that successfully challenged the "separate but equal" doctrine. *McCollum v. Illinois* (1950) was an important test of the First Amendment's disestablishment clause. Pekelis's team also challenged segregation in public and government-funded housing projects, such as the infamous Stuyvesant Town in New York City, where a private developer, the Metropolitan Life Insurance Company, used public grants and tax breaks to build a segregated neighborhood. *Mendez v. Westminster School District of Orange County*, 64 F. Supp. 544 (S.D. Cal. 1946), *aff'd*, 161 F.2d 774 (9th Cir. 1947); "Psychological Data Cited," *Law and Social Action* (September–October 1949): 112; Felix Cohen, "Law and Social Action: Review," *University of Pittsburgh Law Review* 13 (1951–52): 613; "The Editor's Chair," *Indiana Jewish Post*, June 21, 1946; "Columbia U. Brought to Hearing, Denies Charges of Discrimination," *Jewish Post*, May 24, 1946; John Jackson Jr., "Blind Law and Powerless Science: The American Jewish Congress, the NAACP, and the Scientific Case Against Discrimination, 1945–1950," *Isis* 91:1 (March 2000): 89–116; Mark Brilliant, *The Color of America Has Changed: How Racial Diversity Shaped Civil Rights Reform in California, 1941–1978* (Oxford University Press, 2010), 58–88.
10. James Loeffler, "'A Certain Type of Liberalism': Minority Rights in Jewish Liberal Discourse, 1848–1948," in Abigail Green and Simon Levis Sullam, eds., *Jews, Liberalism, Anti-Semitism: A Global History* (Palgrave, 2020), 365–86; David Sorkin, "Emancipation," Simon Rabinovitch, "Integration and Separation," and Lila Berman, "Liberalism," in Shari Rabin and Michael Cohen, eds., *The Oxford Handbook of American Jewish History* (Oxford University Press, 2025), 49–78, 253–68; Tony Michels, "Is America 'Different'? A Critique of American Jewish

Exceptionalism," *American Jewish History* 96:3 (September 2010): 201–24; Pekelis, "Full Equality," 227–28; Will Maslow, "The Law and Race Relations," *Annals of the American Academy of Political and Social Science* 244 (March 1946): 75–81.

11. Alexander Pekelis, "Control of Broadcasting," *New York Times*, November 27, 1946; Pekelis, "Full Equality," 237.
12. Alexander Pekelis, "Group Sanctions for Racism," *New Republic* (October 29, 1945): 569–71.
13. Pekelis, "Group Sanctions," 570; David Riesman, "Democracy and Defamation: Control of Group Libel," *Columbia Law Review* 42:5 (1942): 727–80; PU ACLU, vol. 2186, L. Milner to J. Michael, December 20, 1939; Samantha Barbas, "The Rise and Fall of Group Libel: The Forgotten Campaign for Hate Speech Laws," *Loyola University Chicago Law Journal* 54 (2022): 297–340.
14. Illinois Criminal Code (Revised Statutes of Illinois), Chapter 38, Sec. 471.
15. The law against promoting race hatred also included a second provision banning public displays of lynchings, burnings, or hangings. In the early 1920s, the Illinois attorney general unsuccessfully proposed to use the law to prosecute Henry Ford for his antisemitic *Dearborn Independent* newspaper. In 1942 an Illinois court ruled that it applied as well to literature of any type. Ellen C. Scott, "Black 'Censor,' White Liberties: Civil Rights and Illinois's 1917 Film Law," *American Quarterly* 62:2 (June 2012): 219–47; Woeste, *Ford's War*, 104–6; "Lawyer Charges Henry Ford with Criminal Libel," *Chicago Tribune*, September 9, 1921; *Bevins v. Prindable*, 39 Fed. Supp. 708 (E.D. III. 1941), *aff'd* at 314 U.S. 567 (1941); Steven Zipperstein, *Pogrom: Kishinev and the Tilt of History* (Liveright, 2018), 200–202; National Park Service, *1908 Springfield Race Riot: Special Resource Study* (National Park Service, 2023), 11–12.
16. ILP, Box 5, CCLC Minutes, 1946; AJCP, Box 26, Folder 7, Memo on the Terminiello Decision—July 1947; AJCP, Box 29, Folder 6, Report of Activities—January–May 1948; Seymour Kaplan, "All Is Not 'Hush-Hush' in Chicago," *The Sentinel*, April 18, 1946; *Chaplinsky v. New Hampshire*, 315 U.S. 568 (1942).
17. Terminiello Transcript, 57, 64, 81–83; S. Regensburg, "Fashist Smit un zayn redactor shuldig in kontempt 'af kort,'" *Forverts* (Chicago edition), March 29, 1946; "Court to Jail G.L.K. Smith for Contempt," *Chicago Tribune*, March 29, 1946.
18. Terminiello Transcript, 5; Regensburg, "Fashist Smit."
19. The charge was eventually withdrawn after the priest apologized to the court. Smith was not as lucky. After he distributed a flyer to reporters in which he declared that none of the three "Christian Americans" would receive a fair trial in the communist-controlled Chicago court system, the judge charged him with contempt, sentencing him to sixty days in jail. Regensburg, "Fashist Smit"; S. Regensburg, "Nokh a fashist gefunen shuldig in kontempt af kort' fun heyign rikhter," *Forverts*, March 30, 1946; "Smith Appeals Term," *Jewish Post*, April 12, 1946; Edward Euelenberg, "Jury Finds Terminiello Guilty; Diatribes Against Jews Read to Court," *Jewish Post*, April 5, 1946; Terminiello Transcript, 99; ATP, CTRM 1/01, Terminiello Draft Memoir.

20. Terminiello Transcript, 103.
21. ATP, CTRM 1/01, Terminiello Draft Memoir; Terminiello Transcript, 90; Regensburg, "Nokh a fashist"; Euelenberg, "Jury Finds Terminiello."
22. Terminiello claimed that he taught constitutional law and ethics for two years at Jones Law School. ATP, CTRM 1/01, Terminiello Draft Memoir; Terminiello Transcript, 90; S. Regensberg, "Protestantishe galakhim shveren az zey hobn gefirt pikets gegn Smits' miting," *Forverts* (Chicago), April 3, 1946.
23. James Loeffler, "Anti-Zionism," in Sol Goldberg, Scott Ury, and Kalman Weiser, eds., *Key Concepts in the Study of Antisemitism* (Palgrave, 2020), 39–51; Dmitry Shumsky, *Beyond the Nation-State: The Zionist Political Imagination from Pinsker to Ben-Gurion* (Yale University Press, 2018); Michael Stanislawski, *Zionism: A Very Short Introduction* (Oxford University Press, 2016).
24. Nirenberg, *Anti-Judaism*.
25. Regensberg, "Protestantishe galakhim"; Terminiello Transcript, 116–17, 120, and 123; Euelenberg, "Jury Finds Terminiello."
26. The latter's church had been burned down in 1944 after he ran a campaign to end the anti-Jewish boycott led by Eugene Flitcraft, who had shared the rally stage with Terminiello. Phineas Bilbon, "Strictly Confidential," *Wisconsin Jewish Chronicle*, January 12, 1945; Regensberg, "Protestantishe galakhim"; CTRM 1/01.
27. Regensberg, "Protestantishe galakhim."
28. Regensberg, "Protestantishe galakhim."
29. NARA, QO1-682729345, Docket 272, *Terminiello v. City of Chicago*, 129; S. Regensburg, "Dzhuri rangelt zikh iber a verdict far dem fashistishen galakh Terminielo," *Forverts*, April 4, 1946.
30. S. Regensburg, "Fashist dzherold smit krigt 60 teg in dzhayl," *Forverts*, April 9, 1946; "Jury Convicts Smith Speaker," *Chicago Tribune*, April 4, 1946; Terminiello Transcript; Eulenberg, "Jury Finds"; "Prison for G.L.K. Smith," *Cross and Flag* (April 1946): 752; ATP, CTRM 1/01, Terminiello Draft Memoir.
31. "The First Amendment protects two kinds of interests in free speech," wrote the Harvard legal scholar Zechariah Chafee Jr. in establishing what would become the prevailing theory of the purpose of free speech in the interwar period. "There is the individual interest, the need of many men to express their opinions on matters vital to them if life is to be worth living, and a social interest in the attainment of truth." Zechariah Chafee Jr., "Freedom of Speech in War Time," *Harvard Law Review* 32:8 (June 1919): 958.
32. Harry S. Truman, "Message to the Congress on the State of the Union and on the Budget for 1947," January 21, 1946, The American Presidency Project, www.presidency.ucsb.edu.
33. Fishbein, "Significance of the T. Verdict!"; Jack Fishbein, "The American Jewish Congress Takes Stock," *The Sentinel*, July 4, 1946; Latimer, "The Fight Against Anti-Semitism"; "Creed of Civil Liberties Group Pronounced at Banquet," *The Sentinel*, May 30, 1946; "The Difference between the Congress and the A.D.L.," *Jewish Post*, May 10, 1946.
34. JLC, Box 275, Folder 18, David Rose, "Outline for Antisemitism in the U.S."

(March 1947); Robert Gamzey, "Mile-High View," *Intermountain Jewish News*, April 25, 1946; YIVO AJC, RG 347.14.10, Box 95, Folder 1, S. Fineberg to H. Barron, June 13, 1946.

35. "Enemies of Liberty and Decency," *Chicago Tribune*, February 11, 1946; ATP, CTRM 1/08, Terminiello Draft Memoir; "Tactical Error," *Chicago Daily News*, April 9, 1946; Gilbert Gordon and Max Bressler, "Answers Daily News Editorial," *The Sentinel*, April 18, 1946; Fineberg, *Punishment Without Crime*, 133–35, 234; JLC, Box 272, Folder 10, Memo by Arnold Forster, August 13, 1946.
36. It is an "outrageous distortion of values," Gordon explained at a City Council hearing, to apply the "concept of 'freedom of speech'" to people like Terminiello. "It is perfectly possible to create legislation which will protect the sacred rights of free speech and punish those who abuse these rights by defaming minority groups." A city ordinance would be followed by a statewide statute. Illinois already possessed a law banning "racist publications, but it should be extended to all speech." Gordon had drafted the original Fair Employment Practices Commission bill, and went on to work on desegregation in Chicago housing and antisemitic discrimination in medical school admissions. AJCP, Box 375, Folder 19, "Draft ordinance" and "Memo," June 13, 1946; AJCP, Box 61, Folder 4, B. Miller to W. Maslow, November 3 and November 24, 1947; Gilbert Gordon, "Illinois Assembly to Act on Fair Practices Program," *Chicago Star*, November 16, 1946; "City Council Adopts Anti-Racist Ordinance," *Civil Liberties News* 3 (May 30, 1947): 1; Lawrence Bush, "Gilbert Gordon (1911–2010)," *Jewish Currents* (blog), July 12, 2010.
37. AJCP, Box 835, Folder 17, National Convention Panel Discussion on Racism and Free Speech, May 30, 1946.
38. Pekelis went on to seek to publish a version in the Harvard and Chicago law reviews. The *Harvard Law Review* editor turned him down, saying that such groups lack legal standing because racial groups did not exist as such. A draft law was published by *Columbia Law Review* editor in chief Russell Knapp in 1947. "Statutory Prohibition of Group Defamation," *Columbia Law Review* 47:4 (May 1947): 595–613; Cornell University, Milton Konvitz Papers, Box 12, Folder 2, M. Konvitz to M. Ernst, August 7, 1947.
39. Kelly King-O'Brien, "The Trials of Interracial Advocacy: White-Collar Work, Race, and Inclusion in Post–World War II Chicago," PhD diss., University of Chicago, 2012; "The Extent of Employment Discrimination Against Jewish Workers in the Chicago Area," *Report to the President's Committee on Fair Employment Practices* (United States Committee on Fair Employment Practice, 1946); Arnold Forster, "The Battle Against Bigotry," *The Sentinel*, June 26, 1947; National Community Relations Advisory Council, *Report of the Plenary Session, June 15–17, 1946* (National Community Relations Advisory Council, 1946), 5–8; Robert MacIver, *The More Perfect Union* (Macmillan Company, 1948), 51; *FEPC Final Report* (United States Committee on Fair Employment Practice, 1947), viii.
40. National Community Relations Advisory Council, *Report*, 17–25, 37–45; Amer-

ican Jewish Committee Archives, Z100.CV, "Some Questions of Interest to a Pragmatic Approach on Combating Anti-Semitism [1944]."

41. National Community Relations Advisory Council, *Report*, 17–25; William B. Saphire, "Stopping Hate Pitchmen: Views Differ on Remedy," *Jewish Advocate*, October 31, 1946.
42. G. M. Cohen, "The Editor's Chair," *Jewish Post*, June 21, 1946.
43. Terminiello proposed ambitious plans for a direct mail campaign to blanket the country with books, pamphlets, and a revived edition of his *Crusader* newspaper and issued a call for a new Operation Crusade, boasting of a nation-wide network of paramilitary brigades ready to join law enforcement in combating the Judeo-communist threat. Within a few months, Armstrong embarked on a different scheme to endow a Mississippi college on the condition that the school openly pledge to exclude Jews, Blacks, and Asians. Armstrong disavowed any anti-minority prejudice. "I am anti-Communist," Armstrong asserted, "but only anti-Semitic to the extent that Jews are Communists. I have seen the estimate that 80% of the Jews are Communists . . . If it is true, then I am 80% anti-Semitic." ATP, CTRM 1/01 and CTRM 1/05, Terminiello Draft Memoir; "Smith, Terminiello Spew Hate in St. Louis," *The Sentinel*, June 6, 1946; GWA, AR335–148–29, A. Terminiello to G. Armstrong, October 29, 1945; GWA, AR335–151–27B, G. Armstrong to L. R. Tillman, December 16, 1946; "Anti-Semitism in the South," *Southern Jewish Weekly*, November 7, 1947; GSP, Box 25, G. L. K. Smith to M. St. George, March 22 and May 8, 1948; George W. Armstrong, *World Empire* (The Judge Armstrong Foundation, 1945), 5–6, 120.
44. Feinberg did grant Terminiello one key symbolic victory. He agreed with the defense contention that the counterprotesters were equally responsible for the violence. Their actions should also be "condemned as un-American and as a clear a violation of law as comes to the observation of any court." Still, one crime did not excuse the other. Terminiello's speech broke the law. *City of Chicago v. Terminiello* 396 Ill 41, 71 N.E. 2d 2 (1947); AJCP, Box 26, Folder 7, Memo on the Terminiello Decision, July 1947.
45. Cantwell and his two sons were arrested and convicted for inciting a breach of the peace for playing an anti-Catholic phonograph recording on a New Haven street. Catholic passersby threatened violence in response, leading the men to pack up their stall and depart. Despite their calm actions, their playing of the recording was held to be "acts and words likely to produce violence in others." The court ruled that Cantwell's speech fell under the First Amendment's Free Exercise clause, which applied to state law via the Fourteenth Amendment's principle of equal protection. *City of Chicago v. Terminiello* 396 Ill 41, 71 N.E. 2d 2 (1947); *Cantwell v. Connecticut*, 310 U.S. 296 (1940); Jack Fishbein, "The Significance of the Opinion in Terminiello Case," *The Sentinel*, July 3, 1947.
46. The fact that Terminiello's "listeners did not [all] engage in violence with the angry crowd is immaterial," the Illinois Supreme Court wrote, and the inside versus outside distinction was immaterial. Nor do we find evidence to support

the assertion "that great constitutional questions are involved and sacred constitutional rights are jeopardized." Another petition for rehearing to the Illinois State Supreme Court met the same fate. *City of Chicago v. Terminiello* 396 Ill 41, 71 N.E. 2d 2 (1947); NARA, QO1–682729345, "Separate Typewritten Statement to Accompany Petition for a Writ of Certiorari," September 13, 1948; "Antisemitisher galekh farliert in hekhstn gerikht fun Ilinoiz," *Forverts* (Chicago), March 20, 1948.

47. Opinion polling continued to offer a mixed message about how Americans viewed Jews. A 1947 poll by *Fortune* magazine showed that 36 percent of Americans believed Jews held too much economic power, and 21 percent thought the same of Jews and political power. The pollster Elmo Roper reported that anti-Jewish opinion topped anti-Black racism. On the challenge of polling accuracy and the ambiguity of antisemitism, see MacIver, *More Perfect Union*, 43–51, and "Di letse oysforshung vegen antisemitism in amerike," *Forverts*, April 1, 1948; Chaim Liberman, "Kamf gegen antisemitism," *Forverts*, January 1, 1947; Dovid Einhorn, "Vos iz di beste metod fun kamf gegen antisemitizm?" *Forverts*, January 21, 1947; and Nathan Ziprin, "Off the Record," *Jewish News*, November 7, 1947.
48. "Text of Truman Stadium Speech Blasting G.O.P.," *Chicago Tribune*, October 26, 1948.
49. President Harry Truman Inaugural Address, January 20, 1949, The American Presidency Project, www.presidency.ucsb.edu.

CHAPTER 4: NOT A SUICIDE PACT

1. "What Remains? The Language Remains," in Hannah Arendt, *Essays in Understanding* (Schocken, 1994), 12.
2. Eric Goldstein, *The Price of Whiteness: Jews, Race, and American Identity* (Princeton University Press, 2008), 189–208; Lila Corwin Berman, *Speaking of Jews: Rabbis, Intellectuals, and the Creation of an American Public Identity* (University of California Press, 2009); James Loeffler, "Nationalism Without a Nation? On the Invisibility of American Jewish Politics," *Jewish Quarterly Review* 105:3 (Summer 2015): 367–98; K. Healon Gaston, *Imagining Judeo-Christian America: Religion, Secularism, and the Redefinition of Democracy* (University of Chicago Press, 2019).
3. "Suprim kourt vet di teg entshayden af apil fun farurteyltn shikaga'r antisemit," *Forverts*, February 3, 1949; "Justices Dig into Chicago Speech Case," *Chicago Tribune*, February 2, 1949; AJCP, Box 61, Folder 10, B. Miller to E. Bernhard, February 11, 1949; Library of Congress, Harold Burton Papers (hereafter HBP), Box 168, Folder 9, Oral Argument Notes, February 1, 1949.
4. Karton, the longtime head of the Chicago Corporation Counsel's appellate division, was also the president of the Decalogue Society, the city's association of Jewish lawyers. "Suprim kourt vet di teg entshayden"; "Justices Dig into Chicago Speech Case"; AJCP, Box 61, Folder 10, B. Miller to E. Bernhard, February 11, 1949; HBP, Box 168, Folder 9, Oral Argument Notes, February 1, 1949.

5. "Suprim kourt vet di teg entshayden"; "Justices Dig into Chicago Speech Case"; AJCP, Box 61, Folder 10, B. Miller to E. Bernhard, February 11, 1949; HBP, Box 168, Folder 9, Oral Argument Notes, February 1, 1949; *Smith v. California*, 361 U.S. 147 (1959).
6. Library of Congress, Robert Jackson Papers (hereafter RJP), Box 15, R. H. Jackson to B. Levy, May 9, 1939. For further discussion, see Philip Kurland, "Justice Robert H. Jackson—Impact on Civil Rights and Liberties," *University of Illinois Law Forum* (1977): 551–76, and Brad Snyder, *Democratic Justice: Felix Frankfurter, the Supreme Court, and the Making of the Liberal Establishment* (W. W. Norton & Company, 2022).
7. Robert M. Cover, "The Origins of Judicial Activism in the Protection of Minorities," *Yale Law Journal* 91:7 (1982): 1287–316.
8. "Only 26 per cent of the decisions up to mid-May were unanimous," observed one journalist in 1949, as opposed to "from 84 to 89 per cent" between 1919 and 1935. Clarke Beach, "Court Disappoints Many Liberals," *Washington Post*, May 22, 1949; James E. St. Clair and Linda C. Gugin, *Chief Justice Fred M. Vinson of Kentucky* (University Press of Kentucky, 2014), 156–61; Fred Rodell, "The Chief Justice," *Life* (June 24, 1946): 103, 106. For analyses of the Vinson Court, see Noah Feldman, *Scorpions: Battles and Triumphs of FDR's Great Supreme Court Justices* (Hachette Book Group, 2010), and Melvin Urofsky, *Division and Discord: The Supreme Court under Stone and Vinson, 1941–1953* (Columbia University Press, 1997).
9. Terminiello viewed the ACLU's entrance as a triumph, boasting that he now had "the Reds on my side," since he made no distinction between the ACLU and the CCLC. UC ACLU, Box 41, Folder 3, Minutes, 1945–46, and Statement, November 21, 1946; GSP, Box 17, G. L. K. Smith to R. Baldwin, February 14 and 28, and May 27, 1946; UC ACLU, Box 41, Folder 6, Minutes, May–July 1948; ATP, CTRM 1/01, Terminiello Draft Memoir.
10. *Brief of the ACLU, Amicus Curiae, Arthur Terminiello v. City of Chicago*.
11. Leo Pfeffer, "Defense against Group Defamation," *Jewish Frontier* 13 (February 1946): 6–8; Maslow, "The Law and Race Relations"; AJCP, Box 61, Folder 5, B. Miller to W. Maslow, March 2, 1948; AJCP, Box 61, Folder 4, B. Miller to W. Maslow, November 13, 1947; AJCP, Box 61, Folder 9, B. Miller to W. Maslow, December 22, 1948; AJCP, Box 26, Folder 4, Statement to the President's Committee on Civil Rights by Will Maslow, May 1, 1947. On Maslow, see Svonkin, *Jews Against Prejudice*, 79–81.
12. AJCP, Box 61, Folder 10, American Jewish Congress Amicus brief.
13. AJCP, Box 61, Folder 10, American Jewish Congress Amicus brief; AJCP, Box 61, Folder 4, B. Miller to W. Maslow, November 13, 1947; AJCP, Box 61, Folder 9, B. Miller to W. Maslow, December 22, 1948.
14. During World War II, Murphy personally spearheaded a 1944 national effort to combat Nazi antisemitic propaganda, the National Committee Against Nazi Persecution and Extermination of the Jews. Yet he concluded from the outset that the case did not involve any real constitutional questions of free speech. HBP, Box 168, Folder 9, Notes, February 5, 1949; Box 167, Folder 9; LOC, William Douglas

Papers (hereafter WDP), Box 187, Folder 9, "Question No. 115," and Folder 10, Conference Notes, February 5, 1949; Philip Slomovitz, "Frank Murphy: American Who Understood, Protested Nazi Terror," *Detroit Jewish News*, March 15, 1985; University of Michigan, Frank Murphy Papers, Box 74, F. Murphy to J. Gomen, June 6, 1949.

15. HBP, Box 168, Folder 9, Notes, February 5, 1949.
16. WDP, Box 187, Folder 9, Conference Notes, February 5, 1949; HDP, Box 168, Folder 9, Notes, February 5, 1949.
17. WDP, Box 187, Folder 9, Conference Notes, February 5, 1949; HDP, Box 168, Folder 9, Notes, February 5, 1949.
18. HDP, Box 168, Folder 9, Notes, February 5, 1949; *Nomination of Felix Frankfurter: Hearings Before a Subcommittee of the Committee on the Judiciary, United States Senate, Seventy-sixth Congress, First Session on the Nomination of Felix Frankfurter to be an Associate Justice of the Supreme Court: January 11 and 12, 1939* (Government Printing Office, 1939), 111–12; Weinrib, "Law, History," 290.
19. Melvyn Urofsky, *Felix Frankfurter: Judicial Restraint and Individual Liberties* (Twayne, 1991), 166.
20. WDP, Box 217, Folder 2, Memo #118 on Conference, December 1, 1951; University of Kentucky, Stanley Reed Papers (hereafter SRP), Box 434, Folders 2–3, F. Frankfurter to S. Reed, May 5, 1947 and undated letter; *West Virginia State Board of Education v. Barnette*, 319 U.S. 624 (1943); HBP, Box 168, Folder 9, Notes, February 5, 1949; Urofsky, *Division and Discord*, 233.
21. Burton considered joining Douglas only to change his mind. WDP, Box 187, Folder 16, H. Burton to W. Douglas, April 7, 1949; WDP, Box 187, Folder 10, Question No. 115; University of Kentucky, Fred Vinson Papers, Box 204, Folder 7, F. Felix Frankfurter to F. Vinson, April 9, 1949.
22. Douglas cited the 1931 case *Stromberg v. California*, in which the Court held that the First Amendment applied to symbolic speech and expressive conduct, such as flying political flags. There, too, he explained, no one objected to defective jury instructions, even though their vagueness and breadth became central to the claim that the underlying law used to prosecute was constitutionally defective. Frankfurter would challenge this point in his dissent by saying *Stromberg* was the very opposite. It involved a claim of error, which was not made in *Terminiello. Terminiello v. Chicago*, 337 U.S. 1 (1949). For additional analysis of the Court's reasoning, see Patrick Schmidt, "'The Dilemma to a Free People': Justice Robert Jackson, Walter Bagehot, and the Creation of a Conservative Jurisprudence," *Law and History Review* 20:3 (Autumn 2002): 517–39.
23. "We can only take the statute as the state courts read it," Douglas wrote, arguing that "the gloss which Illinois placed on the ordinance gives it a meaning and application which are conclusive on us." *Terminiello v. Chicago*, 337 U.S. 1 (1949).
24. *Terminiello v. Chicago*, 337 U.S. 1 (1949); University of Kentucky, Fred Vinson Papers, Box 204, Folder 7, Memorandum by the Chief Justice, April 1949.
25. Notably, however, Frankfurter did not join Jackson's dissent. *Terminiello v. Chicago*, 337 U.S. 1 (1949). For a similar critique of Douglas's reasoning, see "Scope

of Supreme Court Review: The Terminiello Case in Focus," *Yale Law Journal* 59:5 (April 1950): 971–78.

26. *Terminiello v. Chicago*, 337 U.S. 1 (1949).
27. *Terminiello v. Chicago*, 337 U.S. 1 (1949).
28. *Terminiello v. Chicago*, 337 U.S. 1 (1949).
29. *Terminiello v. Chicago*, 337 U.S. 1 (1949).
30. *Terminiello v. Chicago*, 337 U.S. 1 (1949).
31. *Terminiello v. Chicago*, 337 U.S. 1 (1949); Sidney Fine, *Frank Murphy: The Washington Years* (University of Michigan Press, 1984), 582.
32. "Press also 'Split' on Terminiello," *Washington Post*, May 22, 1949.
33. WDP, Box 187, Folder 9, L. Field to W. Douglas, May 17, 1949; Library of Congress, Box 298, Folder 5, Hugo Black Papers, W. A. McDonald to H. Black, July 6, 1949.
34. Jackson responded by telling her that "no other letter that I received, and no comment from any source, about the Terminiello case touched the spot the way yours did." RJP, Box 156, Folder 1, B. Margolin to R. H. Jackson, May 17, 1949; Marlene Trestman, *Fair Labor Lawyer: The Remarkable Life of New Deal Attorney and Supreme Court Advocate Bessie Margolin* (Louisiana State University Press, 2016), 110–11; WDP, Box 187, Folder 17, J. Brumberg to W. Douglas, May 27, 1949.
35. "Free Speech Has Limits," *Time* (May 24, 1949): 4; David Lawrence, "Ill. Free Speech Ruling Held to Settle but Little," *Daily Press*, May 21, 1949; "Free Speech Is Fine, But—," *New York Daily News*, May 18, 1949; Robert Grannis, "One Man Says," *Brooklyn Daily Eagle*, May 19, 1949; WDP, Box 187, Folder 17, C. Morgan to W. Douglas, May 23, 1949; ATP, CTRM 1/01, Terminiello Draft Memoir; "Federal Group Libel Legislation: Should Jews and Jewish Organizations Support or Oppose," *NCRAC Legislative Bulletin* (June 10, 1949): 1–7; Tully Nettleton, "Words That Incite: 'Verbal Acts' and the Terminiello Verdict," *Christian Science Monitor*, May 27, 1949.
36. "We confess that we cannot understand from the court's decision what constitutional right enjoyed by defendant compels the reversal of a conviction for words and conduct for which the constitution admittedly grants no immunity," wrote Maslow. The American Jewish Congress had argued that the crime was incitement of the listeners *in* the hall, while the ACLU argued that the violence only took place *outside* the hall. Yet the Supreme Court ignored both questions; "Its opinion went off in a digression which will only serve to befuddle the problem and confuse municipal authorities concerned both with freedom of speech and the avoidance of riots." *Terminiello v. Chicago*, 337 U.S. 1 (1949), Petition for Rehearing, May 31, 1949; Maslow, *Analysis on the Terminiello Decision*, May 19, 1949; YIVO AJC, RG 347.17.12, Box 151, Folder 10, Ben Herzberg, "The Meaning of the Terminiello Decision," June 1, 1949; PU ACLU, vol. 154, H. Levy to E. May 18, 1949, L. Despres to H. Levy, June 27 and August 3, 1949, O. Fraenkel to H. Levy, July 25, 1949, and H. Levy to L. Despres, August 15, 1949.
37. Terminiello's pamphlet *The Illuminati and the Catholic Church* was republished

by the Christian Defense League in 1992, and remains widely available for sale on Christian websites today. ATP, CTRM 1/01, Terminiello Draft Memoir.

38. The Boston Jewish civil rights leader Robert Segal was one who predicted already in May 1949 that the closeness of the decision and Jackson's dissent were "bound to turn the minds and efforts of many persons to the possibility of group libel legislation." "Free Speech Ruling Spur to Race Libel Law," *Jewish Advocate*, May 19, 1949; "Conservatism vs. Liberalism Explained on the Supreme Court," *Lawton Constitution*, June 2, 1949.

CHAPTER 5: A POSTWAR POGROM

1. Chicago History Museum, CC-H91–19493, "CHR Report," Special Report, Chicago Commission on Human Relations, December 1949 (hereafter CHR Report); "White Supremacists Attack Chicago ILWU Official's Home," *Dispatcher*, November 25, 1949; Wisconsin Historical Society, United Packinghouse, Food, and Allied Workers Records, Box 343, Folder 3, Untitled Report (hereafter UPWA Report).
2. Bindman appealed to their Catholic consciences to no avail. Mike Hecht, "Civil Rights on Peoria Street," *Jewish Frontier* 17 (February 1950): 15; UPWA Report; CHR Report; PU ACLU Papers, vol. 129, "Anti-Negro and Anti-Semitic Violence on the South Side (Report)" (hereafter ACLU Report).
3. Hecht, "Civil Rights," 15.
4. UPWA Report; CHR Report; N. Caroline Harney and James Charlton, "The Siege on South Peoria Street," *Chicago Reader*, January 14, 2000; Hecht, "Civil Rights," 15–17.
5. Byron Miller, "Chicago Jewry Learns a Lesson," *Congress Weekly*, January 13, 1950; New York Public Library, Civil Rights Congress Papers, P-60, Undated Press Release; UPWA Report; "Rayoten in shikago tsulib falshern barikht az neger hot zikh arayngetsoygn in vaysn gegent," *Forverts* (Chicago), November 12, 1949; ACLU Report; Harney and Charlton, "Siege"; Helmut Lorsch, "Rabbi Berman Denounces Outbreaks of Racial Riots Here," *The Sentinel*, November 17, 1949; Hecht, "Civil Rights," 16–17.
6. Miller, "Chicago Jewry"; ACLU Report; CHR Report.
7. UPWA Report; Red Holmgren, "Anti-Jewish Violence Sweeps South Side," *National Guardian*, November 21, 1949; New York Public Library, Civil Rights Congress Papers, P70, Press Release, November 17, 1949.
8. A 1947 Chicago government report estimated that at least 200,000 new units were needed to meet the demand for affordable housing. Arnold Hirsch, *Making the Second Ghetto: Race and Housing in Chicago, 1940–1960* (University of Chicago Press, 1998), 23.
9. In the 1948 case *Shelley v. Kraemer*, the Court ruled that racially restrictive covenants banning Blacks, Jews, and others from buying real estate property in some neighborhoods violated the constitutional right to equal protection. "These are not cases, as has been suggested, in which the States have merely abstained from

action, leaving private individuals free to impose such discriminations as they see fit. Rather, these are cases in which the States have made available to such individuals the full coercive power of government to deny" rights "on the grounds of race or color." *Shelley v. Kraemer*, 334 U.S. 1 (1948); Hirsch, *Making*, 24, 41, 53; Miller, "Chicago Jewry," 4; UPWA Report; *Chicago Civil Liberties Committee Newsletter* (September 1, 1944): 1; Wendy Plotkin, "'Hemmed In': The Struggle Against Racial Restrictive Covenants and Deed Restrictions in Post-WWII Chicago," *Journal of the Illinois State Historical Society* 94:1 (Spring 2001): 7–8.

10. Mike Hecht, "Armistice Day in Chicago," *Jewish Life* (January 1950): 6; Beryl Satter, *Family Properties: Race, Real Estate, and the Exploitation of Black Urban America* (Macmillan, 2009).
11. The White Circle League also targeted Jewish businesses in the Englewood commercial district. "Khuligans makhen pogrom oyf nayer shul oyf der Sout Sayd," *Forverts* (Chicago), April 7, 1949; ACLU Report; UPWA Report; Hecht, "Armistice Day in Chicago," 6; ILP, Box 5, CCLC Minutes, 1948–52; "Police Job Fumbled," *New York Daily News*, November 16, 1949; Wisconsin Historical Society, United Packinghouse, Food, and Allied Workers Records, Box 342, Folder 18, Chicago Conference to End Mob Violence Press Release, November 19, 1949; NARA, RG-147, Records of the Selective Service System, 1940-47, "Aaron Morris Bindman."
12. What began as an "anti-Negro and anti-Communist" riot soon revealed "itself as full-blown antisemitism," observed the American Jewish Congress. The American Federation of Polish Jews even called for an emergency unity conference of all Jewish organizations to fight the "growing antisemitic outbreaks across the country." Clifford Wheeler, "Issue Riot Warrants. South Side Alleged Mobsters Face New Charges," *Chicago World*, December 17, 1949; Hecht, "Civil Rights," 15–16; "A ruf vos muz derhert vern," *Morgn Frayhayt*, November 24, 1949; PU ACLU, vol. 129, Chicago Division Executive Committee Minutes, November 17, 1949; ACLU Report; Lorsch, "Rabbi Berman Denounces"; "Who's Who," *Chicago World*, December 10, 1949; AJCP, Box 854, Folder 4, "Morning session of plenary-reports of conference committees, November 13, 1949"; "Peoria Street, Chicago," *The Sentinel*, March 23, 1950; "Is This America?," 3.
13. Yiddish papers commonly referred to it as a pogrom. UC ACLU, Box 343, Folder 3, Mayor's Statement, November 30, 1949; Leo Lerner, "Letter to the Editor," *Indiana Jewish News*, December 29, 1949; "Nayer anti-yidisher un anti-negerishe pogrom in Shikago," *Morgn Frayhayt*, November 13, 1949.
14. "An Open Letter to the Honorable Mayor Martin H. Kennelly," *Chicago Sun-Times*, December 1, 1949; AJPC, Box 854, Folder 4, "Morning session of plenary-reports of conference committees, November 13, 1949"; "Rasen-rayoten oyf Sout-Sayd fun shikago halten on fir teg," *Forverts* (Chicago), November 13, 1949; Lorsch, "Rabbi Berman Denounces"; "Meyer vornt az polis vet ophiten ordenung oyf sout sayd," *Forverts* (Chicago), November 20, 1949; "Vos-zhe klaybt men zikh ton?" *Morgn Frayhayt*, November 17, 1949.
15. On one occasion Bindman reached his block, where he was greeted by a policeman who did not recognize him. "Why don't you people get rid of those

son-of-a-bitches?" the officer asked. That would solve the problem, he said. "I'm one of those son-of-a-bitches, you moron," Bindman replied. New York University, Aaron Bindman Papers, TAM 510, Box 1, "Trade Unions and Automation"; "Peoria Street, Chicago"; Harney and Charlton, "Siege"; University of California, Berkeley, Bancroft Library, Oral History Office, William Sennett, *Communist Functionary and Corporate Executive*, 1981/82, 206–13.

16. David Austin Walsh, *Taking America Back: The Conservative Movement and the Far Right* (Yale University Press, 2024).
17. Walker, *In Defense of American Liberties*, 191–95.
18. UC ACLU, Box 42, Folder 1, Executive Commitment Statement, July 20, 1949; UC ACLU Box 41, Folder 7, ACLU Statement on the Broyles Bills, March 4, 1949; ILP, Chicago Civil Liberties Committee Minutes, June 6, 1950.
19. Randi Storch, *Red Chicago: American Communism at Its Grassroots, 1928–35* (University of Illinois Press, 2007), 186–94.
20. Bindman would not be publicly identified as a communist until the House Un-American Activities Committee held regional hearings in Chicago in September 1952. All the major Jewish civil rights organizations joined with the ACLU in opposing the Mundt-Nixon bill. New York University, Aaron Bindman Papers, TAM 510, Box 1, "Not Just Another Party"; AJCP, Box 833, Folder 16, Joint Statement on the Mundt-Ferguson-Johnston and Nixon Bills, March 30, 1950.
21. An effort to spread the word led the local radio station WMOR to rush to air a special program on which Bindman and other victims narrated their experiences of the violence. Letter from Morton Berman to the *Chicago Daily News*, November 17, 1949; Holmgren, "Anti-Jewish Violence"; Warren Pederson, "Progressive Party Agitators," *Chicago Tribune*, March 24, 1950; Homer Jack, "On Democracy's Battle Front," *Pittsburgh Weekly Courier* (Chicago edition), December 17, 1949; Wisconsin Historical Society, United Packinghouse, Food, and Allied Workers Records, Box 342, Folder 18, S. Williams to H. Jack, December 19, 1949, and Press Release, November 26, 1949; UPWA Report; Sennett, *Communist Functionary*; Harney and Charlton, "Siege"; "Kennelly Blasted by Parley on Mob Violence," *Illinois Daily Worker*, December 4, 1949.
22. On Bindman's block lived six police officers, twenty-two city employees, and a city alderman. UPWA Report; "Judge Blames Race Unrest on Saboteurs' Plot," *Chicago Tribune*, March 14, 1950; University of Pittsburgh, Erroll Garner Archive, Martha Glaser Papers, www.digital.library.pitt.edu, "Race Relations in Chicago."
23. During the violence, journalists noted that "the attacks were well-organized, well-directed . . . and efficiently, at times in almost military fashion, carried out." Keith Wheeler, "A Self-Appointed Fuehrer," *Chicago Sun-Times*, June 12, 1950; Hecht, "Armistice Day in Chicago," 6; UC ACLU, Box 418, Folder 9, J. Beauharnais to L. Johnson and H. Truman, June 24, 1949; Marion Odmark, "Race Racket in Chicago," *Plain Talk* (April 1950): 29–30; UC ACLU, Box 418, Folder 9, Memorandum, February 6, 1950.
24. Odmark, "Race Racket"; Sylvia Alexander, "Founder Admits 'Violence' Aim of Chicago Klan Group," *Illinois Worker*, December 1, 1949; George Sexton, "I Met

with Chicago's Unhooded Klansmen," *Daily Worker* (Illinois edition), December 25, 1949.

25. AJCP, Box 63, Folder 2, CLSA Monthly Report, December 1949; Byron Miller, "Peoria Street Report"; Sexton, "Unhooded," 2A; "The Worker's Exposure," *Jewish Currents* 4 (April 1950): 26; "Accuse Bias Group Head of Defamation," *Chicago Sun-Times*, January 24, 1950; University of Minnesota, National Council of Christians and Jews Papers, Box 8, Folder 7, Frank Kiehne, "Commission on Human Relations Report on White Circle Meeting"; UC ACLU, Box 418, Folder 9, Memorandum, February 6, 1950, *WCLA Bulletin* (May 25, 1950), and ACLU Report on May 25, 1950, meeting; Ralph Roy, *Apostles of Discord: A Study of Organized Bigotry and Disruption on the Fringes of Protestantism* (Beacon Press, 1953), 130; Y. Sigel, "Vikhtigste pasirungen fun der vokh in Shikago: Di groyse maple fun neger-haser un der erfolg fun der komite far besere batsiungen tsvishn negers un vayse in Shikago," *Forverts* (Chicago), June 21, 1952.
26. AJCP, Box 63, Folder 1, B. Miller to W. Maslow, December 5, 1949; AJCP, Box 63, Folder 1, CLSA Minutes, November 22, 1949; UC ACLU, Box 418, Folder 9, E. Meyerding to J. and M. Barton, n.d.; UC ACLU, Box 419, Folder 8, E. Meyerding to A. Matanka, April 2, 1950; Homer Jack, "Chicago's Violent Armistice," *Nation* (December 10, 1949): 571–72.
27. Solomon Fineberg, *Punishment Without Crime* (Beacon Press, 1949), 234; Kirman, "Major Programs," 133–36; AJA, Solomon A. Fineberg Papers, MS-149, Box 3, File 5, "Gerald L. K. Smith," and Box 5, Folder 2, Interview (1974).
28. Naomi Cohen, *Not Free to Desist* (Jewish Publication Society of America, 1972), 345–56; American Jewish Committee Archives, Executive Committee Minutes, April 30, 1950; Svonkin, *Jews Against Prejudice*, 161–78.
29. A year later, the American Jewish Congress adopted a new official position. We oppose "Communism, fascism and all other forms of totalitarianism as destructive of freedom, equality and world peace [and] refrain from association with Communist, pro-Communist and all other [such] groups." AJCP, Box 64, Folder 2, Commission on Law and Social Action Memo, September 15, 1950; AJCP, Box 63, Folder 1, M. Berman to T. Kennelly, December 2, 1949, and S. Jacobs to F. Ptashne, December 7, 1949; Miller, "Chicago Jewry," 4; AJCP, Box 833, Folder 23, Meeting of the Executive Committee, December 11, 1949; AJCP, Box 854, Folder 12, Resolutions Committee Minutes, November 11, 1949.
30. Wisconsin Historical Society, United Packinghouse, Food, and Allied Workers Records, Box 342, Folder 18, Chicago Conference to End Mob Violence Press Release, November 26, 1949, and Memo, December 7, 1949; "Assail City Laxity on Mob Issue," *Chicago Daily News*, December 2, 1949; "New Charges in Disorders," *Chicago Sun-Times*, December 13, 1949; "White Circle's Charter Voided for Racial Hate," *Chicago Tribune*, June 30, 1950; Ted Coleman, "Judge Outlaws Vicious Chicago Hate Gang," *Pittsburgh Courier*, July 8, 1950.
31. On African American reactions to the episode, see Gerald Horne, *Communist Front? The Civil Rights Congress, 1946–1956* (Fairleigh Dickinson University Press, 1988), 145–46; Preston Smith, *Racial Democracy and the Black Metrop-*

olis: Housing Policy in Postwar Chicago (University of Minnesota Press, 2023), 164–67; "Naye klogen gegen 37 mener far rasen-rayoten af shikagor South Sayd," *Forverts*, December 14, 1949; AJCP, Box 63, Folder 2, Chicago Division, Administrative Committee Minutes, December 29, 1949; AJCP, Box 63, Folder 3, S. Jacobs to R. Solovy, February 22, 1950.

32. ILP, Box 5, CCLC Minutes, 1948–52; UC ACLU, Box 340, Folder 9, Conversation Notes.
33. UC ACLU, Box 418, Folder 9, Memorandum, February 6, 1950.
34. Ted Coleman, "Bare 'White Circle' Hate Gang in Chicago," *Pittsburgh Courier*, January 21, 1950; "State's Case Against Racist White Circle League Bogged Down by Official Apathy," *The Worker* (Illinois edition), March 19, 1950; ILP, Box 5, CCLC Minutes, 1948–52; Interview with Daniel Zemel, March 14, 2023; AJCP, Box 63, Folder 6, B. Miller to W. Maslow, May 12, 1950; "Group Libel," *Decalogue Journal* 1:4 (April–May 1951): 9.
35. St. George agreed to take the case even though he remained busy that spring with spillover litigation from the *Terminiello* case. Gerald Smith had sued Judge Samuel Heller and *The Sentinel* for libel. The mock trial included Saul Alinsky and was presided over by Rabbi Ralph Simon, the head rabbi of the rabbinical court of Chicago, a professor at the College of Jewish Studies, and a board member of the CCLC. "Plan 'Trial' of McGarry," *The Worker* (Illinois), April 2, 1950; Ann Prosten, "Fix Blame for Racist Violence, Housing Stall," *The Worker* (Illinois), April 23, 1950.
36. Dogged by allegations of corruption, McGarry would later be demoted to traffic court in 1957. GSP, Box 35, M. St. George to G. L. K. Smith, March 22, 1950; "Hate Leader Charges Bias," *Chicago Defender*, February 18, 1950; Morton Berman, "Voice of the People: Attacks Judge McGarry," *Chicago Tribune*, March 20, 1950; "Peoria Street Trial," *National Guardian*, January 22, 1950; "Victory for Violence," *The Worker* (Illinois), March 19, 1950; Carol Hirsch, "How McGarry Twisted the Peoria St. Facts," *The Worker* (Illinois), March 26, 1950; Gunnar Leander, "McGarry—Product of the 'Whoopee Era,'" *The Worker* (Illinois), April 9, 1950; W. M. Zukerman, "Sequel to Chicago Riot," *Intermountain Jewish News*, March 30, 1950; "Show M'Garry Was More Lenient than Predecessor," *Chicago Tribune*, March 30, 1957.
37. Joseph Tanenhaus, "Group Libel," *Cornell Law Review* 35:10 (Winter 1950): 267–69; Joseph Tanenhaus, "The Protection of Racial and Religious Groups Through the Law of Defamation," MA thesis, Cornell University, 1949, 115–19.
38. Tanenhaus, "Group Libel," 267–69; Jeremy Waldron, *The Harm in Hate Speech* (Harvard University Press, 2012), 204–7. For a recent reevaluation of the incident, see Tony Kushner, *The Jewish Pedlar: An Untold Criminal History* (University of Manchester Press, 2025), 80–83.
39. From the late eighteenth century onward, critics complained that seditious libel allowed for unconstitutional government punishment of political speech, a view expressed by Oliver Wendell Holmes Jr. in his *Abrams v. United States* dissent. *People v. Croswell*, 3 Johns. Cas. 337 N.Y. 1804; *Abrams v. United States*, 250 U.S.

616 (1919); Mrs. B. Sidler, "Truth as a Defense," *Chicago-Kent Law Review* 43:1 (April 1966): 83–91.

40. *Transcript of Record, Supreme Court of the United States, October Term, 1951, No. 118, Joseph Beauharnais, Petitioner, vs. The People of the State of Illinois* (hereafter *Beauharnais Transcript*) (Washington, 1951); Ted Coleman, "Racist Chief Gets Top Penalty—$200 Fine!" *The Worker* (Du Sable edition), May 14, 1950.
41. *Beauharnais Transcript;* Illinois State Constitution (1870), Article II, Section 4; Illinois Revised Statues (1949), Chap. 38, Section 404.
42. "Hold White Circle Meeting in Cicero," *The Worker* (Du Sable edition), May 21, 1950.
43. On the judge's jury instructions and his decision to refuse an instruction to consider whether there existed a "clear and present danger of substantive evil to the public," see Samuel Golden, "Beauharnais vs. People of the State of Illinois," *Decalogue Journal* 3:1 (September–October 1952): 12; *Beauharnais Transcript*; Coleman, "Racist Chief"; "Found Guilty of Defaming Negroes, Fined," *Chicago Daily Sun-Times*, May 5, 1950; "Hate Group Head Fined: All-White Jury Convicts Race Baiter," *Baltimore Afro-American*, May 13, 1950; "Jury Convicts," *Decatur Herald*, May 5, 1950; "Levy Top Fine on 'Fuehrer,'" *Pittsburgh Courier*, May 13, 1950.
44. "Farshpreyter fun rasen-has gefunen shuldig fun a dzshuri," *Forverts* (Chicago), May 1, 1950; "Jury from Which Jews Barred Finds Hate-Peddler Guilty," *National Jewish Post*, May 12, 1950; "Find White Circle Group Boss Guilty," *Chicago Defender*, May 13, 1950.
45. UC ACLU, Box 42, Folders 2–3, Executive Committee Minutes, 1950.
46. UC ACLU, Box 418, Folder 8, H. Levy to E. Meyerding, June 13, 1950, E. Meyerding to J. Beauharnais, July 5, 1950, and J. Beauharnais to E. Meyerding, July 10, 1950; UC ACLU, Box 418, Folder 9, White Circle League Letter to Membership and ACLU Report, May 29, 1950; "Jumping Overboard," *White Circle News*, June 19, 1950, 1.
47. UC ACLU, Box 42, Folders 2–3, Executive Committee Minutes, 1950.
48. UC ACLU, Box 418, Folder 9, Complaint in Quo Warranto; "State of Ill, Revokes Hate Group's Charter," *Afro-American*, July 8, 1950.
49. In its rejected Illinois Supreme Court amicus brief, written by Jewish attorney Alfred Albert, the ACLU cited the contradiction between the Illinois law and a similar New Jersey law recently struck down by the Supreme Court of that state, in the case that would become *Klapprott v. United States*. Albert also offered an argument that was eerily prescient of contemporary arguments about anti-Zionism and antisemitism. "It is our contention that a man has a right to criticize a religious group because of its activities, or a racial group because of its activities. A non-Zionist Jew has the right to take to task a Zionist Jew and in so doing may use the words 'Zionist Jew.' He may use such words so as to group all Zionist Jews together and not any one in particular. Likewise the Negro race will have a perfect right to criticize the conduct of Whites and conversely White people have the right to criticize Negroes. We should not interfere with the right of Protestants to criticize Catholics and vice versa." UC ACLU, Box 340, Folder 8,

L. Des Pres to H. Levy, January 19 and January 30, 1950; ACLU, *Petition and Brief for a Writ of Certiorari to the Justices of the Supreme Court of the State of Illinois.*

50. *The People of the State of Illinois v. Joseph Beauharnais, Brief and Argument for Appellant to the Justices of the Supreme Court of the State of Illinois.*
51. *The People of the State of Illinois v. Joseph Beauharnais, Brief and Argument for Appellant to the Justices of the Supreme Court of the State of Illinois.*
52. The Illinois Supreme Court highlighted the ambiguous link between defamation and violence in the text of the statute. By linking defamatory language to a "breach of the peace or riots," Fulton wrote, the law fell under the "clear and present danger" and "fighting words" exceptions. Yet the statute contained two separate infractions—"breach of the peace or riots" or exposing "the citizens of any race, color, creed or religion to contempt, derision, or obloquy." Two months later, a request for rehearing was denied. SRP, Box 164, Folder 3, Memorandum, Fall 1951; "Race Defamer Loses Appeal," *Chicago Defender*, January 27, 1951.

CHAPTER 6: INSTRUMENT OF DEMOCRACY

1. UC ACLU, Box 518, Folder 3, "The Cicero Riots of 1951," Chicago Council Against Religious and Racial Discrimination Report (July 22, 1951); UC ACLU, Box 418, Folder 8, "Go, Go Cicero!" flyer and E. Meyerding to W. White, July 30, 1951; Arnold Forster and Benjamin Epstein, *The Trouble-Makers* (Doubleday, 1952), 151.
2. YIVO AJC, RG 347.4, Box 2, File 20, H. Kohn to W. Katz, September 20, 1951.
3. PU ACLU, Box 1230, Item 722, Press Release; UC ACLU, Box 418, Folder 8, J. Beauharnais to P. Murray, November 8, 1951; "Rap Indictments in Cicero Rioting," *Chicago Daily News*, September 19, 1951; UC ACLU, Box 551, Folder 3, Homer Jack, "The Cicero Riots of 1951," July 22, 1951.
4. The American Jewish Congress worked closely with the NAACP to coordinate a response. Byron Miller and Morton Berman took the lead in pressuring authorities to dispatch more police and protect the Clark family. AJCP, Box 65, Folder 8, B. Miller to W. Maslow, July 13 and July 17, 1951; UC ACLU, Box 418, Folder 8, I. Shaffer to ACLU Board, July 14, 1951, P. Malin to W. White, July 27, 1951, E. Meyerding to W. White, July 30, 1951, and E. Meyerding to Mrs. A. Alschuler, October 17, 1951; UC ACLU, Box 418, Folder 9, "Notes on Call with Abbot Rosen," August 16, 1951; PU ACLU, Box 1230, W. White to P. Malin, July 16, 1951.
5. "Civil Liberties Explains Its Stand on Freedom of Speech," *Chicago Daily News*, December 17, 1957, 22; Judith Shklar, *After Utopia* (Harvard University Press, 1957); Samuel Moyn, *Liberalism Against Itself: Cold War Intellectuals and the Making of Our Times* (Yale University Press, 2023); Christopher W. Schmidt, *Civil Rights in America* (Cambridge University Press, 2020), 53–75.
6. A similar fear of radicalism led the Court in *Feiner v. New York* (1951) to uphold the conviction, by a 6–3 vote, of a Jewish college student who had publicly urged Blacks to "rise up in arms and fight for their rights." The time, place, and manner of the speech suggested that "a clear danger of disorder was threatened," war-

ranting a breach of the peace charge. *Dennis v. United States*, 341 U.S. 494 (1951); *Feiner v. New York*, 340 U.S. 315 (1951).

7. *Kunz v. New York*, 340 U.S. 290 (1951).
8. Riesman's articles on group defamation directly inspired American Jewish Congress leaders. They even considered using him to draft their amicus brief in the *Terminiello* case. AJCP, Box 61, Folder 9, B. Miller to W. Maslow, December 22, 1948; David Riesman, "The Militant Fight Against Anti-Semites," *Commentary* (January 1951): 11–19.
9. Susan Glenn, *The Jewish Cold War: Anxiety and Identity in the Aftermath of the Holocaust*, University of Michigan Belin Lectures 14 (University of Michigan Press, 2014), 30–31.
10. A Boston-based ACLU lawyer, Albert had fought a major censorship case on behalf of the publisher of Lillian Smith's 1944 book *Strange Fruit*, an explosive novel about racism and interracial love that was banned from the mails by the U.S. Postal Service. He had only just returned from an around-the-world trip to monitor human rights on behalf of the International League for Human Rights, the sibling organization of the ACLU also founded by Roger Baldwin. He was assisted by ACLU staff lawyer Herbert Monte Levy. Herbert Levy, "Bill Might Be a 'Boomerang' Harmful to All Minorities," *Daily Compass*, June 22, 1949, 8; American Civil Liberties Union, *What Do You Mean Free Speech?* (American Civil Liberties Union, 1946); UC ACLU, Box 418, Folder 8, Herbert Monte Levy, "The Case Against Group Libel Legislation," June 1950; *Beauharnais Transcript*.
11. Wines spent his spare time moonlighting on a nationally broadcast live television courtroom drama that he had created. *They Stand Accused* pioneered the ripped-from-the-headlines genre, blending real attorneys with actors to present cases for which a jury picked from studio audience members decided the verdict. The show ran on Sunday evenings from 1949 to 1954 on the DuMont Television Network, filmed in Chicago at WGN studios. SRP, Box 164, Folder 3, Notes; *Beauharnais Transcript*.
12. The *Dennis* standard of "gravity of evil" aligns with the "argument we have been making since the beginning," observed Maslow. The AJC and the ACLU held a joint event in Chicago in mid-November in which Miller moderated a debate between State's Attorney Zemel and ACLU leader John Lapp. AJCP, Box 66, Folder 1, B. Miller to W. Maslow, August 3 and 13, 1951; AJCP, Box 66, Folder 3, B. Miller to W. Maslow, October 26, 1951, Chicago Branch Letter, November 1, 1951, and Chicago Branch Minutes, November 13, 1951; AJCP, Box 559, Folder 4, N. Dershowitz to S. Deutsch, June 13, 1978; Phil Baum, "The Bounds of Free Speech," *Congress Weekly*, February 4, 1952.
13. UC ACLU, Box 418, Folder 8, A. Albert to E. Meyerding, December 4, 1951.
14. UC ACLU, Box 418, Folder 8, H. Levy to E. Meyerding, November 9, 1951, and A. Albert to E. Meyerding, December 4, 1951; "Arguments Before the Court," *U.S. Law Week* (December 4, 1951): 3141–43.
15. UC ACLU, Box 418, Folder 8, A. Albert to E. Meyerding, December 4, 1951; "Arguments Before the Court."

16. UC ACLU, Box 418, Folder 8, A. Albert to E. Meyerding, December 4, 1951; "Arguments Before the Court."
17. "Comrade Zemel Ponders on Chicago Political Parties," *The Sentinel*, May 29, 1952; "Arguments Before the Court"; Alice Dunnigan, "Freedom of Speech—What Is It?" *Atlanta Daily World*, December 16, 1951.
18. *Transcript of Record, Supreme Court of the United States, October Term, 1951, No. 118* (Washington, DC, 1951). Frankfurter also examined the demography of Illinois to quantify the relative size of the African American minority. Harvard University, Felix Frankfurter Papers, Box 48, Folder 6, *Beauharnais v. Illinois* notes.
19. LDP, Box 217, Folder 2, Memo #118 on Conference, December 1, 1951; RJP, Box 173, F. Frankfurter to R. Jackson, n.d.; SRP, Box 164, Folder 3, Notes.
20. Black and Burton had voted for certiorari on this case on grounds that it resembled the 1941 *Klapprott v. United States* case, in which the court overturned a pro-Nazi, German American man's conviction for violating a state law "prohibiting the making of statements inciting, counseling, promoting, or advocating hatred, abuse, violence, or hostility against any group or groups of persons by reason of race, color, religion, or manner of worship," on grounds of vagueness. HBP, Box 208, Folder 21, Conference Notes.
21. Reed had shown a receptivity to Frankfurter's reasoning, conceding that "a socially conscious legislature" might act to prevent group libel. Still, he wondered about the "clear and present danger" issue, asking, "Can a group libel statute, as a language of the statute does, trench on free speech regardless of the likelihood of violence before there is an opportunity for full discussion?" SRP, Box 164, Folder 3, Notes, and H. Burton to F. Frankfurter, January 11, 1952; HBP, Box 209, Folder 13, Notes, September 13, 1951; LDP, Box 217, Folder 2, Memo #118 on Conference, December 1, 1951.
22. *Beauharnais v. Illinois*, 343 U.S. 250 (1952).
23. Among Frankfurter's case notes was a copy of writings by Pekelis and his junior colleague Phil Baum. Harvard University, Felix Frankfurter Papers, Box 48, Folder 6, *Beauharnais v. Illinois* notes; *Beauharnais v. Illinois*, 343 U.S. 250 (1952).
24. *Beauharnais v. Illinois*, 343 U.S. 250 (1952).
25. *Beauharnais v. Illinois*, 343 U.S 250 (1952).
26. *Beauharnais v. Illinois*, 343 U.S. 250 (1952).
27. In his own dissent, Reed, too, acknowledged again that the law recognized "the constitutional power of a state to pass group libel laws to protect the public peace." The crucial issue in this case was the vagueness of the language in the Illinois statute. "If words are to be published criminally," Reed concluded, states must use only "reasonably well defined" terms with commonly "accepted meaning." Both Douglas and Reed, then, seemed convinced that the Constitution permitted laws regulating hate speech. *Beauharnais v. Illinois*, 343 U.S. 250 (1952).
28. RJP, Box 173, R. Jackson to F. Frankfurter, March 1, 1952, and F. Frankfurter to R. Jackson, n.d; *Beauharnais v. Illinois*, 343 U.S. 250 (1952).
29. "Analysis of the Supreme Court Decision in Beauharnais Case and Federal Group Libel Bill," *CLSA Reports*, May 15, 1952.

30. PU ACLU, Box 1102, Folder 38, G. L. K. Smith to R. Baldwin, May 20 and June 2, 1952, R. Baldwin to G. L. K. Smith, May 29 and June 11, 1952.
31. YIVO AJC, RG 347.4, Box 2, File 20, W. Katz to M. Shapiro, September 20, 1951; Letter from Thurgood Marshall, *New York Times*, October 30, 1951, 28; LOC, NAACP Papers, Part 25, T. Marshall to F. Williams, February 26, 1952.
32. Risa Goluboff, *The Lost Promise of Civil Rights* (Harvard University Press, 2010).
33. Earlier, Washington, DC, NAACP leaders had supported the case against Beauharnais on the grounds that he was responsible for lynchings and represented a clear and present danger. But the national leadership had long looked askance at group libel. Library of Congress, National Association for the Advancement of Colored People Papers, Part 18, A. Pekelis to T. Marshall, June 15, 1945, and E. Dudley to A. Pekelis, June 18, 1945; Stanley Robert, "High Court Faces Difficult Decision," *New Pittsburgh Courier*, January 19, 1952; UC ACLU, Box 42, Folder 6, Minutes, May 16, 1952, and Press Release, May 16, 1952; Harry Kalven, "The Law of Defamation and the First Amendment," in University of Chicago, *Conference on the Arts, Publishing, and the Law, May 5, 1952* (University of Chicago Press, 1952), 3–18; Harry Kalven, *The Negro and the First Amendment* (Ohio State University Press, 1965), 7–64.
34. *Beauharnais v. Illinois*, 343 U.S. 988 (1952), Petition for Rehearing.
35. It was also a mistake to liken libel "of racial and religious groups" to obscenity, Marshall argued, as the majority had done in its opinion. "Obscenity never touches upon the political or social issues of the day. But group libel most certainly does."
36. The quartet introduced four identical bills—H.R. 7717 by Javitz, H.R. 7718 by Keough, H.R. 7719 by Klein, and H.R. 7723 by Powell. UC ACLU, Box 419, Folder 1.
37. Murrey Marder, "4 New Yorkers to Introduce Group Libel Measure in House," *Washington Post*, May 5, 1952; "Libel Bill Is Introduced in Congress," *New York Age*, May 10, 1952; "Analysis of the Supreme Court Decision in Beauharnais Case and Federal Group Libel Bill"; Cornell University, Milton Konvitz Papers, Box 96, Folder 20, American Jewish Congress, "Group Libel Legislation," June 5, 1953.
38. Back in Chicago, Zemel was hailed as a hero in the local Jewish and Black communities. He launched a group libel prosecution of Chicago-based antisemite Lyrl Van Hyning, who led the nationwide Christian nationalist Women's Way movement. Samuel Margoshes, "News and Views," *Der Tog*, May 6, 1952; "The Beauharnais Conviction," *Chicago Defender*, May 10, 1952; "Checking the Big Lie," *American Jewish World*, May 15, 1952; S. Dingal, "Di vokh in idishen lebn," *Der Tog*, May 10, 1952; "A vikhtige entsheydung fun suprim kort," *Forverts*, April 30, 1952; "Supreme Court Upholds State Ban on 'Hate' Literature," *Chicago Sun-Times*, April 29, 1952; ILP, Box 5, CCLC Minutes, 1952; Len Hasselson, "Albert Zemel to Address S.S. Meeting," *The Sentinel*, February 19, 1953.
39. "Contracted Freedom," *Washington Post*, May 1, 1952; "Group Libel," *Chicago*

Tribune, May 3, 1952; "Ruling Against Hate-Peddlers," *Chicago Sun-Times*, May 2, 1952; "Latest Supreme Court Decision," *Pittsburgh Courier*, May 10, 1952; E.C. Krauss, "When the Justices Dissent," *Los Angeles Times*, June 5, 1952; "Right to Disagree," *Afro American*, May 10, 1952; B.-Z. Goldberg, "In gang fun gang," *Der Tog*, May 6, 1952.

40. Those fears led the trio of the ADL, the American Jewish Committee, and the American Jewish Congress to assert the absence of antisemitism in the Rosenberg case, in part by pointing to the fact that the judge and prosecutor were both Jewish. Meanwhile, the prosecutor Roy Cohn would go on to become a leading McCarthyite anti-communist and mentor to a younger Donald Trump. Svonkin, *Jews Against Prejudice*, 161–78.
41. "Public Protest Against 'Nuremberg' Bill Is Imperative, Warns N.Y. Paper," *The Sentinel*, May 15, 1952; Jack Fishbein, "The Real 'Trouble-Makers,'" *The Sentinel*, June 5, 1952.
42. Latimer claimed without evidence to have been a member of the party himself for three months in 1936. His revelations came in the context of a two-year fight with the Chicago Bar Association over his quest to become a lawyer. ILP, Box 9, *Transcript of Proceedings, Committee on Character and Fitness, First Appellate Court District of Illinois, October 14, 1955*; ILP, Box 87, Ira Latimer, "The Issue Is Communism" (1960); Matthew Ehrlich, *Dangerous Ideas on Campus: Sex, Conspiracy, and Academic Freedom in the Age of JFK* (University of Illinois Press, 2021); American Jewish Historical Society, New England Branch, Jewish Community Relations Council Papers, I-123, Box 186, Folder 1, Memorandum, November 6, 1959; Walsh, *Taking America Back*, 161–71.
43. "Freedom: Poor Risk," *National Guardian*, December 12, 1949; "Sue Central Figure in Peoria Street Riot on Mortgage and False Arrest," *Chicago Defender*, May 13, 1950; "Suit Demands Foreclosure of Race Row Site," *Chicago Tribune*, March 31, 1950; "Bindman Makes Out-of-Court Settlement in Damage Suit," *Suburbanite Economist*, December 19, 1950; New York Public Library, Civil Rights Congress Papers, N88, C.R.C.-National Board-Reports, 1952; Aaron Bindman, "Participation of Negro Students in an Integrated University," PhD diss., University of Illinois, 1965, 17–18; "Bindman Suggests NAACP File Suit Against University," *Daily Illini*, May 9, 1962; Edward Meyerding, "Defends A.C.L.U.," *Chicago Daily News*, June 21, 1952; "Fan Bias at Rally of Peoria St. Landlords," *The Worker*, May 30, 1952; "Hit Terror Against Families of Chicago Smith Act Victims," *Daily Worker*, November 9, 1951.
44. King-O'Brien, "The Trials of Interracial Advocacy," 314–20.
45. Hillel Rogof, "In itstigen moment," *Forverts*, September 22, 1952; "Bigotry in National Election Deplored," *AJC Committee Reporter*, June 10, 1952.
46. "Hatelers Differ Among Themselves over Whom They Should Attack," *The Sentinel*, July 10, 1952, 1; UC ACLU, Box 418, Folder 8, Flyer, October 1952; Milton Friedman, "The Hate-Monger Conventions," *Jewish Advocate*, July 24, 1952; Elizabeth Dilling, "Reds Threaten Patriot," *Common Sense* (June 1, 1952): 1–4, and "Nationalist Convention," *Common Sense* (June 15, 1952): 1–3; Y. Sigal,

"Vikhtigste pasirungen fun der vokh in Shikago," *Forverts* (Chicago), July 26, 1952; Tsvien, "Idishe interesen: Farvos hobn di idishe tsaytungen azoy venig dertseylt vos es iz forgekumen af der konvenshon fun di antisemiten in Shikago?" *Forverts* (Chicago), July 26, 1952; Boris Smoliar, "Vi halt es mit dem antisemitizm in Amerike?" *Forverts*, June 1, 1952; NAACP and American Jewish Congress *Civil Rights in the United States, 1952: A Balance Sheet of Group Relations* (American Jewish Congress and NAACP, 1952), 137.

47. Congressman Javits tried once more in 1954 to propose a bill for federal legislation. "The Year in Washington," *American Jewish World*, September 19, 1952; Morton Berman, "More Dangerous than Hamanism," *Opinion* 24:2 (January–February 1954): 3; "Rights and Risks Meet," *Jewish Advocate*, August 5, 1954.
48. That ambivalence manifested in a reluctance to fully relinquish the hate speech question. Throughout the 1950s and 1960s, Jewish liberals exhibited a curious pattern of returning to periodic debate over *Beauharnais* and group libel without endorsing it. In 1956, for example, the editors of the *Decalogue* journal of Jewish lawyers of Chicago took the trouble to reprint three student essays from 1946 arguing in favor of group libel accompanied by a note warning against the risks in resorting to such law. AJCP, Box 605, Folder 23, Will Maslow, "The Uses of Law in the Struggle for Equality," October 2, 1954; Leonard Leon, "Group Libel," *Decalogue Journal* 7:1 (September–October 1956): 10; "AJC Committee Notes Dangers," *Times-Picayune*, November 24, 1958; AJCP, Box 837, Folder 20, American Jewish Congress Convention Proceedings, May 30, 1960; AJA, Solomon A. Fineberg Papers, Box 2, Folder 10, Excerpt from NCRAC Report, December 11, 1960, M. Friedman to S. Fineberg and E. Lukas, January 15, 1964, and S. Fineberg to W. Spencer, February 25, 1967.
49. American Jewish Committee Archives, Z138, G. Kellman to J. Slawson, November 4, 1958.
50. Waldron, *The Harm in Hate Speech*, 47–54.
51. Goluboff, *Lost Promise of Civil Rights*, 5.

CHAPTER 7: NEVER AGAIN

1. Skokie Public Library, Attempted Nazi March in Skokie Digital Collection (hereafter SPL), Board Meeting, Part 1, April 25, 1977, Citizens' Comments: Ted Frosch.
2. Illinois Holocaust Museum and Educational Center, Skokie Collection (hereafter IHMEC), 2004.15.4h, National Socialist Party of America Flyer.
3. SPL, Board Meeting, Part 3, April 25, 1977, Citizens' Comments: Ted Frosch and Harvey Schwartz.
4. SPL, Board Meeting, Part 8, April 25, 1977, Citizens' Comments (Fay Waldman).
5. University of Kentucky, Louie B. Nunn Center for Oral History, Jewish Kentucky Oral History Project, Interview with Eugene DuBow by Janice Fernheimer, November 1, 2013; Howard Reich, "Memories of the Skokie That Was," *Chicago Tribune*, December 14, 2008.

6. German records listed his internment as lasting from November 10, 1938, to December 13, 1938. However, U.S. military records indicated that he was only released on February 20, 1939. University of Southern California Shoah Foundation, Ruth Kluger Interview, April 23, 1996; Bundesarchiv, *Gedenkbuch Opfer der Verfolgung der Juden unter der nationalsozialistischen Gewaltherrschaft in Deutschland 1933–1945*, https://www.bundesarchiv.de/gedenkbuch/de; Listenmaterial Dachau, https://collections.arolsen-archives.org/, DocID: 130429387; NARA, U.S. Department of Labor, INS, District Court, Northern District, Chicago Division, Illinois, Petitions for Naturalization, v. 1288, No. 319326–319550, Ca. 1944–1946, No. 147500, May 26, 1939.
7. Ruth Cohn Kluger had personally visited Dachau in 1939 to plead for her brother's release. She took offense at his complete rejection of his Jewish heritage; he in turn accused her of religious fanaticism. Kluger Interview; William Sherman, "The Man Behind the Nazis," *Chicago Daily News*, April 25, 1978; FBI Records: The Vault, Cointelpro White Hate Groups Sub 5 159-9, Part 09, ADL *Memo to Fact Finding Dept*, September 30, 1969; "U.S. Nazi Official Has a Problem: He's Jewish," *Kingsport Times*, July 1, 1970; "Nazi's Actions Pain Jewish Dad," *Charlotte Observer*, July 25, 1977; Marc Wilson, "Nazi Leader's Reward Is 'Respect of Americans,'" *Mt. Vernon News*, July 25, 1977; George Heiner and Bob Copeland, "U.S. Nazis Deify Hitler," *The Stentor*, February 7, 1969.
8. Other hands also drove the swastika vogue. The Soviet KGB dispatched covert agents to spread swastikas as part of a disinformation campaign to link West Germany, Israel, and their allies to the remnants of German fascism. James Loeffler, *Rooted Cosmopolitans: Jews and Human Rights in the Twentieth Century* (Yale University Press, 2018), 230–39.
9. "Rockwell," *ADL Facts* 13:10 (September 1960): 161–66.
10. Beauharnais had drifted into the revived Southern Ku Klux Klan and segregationist circles engaged in church and synagogue bombings in the South. "I salute you, Elijah Muhammad," Beauharnais said in his remarks at the rally. "[S]ince I have learned that Elijah Muhammad is not trying to exterminate the white race and that he does not hate the white race, I have been preaching his teachings in the South among whites." Beauharnais urged Rockwell to abandon the Nazi iconography. "If only George Lincoln Rockwell would wear American symbols," he declared, "I would fight with him shoulder to shoulder." "Black Muslims Hear U.S. Nazi Leader," *Chicago Sun-Times*, February 26, 1962; UC ACLU, Box 257, Folder 4, Edward Marciniak, Memorandum, July 11, 1962.
11. Circuit Court of Cook County, Illinois, County Department–Chancery Division, *Village of Skokie v. National Socialist Party of America et al.*, Transcript of Proceedings, April 28, 1977; Sherman, "Man Behind the Nazis"; John Epperheimer, "Security Police Halt Nazi Leader's Talk," *Daily Egyptian*, February 27, 1968; Richard Avelone, "Nazi Stopped Too Soon," *Daily Egyptian*, February 29, 1968; Interview with Orrin Benn, December 3, 2020; "Carmichael Might Speak Here," *Daily Egyptian*, May 19, 1968; "Crowd Dispersed at Morris' Office," *Daily Egyptian*, May 9, 1968; Frank Collin, "Bring Koehl Back," *Daily Egyptian*,

March 12, 1968; Frank Collin, "Blocking Nazis Bottles Emotion," *Daily Egyptian*, May 29, 1968; "Carmichael Should Debate," *Daily Egyptian*, May 9, 1968.

12. SPL, Mitchell Holzman and Abraham Holtz, "Echoes of a Nightmare" (1987); FBI Records: The Vault, White Hate Groups, Sub 9, 159–9, FBI Chicago Office to J. E. Hoover, June 27, 1968, January 3, 1969, and March 29, 1969; Victor Watia, "Son Says Father Is Liar in Case of Jewish or Not," *Miami Herald*, April 25, 1970; "Denies Jewish Blood, But Dad Claims Otherwise," *The Bulletin* (Oregon), April 24, 1970; "Nazi's Actions Pain Jewish Dad," *Charlotte Observer*, July 25, 1977.
13. UC ACLU, Box 283, Folder 9, *1969 Annual Report of the Midwest Division of the National Socialist White People's Party.*
14. The tortured logic of Collin's racial views was reflected in a statement by his main lieutenant, Richard Tedor. "We consider the Jews to be a racial, an ethnic group of the Caucasian race which we do not classify as white. They are a race, and not a religion. They are more a race of the mind, I think, than of their physical appearance, and sometimes it makes it more difficult to detect them." Holzman and Holtz, "Echoes of a Nightmare"; Heiner and Copeland, "U.S. Nazis Deify Hitler"'; Jim Lukas, "U.S. Nazis Still Active," *Daily Illini*, April 21, 1971; Gail Bernstein, "Ovens in Auschwitz Used to Bake Bread," *Chicago Jewish Post*, April 15, 1977; UC ACLU, Box 953, Folder 7, *Petition for Writ of Certiorari to the United States Court of Appeals for the Seventh Circuit*, 10; Jim Lukas, "NSPA Leader Seeks Revolution," *Daily Illini*, April 23, 1971.
15. FBI Records: The Vault, Cointelpro White Hate Groups Sub 5 159-9, Part 09, ADL Memo to Fact Finding Dept, September 30, 1969, and Chicago FBI Branch to J. E. Hoover, October 6 and 13, November 21, and December 12, 1969; Sherman, "Man Behind the Nazis," 4, 31; "U.S. Nazi Official Has a Problem"; Watia, "Son Says Father Is Liar"; Jack Ouleney, "City's Top Nazi Gets Boot," *Chicago Today*, June 24, 1970.
16. In the 1971 case, the city claimed that Collin's arrest record related to racial violence justified requiring him to use an alternative location outside Marquette Park. In 1975, the city invoked an insurance requirement policy that, while not new, had been inconsistently enforced. Collin claimed that the new rule violated the existing court order. *Collin v. Chicago Park District*, 460 F.2d 746 (7th Cir. 1972); *Collin v. O'Malley*, 452 F. Supp. 577 (N.D. Ill. 1978).
17. UC ACLU, Box 284, Folder 4, Seventh Circuit Order and Mandate, October 4, 1976; Bob Greene, "Chicago's Nazis Switch—Main Target Now Is the Jews," *Chicago Sun-Times*, September 29, 1976.
18. F. Collin to K. Chamberlain, March 20, 1977, UC ACLU, Box 953, Folder 1.
19. Sociologist Nathan Glazer estimated in 1967 that "the present level of anti-Semitism is probably lower in this country than it has been since the 1880s." Nathan Glazer, "Foreword," in Rose Feitelson and George Salomon, *The Many Faces of Antisemitism* (American Jewish Committee, 1967), 8.
20. Baldwin's views on Jews and antisemitism were complex. His 1967 essay was an expansion of an open letter he wrote that same year condemning the spread of antisemitism among younger Black nationalist writers. Yet his own rhetorical

excess continued to lead him into controversy. In a 1970 interview with anthropologist Margaret Mead, Baldwin attacked Israel as an intrinsically murderous, racist regime for its treatment of Palestinians and its own Mizrachi Jewish population. He went as far as to assert, "I have been in America, the Arab at the hands of the Jews," while denying any antisemitic meaning to his statement. Jews have "paid the highest and most extraordinary price for becoming white," Baldwin went on to argue in 1984, surrendering their identity in the process. Yet "the Jewish translation into a white American can sustain the state of Israel in a way that the black presence here can scarcely hope—at least not yet—to halt the slaughter in Africa." James Baldwin and Margaret Mead, *A Rap on Race* (J.B. Lippincott, 1972), 200, 214–16; James Baldwin, "Negroes Are Anti-Semitic Because They're Anti-White," *New York Times Magazine*, April 9, 1967; James Baldwin, "On Being White . . . and Other Lies" in James Baldwin, *The Cross of Redemption* (Pantheon Books, 2010), 136; Ben Ratskoff, "James Baldwin's Black Critique of Jewish Whiteness," *Jewish Studies Quarterly* 27:3 (2020): 249–51.

21. Jonathan Judaken, "So What's New? Rethinking the 'New Antisemitism' in a Global Age," *Patterns of Prejudice* 42: 4/5 (2008): 549–51.
22. Bidol-Padva's work emerged from the field of applied behavioral studies developed by Dr. Kurt Lewin and Dr. Ronald Lippitt, who researched antisemitism and other forms of prejudice in the 1940s and 1950s under the auspices of the American Jewish Congress. She herself would go on to consult to the American Jewish Committee on American Jewish attachment to Israel and direct a nonprofit focused on early Jewish childhood education. "A State Tackles its Prejudice," *Commission on Community Interrelations Newsletter* (May 1946): 1–7; Patricia Bidol-Padva, *Developing New Perspectives on Race: An Innovative Multi-Media Social Studies Curriculum in Racism Awareness for the Secondary Level* (New Perspectives on Race, 1972); Patricia Padva, *Attitudes Towards Israel and Jewish Identity* (American Jewish Committee, 1991); Patricia Bidol-Padva, Michelle Rapchik-Levin, and Eli Schaap, "Project Kavod: Improving the Employment Culture for Jewish Early Childhood Education," *Jewish Education News* (Winter 2006): 19–23.
23. On the larger Jewish civil rights community's reaction to affirmative action, see Marc Dollinger, *Black Power, Jewish Politics: Reinventing the Alliance in the 1960s* (Brandeis University Press, 2018), 59–69. Cheryl Lynn Greenberg argues that beyond any other factor, the issue of affirmative action shattered the Black-Jewish civil rights coalition. Cheryl Lynn Greenberg, "How Affirmative Action Fractured the Black-Jewish Alliance," *Journal of Blacks in Higher Education* 52 (Summer 2006): 85–89; AJCP, Box 12, Folder 17, Report of Executive Director, May 20–24, 1970.
24. The *New York Times* journalist Nina Totenberg observed of the case that "for whatever reason, the whole affirmative action question seems to bring out the worst in Jews and blacks, and their feelings about each other." Several other Jewish groups did join African American civil rights organizations in defending the

policy, notably the Reform movement's Union of American Hebrew Congregations and the National Council of Jewish Women. A fourth group, comprised of Reform, Conservative, and Orthodox rabbis, some of whom had marched with Martin Luther King Jr. in Selma, also entered an amicus brief supporting DeFunis. The ADL went on to stake out an aggressive position against affirmative action, alleging in one lawsuit that it effectively commingled anti-white and anti-Jewish prejudice. AJCP, Box 394, Folder 1, "Affirmative Action—and Reaction" (ca. 1972), 1974 Resolution, and N. Levine to A. Hertzberg et al., January 20, 1977; Yale University, Alexander Bickel Papers, Box 46, Folder 43, "The Anti-Semitic Aspects of Reverse Discrimination" (1973); Louis Henkin, "DeFunis: An Introduction," *Columbia Law Review* 75 (1975): 483–94; Nina Totenberg, "The Painful DeFunis Case Raises the Specters of Racism and Anti-Semitism," *New York Times*, April 14, 1974.

25. In response to a lower court order, DeFunis had been permitted to enroll while his case proceeded and by the time of the Supreme Court oral arguments had nearly reached graduation. *Office of Management and Budget, Directive 15: Race and Ethnic Standards for Federal Statistics and Administrative Reporting (1977).*
26. When the first reports of Collin's plans had surfaced months earlier, the Synagogue Council of the Northwest Suburbs had turned to the ADL for guidance. At the ADL's behest, a statement it prepared was read out in every local synagogue that fall urging Jews to ignore the Nazis and let them protest. This is "a desperate ploy for publicity" by a tiny, powerless group, which must be ignored. "No matter how offensive," the right to protest and leaflet is constitutionally protected. UC ACLU, Box 285, Folder 17, "National Socialist Party of America (Nazis)," Memo, September 30, 1976; Alan Mitchell, "Ignore Nazi March," *Chicago Jewish Post*, April 22, 1977; "4th of July Paradox," *Chicago Jewish Post*, July 1, 1977; AJA, MS-279, Fred Richter Papers (hereafter FRP), Box 1, File 1, Statement of the Synagogue Council of the Northwest Suburbs, October 1, 1976, and Box 1, File 3, ADL Memorandum, September 30, 1976.
27. Mitchell, "Ignore Nazi March."
28. SPL, Board Meeting, Part 14, June 20, 1977, Citizens' Comments: Ruth Schaffner; UC ACLU, Box 811, Folder 1, "Supplemental Statement of Facts."
29. Donald Downs, *Nazis in Skokie: Freedom, Community, and the First Amendment* (University of Notre Dame Press, 1985), 4, 53; "Concern! A Call for Concern," AJA, MS-279, FRP, Box 1, Folder 3; United States Holocaust Memorial Museum, RG-50, Oral History Interview with Harold Zissman, February 28, 2000.
30. FRP, Box 1, Folder 3, Minutes of the Special Committee on Nazis, June 23, 1977; AJCP, Box 559, Folder 2, Trial Transcript.
31. Gordon had gone on to draft an amicus brief used in the *Shelley v. Kraemer* case, before relocating to Skokie in the 1950s, where he helped racially integrate the town. Philippa Strum, *When the Nazis Came to Skokie: Freedom for Speech We Hate* (University of Kansas Press, 1999), 61; Studs Terkel, *Race: How Blacks and Whites Think and Feel About the American Obsession* (The New Press, 1992), 288–91; "Gilbert Gordon Opens Law Office Here," *The Sentinel*, January 5, 1950, 18;

Gerald Rosenbaum, "The Educational Efforts of The American Jewish Congress to Combat Antisemitism in the United States, 1946–1980," PhD diss., Loyola University Chicago, 1992, 29–31, 84–91; AJCP, Box 559, Folder 9, G. Gordon to J. Robison, March 24, 1977.

32. AJPC, Box 559, Folder 2, *Village of Skokie v. National Socialist Party of America et al.*, Emergency Injunction Complaint.
33. AJPC, Box 559, Folder 2, Trial Transcript; Robert McClory, "ACLU Rapped for Aiding Nazis Here," *Chicago Defender*, September 25, 1975, 3; Podcast Interview with David Goldberger, September 17, 2020, www.thefire.org.
34. AJPC, Box 559, Folder 2, Trial Transcript.
35. Joel Albert, *Sefer HaZikaron LeKehilat Yurburg-Lita* (Assistance to Lithuanian Jews, 1991), 48, 259–68.
36. AJPC, Box 559, Folder 2, Trial Transcript; Mary Pious, "Judge Forbids Nazi Event in Skokie, Cites Riot Peril," *Chicago Sun-Times*, April 29, 1977.
37. AJPC, Box 559, Folder 2, Trial Transcript.
38. AJPC, Box 559, Folder 2, Trial Transcript; Pious, "Judge Forbids Nazi Event."
39. UC ACLU, Box 953, Folder 1, "Petition for Issuance of an Emergency Order," April 30, 1977.
40. Strum, *When the Nazis Came*, 59–60.
41. Strum, *When the Nazis Came*, 59–60.
42. All involved $500 fines, and the latter two included the possibility of six-month jail sentences for their violation. AJPC, Box 559, Folder 2, Ordinances.
43. "Heed Their Rising Voices," *New York Times*, March 29, 1960.
44. *New York Times Co. v. Sullivan*, 376 U.S. 254 (1964).
45. Brandenburg established that only meant speech deliberately intended and likely to cause "imminent lawless action" counted as "clear and present danger." The Court went on in *Cohen v. California* to rule that incitement based on "fighting words" applied only in cases in which the speaker's conduct provoked others to acts of violence or disorder. Going even further in *Gertz v. Robert Welch, Inc.* in 1974, the Court ruled that "there is no thing as a false idea . . . Pernicious as an opinion may seem, we depend for its correction not on the conscience of judges and juries but on the competition of other ideas." *Brandenburg v. Ohio*, 395 U.S. 444 (1969); *Cohen v. California*, 403 U.S. 15 (1971); *Gertz v. Robert Welch, Inc.*, 418 U.S. 323 (1974).
46. The First Amendment scholar Lee Bollinger later built a whole theory around this insight, arguing that permitting offensive speech was necessary to provide citizens the opportunity to exercise legal restraint and practice moral critique. Technically, all forms of criminal libel in Illinois were condensed into a provision against breach of peace. Robert Labunski, *Libel and the First Amendment: Legal History and Practice in Print and Broadcasting* (Routledge, 1987), 62; Charles Bowman, "The Illinois Criminal Code of 1961 and Code of Criminal Procedure of 1963," *University of Michigan Journal of Legal Reform* 461 (Spring 1971): 461–75; Downs, *Nazis in Skokie*, 210; David Miller, *1970 Illinois Constitution Annotated for Legislators*, 4th ed. (Legislative Research Unit, 2005), 17; Geoffrey

Stone, "Group Defamation," University of Chicago Law Occasional Paper, No. 15 (1978); Lee Bollinger, *The Tolerant Society: Freedom of Speech and Extremist Speech in America* (Oxford University Press, 1986).

47. The circuit justice responsible for Seventh Circuit appeals, John Paul Stevens, decided to treat the case as if it were a certiorari application and assigned it for full review. The per curiam opinion granted cert and faulted the Illinois Supreme Court for issuing what amounted to a final judgment without examining the case. Justice William Rehnquist, along with Chief Justice Warren Burger and Justice Potter Stewart, dissented on grounds that the Illinois Supreme Court had not issued a final judgment and the U.S. Supreme Court should not have interfered with the stay pending a state hearing on the merits. Another request came in August 1977 from the Skokie government for a stay pending the Illinois Supreme Court's review; Stevens denied it. *National Socialist Party of America v. Village of Skokie*, 432 U.S. 43 (1977); LOC, Stevens Papers, Box 69, Folder 9, Memo, August 26, 1977; Lesley Oelsner, "High Court Upsets a Ban in Illinois on Parade by Nazi-Styled Group," *New York Times*, June 16, 1977.
48. AJPC, Box 559, Folder 6, Minutes of the Special Committee Meeting on the Nazis, June 23, 1977; Eugene DuBow, "The Threatened Nazi March in Skokie and the Jewish Reaction," MA thesis, Hebrew Union College–Jewish Institute of Religion, 1980, 28; A. Abbot Rosen, "Skokie, Illinois—Nazis," July 28, 1977, and ADL Memorandum, April 7, 1978, ADL files; Roger Simon, "Another Side of the Nazi Rights Issue," *Chicago Sun-Times*, August 16, 1977.
49. Despite their quarantine policy, the ADL had previously supported the use of injunctions against George Lincoln Rockwell in the 1960s in Chicago on grounds that antisemitic protests outside synagogues violated Jewish civil rights. Circuit Court of Cook County, Chancery Division, *Sol Goldstein v. Francis Joseph Collin*, 77 CH 4367, Class Action Complaint.
50. Freedman borrowed the name from the Dutch Jewish psychiatrist and Holocaust survivor Joost Meerloo, who had coined it to describe the mental anguish suffered by those brainwashed by totalitarian regimes. For a sophisticated theoretical treatment of antisemitism as emotional sadism, see Susannah Heschel, "Erotohistoriography: Sensory and Emotional Dimensions of Antisemitism," in Scott Ury and Guy Miron, eds., *Antisemitism and the Politics of History* (Brandeis University Press, 2023), 65–86. Circuit Court of Cook County, Chancery Division, *Sol Goldstein v. Francis Joseph Collin*, 77 CH 4367, Affidavit of Freedman; Joost A. M. Meerloo, "The Crime of Menticide," *American Journal of Psychiatry* 107:8 (February 1951): 594–98.
51. "You must realize we're not talking about free speech," echoed one of Goldstein's lawyers, Gerald Leval; "this group is seeking to inflict emotional harm to a certain group of people, the World War Holocaust survivors . . . who have undergone an experience unequalled in history." The march would be "a psychic assault which would bring to the survivors' feelings of anxiety, terror, shame, guilt, withdrawal, alienation, and a paralyzing sense of helplessness." Douglas Kneeland, "Skokie's Jews See Nazi Threat as Real," *New York Times*, July 8, 1977; Diane Dubey,

"Censure ACLU Position," *Skokie Life*, September 29, 1977; Nat Hentoff, "Nazis March Toward the First Amendment," *Village Voice*, August 1, 1977.

52. Hentoff, "Nazis March Toward the First Amendment."
53. Circuit Court of Cook County, Chancery Division, *Sol Goldstein v. Francis Joseph Collin*, 77 CH 4367, Trial Transcript; Diane Dubey, "Censure ACLU Position"; Saundra Saperstein and Steve Marshall, "Confrontation in Court: Nazi Turmoil Grows," *Chicago Tribune*, July 5, 1977.
54. Circuit Court of Cook County, Chancery Division, *Sol Goldstein v. Francis Joseph Collin*, 77 CH 4367, Trial Transcript.

CHAPTER 8: HOLOCAUST TRAUMAS

1. UC ACLU, Box 258, Folder 6, F. Collin to J. Matzer Jr., June 22, 1977; ADL Memorandum, April 7, 1978; AJPC, Box 559, Folder 9, B. Goldberg to J. Robison, August 3, 1977; "JDL Threatens to Halt Nazi Parade," *Taylorville Daily Breeze Courier*, June 29, 1977.
2. Letter to the Editor from David Fisch, *Jewish News of Northern California*, July 27, 1973; "Jewish Defense League: Exploiter of Fear," *The Sentinel*, July 23, 1970; "Kahane Calls Violence Necessary," *New York Times*, July 5, 1977; Downs, *Nazis in Skokie*, 59; Peter Novick, *The Holocaust in American Life* (Oxford University Press, 1999), 159.
3. Local Jewish leaders had canceled their own official "patriotic American rally" to avoid stoking more fear and conflict whereas Kahane called on Jews to protest the Nazis and boycott the ACLU, which he deemed "a group of liberal fools who would be the first to be gassed by those they help." "Fund Leader Denounces JDL," *Exponent* (Philadelphia), July 15, 1977; "Kahane Blasted by Skokie Jews," *Jewish News of Northern California*, July 16, 1977; "JDL Plans July 4th Counter-March," *Skokie Life*, June 26, 1977; Hentoff, "Nazis March Toward the First Amendment"; IHMEC, Albert Smith Scrapbook, F. Richter to JDL, March 16, 1978. On the complex origins of Kahane's radicalism, see Shaul Magid, *Meir Kahane: The Public Life and Political Thought of an American Jewish Radical* (Princeton University Press, 2021) and Natasha Roth-Rowland, "'Not One Inch of Retreat': The Transnational Jewish Far Right, 1929–1996," PhD diss., University of Virginia, 2023, 124–79.
4. As a member of the Illinois legislature, Mikva had led the 1961 overhaul of the state criminal code that eliminated group libel as an offense. "Don't Allow Them to Destroy July 4th," *Skokie Life*, June 30, 1977; Bonnie Pechter, *Nazis in America: A Study of Jewish Common Sense* (Jewish Defense League, 1978); "Rabbi Suggests Taking to Streets Against Nazis," *Daily Illini*, June 23, 1977; Judy Agusti, "If the Nazis Win Now, May Win Again," *Daily Illini*, June 29, 1977; Allen Feuerstein and Harold Allston, "Not in Skokie," *Daily Illini*, July 7, 1977; Sanford Horwitt, *Conversations with Abner Mikva* (University of Kansas Press, 2018), 85; FRP, Box 1, Folder 3, "Confronting the Nazis"; IHMEC Albert Smith Scrapbook, A. Lapping to A. Smith, June 28, 1977.
5. "I am not Jewish, and I am here," said Etta Alejandro, who had traveled two hours

by public transit from the city to be there. Alejandro came ready for violent confrontation. "I am a fighter, not a lover," she told a reporter, adding, "'Ignore it and it will go away' . . . was the exact mentality of the Germans in the 1930's." Roger Simon, "JDL Has Day in the Skokie Sun," *Chicago Sun-Times*, July 5, 1977; Jeff Lyon, "Demagogs Play on Skokie Fears of Nazi Threat to March," *Chicago Tribune*, July 5, 1977; "King Group Slates Pro-Jewish March," *Chicago Defender*, June 29, 1977.

6. Mike Lavelle, "We Owe Something to the Nazis," *Chicago Reader*, June 30, 1978.
7. "The unique dimensions of the Nazi atrocity, an atrocity that finds no parallel before or since," argued one Chicago rabbi, "places the Nazis in a category where they have no claim to defense by a civil libertarian group." "There's No Justification for the ACLU Defense of Nazis," *The Sentinel*, February 16, 1978; Agusti, "If the Nazis Win Now"; Zissman Interview.
8. Judith Shklar, *Legalism: Law, Morals, and Political Trials* (Harvard University Press, 1964).
9. Alexander Bickel, *The Morality of Consent* (Yale University Press, 1976), 72–73. On Bickel's view of *Beauharnais* and the *Pentagon Papers*, see Alexander Bickel, "The 'Uninhibited, Robust, and Wide-Open' First Amendment," *Commentary* (November 1972): 60–67.
10. "The fundamental issue raised by Skokie is not the affront to the Jewish citizens there, though that is serious enough," Bork said in a 1977 speech, "it is whether a creed of that sort ought to be allowed to find voice anywhere in America." Robert Bork, "The Individual, the State, and the First Amendment," Ronald Reagan Presidential Library, Digital Library Collections, www.reaganlibrary.gov. This argument built on his famous 1971 article "Neutral Principles and Some First Amendment Problems," *Indiana Law Journal* 47:1 (1971): 1–35. See also Mark Campisano, "Note: Group Vilification Reconsidered," *Yale Law Journal* 89:2 (December 1979): 308–32; Mark Campisano, "On 'Group Vilification Reconsidered,'" *Yale Law Journal* 89:7 (June 1980): 1452–53; Mark Campisano, "Civil Liberties, Beyond the Anecdotes," *Wall Street Journal*, October 20, 1988.
11. The conservative Republican columnist George Will similarly called for banning the march, using the opportunity to take a swipe at the amorality of left liberalism, "a philosophy that yields the essential task of philosophy—distinguishing truth from error—to the 'market,' which measures preferences (popularity), not truth . . . the logic of liberalism is that it is better to be ruled by Nazis than to restrict them." Hadley Arkes, "Marching Through Skokie," *National Review* 30:19 (May 12, 1978): 588; "No Free Speech Rights for Nazis: Panelists," *American Bar Association Journal* 64:9 (September 1978): 1335; Hadley Arkes, *The Philosopher in the City: The Moral Dimensions of Urban Politics* (Princeton University Press, 1981); George Will, "Nazis: Outside the Constitution," *Washington Post*, February 2, 1978.
12. Leo Strauss, *What Is Political Philosophy and Other Studies* (The Free Press, 1959).
13. Davis called for using the 1871 Civil Rights Act to allow victims of the Nazis and Ku Klux Klan to sue for material damages. Fania Davis, Doris Brin Walker, and Ann Fagan Ginger, "Opposing Right-Wing White Supremacist Groups," in Ann Fagan Ginger and Eugene Tobin, eds., *The National Lawyers Guild: From*

Roosevelt Through Reagan (Temple University Press, 1988), 338–40. For other leftist reactions, see "SL Blasts ACLU Defense of Fascists," *Workers Vanguard*, June 3, 1977; Sam Pevzner, "Skokie: A Lesson in Combatting Nazis," *Jewish Currents* 31 (October 1977): 7. For a recent progressive critique of the First Amendment, see Louis Michael Seidman, "Can Free Speech Be Progressive?" 118:7 *Columbia Law Review* (2018): 2219–50.

14. Richard Delgado, "Words That Wound: A Tort Action for Racial Insults, Epithets, and Name-Calling," *Harvard Civil Rights–Civil Liberties Law Review* 17: 133 (1982): 181; Mari Matsuda, Charles Lawrence III, Richard Delgado, and Kimberlé Williams Crenshaw, *Words That Wound: Critical Race Theory, Assaultive Speech, and The First Amendment* (Columbia University Press, 1993).
15. UC ACLU, Box 953, Folder 3, Philip Kurland, "*Village of Skokie v. National Socialist Party of America*: A Dissent," March 19, 1978; Susan Malaskiewicz, "Nazi March May Be Illegal, Kurland Tells Hillel Group," *Chicago Maroon*, April 7, 1978; UC ACLU, Box 284, Folder 1, *Collin v. O'Malley*, notice of filing; Carl Cohen, "Genocide and the Nazis: The Case Against Group Libel," *Nation* (June 24, 1978): 757–61.
16. Carl Cohen, *A Conflict of Principles: The Battle over Affirmative Action at the University of Michigan* (University of Kansas Press, 2014), 2–6; Cohen, "Genocide and the Nazis"; Stone, "Group Defamation," 11.
17. Jewish critiques were echoed in reverse by African American groups who complained of Jewish hypocrisy. Charles Sims, "On 'Group Vilification Reconsidered,'" *Yale Law Journal*, 89:7 (June 1980): 1450–51; Belth, *Promise*, 203–4; AJCP, Box 559, Folder 9, M. Stern to L. Lusky, May 5, 1978, and N. Morawetz to N. Dershowitz, April 8, 1980; Zemel Interview; Interview with Aryeh Neier, November 12, 2020; Harvey Schechter, "The Skokie March: 1st Amendment Wasn't Meant to Protect Advocates of Murder," *Los Angeles Times*, May 14, 1978.
18. "Proud ACLU Member Defends Nazi Distribution of Hate Literature," *The Sentinel*, March 24, 1960; UC ACLU, Box 327, Folder 6, S. Heller to D. Goldberger, 1977; Elie Wiesel, "What Did Happen to the Six Million?" *Wisconsin Jewish Chronicle*, December 8, 1977; Andrea Horwich, "Wiesel: Hope in Education," *Cardunal Free Press*, December 6, 1977; James Adams, "Jewish Author Censures ACLU Support of Nazis," *St. Louis Post-Dispatch*, February 1, 1978; Jack Germond and Jules Witcover, "Should a Jewish Lawyer Defend a Nazi?," *Chicago Tribune*, August 5, 1977.
19. Robert McClory, "ACLU Rapped for Aiding Nazis Here," *Chicago Defender*, September 23, 1975.
20. Roger Simon, "His Stand for Right Not Sitting Well," *Chicago Sun-Times*, August 14, 1977; UC ACLU, Box 953, Folder 3, David Goldberger, "The 'Right to Counsel' in Political Cases: The Bar's Failure," February 23, 1978; Jonathan Braun, "Mass Exodus of Jews Threatens ACLU Over Skokie Nazis," *New York Jewish Week*, August 21, 1977; UC ACLU, Box 82, Folder 10, J. Miller to S. Waxman, November 6, 1979; "The Nazis in Skokie," *Chicago Defender*, June 26, 1977; David Hamlin, "Swastikas & Survivors: Inside the Skokie-Nazi Free Speech Case," *Civil Liberties Review* 4:6 (March/April 1978): 8–33; "ACLU Office Hit by

Kahane Sit-in," *The Sentinel*, May 1, 1977; FRP, Box 1, Folder 2, D. Goldberger to E. DuBow, March 16, 1978; Roger Simon, "Nazis' Defender Still Feels the Pain," *Chicago Sun-Times*, November 12, 1981; Interview with Steven Lubet, August 30, 2024; Germond and Witcover, "Should a Jewish Lawyer Defend a Nazi."

21. Dubey, "Censure ACLU Position," David Goldberger, "Would You Defend an Unpopular Cause?" *Barrister* 5:1 (1978): 46–52; David Goldberger, "Skokie: The First Amendment Under Attack by Its Friends," *Mercer Law Review* 29:3 (1978): 761–72; PU ACLU, Box 754, Goldberger Lecture draft, August 31, 1977.
22. Walker, *In Defense of American Liberties*, 333–34.
23. "The people who most need the ACLU to defend the rights of the Klan are the blacks," Neier would add. "The people who most need the ACLU to defend the rights of Nazis are the Jews." PU ACLU, Box 1872, Folder 5, G. Tucker to A. Neier, November 23, 1977, A. Neier to G. Tucker, November 29, 1977, S. Listfield to A. Neier, October 23, 1977, and A. Neier to S. Listfield, November 15, 1977; Strum, *When the Nazis*, 86; Neier Interview.
24. Neier Interview; PU ACLU, Box 754, Folder 15, A. Neier to A. Reitman, August 31, 1977, and B. Brickner to A. Neier, September 16, 1977; PU ACLU, Box 754, Folder 10, S. Waxman to *Chicago Sun Times*, n.d.; UC ACLU, Box 82, Folder 10; "Support for ACLU Is Urged," *Chicago Tribune*, August 26, 1977.
25. Nat Hentoff, *Free Speech for Me—But Not for Thee: How the American Left and Right Relentlessly Censor Each Other* (HarperCollins, 1992), 250–51.
26. On Jewish commemoration, see Hasia Diner, *We Remember with Reverence and Love: American Jews and the Myth of Silence after the Holocaust, 1945–1962* (New York University Press, 2009); Rachel Deblinger, *Saving Our Survivors: How American Jews Learned about the Holocaust* (Indiana University Press, 2025). On American public consciousness, see Jeffrey Alexander, "On the Social Construction of Moral Universals: The 'Holocaust' from War Crime to Trauma Drama," *European Journal of Social Theory* 5:1 (2002): 5–85; Novick, *Holocaust in American Life*; Edward Linenthal, *Preserving Memory: The Struggle to Create America's Holocaust Museum* (Columbia University Press, 2001), 18.
27. Samuel Moyn, *The Last Utopia: Human Rights in History* (Harvard University Press, 2010), 120–75; Barbara Keys, *Reclaiming American Virtue: The Human Rights Revolution of the 1970s* (Harvard University Press, 2014); Roger Simon, "JDL Has Day in the Skokie Sun," *Chicago Sun-Times*, July 5, 1977; IHEMC, Smith Scrapbook.
28. The ACLU had argued that "the swastika has substantive content and serves as a 'shortcut from mind to mind,' conveying an actual idea, not a mere abusive attack." AJPC, Box 559, Folder 2, Illinois State Court of Appeals, 1st Division, July 12, 1977, per curiam opinion.
29. Rosen had reluctantly realigned the ADL with Skokie on grounds of supporting the survivors, despite his personal reservations about the legal strategy. Rosen, "Skokie, Illinois"; A. Abbot Rosen, "Hatred on the March," *ADL Bulletin* (October 1977): 3; Interview with Joshua Rosen, November 22, 2024.
30. The ACLU tried without success to secure a writ from the Supreme Court for

expedited review of the injunction case but did win a review by the Illinois State Supreme Court.

31. AJCP, Box 559, Folder 2, Illinois State Court of Appeals, 1st Division, Trial Transcript and ACLU Brief, July 12, 1977, and Appellate Court Decker opinion.
32. AJCP, Box 559, Folder 2, Illinois State Court of Appeals, 1st Division, Trial Transcript; Interview with Ross Harano, August 21, 2024; "Chicago JACL Blasts Racism in Nazi Demo," *Pacific Citizen*, June 16, 1978; "The Nazis in Skokie," *Pacific Citizen*, June 23, 1978.
33. AJCP, Box 559, Folder 2, Illinois State Court of Appeals, 1st Division, Trial Materials.
34. On the question of trial strategy, see AJCP, Box 559, Folder 10, N. Dershowitz to N. Levine, January 4, 1978.
35. AJCP, Box 559, Folder 2, Illinois State Court of Appeals, 1st Division, July 12, 1977, Suppl. facts memo; Harano Interview; Gilbert Gordon, "Cohen vs. Skokie: An Exchange," *Nation* (May 6, 1978): 522; Owen Fiss, "Groups and the Equal Protection Clause," *Philosophy and Public Affairs* 5 (1976): 148.
36. *Skokie v. Nat'l Socialist Party of America* 69 Ill. 2d 605 (1978), 373 N.E.2d 21.
37. *Beauharnais* rested on two pillars: injury to group reputation and likelihood of violence. *Sullivan* had shrunk the reputational injury standard so that it would not apply in this case. Meanwhile, the language involved here did not appear "so extremely likely to cause violence as to" qualify as "inherently productive of violence." *Collin v. Smith*, 447 F. Supp. 676 (N.D. Ill. 1978); AJCP, Box 559, Folder 7, Marc Stern, Memorandum on Skokie.
38. JLC, Box 165, Folder 23, *CLSA/UA Reports*, March 3, 1978.
39. AJCP, Box 559, Folder 9, Howard Carroll Fact Sheet, S.B. 1811 "Criminal Group Defamation"; UC ACLU, Box 953, Folder 1, Draft legislation documents; AJCP, Box 559, Folder 10, J. Robison to N. Dershowitz, May 22, 1978.
40. The Senate approved the Carroll "Group Libel" bill 44–10, with 3 present votes, and the Nimrod "Crowd Disturbance" bill 40–14, with 4 present. Nathan Dershowitz, the director of the American Jewish Congress's legal commission, expressed skepticism that either bill would pass constitutional muster or solve the problem. *Illinois 80th General Assembly* transcript, May 10, 1978; AJCP, Box 559, Folder 9, Carroll Office Press Release, May 10, 1978, 559; AJCP, Box 559, Folder 10, J. Robison to N. Dershowitz, May 22, 1978.
41. "Any exception . . . to the First Amendment which we might be tempted to fashion for these particular persuasive circumstances," added Judge Harlington Wood in his concurrence, "would . . . remain a dangerous and unmanageable precedent in our free and open society." *Collin v. Smith*, 578 F.2d 1197 (1978).
42. Where Sprecher formally dissented was on the matter of the insurance requirement. Such a law was a legitimate move by the village government, which "has a right and a duty to protect its citizens and property in this reasonable manner." Given the potential for violence and destruction, imposing such a requirement on an extremist group seeking to stage a protest march was justified. *Collin v. Smith*, 578 F.2d 1197 (1978).

CHAPTER 9: SYMBOL OF THE WORLD

1. AJCP, Box 559, Folder 7, J. Doyle to N. Dershowitz, May 12, 1978.
2. FRP, Box 1, Folders 2–3, Letters and Memos.
3. The committee replaced an earlier effort, the Special Committee on Nazis, established in 1977 under the auspices of the Chicago Jewish Public Affairs Committee, a local Jewish communal relations agency. AJCP, Box 559, Folder 10, N. Dershowitz to N. Levine, July 20, 1977, and S. Goldstein to PAC, March 27, 1977; DuBow, "The Threatened Nazi March," 43; JLC, Box 165, Folder 23, Jewish Federation of Metropolitan Chicago Press Release, March 8, 1978.
4. Sheryl Adelman Kimmel, "The Changing of the Guard: A Case Study of Maynard I. Wishner as an American Jewish Communal Leader," MA thesis, University of Kansas, 1995, 215–16; FRP, Box 1, Folder 2, Summary Report, Committee on Jewish Security, February 27, 1978; AJCP, Box 599, Folder 9, S. Goldstein to PAC, March 27, 1977; FRP, Box 1, Folder 3, Memo, April 18, 1978; SPL, PAC Press Release, February 23, 1978; DuBow, "The Threatened Nazi March," 70.
5. Similar divisions surfaced within the American Jewish Congress, ADL, Jewish Labor Committee, National Council of Jewish Women, Union of American Hebrew Congregations, and others. Kimmel, "The Changing of the Guard," 128–41; Boris Smolar, "Anti-Semitism and AJC: A Jewish Predicament," *Wisconsin Jewish Chronicle*, October 20, 1977; Maynard Wishner, "American Nazis and the First Amendment," *Sh'ma* 7 (September 2, 1977): 134; DuBow, "The Threatened Nazi March," 56–62; FRP, Box 1, Folder 2, Meeting of Subcommittee on Individual Liberty and Jewish Security, May 10, 1978, and NCRAC Resolution; David Dalin, "Jews, Nazis, and Civil Liberties," *American Jewish Year Book* 80 (1980): 18; AJCP, Box 559, Folder 9, J. Robison to G. Gordon, March 29, 1977; Rosen "Skokie, Illinois."
6. Skokie residents were themselves divided over the march and counterprotest plans. According to a March poll, 63 percent did not think the Nazis should be legally allowed to march with swastikas at all. A May poll offered a more complex picture: 57 percent of Skokie residents thought that the Nazis possessed no legal right to march (67 percent of Jews, 44 percent of non-Jews), and 87 percent felt that even if legal, the march was unacceptable (92 percent of Jews, 79 percent of non-Jews). Dennis Byrne, "Hold Counterdemonstration Elsewhere: Skokie Residents," *Chicago Sun-Times*, March 12, 1978; John J. Camper, "Who Scored in Skokie?," *National Jewish Monthly* (July–August 1978): 33; IHMEC, NSPA Press Release, May 23, 1978; AJCP, Box 559, Folder 10, N. Dershowitz to N. Levine, May 24, 1978; AJCP, Box 559, Folder 9, M. Silver to N. Levine and N. Dershowitz, May 11, 1978; FRP, Box 1, Folder 2, L. Montrose to F. Richter, February 2, 1978; Roger Simon, "He Hits Without Hate," *Chicago Sun-Times*, June 12, 1978; "Young Blacks Wanted to Oppose Nazi March," *Elyria Chronicle-Telegram*, May 27, 1978.
7. DuBow, "The Threatened Nazi March," 131, 137; JCPA, Box 559, Folder 9, R. Epstein to A. Chernin, May 9, 1978.

8. "Erna Gans Hasn't Forgotten About the Holocaust," *Kalamazoo Gazette*, April 17, 1978; Jeffrey Shandler, *While America Watches: Televising the Holocaust* (Oxford University Press, 1999), 159–78.
9. FRP, Box 1, Folder 2, Public Affairs Committee Memo, June 26, 1978, and H. D. Kirk to F. Richter, June 6, 1978; FRP, Box 1, Folder 3, Laurence Charney Notes, April 15, 1978; DuBow, "The Threatened Nazi March," 122.
10. FRP, Box 1, Folder 2, L. Montrose to F. Richter, February 2, 1978.
11. FRP, Box 1, Folder 2, Summary Reports, February 14 and February 21, 1978, "The Skokie March—A Battle Plan," "Proposal for Dealing with Nazi Demonstration," February 20, 1978, Planning Notes, April 5, 1978; FRP, Box 1, Folder 3, Karl Weiner, "A Recommendation"; AJCP, Box 559, Folder 7, J. Doyle to N. Dershowitz, May 12, 1978.
12. IHMEC, NSPA Press Release, May 23, 1978; AJPC, Box 559, Folder 10, N. Dershowitz to N. Levine, May 24, 1978; DuBow, "The Threatened Nazi March," 137.
13. The Skokie team had previously sought an emergency stay from the Seventh Circuit, who voted 2–1 against granting it. Judge Sprecher again dissented, invoking *Beauharnais*. For an argument that *Beauharnais* remained good law, see Kenneth Lasson, "Group Libel Versus Free Speech: When Big Brother *Should* Butt In," *Duquesne Law Review* 23:1 (1984): 77–130.
14. *Collin v. Smith,* U.S.S.C. 77-1736, Petition for Certiorari.
15. Library of Congress, John Paul Stevens Papers (hereafter JPSP), Box 69, Folder 9, Memorandum, August 26, 1977; Library of Congress, Harry Blackmun Papers, Box 289, Memorandum from J. P. Stevens, June 9, 1978, and R. Glushien to H. Blackmun, June 9, 1978.
16. The legal officer's memo recommended that the justices grant Skokie a stay pending certiorari to consider the legal questions. Halting a march, even one delayed for over a year, he reasoned, would pose little material harm to Collin's equity interests since the march was not tied to any specific date or event. JPSP, Box 63, Folder 15, Conference Memorandum by Marc Richman, June 9, 1978; *Lemon v. Kurtzman*, 403 U.S. 602 (1971); *Gertz v. Robert Welch, Inc.*, 418 U.S. 323 (1974).
17. AJPC, Box 559, Folder 10, W. Maslow to N. Levine, June 24, 1977, and M. Wekselman to A. Goldstein, October 26, 1977; AJPC, Box 559, Folder 6, "Preliminary Statement" and Meeting Notes, November 1977; AJPC, Box 559, Folder 9, B. Epstein to N. Levine, January 19, 1978; AJPC, Box 641, Folder 15, Minutes of Governing Council Meeting, January 8, 1978; ADL Files, Memos, September 20, 1977, and April 7, 1978; Rosen, "Skokie, Illinois"; American Jewish Committee Archives, Milton Ellerin, "American Nazis—Myth or Menace?," November 22, 1977; Marc Stern, "The Dilemma of Skokie," *Institute for Jewish Affairs Research Report* (August 1978); Marianne Sanua, *Let Us Prove Strong: The American Jewish Committee, 1945–2006* (Brandeis University Press, 2006), 253–54; YIVO, RG 347.6.38, Box 84, Folder 23, Memo, June 14, 1978.
18. Bob Secter, "House Panel Rejects Bills to Bar Nazi March," *Chicago Sun-Times*, June 6, 1978; Bob Secter, "House Won't Hear Bills to Block Nazi March," *Chi-*

cago Sun-Times, June 14, 1978; Robert Edelman, "Ideology Battles Flare on Nazi March Issue," *Decatur Daily Review*, June 7, 1978.

19. DuBow, "The Threatened Nazi March," 122; DuBow Interview.
20. Stern, "Dilemmas"; FRP, Box 1, Folder 2, Public Affairs Committee Report, June 26, 1978; "Nazi Cancels Plan for Skokie March," *Washington Post*, June 23, 1978.
21. DuBow claimed that the federation had intimidated Collin by privately telling him the extent of preparations for a mass casualty event. DuBow Interview; Jim Casey, "Man Arrested in Plot to Fire-bomb Nazi HQ," *Chicago Sun-Times*, June 23, 1978; Larry Green and Michael Seiler, "Nazi Group Drops Plans to March at Skokie Sunday," *Los Angeles Times*, June 23, 1978.
22. Steven Lubet, "Update: Nazis in Chicago," *Jewish Veteran* (November–December 1979): 15; Barbara DeKovner-Mayer, "Skokie and Chicago," *Israel Today*, July 7, 1978; Judith Michaelson, "Protecting Nazis Enrages Victims," *Buffalo News*, June 25, 1978.
23. Lubet, "Update," 16; Lubet Interview.
24. *Smith v. Collin* 436 U.S. 953 (1978); JPSP, Box 63, Folder 15, Order, June 12, 1978; UC ACLU, Box 953, Folder 6, Stevens Order; AJPC, Box 559, Folder 9, J. Torshen to N. Dershowitz, June 16, 1978.
25. Leo Sauvage, "A Matter of Rights? Talking with American Nazis and Their Defenders," *New Leader*, August 14, 1978; Max Wiley, "The Law, the Press and the Nazis," *Chicago Journal*, July 19, 1978; FRP, Box 1, Folder 3, Goldberger Fundraising Letter.
26. Stern, "Dilemmas"; "Liberalism and the Jews: A Symposium," *Commentary* (January 1980): 15-82; Irving Louis Horowitz and Victoria Curtis Bramson, "Skokie, the ACLU and the Endurance of Democratic Theory," *Law and Contemporary Problems* 43:2 (Spring 1979): 328–49.
27. On the success of the letter, see Walker, *In Defense of American Liberties*, 329–30; FRP, Box 1, Folder 3, Goldberger Fundraising Letter.
28. FRP, Box 1, Folder 2, March 9, 1978, Minutes of Synagogue Council Board Meeting; SPL, June 19, 1978, Citizens' Comments: Sol Goldstein.
29. DeKovner-Mayer, "Skokie and Chicago"; Howard Goodman, "Death Camp Survivor Sees Battles Ahead," *Oregon Statesman*, June 23, 1978; Sauvage, "A Matter of Rights?"; United States Holocaust Memorial Museum, RG-50, Oral History Interview with Erna Gans, June 15, 1981.

CHAPTER 10: JEWS WILL NOT REPLACE US

1. *Sines et al. v. Kessler et al.* (3:17-cv-00072), District Court, W.D. Virginia, Trial Transcript, day 8 (hereafter Sines Transcript); Dix Transcript.
2. UVAA, Jonathan Martin, "Clips from Rotunda"; Dix Transcript; "Reflections on August," September 1, 2017, *Brody Jewish Center Blog*, www.brodyjewishcenter.org; Diane D'Costa Facebook post, September 30, 2020.
3. Dix Transcript.
4. Bonnie Gordon, "In the Aftermath of Charlottesville," *AMS Musicology Now Blog*,

musicologynow.org, September 8, 2017; Interview with Rachel Schmelkin, February 15, 2024; UVAA, Keith Weimer, "Friday Night: My Experience"; Timothy Heaphy, *Independent Review of the 2017 Protest Events in Charlottesville, Virginia* (Hunton & Williams, 2017) (hereafter *Heaphy Report*), 115.

5. *Heaphy Report*, 118–21, 133.
6. D'Costa Facebook post, September 30, 2020.
7. Michael Barnett, *The Star and the Stripes: A History of the Foreign Policies of American Jews* (Princeton University Press, 2016), 202.
8. Dix Transcript; UVAA, John Hermsmeier, "Mass Prayer Service at St. Paul's Memorial Church," August 11, 2017.
9. Spencer Hawes, *Summer of Hate: Charlottesville, USA* (University of Virginia Press, 2018), 28–29.
10. The ADL originally categorized bias crimes under the heading "Ethnic Vandalism and Intimidation." The ADL also called for local and state governments to adopt specific policies mandating "bias crime reporting and training." The roots of such legislation could be traced to the 1968 Civil Rights Act, which made it a federal crime to injure, intimidate, or interfere with another person's exercise of core rights on the basis of "race, color, religion, or national origin." 18 U.S.C. § 245(b)(2); Anti-Defamation League, *1981 Audit of Anti-Semitic Incidents* (Anti-Defamation League, 1981), 3–6 and appendix; Steven Freeman, "The Anti-Defamation League and the Evolution of Hate Crime Laws," *Lewis and Clark Law Review* 27:4 (2024): 1038; Steven Freeman, "Hate Crime Laws: Punishment Which Fits the Crime," *Annual Survey of American Law* (1994): 581–85; Anti-Defamtion League Archives, Memo by Jeffrey Sinensky and David Raim, December 28, 1981.
11. By 1982, eight states had enacted new laws. The number rose to thirty-one by 1988. A third smaller category of such laws made parents responsible for damages of their underage children. Federal legislation included the 1990 Hate Crimes Statistics Act, the 1994 Hate Crimes Sentencing Enhancement Act, the 1997 Church Arson Prevention Act, and the 2009 Hate Crimes Prevention Act. For overviews, see Ryken Grattet and Valerie Jenness, "The Birth and Maturation of Hate Crime Policy in the U.S.," *American Behavioral Scientist* 45:4 (2001): 668–96 and James Jacobs and Kimberly Potter, *Hate Crimes: Criminal Law and Identity Politics* (Oxford University Press, 1998).
12. The debate led to a larger focus on the definition and measurement of antisemitism in the mid-1980s. Edward Shapiro, *A Time for Healing: American Jewry since World War II* (Johns Hopkins University Press, 1992), 28–59; Ellen Cates, "Anti-Semitism Said on Rise," *Houston Chronicle*, January 8, 1981; Anti-Defamation League Archives, Press Release, December 8, 1979; Clara Lewis, *Tough on Hate? The Cultural Politics of Hate Crimes* (Rutgers University Press, 2014), 30; Ryken Grattet and Valerie Jenness, *Making Hate a Crime: From Social Movement to Law Enforcement* (Russell Sage Foundation, 2001), 48–49; AJPC, Box 541, Folder 18, Minutes of the Meeting of NCLS, December 9, 1980, and February 23, 1981;

Interview with Nathan Perlmutter in Cohen and Wexler, *"Not the Work of a Day,"* vol. 1, 130–31.

13. Kathleen Belew, *Bring the War Home: The White Power Movement and Paramilitary America* (Harvard University Press, 2019); Anti-Defamation League, *Shaved for Battle: Skinheads Target America's Youth* (Anti-Defamation League, 1987); Anti-Defamation League, *The Hate Movement Today: A Chronicle of Violence and Disarray* (Anti-Defamation League, 1987).
14. Steven Freeman, *Civil Rights Division Policy Background Report* (Anti-Defamation League, 1990), 2.
15. The ADL soon joined with gay rights organizations to expand the statutes to include sexual orientation; Marlene Young and John Stein, "The History of the Crime Victims' Movement in the United States" (December 2004), www.ncjrs.gov; *Final Report of the President's Task Force on Victims of Crime* (The Task Force, 1982), vi, 20.
16. Susan Gellman, "Sticks and Stones Can Put You in Jail, But Can Words Increase Your Sentence? Constitutional and Policy Dilemmas of Ethnic Intimidation Laws," *UCLA Law Review* 39 (1991): 333–96; Monroe H. Freedman and Eric M. Freedman, eds., *Group Defamation and Freedom of Speech: The Relationship Between Language and Violence* (Praeger, 1995); AJPC, Box 632, Folder 11, R. Lifton to A. Goldstein, September 1, 1988, and M. Stern and L. Waldman to H. Siegman, May 5, 1988.
17. *R.A.V. v. City of St. Paul*, 505 US 377 (1992); *Wisconsin v. Mitchell*, 508 U.S. 476 (1993).
18. The first municipality within Virginia to pass an anti-swastika statute was Charlottesville, in the wake of a 1960 vandalism attack on Congregation Beth Israel's building. The state's 1952 law on cross burning had applied only to private property; in 1968 it was expanded to cover public property. The 1983 law was cosponsored by State Delegate Mary Sue Terry, who went on to become the first woman elected to statewide office in Virginia as attorney general. Va. Code Ann. § 18.2–423.1 states, "It shall be unlawful for any person or persons, with the intent of intimidating another person or group of persons, to place or cause to be placed a swastika on any church, synagogue or other building or place used for religious worship, or on any school, educational facility or community center owned or operated by a church or religious body." A 2025 amendment added private property and exempted Hindu and other religious symbols. "Virginia's Jews Suffer New Wave of Vandalism," *Daily News Record*, January 26, 1982; "Hate-Crime Law Dismissed High Court Argues Right to Free Speech," *Daily Press*, June 23, 1992.
19. *Virginia v. Black*, 538 U.S. 343 (2003); Rodney Smolla, *Confessions of a Free Speech Lawyer: Charlottesville and the Politics of Hate* (Cornell University Press, 2020), 189–211.
20. "It is not just hate speech," countered Hurd. "In the hands of the Klan, the message [of a burning cross] is the law cannot help you if you're black or Catholic or

Jewish or foreign-born, or we just don't like you, and if you try to live your life as a free American, we are going to kill you . . . That is the message of cross-burning backed up by 100 years of history." *Virginia v. Black* 538 U.S. 343 (2003), Trial Transcript.

21. By contrast the American Jewish Congress decided not to enter the case. *Brief of Amicus Curiae of Anti-Defamation League et al., Virginia v. Black 538 U.S. 343* (2003); *Brief of Amicus Curiae Thomas Jefferson Center for the Protection of Freedom of Expression, Virginia v. Black 538 US 343* (2003); AJPC, Box 852, Folder 35, American Jewish Congress Executive Committee Meeting Minutes, June 10, 2002.
22. The case scrambled the Court's typical left-right positions. Four justices joined Justice O'Connor in saying that while the state could still ban cross burning in principle, the wording of its statute was too broad. Strikingly, Justice Clarence Thomas, a Black conservative who had consistently stressed the need for a color-blind view of law, departed from this philosophy. He offered an argument about the exceptional character of cross burning that reflected precisely critical race theorists' view of discrimination's unique harm to minorities. *Virginia v. Black* 538 U.S. 343 (2003); Guy-Uriel Charles, "Colored Speech: Cross Burnings, Epistemics, and the Triumph of the Crits?," *Georgetown Law Journal* 93:2 (January 2005): 575–632.
23. Beverly N. Williams, "Church Vandal Sentenced to Five-Year Prison Term," *Daily Press*, March 9, 1995.
24. Hawes, *Summer of Hate*, 109.
25. Interview with Tom Gutherz, February 5, 2025; Hawes, *Summer of Hate*, 110.
26. Tamar Bar-On, "Richard B. Spencer and the Alt Right," in Mark Sedgwick, ed., *Key Thinkers of the Radical Right: Behind the New Threat to Liberal Democracy* (Oxford University Press, 2019), 224–41; Axel Öberg, "Meet the White Nationalist Trying to Ride the Trump Train to Lasting Power," *Mother Jones* (October 27, 2016).
27. Joseph Goldstein, "Alt-Right Gathering Exults in Trump Election with Nazi-Era Salute," *New York Times*, November 20, 2016.
28. Phyllis Leffler, "Insiders or Outsiders: Charlottesville's Jews, White Supremacy, and Antisemitism," *Southern Jewish History* 21 (2018): 93; Kirt Von Daacke and Ashley Schmidt, "When the KKK Flourished in Charlottesville," in Kirt von Daacke and Andrea Douglas, eds., *After Emancipation: Racism and Resistance at the University of Virginia* (University of Virginia Press, 2024), 65–78; *City of Charlottesville Blue Ribbon Commission on Race, Memorials, and Public Spaces* (City of Charlottesville, 2016), 105–26; Jalane Schmidt, "Excuse Me, America, Your House Is On Fire: Lessons from Charlottesville on the KKK and 'Alt-Right,'" *Medium* (June 27, 2017); Michael Signer, *Cry Havoc: Charlottesville and American Democracy under Siege* (Public Affairs, 2020), 92–98.
29. Deborah Baker, *Charlottesville: An American Story* (Graywolf Press, 2025), 25–101; Ian Shapira, "Inside Jason Kessler's Rise in White Nationalist Movement," *Washington Post*, August 11, 2018.

30. "This is not like a genocide of yesteryear," added Spencer. "This is not a war with bullets and trenches, this is a psychological war, a moral war. We will fight it on the battlefield where the war is taking place. That is the battlefield of symbolism." Then, a group from Identity Evropa unfurled a banner that read, "You will not replace us." *Heaphy Report*, 80; "Spencer & Enoch at Charlottesville, VA (13 May 2017)," www.youtube.com, May 13, 2017; Hawes, *Summer of Hate*, 109–111.
31. Jamelle Bouie, "Why Richard Spencer Matters," *Slate* (May 22, 2017); *Heaphy Report*, 26–28; Signer, *Cry Havoc*, 120; Hawes, *Summer of Hate*, 110–13.
32. *Heaphy Report*, 26–28; Jason Kessler, *Charlottesville and the Death of Free Speech* (Dissident Press, 2024), 97–98.
33. *Sines v. Kessler*, Second Amended Complaint.
34. *Sines v. Kessler*, Second Amended Complaint.
35. "I know your afflictions and your poverty," Jesus tells his followers in *Revelation* 2:9. He then proceeds to identify the reason: I know "the blasphemy of those who say they are Jews, and are not, but are a synagogue of Satan." Two millennia later, as America became progressively less white and increasingly mixed-race in the 2010s, white supremacists returned to this ancient trope of Jewish malevolence. It was precisely because of the relatively small number of Jews in the United States—less than 2.5 percent of the American population in 2017—and their ambiguous place vis-à-vis whiteness and Christianity, that Jews became a focal point for fantasies about race, power, and inequality in America.
36. Leonard Zeskind, "Michael Hill from the League of the South to Speak in Charlottesville," July 23, 2017, Institute for Research and Education on Human Rights Blog, www.irehr.org.
37. Graham Moomaw, "22 Arrested, Tear Gas Deployed as Ku Klux Klan Rallies in Charlottesville," *Richmond Times-Dispatch*, July 8, 2017; Sarah Lazare, "'Not Here, Not in My Town': Charlottesville Black Lives Matter on Why We Must All Resist Fascism," *In These Times* (August 14, 2017); Signer, *Cry Havoc*, 171–72; Michael Signer, Facebook post, July 8, 2017.
38. "Charlottesville Mayor Holds Rally to Declare City Capital of Resistance," www.nbc29news.com (January 31, 2017).
39. Yair Rosenberg, "Charlottesville Mayor Mike Signer Ran Away from His Jewish Identity for Years. Then He Reclaimed It and Faced Down Nazis," *Tablet* (March 22, 2018); Gutherz Interview; Signer, *Cry Havoc*, 80, 99, 123.
40. *Heaphy Report*; Signer, *Cry Havoc*, 144; Smolla, *Confessions*, 106–9.
41. The local interfaith clergy group Solidarity Cville issued a statement denouncing the police. "Injured Community Members Expose Police Brutality at July 8 Anti-Klan Protest in Charlottesville," July 14, 2017, www.solidaritycville.com; Michael Signer, Facebook post comments, July 8, 2017; *Heaphy Report*, 62.
42. Signer, *Cry Havoc*, 147–48.
43. Sharon Bernstein, "Mayor of Virginia City Targeted by Anti-Semitic Tweets After Criticizing Marchers," Reuters, May 14, 2017; Marc Mazique, "On Not 'Taking the Bait,'" *Black, Whole* July 10, 2017, http://www.black-whole.org; David Straughn, "I Rebuke You, Charlottesville," *Parle* (June 8, 2017), www.parlemag

.com; Mark Mazique, "7/17/2017 Statement to Cville City Council," *Black, Whole* (blog), July 28, 2017, http://www.black-whole.org; Hawes, *Summer of Hate*, 163.

44. Signer, *Cry Havoc*, 98, 120, 190–91.
45. *Heaphy Report*, 203.
46. Rachel Schmelkin, "After Charlottesville: A Sermon for Rosh Hashanah," September 21, 2017, *CBI: From the Rabbi* (blog), www.congregationbethisrael.wordpress.com; Interview with Schmelkin.
47. Schmelkin Interview; Dahlia Lithwick, "Drowning Out the Hate," *Slate*, August 17, 2017; Gutherz Interview.
48. See, for instance, *Clark v. Commun. for Nonviolence*, 468 U.S. 288 (1984); *Ward v. Rock Against Racism*, 491 U.S. 781 (1989).
49. *Citizens United v. FEC*, 558 U.S. 310 (2010); *Snyder v. Phelps*, 562 U.S. 443 (2011).
50. Kessler, *Charlottesville*, 131–32.
51. *Sines v. Kessler*, First Complaint.
52. On First Amendment deliberations at the time, see Signer, *Cry Havoc*, 175–76.
53. On the advice of the law firm Boies Schiller, Signer and the city made no mention of the content of the speech, including antisemitism and racism, or Signer's Jewishness, to avoid giving pretext for a viewpoint discrimination claim. Signer, *Cry Havoc*, 180, 186–88, 191–93; "'Unite the Right' Rally Could Be Largest White Supremacist Gathering in a Decade," August 7, 2017, https://www.adl.org/resources/blog/unite-right-rally-could-be-largest-white-supremacist-gathering-decade.
54. *Jason Kessler v. City of Charlottesville and Maurice Jones* (WL 3469956), W.D. Va., August 11, 2017; Smolla, *Confessions*, 68–69; Joseph Goldstein, "A.C.L.U. Wrestles with Its Role in Defending 'Groups We Detest,'" *New York Times*, August 18, 2017; Hawes, *Summer of Hate*, 152–53; Dahlia Lithwick, "What the ACLU Should Stand for in Trump's America," *Slate* (September 8, 2017).
55. Claire Guthrie Gastañaga and Steve Levinson, "Why We Represented the Alt-Right in Charlottesville," *Richmond Times-Dispatch*, August 26, 2017; Hawes, *Summer of Hate*, 147; *Heaphy Report*, 148; Signer, *Cry Havoc*, 148, 199.
56. The Department of Homeland Security had also issued a bulletin on August 9, but it was not sent to Charlottesville. The bulletin focused on the two earlier Charlottesville rallies to emphasize that both white supremacist groups and Antifa (described as "anarchist extremists") had plans for violence. Signer, *Cry Havoc*, 198–99; Josh Meyer, "Virginia Received DHS Warning Before Charlottesville Rally," *Politico* (August 29, 2017); *Heaphy Report*, 110–11; Baker, *Charlottesville*, 218–20, 245–49; Homeland Security Office of Intelligence and Analysis, "Domestic Terrorist Violence at Lawfully Permitted White Supremacist Rallies Likely to Continue," August 9, 2017; Will Parrish, "Police Targeted Anti-Racists in Charlottesville Ahead of 'Unite the Right' Rally, Documents Show," *Shadowproof* (March 7, 2018).
57. Just before midnight on Friday evening, Signer did ask attorney Craig Brown to return to federal court to seek an injunction. Brown told him it was too late. University leaders conceded their failure to use the law effectively. Matthew

Kesselman, "A Dean Groves Talk: The Balance Between Free Speech & Bias," September 28, 2017, https://www.wuvanews.com/dean-groves-talk-balance-free-speech-bias/; *Heaphy Report*, 120, 205; UVA Dean's Working Group, *The University's Response to August 11, 2017: Observations and Improvements* (September 11, 2017); Alexis Gravely, Thomas Roades, and Eliza Haverstock, "An In-Depth Look at the BSA Demands," *Cavalier Daily*, August 31, 2017.

58. George Gittleman, "After Charlottesville," August 16, 2017, *Congregation Shomrei Torah* (blog), www.cstsr.org; Alan Zimmerman, "In Charlottesville, the Local Jewish Community Presses On," August 14, 2017, www.reformjudaism.org; Signer, *Cry Havoc*, 150.
59. Schmelkin Interview; Gutherz Interview.
60. Lithwick, "Drowning Out the Hate."
61. Stephen Lurie, "The Dismal Failure of Jewish Groups to Confront Trump," *New Republic*, October 24, 2017; ADL Advisory Regarding Charlottesville, VA Protests, August 11, 2017.
62. Signer, *Cry Havoc*, 208; Dahlia Lithwick, "Yes, What About the 'Alt-Left'?" *Slate* (August 16, 2017); Smolla, *Confessions*, 105; *Heaphy Report*, 131; Schmelkin Interview; Gutherz Interview; Interview with Hannah Pearce, February 28, 2025.
63. *Sines v. Kessler*, First Amended Complaint.
64. *Sines v. Kessler*, First Amended Complaint.
65. *Heaphy Report*, 126–32.
66. Signer, *Cry Havoc*, 208; *Heaphy Report*, 87, 121, 124; Smolla, *Confessions*, 177–79.
67. Tom Gutherz, "Charlottesville: Before and After," in Michael Cheuk, ed., *Standing Up to Hate: The Charlottesville Clergy Collective and the Lessons from August 12, 2017* (Nurturing Faith, 2023), 22; Gutherz Interview; Pearce Interview.
68. Signer, *Cry Havoc*, 215; Nathan Guttman, "What a Jewish Journalist Saw in Charlottesville," *Forward*, August 13, 2017; Ron Kampeas, "Hate in Charlottesville: The Day the Nazi Called Me Shlomo," *JTA*, August 13, 2017.
69. UVAA, Megan, "Medic Respite Park at McGuffey."
70. Gutherz Interview; Pearce Interview; Schmelkin Interview.
71. Sines Transcript, Day 1.

CHAPTER 11: PRIVILEGED HATRED

1. Donald J. Trump, "Remarks on Signing the VA Choice and Quality Employment Act of 2017 in Bedminster, New Jersey," August 12, 2017, The American Presidency Project, www.presidency.ucsb.edu.
2. Julia Manchester, "White House Clarifies: We Condemn All Violence," *The Hill*, August 13, 2017. This was followed by a statement read out by Trump in person at the White House on August 14 that echoed the same language. Donald J. Trump, "Remarks on the Situation in Charlottesville, Virginia," August 14, 2017, The American Presidency Project, www.presidency.ucsb.edu.
3. Donald J. Trump, "Remarks on Infrastructure and an Exchange with Reporters in New York City," August 15, 2017, The American Presidency Project, www

.presidency.ucsb.edu; Annie Karni, Eliana Johnson, and Nolan D. McCaskill, "Trump Blows Up Damage Control as He Blames 'Both Sides' for Charlottesville," *Politico* (August 15, 2017); Lithwick, "Yes, What About the 'Alt-Left'?"

4. Karni, Johnson, and McCaskill, "Trump Blows Up Damage Control."
5. "U.S. Rights Group Rethinks Defending Hate Groups Protesting with Guns," Reuters, August 17, 2017.
6. "Message from the University of Virginia," August 12, 2017, https://news.virginia.edu.
7. Karl Shapiro, *Poems, 1940–1953* (Random House, 1953), 152, 89. On the background to the poem, see Joseph Reino, *Karl Shapiro* (Twayne, 1981), 78–85. On the intertwined fates of Jew and Black in the Southern white supremacist imagination, and the question of Jewish whiteness, Leonard Rogoff, "Is the Jew White? The Racial Place of the Southern Jew," *American Jewish History* 85:3 (September 1997): 195–230. The long history of fusing race and religion to form whiteness in Virginia is discussed in Rebecca Goetz, *The Baptism of Early Virginia: How Christianity Created Race* (Johns Hopkins University Press, 2012). On the history of Jewish life in Charlottesville, see Phyllis Leffler, *From Civil War to Civil Rights: The Jewish Experience in Charlottesville* (Charlottesville Historical Society, 2019).
8. Gregory Dorr, "Segregation's Science: The American Eugenics Movement and Virginia, 1900–1980," PhD diss., University of Virginia, 2000, 584–86.
9. "[N]othing is more certainly written in the book of fate than that these people are to be free," he wrote in his 1821 draft memoirs, "nor is it less certain that the two races, equally free, cannot live in the same government." T. Jefferson to W. Roscoe, December 27, 1820, in Andrew Lipscomb and Albert Bergh, eds., *The Writings of Thomas Jefferson* (Thomas Jefferson Memorial Association of the United States, 1904), vol. 15, 330; Thomas Jefferson, *Notes on the State of Virginia*, Query XIV (London, 1785); T. Jefferson to T. Cooper, September 10, 1814, in J. Jefferson Looney, ed., *The Papers of Thomas Jefferson: Retirement Series* (Princeton University Press, 2010), vol. 7, 652; Thomas Jefferson, *Notes on Early Career*, February 8, 1821, in J. Jefferson Looney, ed., *The Papers of Thomas Jefferson: Retirement Series* (Princeton University Press, 2020), vol. 17, 328.
10. It would be "a cruel addition to the wrongs which that injured sect have suffered" to require Christian worship or religious study as a condition of admission, he added. T. Jefferson to J. Marx, July 8, 1820, in J. Jefferson Looney, ed., *The Papers of Thomas Jefferson: Retirement Series* (Princeton University Press, 2019), vol. 16, 93; T. Jefferson to I. Harby, January 6, 1826, *Founders Online*, National Archives, www.founders.archives.gov.
11. Despite Jefferson's very different views of Blacks and Jews, the two groups remained enmeshed in Virginian history. That entanglement was exemplified in Jefferson's own family. His son with Sally Hemings, Eston Hemings, was freed from slavery upon Jefferson's death in 1826. He went on to marry Julia Ann Isaacs, the daughter of local white Jewish merchant David Isaacs and his common-law wife, Nancy West, a free mixed-race businesswoman. Julia Ann

and Eston eventually moved to the Midwest, adopted the last name Jefferson, and severed all connections to their Jewish and Black heritage, identifying as white Christians. James Loeffler, "The Jewish Grandchildren of Sally Hemings and Thomas Jefferson," UVA *Thoughts from the Lawn* (blog), November 9, 2020, www. engagement.virginia.edu; Joshua Rothman, *Notorious in the Neighborhood: Sex and Families Across the Color Line in Virginia, 1787–1861* (University of North Carolina Press, 2003), 57–87; Jonathan Sarna, "The 'Mythical Jew' and the 'Jew Next Door' in Nineteenth-Century America," in David Gerber, ed., *Anti-Semitism in American History* (University of Illinois Press, 1986), 69–70; Robert Healey, "Jefferson on Judaism and the Jews: 'Divided We Stand, United, We Fall!'" *American Jewish History* 73:4 (June 1984): 359–74; Nirenberg, *Anti-Judaism*, 322–25, 352–59.

12. James Lawrence Cabell, *The Testimony of Modern Science to the Unity of Mankind* (New York, 1859), 243, 306–7; Harry Gamble, *God on the Grounds: A History of Religion at Thomas Jefferson's University* (University of Virginia Press, 2020), 63.
13. The most extensive account of twentieth-century antisemitism at UVA can be found in Dorr, "Segregation's Science," 578–96. Karen Parshall, *James Joseph Sylvester: Jewish Mathematician in a Victorian World* (Johns Hopkins University Press, 2006), 66–76; Lewis Feuer, "America's First Jewish Professor: James Joseph Sylvester at the University of Virginia," *American Jewish Archives* 36:2 (November 1984): 152–201.
14. Phyllis Leffler, "Insiders or Outsiders," 87–88; Baskind, *Moses Jacob Ezekiel*, 131–60.
15. Paul Brandon Barringer, *The American Negro: His Past and Future* (Edwards & Broughton, 1900), 7.
16. Typical of American white supremacist thinkers, Lewis treated the supposed racial purity Jews had maintained through the millennia as both a model for white Anglo-Saxons and a mark of inferiority and tribal hostility. During the Holocaust, he strenously opposed student efforts to stage anti-Nazi rallies on grounds that "pro-Jew propaganda" would only offend the large proportion of pro-Nazi UVA students and provoke more anti-Jewish racial prejudice. Dorr, "Segregation's Science," 579, 584–86; Leffler, "Insiders or Outsiders," 94; "Biologist Supports Curb on Immigrants," *New York Times*, April 6, 1924.
17. John Kasper, *Charlottesville Attack* (Seabord White Citizens Council, 1956); Milton Friedman, "Is Integration at Root of Swastika Smearing?" *The Sentinel*, March 16, 1960; Leffler, "Insiders or Outsiders," 101; Murray Friedman, "Virginia Jewry in the School Crisis: Anti-Semitism and Desegregation," in Leonard Dinnerstein and Mary Dale Palsson, eds., *Jews in the South* (Lousiana State University Press, 1973), 340–50.
18. The Farmington controversy sparked fierce resistance from some alumni. One response captured the backlash: "UVA is for Virginians," wrote alum John Gill, "not just for Jews, not just for Negros or whatever the cherished minority of the month happens to be." B. Drummond Ayres Jr., "Head of UVA Stirs Racial Dispute," *New York Times*, December 10, 1975, 57; University of Virginia, Special

Collections, MSS12674a, Box 1, Folder 3, J. A. Gill to F. Hereford, October 9, 1974; Claudrena Harold, "No Ordinary Sacrifice: The Struggle for Racial Justice at the University of Virgina in the Post–Civil Rights Era," in Louis Nelson and Claudrena Harold, eds., *Charlottesville 2017: The Legacy of Race and Inequity* (University of Virginia Press, 2018), 133–45.

19. In 2016, antisemitic graffiti on an apartment building in which Jewish students lived near campus prompted alarm. Interview with Vanessa Ochs, February 3, 2025; Interview with Truman Brody-Boyd, August 13, 2025; Email from V. Ochs to J. Loeffler, February 4, 2025; Anne (Nava) Grant, "Too Jewish but Not Jewish Enough: Anxieties of Self-Presentation and Self-Perception at the University of Virginia," BA thesis, University of Virginia, 2012.
20. Kirt von Daacke and Andrea Douglas, "Introduction: Twenty-First-Century Truth-Telling," in von Daacke and Douglas, *After Emancipation*, 1–16.
21. Eric Ward, "Skin in the Game: How Antisemitism Animates White Nationalism," *The Public Eye* (Summer 2017). See also Eric Ward, "Skin in the Game Revisited," *Lewis and Clark Law Review* 27:4 (2024): 1045–57.
22. Truman Brody-Boyd, "Responding to Hate and Violence on our Doorstep," *Cavalier Daily*, August 13, 2017; Brody-Boyd Interview.
23. "Demands of the 'March to Reclaim Our Grounds,'" August 21, 2017, www.virginiaequitycenter.org.
24. Ochs Interview; Gabriel Finder, "UVA's Jewish Studies Program Reacts to Tragic Events in Charlottesville," n.d., www.associationforjewishstudies.org.
25. Brody-Boyd Interview.
26. The Constitution of the Minority Rights Coalition at the University of Virginia, https://virginia.presence.io/organization/the-minority-rights-coalition; Brody-Boyd Interview; Interview with Maya Nir, August 8, 2025; Interview with Jenna Wichterman, September 11, 2025; Muslim Students Association Statements, September 12 and December 7, 2017, April 3, 2018.
27. Meghan Tonner, "Student Council Introduces Specialized Vice Chair for Women, Gender Affairs," *Cavalier Daily*, April 27, 2017; Anna Pollard, "After Violence in Charlottesville, Student Groups Weigh in on Next Steps," *Cavalier Daily*, August 22, 2017; Minority Rights Coalition Facebook post, April 17, 2018.
28. Jewish Leadership Council Statement, March 2, 2018; Brody-Boyd Interview.
29. Wichterman Interview.
30. Reservists on Duty had been founded specifically as a counterweight to the Breaking the Silence organization, which collects testimonies from Israeli soldiers about human rights violations committed during military service. Scott Jaschik, "Who Gets Shouted Down on Campus?" *Inside Higher Ed* (February 25, 2018); "BDS on Campus Leads to Physical Violence," Reservists on Duty Facebook post, December 25, 2018; Interview of Amit Deri by Marc Golub, Jewish Broadcasting Service Facebook post, September 15, 2016.
31. Brody-Boyd Interview; "What Happened Last Night?—Protest @Hoos for Israel Event," WUVA News, www.youtube.com, February 23, 2018.
32. The Hillel leadership echoed this with a statement. "While free speech and the

ability to protest are important aspects of college life, we are disappointed that protesters refused to engage in conversation and instead continued to shout intimidating and hostile slurs directed at students, staff, and panelists." Jake Gold, "Pro-Palestine Protest Interrupts Brody Jewish Center, Hoos for Israel Event," *Cavalier Daily*, February 23, 2018; Baruch Nutovic, "Response to Clark Hall," March 14, 2018, www.lawweekly.org; Brody Jewish Center–Hillel Statement, February 23, 2018.

33. Jaschik, "Who Gets Shouted Down."
34. Students for Peace and Justice in Palestine at UVA Statement, February 27, 2018.
35. UVA Students United Statement, February 27, 2018.
36. Amit Deri, CEO of Reservists on Duty, trumpeted the incident as unequivocal proof that "anti-Israel activists are a violent group whose goal is to intimidate and silence Jewish students and the pro-Israel voice on campus." His group peddled unsubstantiated claims that campus anti-Zionist activism led directly to physical violence in a video juxtaposing an image of the 2017 Unite the Right rally with keffiyeh-clad students. Lidar Gravé-Lazi, "Pro-Palestinian Protesters Disrupt IDF Reservists at U.S. College Campus," *Jerusalem Post*, February 26, 2018; "August 11 Survivors Demand Justice," UVA Students United Facebook video, May 21, 2018; Reservists on Duty Facebook post, December 25, 2018.
37. Minority Rights Coalition Statement, March 2, 2018.
38. Brody-Boyd Interview.
39. Diane D'Costa, "MRC Delegitimizes Its Organization with Decision to Reject the JLC," *Cavalier Daily*, March 13, 2018.
40. "Editorial Board: New MRC leadership should find solution with JLC," *Cavalier Daily*, April 5, 2018.
41. Loeffler, "Anti-Zionism"; Scott Ury, "Strange Bedfellows? Anti-Semitism, Zionism, and the Fate of 'the Jews,'" *American Historical Review* 123:4 (October 2018): 1156.
42. Loeffler, *Rooted Cosmopolitans*, 230–60.
43. United Nations Archives, UN Doc A/RES/3379.
44. Kenneth Stern, *Anti-Zionism: The Sophisticated Anti-Semitism* (American Jewish Committee, 1990), 29.
45. On the origins of IHRA, see Larissa Allwork, *Holocaust Remembrance Between the National and the Transnational: The Stockholm International Forum and the First Decade of the International Task Force* (Bloomsbury, 2015).
46. "IHRA Non-Legally Binding Working Definition of Antisemitism," May 20, 2016, www.holocaustremembrance.com.
47. Derek Penslar, "Who's Afraid of Defining Antisemitism?" *Antisemitism Studies* 6:1 (2022): 133–46.
48. Brief *Amicus Curiae* of the Louis D. Brandeis Center, *Fisher v. University of Texas*, 70 U.S. 297 (2013).
49. Kenneth Marcus, "Jurisprudence of the New-Antisemitism," *Wake Forest Law Review* 44: 2 (Summer 2009): 374–75, 384.
50. Marcus, "Jurisprudence of the New-Antisemitism," 374–75, 384; Lila Corwin

Berman, *Who Is American? Belonging and the Question of Jewish Citizenship* (Princeton University Press, 2026), 215–16.

51. Leadership Conference on Civil Rights, "Oppose Confirmation of Kenneth Marcus for Assistant Secretary for Civil Rights," January 11, 2018.
52. Kenneth L. Marcus and Sitara Kedilaya, "The Very Foundations of the University," *AAUP Journal of Academic Freedom* 4 (2013).
53. "ADL is careful to not conflate general criticism of Israel or anti-Israel activism with anti-Semitism," it wrote in presenting its findings. "However, Israel-related harassment of groups or individuals may be included when the harassment incorporates traditional anti-Jewish references, accusations and conspiracy theories. Also included are cases of picketing of Jewish religious or cultural institutions for purported support for Israel." *2017 Audit of Anti-Semitic Incidents*, www.adl.org.
54. Donald J. Trump (1st Term), "Statement on the Observance of International Holocaust Remembrance Day," January 27, 2017, The American Presidency Project, www.presidency.ucsb.edu; Julie Hirschfield Davis, "After Weeks of Silence, Trump Condemns a Rise in Anti-Semitic Threats," *New York Times*, February 22, 2017; Donald J. Trump, Executive Order 13899—Combating Anti-Semitism, December 11, 2019, The American Presidency Project, www.presidency.ucsb.edu.
55. Kenneth Stern, "I Drafted the Definition of Antisemitism. Rightwing Jews Are Weaponizing It," *Guardian*, December 13, 2019.
56. Hira Azher, "Moving Beyond Free Speech—Why I Say F—k U.Va.," *Cavalier Daily*, October 13, 2020.
57. James Bacon, "A Backlash at Last," www.baconsrebellion.com (September 18, 2022).
58. Free speech controversies had continued to roil the university since 2018, especially after then-President Sullivan announced a new policy of banning non-affiliates from public speeches on Grounds without prior permission. The policy had been implemented after Jason Kessler decided to provoke his opponents by live-tweeting from the law library. Andy Humm, Letter to the Editor: "Free Speech Hypocrite Bert Ellis Canceled Speaker in 1975," *Cavalier Daily*, August 29, 2022; Eva Surovell, "Ellis at Center of Controversy over Eugenicist Speaker While at U.Va., Archives Show," *Cavalier Daily*, August 18. 2022; Eric Willersdorf, "Unfounded Attacks Should Not Tarnish Board of Visitors Appointment Processes," *Jefferson Independent*, September 21, 2022; Susan Svrluga, "When a U-Va. Alumnus Read His Bible on the Steps of the Rotunda, the School Called Police," *Washington Post*, May 11, 2018.
59. James Ryan, "Addressing Free Speech and the University," September 20, 2020, www.news.virginia.edu; T. Heaphy to J. Murray Jr., September 29, 2020, www.news.virginia.edu.
60. Hira Azher tweet, October 12, 2020, including online recording.
61. UVA Student Council FR20-27, A Resolution Calling for Action and "Moving Beyond Free Speech."

62. UVA Student Council FR20–30, A Resolution Denouncing Repeated Instances of Racist Statements by Professors at the University.
63. Susan Svrluga, "College Alumni Groups Spread Nationally to Counter 'Cancel Culture,'" *Washington Post*, July 24, 2022; Joel Gardner, "The Greatest Threat to Academic Freedom and Integrity in UVa's History," October 15, 2020, www.jeffersoncouncil.org.
64. Joel Gardner, *From Rebel Yell to Revolution: My Four Years at UVA, 1966–1970* (Brandylane Publishers, 2018); Gardner, "Greatest Threat"; Joel Gardner, "Uva's Administration Has Willfully Ignored Its Longstanding Antisemitism Problem," December 12, 2024, www.jeffersoncouncil.org; J. Gardner to J. Ryan, October 15, 2020, www.jeffersoncouncil.org.
65. "Joel Gardner," *The Schilling Show*, www.youtube.com, December 20, 2024.
66. Alexander Tsesis, "Remembering Charlottesville 2017 and Engaging Black-Jewish Alliances," *Virginia Law Review Online* 105 (November 2019): 149–54; Email from T. Stone to E. Magill, March 30, 2021; Phone Conversations with Thatcher Stone, March 28, April 6, 2021; Email from J. Loeffler to M. Halvorson-Taylor, December 1, 2021; Email from J. Loeffler to K. John, September 14, 2021; Jewish Student Leadership Statement on Student Council Presidential Candidate Gavin Oxley, March 17, 2021.
67. Jonathan Sarna, "A Scholar of American Anti-Semitism Explains the Hate Symbols Present During the US Capitol Riot," *The Conversation*, January 8, 2021, www.theconversation.com.
68. Kelly Kauffman, "University Names New Committees on Free Speech and the Historic Landscape at UVA," *UVA Today* (February 8, 2021).
69. Caroline Newman, "'Common Ground on Our Grounds': Bridging Political Differences," *UVA Today* (May 12, 2021).
70. Lauren O'Neil, "Students Donate, Protest in Response to Conflict Between Israel and Palestine," *Cavalier Daily*, June 1, 2021; Arab Students Organization Instagram post, May 11, 2021; Nir Interview.
71. Hoos for Israel Statement on the Current Situation in Israel and Gaza, May 14, 2021; SJP Statement on occupied Palestine, May 18, 2021.
72. "UVA Statement on Free Expression and Free Inquiry," June 2021, www.freespeech.virginia.edu.

CHAPTER 12: TRIAL WITHOUT END

1. Sines Transcript, Day 4; Charlottesville Trial Press Pool Working Document.
2. Risa Goluboff, "'Charlottesville' as Legal History," *Journal of American Constitutional History* 1:2 (Spring 2023): 117–37.
3. Sines Transcript, Day 4.
4. Sines Transcript, Day 4; Monroe Trombly, "In a Suburban Cincinnati Office Park, White Nationalists Have Found Their Lawyer—And an Ally," *Cincinnati Enquirer*, March 6, 2018.

5. Sines Transcript, Day 4.
6. Sines Transcript, Days 1 and 4.
7. Sines Transcript, Day 4.
8. Sines Transcript, Day 4.
9. Sines Transcript, Day 4.
10. *Brown v. Invisible Empire Knights of the Ku Klux Klan* (No. CV-80-1449), S.D. Ala. 1989.
11. Interview with Kevin Lipson, November 11, 2020.
12. Lipson Interview; AJPC, Box 557, Folder 8, Memo from Andrea Klausner to Members of the National Legal Committee, May 23, 1986.
13. The American Jewish Congress and the NCRAC chose not to enter the case. ADL Archives, Internal Memo, 1986; AJPC, Box 557, Folder 6, Memo to CLSA Executive Committee from Marc Stern, April 4, 1986; AJPC, Box 557, Folder 8, Memo by Ron Krauss, June 30, 1986.
14. *Shaare Tefila Congregation v. John William Cobb*, 481 U.S. 615. 107 S.Ct. 2019.
15. "He felt [racism] doubly," recalled Marshall, "because he was blond and blue-eyed . . . He could have passed for white, and a lot of times he would get into a big fight because someone would think he was white." *Shaare Tefila Congregation v. John William Cobb*, Trial Transcript; Charles Zelden, *Thurgood Marshall: Race, Rights, and the Struggle for a More Perfect Union* (Taylor & Francis, 2013), 26.
16. The case also offered a harbinger of the Court's path toward textualist originalism, the conservative constitutional theory that the historical meaning of the law must govern its application in all subsequent instances. Yet here, originalist reasoning led not to restriction but to an expansion of civil rights protection. Naomi Cohen, "Shaare Tefila Congregation v. Cobb: A New Departure in American Jewish Defense?," *Jewish History* 3:1 (Spring 1988): 98–108; Annalise Glauz-Todrank, *Judging Jewish Identity in the United States* (Rowman & Littlefield, 2023), 131–32, 137; Martha Minow, *Making All the Difference: Inclusion, Exclusion, and American Law* (Cornell University Press, 1990), 46, 55.
17. Cohen, "Shaare Tefila Congregation."
18. David Schraub, "White Jews: An Intersectional Approach," *AJS Review* 43:2 (2019): 379–407.
19. Marcus, "Jurisprudence of the New-Antisemitism"; Stephen Halpern, *On the Limits of the Law: The Ironic Legacy of Title VI of the 1964 Civil Rights Act* (Johns Hopkins University Press, 1995).
20. Interview with Roberta Kaplan, March 25, 2025; Interview with Karen Dunn, August 22, 2025.
21. *Sines v. Kessler*, Memorandum Opinion, July 9, 2018.
22. Kaplan Interview.
23. Pearce Interview; Kaplan Interview.
24. Since no one had physically touched the synagogue, even though its Torah scrolls had to be removed, its "property rights" were not impinged. *Sines v. Kessler*, Memorandum Opinion, July 9, 2018.

25. "Michael Bloch, Civil Rights Attorney," *Real Ones with Jon Bernthal*, www.youtube.com, March 24, 2022.
26. Sines Transcript, Day 5.
27. Sines Transcript, Day 19.
28. Sines Transcript, Day 4.
29. Sines Transcript, Day 14; Expert Report of Kathleen Blee and Peter Simi, July 21, 2020.
30. Sines Transcript, Day 8.
31. Sines Transcript, Day 8.
32. Sines Transcript, Day 8.
33. *Sines v. Kessler*, Motion in Limine by Christopher Cantwell, September 13, 2021; *Sines v. Kessler*, Motion by Christopher Cantwell, September 22, 2021; *Sines v. Kessler*, Letter to the Court, September 22, 2021; *Sines v. Kessler*, Motion in Limine by Christopher Cantwell, October 8, 2021.
34. Sines Transcript, Day 8.
35. Sartre, *Anti-Semite and Jew*, 13.
36. *Sines v. Kessler*, Motion in Limine by Christopher Cantwell, September 13, 2021.
37. Gutherz Interview.
38. Young Americans for Freedom Instagram post, October 3, 2021; James Bacon, "Defending Mr. Jefferson," www.baconsrebellion.com (October 27, 2021); Rahul Sharma, "YAF Hosts Prominent Conservative Alumni for Event Promoting Legacy of Thomas Jefferson," *Cavalier Daily*, November 1, 2021.
39. Glenn Youngkin Facebook campaign ad, May 4, 2021.
40. Ron Kampeas, "Glenn Youngkin, GOP Nominee for Virginia Governor, Accuses George Soros of Filling School Boards with 'Disguised' Political Operatives," *JTA*, October 21, 2021; Democratic Party of Virginia press release, "Donald Trump Supports White Nationalists. Does Glenn Youngkin Agree?" (October 19, 2021); Michelle Boorstein and Laura Vozzella, "Youngkin Accused of Antisemitism after Claims on Soros 'Operatives,'" *Washington Post*, October 24, 2021; Ron Kampeas, "Democrats Trying to Make Antisemitism a Key Issue in Virginia's Governor's Race," *JTA*, October 18, 2021.
41. Shira Hanau, "Protesters Posed as Neo-Nazis to Target the GOP Nominee in Virginia's Governor Race," *JTA*, October 31, 2021.
42. Ron Kampeas, "Kamala Harris 'Strongly Disagrees' with Student Who Said Israel Was Carrying Out Ethnic Genocide," *JTA*, October 1, 2021; Glenn Youngkin tweet, September 30, 2021; Youngkin campaign press release, "Youngkin Announces Plan to Combat Anti-Semitism in Virginia," June 17, 2021.
43. Executive Order #1 (2022), "Ending the Use of Inherently Divisive Concepts, Including Critical Race Theory, and Restoring Excellence in K–12 Public Education in the Commonwealth"; Charlottesville Public Schools Convocation Speech of Dr. Rosa Atkins, August 15, 2017; C. J. Paschall, "Dr. Atkins Named Chief Diversity, Opportunity and Inclusion Officer," www.29news.com, July 15, 2022.

44. Executive Order #8 (2022), "Establishing the Commission to Combat Antisemitism"; Jewish Community Advocacy Day, Gov. Glenn Youngkin remarks, www.youtube.com, February 2, 2022.
45. *Combating Antisemitism in Virginia: Report of the Commission to Combat Antisemitism* (December 5, 2002); Andrew Lapin, "Virginia Antisemitism Commission Blasts Israel Boycotts and Indirectly Critiques Trump," *JTA*, December 9, 2022.
46. Elizabeth Beyer, "The Free Speech Summit That Wasn't," *Petersburg Progress-Index*, December 3, 2023.
47. Sines Transcript, Day 19.
48. Sines Transcript, Day 19.
49. Sines Transcript, Day 19.
50. Sines Transcript, Day 19.
51. Sines Transcript, Day 19.
52. Sines Transcript, Day 19.
53. Sines Transcript, Day 19.
54. Sines Transcript, Day 19.
55. Sines Transcript, Day 19.
56. Sines Transcript, Day 19.
57. The judge rejected defense motions to suspend the verdict on First Amendment or procedural grounds, writing, "Plaintiffs introduced substantial evidence that defendants sought violence, planned for violence, sparked violence, engaged in violence, and afterwards, glorified the violence." Hawes Spencer, "Judge Trims Sines v. Kessler Punitive Award from $24 Million to $350K," *Daily Progress*, January 11, 2023; *Sines v. Kessler*, No. 23-1119 (4th Cir. 2024).
58. Hingely did not close the door to future prosecutions, but suggested they were unlikely. Eduardo Medina, "Torch Carriers in 2017 Charlottesville Rally Are Indicted," *New York Times*, April 18, 2023; Avery Davis, "2017 Torch Rally Prosecutions Likely at an End, Albemarle Commonwealth's Attorney Said," www.29news.com, April 11, 2025.
59. Elena Kagan, "Regulation of Hate Speech and Pornography after R. A. V.," *University of Chicago Law Review* 60 (1993): 883.
60. For another important argument that hate speech should be considered a violation of the free speech rights of its targeted victims, see Owen Fiss, "The Supreme Court and the Problem of Hate Speech," *Capital University Law Review* 24:2 (1995): 181–91; Kagan, "Regulation of Hate Speech," 887.
61. For a more promising view of the potential for dignity torts, see Rachel Bayefsky, *Dignity and Judicial Authority* (Oxford University Press, 2024).
62. *Swords into Ploughshares*, https://www.sipcville.com/about.
63. Charlottesville City Council Meeting, December 6, 2021, www.charlottesvilleva.portal.civicclerk.com; "The Summer of Hate: One Woman's Story Navigating the Aftermath," The Center at Belvedere, www.youtube.com, September 17, 2020.
64. Tom Gutherz, "Sines vs. Kessler—An Open Letter from Rabbi Tom Gutherz," October 24, 2021.

65. *Swords into Ploughshares 2024 Community Engagement Report* (Charlottesville, 2024), 2.

AFTERWORD

1. Sarah Jaffe, "A Long History of Antifascism Is Driving the Jewish Demand for Gaza Cease-Fire," *In These Times*, December 15, 2023.
2. Jason Armesto, "'Family and Friends, Murdered, Injured': Hundreds Gather at UVa to Mourn Bloodshed in Israel," *Daily Progress*, October 11, 2023; *Goldstein v. The Rector and Visitors of the University of Virginia*, 3:24-cv-00036 (W.D. Va.).
3. Open Letter from Anti-Zionist NYU Jewish Law Students to Dean Trevor Morrison, April 19, 2022; *Goldstein v. The Rector and Visitors of the University of Virginia.*
4. The ADL, which had long maintained that anti-Zionism was not inherently antisemitic, abandoned that position in 2022 when leader Jonathan Greenblatt declared otherwise. "Remarks by Jonathan Greenblatt to the ADL Virtual National Leadership Summit," May 1, 2022, www.adl.org.
5. James Bacon, "Miyares Calls for Moral Clarity Regarding Pro-Hamas Demonstrators," www.baconsrebellion.com (November 19, 2023); Jason Armesto, "UVa Students, Faculty Named in Blacklist, Accused of Antisemitism Without Evidence," *Daily Progress*, April 27, 2024; Stephanie Saul, "Inside the Conservative Campaign That Took Down a University President," *New York Times*, July 14, 2025.
6. The current legal landscape has only just begun to engage these questions. For the most important recent cases, see *Pauker v. Heart Consciousness Church, Inc.* (3:25-cv-02852), N.D. Cal. 2025; *Gartenberg v. The Cooper Union for the Advancement of Science and Art* (1:24-cv-02669), S.D. N.Y. 2025; *Frankel v. Regents of the University of California* (2:24-cv-04702-MCS-PD), C.D. Cal. 2025; *American Association of University Professors v. Rubio* (1:25-cv-10685), D. Mass. 2025. For legal discussion of recent developments, see Benjamin Eidelson and Deborah Hellmann, "Antisemitism, Anti-Zionism, and Title VI: A Guide for the Perplexed," *Harvard Law Review Forum* 139:1 (November 2025): 1–24; Zalman Rothschild, "Anti-Zionism, Antisemitism, Antidiscrimination," *Indiana Law Journal* (2026) (forthcoming); Jacob Gersen and Jeannie Suk Gersen, "The Six Bureaucracy," *Harvard Public Law Working Paper 25-20* (March 30, 2025).

ACKNOWLEDGMENTS

Jewish history, the great scholar Salo Baron once observed, is actually the story of what happens *between* the pogroms. Those words drew me to this profession. I became a historian to tell the stories of how past generations lived, not how they died. While I still believe Baron was right, I would offer an addendum: History is also the chronicle of catastrophes, and how societies choose to reckon with them. Writing this book about how Americans have encountered and responded to prejudice and violence has taken me through the intersecting realms of history, law, and politics, a journey that would have been impossible without the knowledge, generosity, and steadfast support of many people.

I am profoundly grateful to my editor at Metropolitan Books, Riva Hocherman, who believed in this project from the outset, and guided it toward its final form with an exceptional blend of expertise, wisdom, principle, and grace. Alex Foster, Chris O'Connell, and Chris Sergio deftly guided the publication process at Metropolitan Books/Henry Holt, while Joshua Rubins of Duane Morris provided astute legal and literary counsel. Don Fehr and his team at the Trident Media Group offered wisdom and unwavering support. Leah Paulos at PressShop has steered me through the media maelstrom with expert skill and good humor.

The book has been profoundly shaped by extraordinary readers—Lila Berman, Lisa Leff, Joshua Leifer, Yosef Malka, Samuel Moyn, Daniel B. Schwartz, Eliyahu Stern, and Laura Weinrib—each of whom brought penetrating intelligence and unstinting care to these pages. And they read quickly but closely, another gift in this hurried age.

If these readers honed my arguments, a wider circle of interlocutors helped generate them. This book's core insights emerged from conversations with a generous roster of scholars and thinkers: Zachary Braiterman, Carolyn Dean, Carrie Filipetti, Noah Feldman, William Forbath, Jennifer Geeter, Sarah Gershman, Dan Gordon, Susannah Heschel, Amos Hochstein, Sarah Hurwitz, Randall Kennedy, Amalia Kessler, Linda Kinstler, David Luban, Martha Minow, David Myers, Karen Naimer, Reut Paz, Derek Penslar, Riv-Ellen Prell, Simon Rabinovitch, Zalman Rothschild, Jason Rubenstein, Esther Schor, Joshua Shanes, Daniel Silverberg, David Sorkin, Ronit Stahl, Farah Stockman, Nomi Stolzenberg, Jeffrey Veidlinger, and Victoria Woeste. Two deserve particular mention: Dahlia Lithwick, who urged me to unravel the myths of Charlottesville, and Franklin Foer, who insisted I tell the story of what America is rather than what it wants to be.

Such vital exchanges require nurturing environments, and three institutions provided the intellectual community this book needed to grow. At the University of Virginia—a community still reeling from Charlottesville—colleagues in history, Jewish studies, and law helped me think through these urgent questions. I particularly thank Asher Biemann, Jennifer Geddes, Risa Goluboff, Claudrena Harold, William Hitchcock, Leslie Kendrick, Phyllis Leffler, Christian McMillen, Neeti Nair, Vanessa Ochs, and Micah Schwartzman. At Johns Hopkins University, I have found a wonderful new professional home in the History Department and the Leonard and Helen R. Stulman Jewish Studies Program. Nathan Connolly and Martha Jones engaged me in vital conversations about race and law in American history. Inviting me into the Shalom Hartman Institute of North America, Yehuda Kurtzer challenged me to explore how words shape the moral imagination. At the Kogod Research Center, I benefited from rich intellectual exchange with Hartman leadership Justus Baird, Elana Stein Hain, Donniel Hartman,

Sara Labaton, Joshua Ladon, Rebecca Schwartz, and Claire Sufrin, and learned much while studying liberalism and antisemitism with seminar fellows Leora Batnitzky, Flora Cassen, Christine Hayes, Michael Helfand, Meirav Jones, Shaul Magid, Daniel May, Masua Sagiv, Yoav Schaefer, and Rivka Press Schwartz.

Several publications provided opportunities to develop the ideas in this book, including *The Chronicle of Higher Education*, *The Forward*, *Newsweek*, *The Wall Street Journal*, and *Sources*—where Claire Sufrin encouraged the piece that helped me engage our contemporary reality. Above all, I thank Yoni Appelbaum at *The Atlantic*, an extraordinary editor and historian, whose early receptiveness and incisive questions helped clarify the stakes of this history. While reporting on the 2021 *Sines v. Kessler* trial for *The Atlantic*, I was immersed in both a landmark legal proceeding and a community of perceptive journalists, among them Jonathan Katz, Lyz Lenz, Neil MacFarquhar, Christopher Miller, Ian Shapiro, and Ellie Silverman, whose methods and insights both complemented and challenged my own historical approach.

Presenting this work-in-progress at universities and institutes worldwide has deepened my thinking immeasurably. I thank the following institutions for providing forums to test and refine this book's arguments: Amherst College; Centro Primo Levi; the Georgetown University McCourt School of Public Policy; the Harvard Law School Julis-Rabinowitz Program on Jewish and Israeli Law; the *Law v. Antisemitism* Conference; the *Seeing Antisemitism Through Law Initiative* at the Leibniz Peace Research Institute; the New York University Center for Antisemitism Studies; the Northeastern University Jewish Studies Program; the Syracuse University Jewish Studies Program; Touro College of Law; the University of Florida Bud Shorstein Center for Jewish Studies; the University of Minnesota Center for Jewish Studies; the Carolina Center for Jewish Studies at the University of North Carolina; the University of Pennsylvania Katz Center for Advanced Jewish Studies; the University of Wisconsin–Madison Mosse/Weinstein Center for Jewish Studies; the University of Wisconsin–Milwaukee Stahl Center for Jewish Studies; the Weitzman National Museum of American Jewish History; and the Yale University Program for the Study of Antisemitism.

Conducting this research during Covid's peak would have been impossible without dedicated research assistants who unearthed materials nationwide: Adam Abergel, James Breen, Erin Faigen, Elena Hoffenberg, Max Klein, Eliana Koren, Yosef Malka, Kalle Masci, Natasha Roth-Rowland, and Avi Segal. Fellow scholars John Q. Barrett, David Koffman, Isabelle Levy, Marlene Trustman, and Matthew Williams generously shared sources and research leads, while Judge Nael Abouzaki of the Henrico County Court courteously provided the *Commonwealth v. Dix* trial transcript.

The librarians and archivists who made sources available proved indispensable. I thank Dana Herman at the American Jewish Archives; Lauren Vandenberg at the Anti-Defamation League Archives; Emily Mohney, Kelley Szany, and Arielle Weininger at the Illinois Holocaust Museum & Education Center; Kimberly Hazlett and Eileen Karsten at the Lake Forest College Donnelley and Lee Library; Mackenzie Zalin at the Johns Hopkins University Sheridan Libraries; and Kaidin Phelan at the Legacy of the Plains Museum. Additional libraries and archives that provided crucial materials include: the Albert and Shirley Small Special Collections Library and August 2017 Archive at the University of Virginia; the American Jewish Committee Archives; the American Jewish Historical Society; the Arolsen Archives; the Bancroft Library at the University of California, Berkeley; the Center for Jewish History; the Chicago Historical Museum; the Chicago Public Library; the Cook County Court; the Cornell University Archives; the Federal Bureau of Investigation Vault; the Hanna Holborn Gray Special Collections Research Center of the University of Chicago; the Harvard Law School Library; the Historical Jewish Press Archive of the National Library of Israel in partnership with Tel Aviv University; the Library of Congress Manuscript Division; the Loyola University Chicago Archives and Special Collections; the National Archives and Record Administration; the New York Public Library; the Princeton University Libraries Special Collections; the Hesburgh Libraries of the University of Notre Dame; the Skokie Public Library; the Special Collections Research Center and Louis B. Nunn Oral History Center of the University of Kentucky; the Tamiment Library at New York University; the United Nations Archives; the United States Holocaust Memorial Museum; the Bentley Historical Library of the University of Michigan; the University of Pittsburgh Library Archives and Special Collections; the University of Southern California Shoah Foundation; the University of Texas at Arlington Archives and Special Collections; the Wisconsin State Historical Society; and the YIVO Institute for Jewish Research.

Beyond archival sources, many individuals shared their stories and perspectives through interviews and conversations. While not all these exchanges appear in the final book, each enriched my understanding of this history.

For permission to reprint materials, I am grateful to the family of Justice Robert H. Jackson for the poem found in his papers and to Kathy Shapiro and the Karl Shapiro estate for allowing me to publish an excerpt from his poem "University."

Finally, I turn to those whose support sustained me throughout this journey. Writing a book requires navigating between the excitement of historical discovery and the craft of storytelling. Jeremy Eichler traveled this path with me near daily, patiently enduring my writerly worries and sharing my joy when passages came alive. His extraordinary generosity—as writer, scholar, and friend—sustained this project from beginning to end. Above all, his keen ear for the voices from the past helped transform the noise of time into the sound of history.

I dedicate this book to my family. My parents, Robert and Jane Loeffler, have provided unwavering love and support, with my father sharing formative memories of growing up in Chicago during the 1940s and 1950s. My brother Charles has been a wonderful companion on our parallel journeys into the legal past, as have Amy and Peter. The Lebenson clan—Ira and Cecile, Julie and Lawrence, Matthew and Carly, and my delightful nieces—have sustained me with joy and laughter, insisting I occasionally close the books and join the party outside.

Rachel, my wife, brings what every writer most needs: genuine curiosity and moral clarity. She reads with anticipation, eager to know what happens next, while her ethical compass keeps me true to what matters most.

David, Eli, and Talia have lived through this book's many twists and turns. Instead of reading it, they talked it through every night—willingly and unwillingly—at the dinner table for eight years. In the process, their penetrating questions, both innocent and shrewd, taught me to think and rethink the meaning of the past in the present. If I have left many questions open in this book, it is my hope that they will help answer them as we strive toward a more just future.

INDEX

ABOUT THE AUTHOR

An award-winning historian, James Loeffler is the Felix Posen Professor of Modern Jewish History at Johns Hopkins University and the author of *Rooted Cosmopolitans: Jews and Human Rights in the Twentieth Century*. Previously he taught at the University of Virginia and served as Dean's Visiting Scholar at Georgetown University Law Center. Loeffler is currently a Kogod Senior Research Fellow at the Shalom Hartman Institute of North America. His writing has appeared in *The Atlantic*, *The New York Times*, *The Washington Post*, *The Wall Street Journal*, and *The New Republic*. He lives in Washington, DC, with his family. For more information, visit jamesloeffler.com.